Single Mother By Choice

Written by Sachele Gayle

Dedications

I dedicate this book to my daughters, Ayanna and Aniyah. At present you are both only 4 and 1 year of age and the reason I decided to start writing this book. You are my motivators and by the time you are old enough to read this book I pray that you have both established yourselves as strong independent girls or women. If not, don't worry, there is still time and it is never too late.

I also dedicate this book to all women who have had to be mothers and fathers to their children and also to the fathers who have fought to take an active part in your child or children's life. No matter what your circumstances are, you are amazing, and your children are the proof of that.

To all the women that are looking for inspiration in order to leave a toxic relationship, you are the strength that you need. I hope this book provides you with the support and the guidance that you need and are currently looking for.

I dedicate this book to you also.

To anybody feeling stuck in life, remember, you are responsible for your destiny. Decide what you want or need and make the plans to work towards your positive change. After years of feeling, stuck, fed up and sometimes depressed, I have found my happiness and you can too.

I hope this book inspires all readers to accomplish what it is you want out of **YOUR** life.

"My whole life was and is to try and make something of my life pertaining to our community as a people more importantly the Family.

Obviously you have no regards for "children in the middle" you have proven that they don't matter to their Father or even still both parents in turmoil within relating to each other.

I have tried everything in my power to keep the peace with you over the decades but nothing seems to work:-

- Advising and planning ways to enhance the family home.
- Communicating which is paramount / you never want to interact verbally regardless.
- Keeping my distance/your happy enough to keep the children away.
- Avoiding derogatory remarks towards you / you continue to throw verbal abuse.
- Suggested counselling / it never happen for whatever reason!

The list goes on but I'm trying to hit the main points!

Families is not just about being together in the same household, when there is a breakdown within, how do both parties rectify a peaceful solution for everyone's benefit?

I have gone around you to see my son as you keep hiding him and every time I see him, he is in need of support, clothing and guidance.

My second son was in a state late last year ,coming in to the early part of this year. I have put him on the straight and narrow, he was giving you some problems at home, that's why I took him and as you can see he's trying to do his best. Presently he is missing out on opportunities I have sorted out for him regarding his career.

My first son is not 100% but getting on with his life, your support regarding me and him wasn't there, that is why he doesn't understand me being upset with his hygiene, cleanliness and untidiness in his environment at home.

Stepping in the house on Father's Day doesn't justify your violent actions to attempt to stab me in front of my boys. I stayed away, because that's what you wanted, plus you wanting to rip my sons clothes of his back, because I bought them. I visited because of my concern for my last son. I wanted to ask you to stop your torment towards me, as I did notify you in every way of his weariness over the weekend. You are always trying to wind me up.

Remember when I said you're an aggressive woman, I have always had to stand up to you in the past imagine my frustration. Even now you're trying to aggravate me by bringing out the violence, emotionally, but not anymore. I now understand it's not the way as I've matured in life.

Baby Mothers where ever you are getting your information from plus all the other garbage past and recent cannot answer that for you.

Conclusion:

- The children love both of us, but you've proven it hurts you to see that I will not give up on being close with them. That is why all these decades you have tried to destroy the bond between us.
- The hate you have and the bitterness only destroys what is around you and more importantly yourself.
- Being vindictive will not solve anything only turmoil.
- You know I would and do give my last penny to the children that is why I'm broke always being inconvenienced cause I don't want to see them suffer.
- This is not about me and you anymore, but you refuse to understand the children are feeling things mentally.

Remember you've been back and forth at mines in the latter years and you still couldn't talk to me regarding our relationship ("Quote" I Don't know what to do with you!). I'm only giving pointers.

Anyway as you know I'm not one to dwell in the past it doesn't solve anything. Yes! I've made mistakes, but you keep using the children as pawns or a tug of war, what is this going to solve, this is the area where you need to look upon.

I ask you to watch this educational DVD to the very end as it changes into the more recent.

Yes! You may not give a damn cause it's me who handed it to you.

The venom you have for me "God help me!"

This is not to dictate or condemn just a brief message to the awareness of your subconscious which you have always disapproved regarding me as a conscious person." 20/06/12

What you just read is a letter my father sent to my mother.

When I found this, I knew it had to be included in this book. This letter sets the tone of the subject I am talking about. In this book I will explain how my parent's toxic relationship has affected me and the decisions I have made as an adult.

I am now a parent, with the trauma of seeing and hearing things no child should. I am trying my very best not to let history repeat itself. But, it seems in my case, history really is trying to repeat itself.

Introduction

A Little Bit About Me

I was born 31st July 1985. The first out of four children and the only girl. I used to tell my brothers this made me special twice.

I was raised in a two-parent home, and from my earliest childhood memories, everything was great. My brother came along when I was two and for eight years, it was just me and him.

My mum did not work when I was growing up and my father was Self Employed, he actually still is. During this part of my childhood, my parents were very present. Mum would be there to bring my brother and I to school. She would be at home when we returned and dinner would already be prepared. Dad would come home in the evenings and I was always happy to hear his keys enter the lock. I actually remember running down stairs to greet him whilst shouting "Daddy". He would always pick me up and swing me in the air whilst spinning 360 degrees.

I am 37 years old and still smile when these memories appear in my thoughts. My 2nd brother was born in 1995. I was 10. I remember the day mum told us she was expecting. I was so happy and really wanted a little sister. When I heard she had a boy I was so disappointed, but fell in love with him the moment I met him.

In 2001, my third and final brother was born. I was 16 and this is when the troubles between my parents began.

The Beginning of The End

My 3rd brother being born was the beginning of the end for my parents. My dad was not happy that my mum decided to continue with the pregnancy. My mum was still unemployed and raising us on benefits. My dad was and still is very ambitious. During my childhood he taught Martial Arts and worked in the printing trade. Though my dad was there throughout my childhood, and contributed to raising me, he was not really a family man. His aim in life was to be successful and he believes the number of children he and my mother had, had a negative impact on his personal goals and "slowed him down". Due to this he did not acknowledge my brother for six weeks.

My mum had a caesarean section and needed a 6-week recovery window. During this time, my dad was nowhere to be seen. As previously mentioned, I was 16 and was completing my GCSE's. I had to stay focussed at school. The only help my mum had was from my brother. The eldest one. He looked after my mum for 6 weeks and did things no 14-year-old boy should have to do as well as see things no 14-year-old boy should see.

As far as I am concerned, this was very self-fish of my dad. Regardless of whether he wanted mum to keep him or not, he arrived. My dad should have put his annoyances to a side and be there for his partner and new born son. To this very day, my brother has issues with my dad and his treatment of mum.

My mum turned 40 two months after my brother was born. Once again, dad was nowhere to be seen. On her birthday, I remember this day very vividly. Mum was sat in the kitchen, in the dark, having a smoke all by herself. I could tell she was in very deep thought. I felt really bad for her. She didn't even receive a phone call from dad and she did not call him either. But mum being mum, kept smiling. Deep down, I know she was hurting, but she did not show it.

Between the ages of 16 and 21 all my parents did was argue and fight. Sometimes the fights were really bad and would spill on to the streets, neighbours watching, not being discreet at all. I would be woken up out of my bed by shouting and things breaking. Dad once gave mum a black eye. He tried to justify this by saying the black eye was an accident. Mum and dad had been fighting and he managed to get her to the floor. He claims mum bit his shin and that's when his foot connected with her eye.

I have seen my mum attempt to stab my dad. The most high was looking after her this day, because this is the moment, I learned what the saying saved by the bell actually means. They were arguing and when dad's back was turned, she picked up the knife and raised her hand. At this point, my brothers and I had had enough and neither of us attempted to stop her. Just as she was going to bring her arm down and strike him with the knife, the police knocked the door. The neighbours must have heard the commotion and called them.

Eventually their relationship came to an end and mum got her keys back from dad. This did not affect my brothers and I, because for as long as I can remember, my dad had his own place and always came and went as he pleased.

After dad left for good, the next issue that would cause major conflict between my parents was access to my youngest brother. Mum stopped all contact and would not allow dad to see him. When speaking with her, she claims she did not. But I disagree with her. Dad had a habit of turning up unannounced. Mum would pretend she was not home. If dad would ask to have him, she would pretend she was busy. At the time, I would judge my mum's actions as I believed she was wrong for what she was doing. But now I am a mother of my own children, I totally understand her reasoning behind her behaviour. I am not saying it is right and I do not condone children being kept from their fathers without good reason, such as domestic or sexual abuse, but I understand why she behaved in such a way. I will explain why a little later in this book.

Moving forward from this introduction I am going to be explaining and expressing how my upbringing and the conflict I witnessed between my parents has shaped me as an individual. I have made decisions based on what I witnessed in my teenage years and early twenties. I refuse to let my daughters grow up in and around conflict, as well as negative energy.

The title single mother by choice describes my current circumstances. I am a single mother by choice and as you continue to read this book, I hope I can inspire and motivate you too take charge of your life, happiness and wellbeing.

Chapter 1

My First Daughter

My first daughter, Ayanna was born on 14th March 2018. I was 32 and an old mum by society's standard. Her father and I were not in a relationship, but she was planned. How can you plan a baby when you are not in a relationship with the father? I envision most people asking me. Let me explain.

After all the conflict between my parents growing up, I promised myself, no child of mine will ever witness, what I had to. Looking at my own relationships, before I met my daughter's father, I had 3 failed relationships within a time frame of 10 years. 2 years with one partner, 3 years with another partner and 5 years with the last partner.

Whilst I was in these relationships, I did become rather broody. But I felt like I could not have a baby with either of those men, because in my eyes, we would not be the perfect family. I know now, there is no such thing as the perfect family, but I do not regret ending these relationships.

The reason as to why these 3 relationships failed is merely due to the fact that I put myself first. Some may call this self-fish, but I know what I want from a relationship and neither of those men could give it to me. Stability, loyalty, trust, maturity and most of all compromise.

Relationship 1, Together, For Two Years.

I was 19 when this relationship started. I was in college studying Business and had a part time job in a wine store. Thinking back to that time, I can see, I was still finding myself.

I thought my boyfriend was 18. That is what he told me when we met. We were about 6 months into our relationship and he decided to confess his real age. He was 16. I didn't believe him at first, it was not until he presented me with his college ID that I realised our relationship started off as a lie. This was red flag number 1. Regardless of the situation, we stayed together.

The 3 years between us was not really an issue. After all, my mum is 3 years older than my dad. But my main issue with this particular relationship was the fact that I felt like my partner had no ambition. He loves his local area and is practically a "Road Man". For those that do not know, a road man is somebody who hustles to make his money. This can be in the form of selling drugs, stolen goods and committing fraud. There are plenty other ways road men make their money, but these are just a few examples. In addition to this they live by certain street codes. These can consist of not being able to go into other areas outside of NW London, or in some cases, not being able to go to other parts of NW London. Coming from the heart of NW London, our environment had a huge impact on the way he lived his life. But that lifestyle was not and still is not for me.

Another issue I had with him was him not having enough time to spend with me. Road men put their business on the streets before their relationship, after all, this is how they earn a living.

I have nothing bad to say about him as a person. He is a wonderful individual with a good heart and after 17 years, believe it or not, we are still friends. But looking at his life now, not much has changed. He has a job, but is still a road man doing his side hustle. His current girlfriend complains about the same things I complained about when we were together. Though I was confident in my decision to end the relationship, seeing how things are with him in this present day, I firmly believe that I made the right decision.

<u>Relationship 2, Together, For Three Years</u>

This relationship was with another man from NW London, he was also a road man and was younger than me also.

I was going to university when this relationship started and our lives could not have been more different, but I did like him, so thought I would give it a go. This partner was also very caring and had a good heart, but he was jealous as well as possessive and I believe he came to be obsessed with me.

His mother had a genuine dislike for me. She accused me of stealing my boyfriend's money after he gave me his bank card to look after. I was at home, completing an essay for university and I received a phone call from my boyfriend. He told me his mum was on his way to my house, because she thinks I stole his money. Within 15 seconds of him saying money, my mum's door knocked. There she was, shouting at me, asking me where his money was, telling me I am a thief and all sorts.

I was so confused when this happened. I honestly had no idea what she was talking about. Whilst she was shouting at me, I was thinking to myself, here I am trying to better my life, sitting at home, completing an essay and trouble is coming to find me. She really caused a scene at my mums' front door. Neighbours were peeking out of their windows, standing at their front doors and everything. I was so upset I finished with him there and then. How could he let his mum come to my house like that? He must have believed I was guilty, because, if he thought I was innocent, he would be telling his mum this. He just stood there letting her shout the odds.

My mum was not home when this happened, but when she found out, she was round his mum's house like lightening. I stayed at home as I had had enough drama for one evening. My brother actually went with her and his feedback of the incident was not very positive.

Regardless of what happened, we got back together after a short amount of time apart. He expressed that he knew I had nothing to do with the money that left his account. He also said I should not judge him by his mother's actions, as she is her own person and he could not have forcibly stopped her from leaving his home to come to mine. So, I gave him the benefit of the doubt.

I never did find out what happened, but I believe one of his brothers had something to do with it. All siblings had the same initials. D BEN. In my heart, I know one of his brothers did this to him and allowed me to take the blame.

I finished University in July of 2009. Six months after I graduated, I got a job in a school. The school was based in Newham, East London and this was my ticket out of my mother's house. After being in employment for 6 months, I managed to secure a one-bedroom flat on a six-month tenancy. I did not ask or even suggest to my boyfriend that he move in with me. He just decided he was coming along. There was no conversation, nothing, he just moved in. Now, at the time, I had no issue with this. We had been together for about two years and I just went along with the program.

I did not realise this at the time, but him moving in with me without any form of discussion was a red flag that I cannot believe I missed.

In his mind, he believed he had to move in with me, when, he actually did not. Us living apart would not of affected our relationship in any way. But he believed it would, he had to be close to me at all times. One of the main reasons we separated was due to the fact that he was possessive. I remember one occasion where he followed me to university and actually sat through my Drama, workshop. This was the result of an argument we had before I had to go to class and he did not believe I was going to Uni, so he said he was coming. This was red flag number 3.

During those 6 months of us living together all we did was argue. All he wanted to do was be where I was. If I was going to visit a friend it was an issue. He would then go back to his foolish ways of linking up with the "Man Dem" and doing nothing but smoke cannabis and drink strong alcoholic drinks. My life was moving in the right direction. I had a new job, new flat, was meeting new people and going new places. Meanwhile, he had previously lost his job and was struggling to find one he liked. I was at work and he was at home. This affected him. I think he thought I was leaving him behind, but he never expressed this to me. I just knew. I used to speak to him about what he wanted out of life, he did not know. He was only educated up to GCSE level. He had no trade and all he knew was the streets. He could not manage the direction my life was moving in. After the tenancy ended, I moved out into a shared house and broke it off with him. He never took it very well; it ended up being a really nasty break up. He was very immature during our break up and I was so glad when it all officially ended.

This relationship taught me, you can take the man out of the streets, but you can't take the streets out of the man. We never wanted the same things; this relationship would have never worked. Like my last partner, he was a product of his environment. Change was too much for him.

Relationship 3, 5 years together

Whilst I was living in the shared house my room mates and I became quite close. I met my next partner at a christening. He was friends with one of my room mates and cousin with one of our neighbours.

This man was very different compared to my last two exes. He was from Ghana. I had only ever been with boys from London, but he was so different to anybody I had ever met in the past. Another positive is he was 5 years older than me. Both of my exes were younger than me, so this time around I believed I had caught me an actual man. I was 24 and he was 30. In my head, he was already established in life and if this was to work, we would have to work as a team to ensure we get the best life together.

Whilst I was thinking all of these happy thoughts, my day dream was gate crashed by a comment he made informing me he had a baby. When I heard baby, I was shocked. I was 24, nowhere near ready to become a step mother. I always ran from men who had kids, because usually, with children, baby mother drama was not far behind. I hated baby mother drama. I had seen some of my friends go through it. At this moment, I should have run, but I didn't. I failed to follow my instincts. If only I did, I would have saved myself 5 years of DRAMA and I am talking a lot more than baby mother drama.

When we met, his daughter was only 3 months old. He told me his relationship with her mother was over. I didn't doubt this as I had no reason too. He explained they had a dysfunctional relationship and that she is also bisexual. I respected him for telling me all of this, as I believe he did not have too. Either way, they had a healthy co-parenting relationship.

We used to spend all of our time together. He practically moved into my room. One day, the door knocked and there were 2 men delivering a washing machine. I was confused. The person the delivery was for did not live at this address so I sent it away. My boyfriend said I should have kept it, but I said no. I did not think anything of it, until about 2 days later it was being redelivered to the same person. The delivery men said they had to deliver it so I said OK. I spoke to all my room mates and nobody knew anything of this washing machine. We had a washing machine that worked perfectly fine, we did not need one. My partner said he would sell it and I said OK.

When we met, he told me he worked with computers. But I could not understand why this man was never at work and always free. One day we were in my kitchen cooking and I had a light bulb moment. I remember shouting out "you aint got no papers". He was shocked, but did not deny it. It all started to make sense. He did not work, because he could not work. He came to England on a student Visa and he let it expire and never went back to Ghana. I was furious when I found out. I remember thinking, yet, another relationship started on a lie. I remember saying "don't expect me to marry you" and I was serious. We have all heard those stories about men from abroad using English women to claim British Citizenship. I was not going to be one of those women.

After about a year, some of the girls in the house used to complain about his presence. The house was for single women only and couples were not allowed to live there. He was with me 24/7 so I decided it was time to get another flat.

Together we moved into a one-bedroom flat in Goodmayes, Ilford. He was a great boyfriend in the sense that he would come home at a decent hour, he cooked, he was clean, he loved me and looked after me very well, I was just really frustrated with his financial situation. I paid all the rent and the bills as I was the only person who was working. As previously mentioned, he couldn't work, so he would hustle. Do fraud, bet on football, sell a little bit of weed and so on. He also had a child to look after, there were no consistency in his finances and this annoyed me. This caused arguments because he was not even trying to get out of his situation. He was happy to hustle. I used to ask him, when are you going to sort your status out and he would just say soon. There was no urgency to want to better himself and this upset me.

In addition to this, the mother of his child used to do my head in. I remember she once turned up unannounced. She literally dumped her baby on me. My boyfriend was not home and I called him fuming. He came home straight away to look after his child. He was a good dad and he loved his daughter very much, but their situation was very complicated. She was from Tanzania and also had no papers. But the difference is, she worked, she had a job. She was a good mother and loved her daughter too, but she had issues and serious anger management issues.

She got this boyfriend. She used to put all his pictures on Facebook and tag him. He would be posing with her daughter and she would write comments like "look at my baby with her daddy." I used to frown upon this, but it was not my place to say anything, so I kept my mouth closed.

There was an incident, where she and the boyfriend had an argument and he called the police on her. She was charged with affray. That poor little girl is what I used to think to myself.

She came to our house once. It was around Christmas time and we were having a bit of a drink, eating food and just enjoying the festive period. It was time to drop them home and whilst in the car, she kissed me and told me that she fancied me. I was in shock. I am your ex's girlfriend. He is the father of your child; how can you kiss me like that? If you want us to have an affair you got another thing coming. All of this was going through my head. But after that moment I knew that was the last time she would be coming over to my house.

I don't remember ever telling my boyfriend what happened. But he knew that I had gone off her. He stopped talking to me about her and I was grateful, because deep down I felt like he still had some feelings for her. After all, she did give him his first child. Being totally honest, I was slightly jealous and had a fear that she wanted him back. But I did not express this to him, because I did not want to be seen as the jealous girlfriend. I understood that they shared a child and that co-parenting means communication at all times, sometimes at crazy hours of the night. As far as I am concerned, I had to keep my feelings to myself, because the baby was the priority. I did not expect him to put my feelings before his responsibility as a parent, but what I did expect was honesty. This is something he could not do. Be honest. I am going to give you 3 separate scenarios of his dishonesty.

scenario 1.

I went through his phone and found some texts between him and his daughter's mother.

He was telling her to pack what she can manage and to meet him on the estate. Her responses were not there, so I believe he had deleted them. He went on to say "she is leaving in 10 minutes" "she drives right through the estate". When I had seen these, I got so mad I confronted him right away.

He said she had been kicked out of her accommodation and had nowhere to go. If this was the case, why was he conspiring behind my back? why could you not be honest with me and tell me the truth? Yes, I disliked her, but she had a baby. If he was to tell me his daughter and her mother are currently homeless, I would not have said she can't come here. I may not have liked it, yes, I most likely would have complained, but at the end of the day, the baby's safety would have been my main concern. Him feeling like he could not be honest with me from the get go really hurt me.

Scenario 2

He had arranged a drug deal that I had known nothing about. This is funny, because it was actually my birthday. No card, no present, no date, he disappeared. Sounds Familiar, doesn't it?

Turns out the drug deal went wrong and the customers attempted to pay him with fake money. A fight ensued he was roughed up escaped and managed to get himself to hospital. Whilst at the hospital he contacted another set of men who was involved in this drug deal also. They turned up at the hospital, he had not even been seen to when he went outside and was kidnapped.

These men held him for 24 hours and beat him. They also burned his cheek with a hot iron. The next time I saw him, he was a mess and once again, I was fuming. I knew nothing about what he was planning and if he had been honest with me, I would have told him the whole deal seems dodgy. But once again, you are involved in something you know I will not condone and because you don't want to hear what I have to say, you decide to go ahead and do it anyway. I had no pity for him. It may sound harsh, but it is the truth. He made his bed; I left him to lay in it.

This was a massive case. It made the local newspapers, he testified against all parties and each individual involved, were sent down and given time. This was a sort of blessing in disguise for him, because the judge awarded him his indefinite leave to remain. After many years living illegally in Britain, he was awarded his stay after being battered and burned with an iron. You cannot make this up.

After this incident I moved out of the flat. I watch a lot of Gangster movies and my mind was going mental. I was thinking, he "snitched" they can send their people to come and get me, they know where we live. There is no way I was living in that flat after that case had ended. I didn't even go to any part of the trial. I did not want them to see my face. My safety was my main priority, so off I went. Believe me, he was not far behind. He did not move in though. After living him for 2 and half years and paying all bills on my own, there was no way I was letting him live with me again, at least, not until he sorted his life out.

Scenario 3

This was the last straw for me. He had managed to secure a room in a flat and I would spend a lot of time there as it was around the corner from where I was working and very convenient. At the same time, he had been with me throughout every property I had lived in, I was glad that I could actually say I am going to my boyfriends.

One day I went through his phone. I did this, because his behaviour was not right. He was just acting off, going out and not saying where ETC. Just call it woman's intuition. I found some naked photos of him. When I did all my investigations, I could see that he was sending these naked photos to other men. To say I was shocked is an understatement. I was asking myself a whole heap of questions. Is he gay? has he been sleeping with men behind my back? Before I confronted him, I took the number of one of the men he was speaking with. I contacted him via text and explained who I was and asked him how he knew my boyfriend. He told me, that he had met him in a gay bar and that they had met for a drink. He expressed that nothing happened, but did say he attempted to sell him some cocaine. After everything he had been through with the kidnap, I could not believe that he had gone back to selling drugs, especially since he had been given permission to reside in England. Once again, I was mad.

I confronted him and he confessed that he was told he would be able to make more money from Cocaine if he targets the gay clubs. If this was the case, why the secrecy? Why did he not tell me what his plans were. I did not believe him and this scenario, ended our relationship.

This brings me back to my first daughter's father. We met on an online dating site. After having 3 failed relationships in the last 10 years, I was finished with them. I was just looking for something casual.

When I met my first daughters' father, I instantly liked him. He was good looking, had a job and was a father to 2 children. A girl and a boy. His daughter lived in Germany. He used to be in the Army and was placed in Germany for a few years. He explained that he did not have much contact with his daughter as he and her mother did not speak. He explained they were in a relationship and he decided to move back to the UK.

His 2nd son lived in Northampton and he had regular contact with this child. He and his son's mother got on quite well. I liked this.

We started seeing each other and I fell pregnant quite quickly. We planned this pregnancy. He knew I was broody and expressed that he wanted to give me a child. I accepted, because I could see how much of a good father he was. By this time, he had reconnected with his daughter in Germany. I thought to myself, he is actually trying to re-establish contact. This was a huge positive for me. We were not in a relationship and I was happy to have a co-parenting arrangement with him.

One night we were at my flat and my father called me. We were just having a normal conversation and then we started speaking about my pregnancy. I mentioned the father was with me and he asked to speak to him. I could not hear exactly what my father was saying to him, but I had an idea. My father is quite over protective of me. Anytime there is a man in my life, my father feels like he needs to give him "the talk". That is exactly what my dad did and

Ayanna's dad did not appreciate this. I had no idea at the time though. He waited until the next day to tell me. But he told me via What's App and whilst I was at work.

This did not sit right with me. Why did he wait a whole 24 hours to say something? Why did he not just be open an honest with my dad on the phone? This upset me.

We had a dispute about the situation. I told him he should have told my dad what he told me. He said that he did not appreciate my dad dictating to him. He felt like my dad was treating him like a child. He felt like he should not have to say anything to my dad. I disagreed with this. If you are so much of a big man, why can you not express yourself to your child's grandfather man to man.

After this dispute, he ghosted me throughout the rest of the pregnancy. Prior to this dispute, I remember him telling him to let him know when I started getting uncomfortable and needed a little more support. I did this when my maternity leave started.

I was due 16th March 2018. I wanted to work up until the very last minute. I was unable to do this, because I suffered from SPD during my first pregnancy. SPD is a very painful condition that occurs during some pregnancies. It affected me badly. I was unable to walk up and down the stairs, getting in and out of the car was painful, getting in and out of bed was painful, just attempting to sit on the toilet or get off the sofa was really painful. It had me in tears most days. To make matters worse, where I was living at the time had a communal laundry room, as none of the flats had plumbing for individual washing machines. I lived on the top floor; the laundry room was on the ground floor and there were no elevators. At this point in my pregnancy, I needed him and he was nowhere to be seen.

Eventually, I sent him a message, explaining that I needed some help. There was no response to this message, so then, I decided and actually accepted that I was on my own and that I just have to continue dealing with this by myself. My mother eventually came and practically moved in with me.

I remember a false alarm and my dad contacted him on my behalf. He did not respond to my dad, but he did send me a message asking if I am OK. I remember thinking, you have a cheek. But, for the sake of my unborn daughter, I responded and from there onwards, it was like, nothing ever happened.

My daughter was born 14th March 2018 vis C section. I was in labour for 48 hours and had only dilated 5cm. the hospital refused to give me the epidural, so I requested the Caesarean, because I was so tired and after 2 full days, I wanted the baby out. Her dad was not present, because he was having car troubles and was unable to make it to the hospital. My daughter was born in Basildon hospital in Essex, UK. Yes, the hospital is in the sticks and without a car it is difficult to get to. But, if he really wanted to be present for his daughter's birth, I believe he could have.

I was in the hospital for a whole week after she was born. We were both at risk of developing Sepsis and because of this, we were both on antibiotics. I hated my time in hospital. I remember breaking down, because I was seeing other mums come and go the same day their child had been born. I was stuck in a hospital bed, still suffering from the SPD as it takes a few weeks after your baby has been born for the condition to go completely. Her dad eventually came to see us about 4 days into my stay.

When we were discharged, he came and collected us. After being home for about 2 weeks, he would come and see us regularly. If I wanted to go out, I could call him and he would be more than happy to come and stay with his daughter. We had the perfect co-parenting relationship. He was paying maintenance, would call us regularly as well as come and spend time with us.

One evening, he messaged me, telling me he was losing his job due to an error he made at work. He was an IT engineer and whatever the error was, it caused a major failure and he resigned instead of waiting to be let go. He started job hunting. He was saving to buy a house and he had child maintenance to pay for his other children, he really needed a job. He managed to secure a position in Amsterdam. When he told me, I remember thinking Amsterdam. I remember thinking, he is doing to me, what he did to his first daughters' mother, the one in Germany. Luckily, we were not in a relationship and this decision, did not affect me in any way. I just thought, what about your daughter?

Regardless, I understood his situation and would not hold it against him. So, within 4 weeks of him giving me the news, he was gone. But he maintained contact with us. he would video call every other day; he was still paying his child maintenance and the both of us got on with our lives.

At this moment in time My baby was not even a year old yet. But he had to do, what he had to do.

Chapter 2

My 2nd daughter

Sometime had passed and I had met someone. I was on my way to a party and my mum was babysitting for me. I went to the shop to buy my friend a birthday card and there, was where I met the father of my 2nd child. This scenario was completely different.

after being sworn off relationships, I decided to give it another go. This man was really nice and the most important thing for me was the fact that my daughter liked him and he treated her well.

We met in February and by April, we were an item. We spent all of our free time together. When we met, I was still living in Essex. I moved out of that flat and into my mother's house temporarily.

I do not know what it was I liked about this man and I do not know why I went back on my own word and started a relationship with him, but I really fell for him.

Once again, I noticed the red flags from the beginning of our relationship, but did not think anything of this.

Red flag number 1

I could never get hold of him. Any time I would call, his phone would be off. We both worked in the week and hardly saw one another. Its common practice to speak with your partner at the end of each day, or, every other day at least. After not seeing or speaking with each other for the week, he would just turn up and knock the door on a Saturday morning.

Reflecting on this now, I guess, I am at fault also. I never expressed that this annoyed me. I now believe, I should have. Communication is very important in a healthy relationship. I believe, if I had communicated this to him from the beginning, his response may have shown me he was not the man for me. Instead, I ignored it, because I did not want to come across as clingy or needy. I know I am neither of these, and, because I wanted this relationship to work and be successful, I feel like I lowered my standards. This is something nobody should have to do in a relationship.

Anyway, after living with my mum for about 6 months. I decided it was time to get another place of my own. I managed to secure a tenancy on a 2-bedroom flat. We did not move in together, but after about 4 weeks, he gave up his tenancy and moved in with me. Once again, without any prior discussion, but I did not mind this, as I really liked this man and wanted this relationship to work out.

The first year of our relationship was great. We would both go out to work and spend time together in the evenings. He would get home later than me. I worked in a school and would get home about 5pm. He was self-employed and would get home no later than 10pm.

Red flag 2.

One evening, he never came home. No phone call, no prior conversation to say he would be out all night, he just did not show. I was worried. His phone was off, I was thinking the worst. The next morning, I got up and went to work as normal, and kept trying to call him. I still could not get through. At this moment in time, I thought something bad had happened to him, so I called his mum. She had not heard from him either and was just as worried as I was. She even mentioned calling the police to report him missing. Eventually, he called me. He was apologetic and explained he had fallen asleep at a friend's house. Fair enough.

I am not one to hold grudges. After his explanation, life continued as it should.

Red flag number 3

In February of 2020, he announced he was going to Jamaica. This was not my issue. My issue was that he booked and paid for his flight and didn't even ask as to whether I would be interested in coming along. I found this weird and strange. I would like to think, the normal thing to do, is to speak with your partner about your plans? He could have said, "I am planning on going to Jamaica". He did not even do this; he just booked his flight and went.

During this time, I discovered I was pregnant. But this pregnancy ended in a miscarriage. I was carrying twins and was devastated. I ended up dealing with this on my own, because he was in Jamaica at the time of my miscarriage. I remember calling him to notify him of what had happened and I was in tears. His response was, there is no point in being upset, its life, these things happen. Wow, was my thought! I expected him to be as upset as I was, to tell me, not to worry, everything will be OK, I am here for you. All I received was, that's life. Maybe that was his way of dealing with the loss. But thinking back, I really needed him emotionally and he was not there.

He landed back in the UK on 10th March 2020. I remember this day specifically, because this was the day, I was supposed to have my 12-week scan.

When he returned, we did not discuss the miscarriage. Life continued as if nothing ever happened.

The 15th of March 2020 was my 1st daughter's 2nd birthday. She was having a party at home and all of my friends and family were invited.

After all the preparations had been completed and we were waiting for our guests to arrive, he said, he was leaving. This angered me, and for the first time in our relationship, I lost it with him.

I do not remember word for word what it was I said exactly. But I do remember stating that I care too much and from this point onwards, I will stop caring.

I could not understand, why, he would not want to stick around for my daughter's 2nd birthday, his step daughter, whom he had grown a very close bond with.

I remember, just ranting and raving. He did not respond, he just ended up staying.

A couple of hours later, the party was in full swing. All guests had arrived, we were eating, drinking and socialising, then, my phone rang. It was the father of my eldest daughter. He was calling to wish her a happy birthday. I answered the phone for her and was attempting to get her attention, so, she could speak with her father. My then boyfriend, called me to one side. I handed the phone to a friend and asked her, if she could help Pumpkin to continue speaking with her father.

I went into the bedroom, where he was waiting and he asked me a strange question. The question was "Are you having a party for your daughter or for your baby father?" I was confused and immediately asked him, what he was speaking about. He expressed that he was not happy at the fact that my daughter's father had called to wish his daughter a happy birthday. I was stunned. In my head, I'm thinking, you have really called me away from my daughter's birthday party, to tell me that you have an issue with her father calling her. Truthfully, I really wanted to curse him out. But I was raised better than that and I believe in having decorum. This scenario, shown, me, he had none.

I remember responding by saying, he is wishing her a happy birthday, what is the problem? He basically, told me to hang up the phone. At this point, I walked away from him and went back into the party and acted as if all was well. There was no way, I was going to spoil my daughter's big day, due to her step fathers' insecurities.

By the time, I returned to the party, her phone call with her father had ended. I was glad, because, there was no way, I was going to back into the front room of my home and tell my daughter that she must stop speaking to her dad. Only, the most high knows how that would have played out.

That evening after everybody had left, I confronted him. Nothing he said made any sense to me. He was just ranting and told me that he feels uncomfortable when Ayanna's father phones my phone. He suggested I install What's App on her tablet, so her dad can call her directly. I explained, that this will not make a difference, as, I will still need to answer the call for her. Regardless, I took his feelings into consideration and installed what's app on Ayanna's tablet.

I informed Ayanna's dad and he started calling her every other day via her tablet.

Ayanna's birthday was celebrated at the beginning of the Pandemic. Covid had only just hit the headlines. Her dad was actually meant to be there as he had booked a ticket to fly to the UK. He informed me that he will be there for her birthday and I planned on letting Aniyah's dad know.

He eventually changed his mind and expressed that he feared getting stuck in the UK. I understood completely and I did not begrudge him for not being there. But I did plan on having the two men meet one another at the party.

I was yet to inform him of the fact that I was in a relationship with somebody. He had no idea, that his daughter had a step father. I was planning on telling him as soon as I could, but I had doubts about the relationship and was unsure as to whether it would last, so decided not to say anything until I knew for sure that we were solid.

Most fathers get really protective, when their daughters are around their mothers' partner. As a single parent, I understand this. If any of my daughter's fathers, were to get into new relationships, I would want to be informed. I would want to meet their new partner, as I would like to ensure she is suitable to be around my child.

I never managed to tell him about my boyfriend, but he did find out.

One evening, Ayanna was on the phone to her father, when my partner returned home from work. He came in and went into our bedroom. The conversation, between Ayanna and her father continued. I did not see the need to end the conversation, just, because he has returned home.

I asked Ayanna's father how his other children were. A moment later, my boyfriend entered the room and asked me, in front of my daughter, "what type of conversation is this?"

Please remember, Ayanna's father has no idea I was in a relationship and I had not mentioned it to him. Understandably, this was a shock to his system.

After that question was asked, Ayanna's dad asked me who he was. I then went on to explain that he was my boyfriend and that we had been together for year. I could see the shock on his face. At this point, Aniyah's dad returned and was saying something to Ayanna's dad and they just started arguing.

At this point, I was mad with Aniyah's dad, but my Ayanna was still present and witnessing all of this, so I hung up. I then went off on my partner and told him how rude and disrespectful he was. How can you interrupt the conversation a child is having with her father, because, you do not want me to speak with him. She was two years old. What two-year-old can hold a full conversation, without the guidance of a parent?

I was really upset, angry and had felt disrespected. If he had any form of decorum about him, he would have waited until the conversation had ended to ask me about my conversation. Furthermore, he was in the next room and could hear everything word for word. He had no business, leaving the bedroom to attempt to involve himself in his step daughter's conversation with her father. This is when I realised, this man's insecurities ran deep.

I had been in his position once before, when I was seeing the Ghanian. Not once did I say to that man, he could not speak with his daughter's mother. I had no right to do so. Any adult with sense, should know when two people share a child, there will forever be some form of communication, even if its via email. Well, I speak for those that understand what a healthy co-parenting relationship is.

At this point, Ayanna's father was calling me, constantly. I did not answer, because my boyfriend and I were arguing.

About 30 minutes later, I receive a call from my mum. Straight away I knew, Ayanna's dad had contacted her. I remember thinking to myself, why did I not just tell him about my relationship? Though I was upset with Aniyah's dad for causing all of this, I had to take some responsibility. If Ayanna's dad had known there was a man in my life and around his daughter, maybe things would have played out differently. I guess we will never know.

I answered my mums call and we were speaking, whilst, Aniyah's dad and I were still arguing. Mum, said she would be coming over the following day to speak with us both.

That night, I could not even look at him. I could not believe how he behaved in front of Ayanna. Especially since I had expressed everything I had witnessed growing up with my own parents. He knew how much I hated my daughter seeing us argue and I felt like he disregarded my feelings. His insecurities, were more important. I remember thinking, this relationship is over, he has to go.

Whilst he was sleeping, I took my house keys off his keyring. Prior to this argument, I had attempted to break it off with him before. He would never leave. So, this time, I thought I would move in silence. I assumed, him not seeing the keys on the ring, would have confirmed to him that we were through.

He awoke in the morning and went to work as usual. There was no dialogue between us, I was disgusted by his behaviour and really just wanted this man out of my life. He was a child, who was unable to cope with the fact that my child's father and I had a healthy co parenting relationship. At one point, he actually accused me of having feelings for him, accused me of sleeping with him, the one time, I carried my child to Amsterdam, to visit her dad. This was at the beginning of our relationship, not once, did he voice to me that he had an issue with me taking Ayanna to Amsterdam. But, in his unstable mind, he was thinking, I was out there cheating on him, but yet, said nothing.

He once told me not to speak with him, he further went on to say, anytime, I am on the phone to Ayanna's dad and he returns home, I must end the conversation. This did not sit right with me. When we first got together, Ayanna's dad and I would speak on the phone in front of him. Once again, he never voiced that he did not like this. If he had, I would have known, he was not the man for me.

Those were all red flags and our relationship should have ended before Aniyah, came along. Everything happens for a reason I guess.

My mum arrived whilst he was at work, but she was not alone. Two of my brothers were with her.

After a while, he eventually returned home from work. The bell rang and I knew it was him. I told my brothers to let him in. As soon as he entered the flat, I heard my brother say “I need to talk to you man” his response was “about what?” Then, my brother responded “yesterday”. That’s all I remember. They entered the kitchen, where they tried to reason with him and explain, why he was in the wrong. He was not having any of it, he firmly believed that he did nothing wrong and that me and my child’s father should not have any communication what so ever.

He believed, because he was in her life physically, he should have more rights over her dad. I whole heartedly disagree with this. Yes, her father was not there physically. But we live in the age of technology. She saw and spoke to her father every other day via video calls. He was not an absent father. He paid his child maintenance and communicated with her regularly. When she was naughty, I could call him and have him speak to her about her behaviour. Her behaviour at home and at nursery. Her step father hated this. He believed; he should be the one to chastise her when she is misbehaving.

I would allow him to tell her off when she needed it. One thing I believe is that children should have respect for all adults. But he was not allowed to put his hands on her of course, and, if he was to chastise her, I would set boundaries. He is a Jamaican man. Jamaicans are very strict when it comes to discipline. I am a firm believer in discipline, but we had very different ideas of what was suitable discipline was for a 2-year-old.

He felt like, I would choose her actual father over him, when it came to discipline. He did not like this, and stated, it was because he was the one who was physically there with her. Though I have some understanding of what he meant, why could he not communicate that to me prior? Why could he not let me know that he did not want to stay for the party, because he would feel uncomfortable if Ayanna’s dad was to be in attendance or give her a call?

When reflecting on the entire situation, it all started to make sense. This is why you did not want to stay at the party. If he had expressed this to me, I would not have ranted at him the way I did. I would have respected this and let him go. At that time, all he did was say "I am going". No explanation, nothing. If he had been honest with me, we would have saved all of this headache.

I then informed my family of what he had done on Ayanna's 2nd birthday. I informed him that her dad was meant to attend and was unable to make it. I told him this, because I wanted to hear his reaction. He went on to say, he would not have allowed him to enter the house.

Remember, this man moved in with me, I paid all the bills for the property and the tenancy agreement was in my name. How dare you tell me; he would not have been allowed in. He was dictating to me. I responded by telling him if I have to choose between you and my daughter having a healthy relationship with her father, I will always choose my daughter and her father every time.

In front of my brothers, I went on say, if Ayanna's dad ever came over from Amsterdam to see his daughter, I will let him in my home and there is nothing he can do about it. He did not like this, he could see that he would not get his own way with me and I told my brothers to ensure this man has left my house, before they go.

The conversation ended, with no conclusion and he packed a bag and left for a couple of days.

During his absence, I was trying to repair things with Ayanna's father. I was on his side and could understand why he was so angry. He told my mum, if he ever saw my partner, he would "buss his head" in other words, cause him some serious physical harm. He told my mum that he will no longer be calling Ayanna and that she, must make sure, Ayanna calls him. This did not sit right with me.

Yes, I understand your grievance and I understand why you are vexed. But do not, stop calling your child, because you had an argument with the step dad. Your daughter is 2 years old. She is not even speaking in sentences yet. How can you expect her to call you. That's your responsibility as the father. Not hers.

I decided, to let Ayanna call her dad. He took a long time to answer, but he eventually did. I was nowhere to be seen, just in the background. No word of a lie, he said "hello baby" then proceeded to end the conversation. She seen him for approximately 30 seconds.

He then called my mum, complaining that Ayanna called him and that he has not heard from me since the whole fiasco, so I decided to send him an email, as he had blocked my number.

Below, is the email I sent to her father.

I know you are upset and you have every right to be. What he did was out of order, rude and disrespectful. Believe me when I tell you I was very upset and angry with him and this caused us to argue,

I explained to him that he had no right to interfere in our conversation and I have told him that he can fuck off if he does not like the fact that my child's father and I can hold a conversation. I am holding my hands up, yes, I should have told you I was in a relationship and that there is a man around Yanna, but like I said previously, I was not sure whether it was going to work and did not want to mention anything without being absolutely sure we were solid. I am apologising to you for not letting you know sooner.

I understand why you want to mash him up and you have every right to feel that way. But I will not let that happen. I will not allow Yanna to witness the adults in her life fighting.... I witnessed that shit growing up and I promise you, she will not go through what I went through as a child. It can affect her in ways you can't imagine and her welfare is my main concern.

What happened has happened, my mum and my brothers have your back, as do I. I do not want this 1 incident to ruin the relationship you have with your daughter, it's unfair on her. She has been asking for you. What do I tell her? Daddy does not want to call you because he is upset with mummy? come on Real. Be upset with me, that is fine, we don't ever have to speak again if that's what you want, but do not take it out on Tashai. She is innocent in all this

When you want to see Yanna I will drop her to my mums. I am sorry, but I cannot let you know where I live as I want to keep the peace and do not want you 2 big ass men fighting over bull shit. I have instructed my mum not to ever bring you to my house or tell you where I live.

Yanna loves and misses you and I know you miss her too. Please don't let that fool and his insecurities break what you and Yanna have. If you choose to not contact her, obviously that's your choice, but remember, you will be missing out on watching her grow and flourish. She is a beautiful little girl and I don't want her to grow up with resentment towards you. That can easily happen. I know you told my mum to let Yanna call you when she is there. But you are the parent, you need to keep the contact with her. It's not Yanna's responsibility to call you, it's yours to call her. Well, until she is old enough to pick up the phone and call you herself.

Like I said previously, Yanna is my main concern. I am going to let pumpkin call you tomorrow, I hope you answer, if not, I know where she stands with you and you will never hear from her again. But I will never stop you from seeing her, I promised you that before we had her and I meant it.

After sending him this email, I understood that he needed some space and I left him alone. He stopped communicating with Ayanna completely. I have done everything to get her reacquainted with him again, but to no avail.

I finally accepted, this man has put his ego and pride before his daughter. There is nothing more I can do.

After a week or so, Ayanna's step dad returned home and we sorted things out. I was still very angry with him, but we had a heart to heart, where he informed me of an unfortunate incident that I believe is the root cause of his insecurity.

He told me that he was once in a relationship and his girlfriend at the time fell pregnant. A few weeks after the baby was born, a note was dropped through the letter box, which read "I want to see my baby". After reading this note, he packed his bags and left.

I did feel sorry for him and I did have a lot of pity for him, but this shown me that this man is really damaged. Imagine the unanswered questions he has. After reading a note like that, you just walk away? No discussion, no DNA test. You just leave. No wonder you have issues with my daughter's father being in my home. You are judging me, by her standards. I expressed to him that I would never do that to him, but this man was damaged beyond repair.

I still believed I could help him. Due to what he confessed to me; we got back together. It was not out of pity. But, due to the fact that I loved this man and I believed he loved me too. I really thought I could help him heal and overcome his insecurities. He did not have to open up to me, but he did and I respected that.

So, life continued. Ayanna's father stopped calling her after this whole fiasco. Currently as I write this book, it has been two years and she still have not heard from him. I have attempted to reach out to him many times, even after changing my phone number, but he does not respond.

I understand his gripe with me. Be upset with me, that is OK. But, to cut your daughter off completely, because of her step father, shows me, I was your main interest. How else am I supposed to think.

Regardless of what occurred between her stepfather and you, you should still maintain the contact with your child. The baby is innocent in all of this. So, your ego and pride comes before your daughter?

Anyway, after about 3-4 weeks, I discovered I was pregnant again. Due to the previous miscarriage, I was very anxious and I booked myself a private scan. That miscarriage, was actually a Blighted Ovum. This is when, a conception occurs, but the body recognises there is an issue with the foetus and eventually, the foetus is absorbed by the body.

I did not want to get all excited by this pregnancy, only to discover there is no baby, again. The scan was booked and I informed my partner that I had booked this scan, where it was and the time of my appointment. The day of the scan he was a no show. I was not upset. Slightly disappointed, but to be honest, I expected this.

Throughout our relationship, he always prioritised work over my daughter and I. He missed this appointment, because of work. Now, I have no issue with a hardworking man. He had a wonderful work ethic and I loved this about him. But he did not have a work life balance. Work, came before everything.

When I returned home from the scan, I sent him a text message. It read, thank you for coming to the scan today. There was no response to my message. When he returned home, he tried to gaslight me and said "why, didn't you remind me about the appointment?"

This baby was his first child, I didn't think I had to remind him. I refuse to be blamed for something that he forgot. I remember shouting at him and saying "If, I have to remind you about something as important as the private scan of your first child, you are showing me, what is really important to you and what your priorities actually are". Once again, he said nothing.

I know he felt guilty, but failed to say this and failed to address the fact that I was upset with him. He just let me sulk, and, sulk, I did.

I was pregnant throughout the Pandemic. We were going through lock down, I was working from home, in my first trimester, suffering from severe morning sickness and still being a mum to a 2-year-old. During this time, my partner was still working. I was home alone for practically most of my pregnancy. Don't get me wrong, some evenings, he would come home and prepare dinner, some Sundays, he would stay in and cook, but there was no consistency.

I remember a specific incident, where we had an issue with the electricity and I had to call for a repair. I was on the phone to the repair man, when my partner called me. I answered his call and told him to wait on the line, whilst I continued speaking with the Electrician. At the end of the phone call with the electrician, I went back to his call and he asked me who I was speaking with. I explained that it was the electrician and that he was on his way to carry out a repair and he told me he was coming home.

There was another occasion where he did this. We once had an issue with bed bugs. Only the most high knows where they came from, as I had never dealt with anything like this before. I did some research and found a pest control company with brilliant reviews. I did not hesitate to get in contact with them and made booking for the house to be treated. Believe, this man, my boyfriend took the whole day off work, because, he did not want me to be alone in the house with the fumigator.

Now, why am I telling you this? I was in my first trimester of pregnancy, still working, and looking after a 2-year-old. Every morning, he would see me throw up, whilst he was getting ready for work. Not once, did this man take the day off, or even the morning off work, to stay with me. But yet, you can take the day off work, because we have a fumigator coming to deal with our infestation. You can leave work, because I have an electrician coming to the flat to make some repairs. If this is not insecurity at its finest, then I do not know what is.

This is the behaviour that I now reflect on, when I am in deep thought and it shows me, this man had and probably still has some serious issues, with trust. I really believe it stems from what he told me about his ex-girlfriend.

Well, the pregnancy continued and on 24th of December 2020, my contractions started. He was very thoughtful during the early part of my labour. He went to work and brought me with him. We dropped my daughter off with my mum and that evening I went to the hospital.

Aniyah was born 26th December 2020. I could tell he was excited. As soon as the baby came out, he was on the phone to his mum and my dad. He cut the cord, had skin to skin contact with her and then he left for a little while. I was not upset that he left. After all, he had been with me for the whole 48 hours of labour and let's not forget, it was during Christmas too.

He was back after about 4 hours. Baby and I were discharged and off we went. His family wasted no time in introducing themselves to Aniyah. They were at my flat the next day. I was so tired and was not in the mood for visitors. But I understood the excitement. This was His mum's 3rd granddaughter, but she was special, because, she was her son's 1st. His sisters first niece and her daughters, first cousin. I could have done with them giving me at least a week. But I did not voice this.

The first two weeks was ok. Aniyah's dad was still going to work, and we had an arrangement, where he would return home and look after Aniyah until 2am, just so I could get some sleep. Then, I will take over.

Every morning he would wake up and take her for a walk, then bathe her and go to work. This arrangement worked fine for me, and, I thought he was happy with this arrangement too as it was something we both agreed.

On New Year's Day his family came over for dinner. All was well, my dad and his partner were in attendance and we had a good evening. After everybody had left, I went to lie down. He entered our room with the baby sat on the bed and said "You need give your daughter a bed time". I asked him what he was talking about and he just started yelling. He was telling me, my daughter was misbehaving the previous night, when he had Aniyah and when he was telling her to go to bed, she was telling him no.

I then said, so, "why tell me now and why are you shouting?" He then started speaking to me in patois. Once again, this man had confronted me about something that had bothered him and once again I was confused.

During this time, as previously mentioned, we were going through a pandemic and my daughter and I had no routine. I was not at work; she was not at nursery and she had no official bed time. At that time, I let her go to bed when she was tired.

Now, I have no issue with this man sitting me down to talk to me about my daughter's behaviour. But, why could he not communicate this to me without cursing, arguing with me and shouting at me. Why always in front of the children. I remember responding by asking him what his problem was. I told him, that he needs to speak with me when sober. He had had a drink you see and anytime he drank, he became argumentative.

I also believe he was struggling with his transition into fatherhood. He was a man who liked to go to work, go see his friends after work, have a drink and a smoke, then return home at stupid o clock. He knew, being a father now, meant he had to be more responsible, but he could not manage. He did not tell me this, I just feel it in my heart. This man did not speak openly about his emotions, he kept everything to himself. This was a contributing factor to this relationship ending, but we are not there yet.

During our argument, his mother called him and he explained that we were arguing. She asked to speak with me and I explained the alcohol is a contributing factor to this and that I will not be speaking to him whilst he is behaving like this in front of my children. He took the phone from me and told his mother that he feels like he cannot say anything to me about Ayanna's behaviour without me getting upset. There was some truth to this. He always had something to say about my daughter and her behaviour. But I always used to remind him that she is two years old and she is going through the terrible 2 phase. Being a Jamaican man, he did not believe, in the terrible twos. In Jamaica, either, your child is behaving or not. Regardless of age, they expect children to be seen and not heard.

I explained to him I will not be raising my daughter like this and that I will not be chastising my daughter on his say so. He did not like this.

I can understand where he is coming from, but he was misunderstood. I had no issue with us discussing my child's behaviour. But that is what he could never do. Have a discussion.

I was once a stepmother. I had been in his shoes. But his belief was due to the fact that he is the stepfather, I must raise my daughter in the way he wants me too. I disagreed with this.

My daughter will be raised with manners and be raised to respect those older than her. This included him. Anytime, she misbehaved and I did not punish her the way he wanted me too, he would turn around and tell me, he feels like he cannot tell me anything about her. This is just, because, he was not getting his own way. Relationships and co-parenting are all about compromise. No parent, should dictate to another how their child should be raised or dealt with in times of discipline. Both parents should be able to have an amicable discussion and come to some form of agreement. Where an agreement cannot be reached, I do not believe in arguing about it. This solves nothing. I remember explaining all of this too him, but it all fell on deaf ears.

Whilst he was talking to his mum, he left. I let him go. I understand what it is like to want to remove yourself from an environment, because you need some time to yourself. I respected this. I did not call him nor text, I just let him go.

I firmly believe in letting somebody walk away when they want to. In my mind, I was telling myself, he can come back when he is ready.

That night, it was just me and my daughters. I remember, Aniyah slept from 1am right through to 5am...That was the most sleep I had had since she was born. The Peace I experienced that one night he was not there was amazing. This was the peace I missed.

The following day he returned. He let himself in with the key and came and sat on the dining table in the front room. I did not say anything to him and he said nothing to me neither. We just sat there in silence. By now, I had figured out his game and I was not going to play it with him. At the time, I remember thinking, I am too old and too mature for this bullshit!

I was sat on my sofa, watching my TV and he was on the chair by the dinner table. After approximately 20 minutes of silence, he went into the bathroom and removed his toiletries, wrapped them in cling film and put them in his suitcases.

His suitcases were already packed from a previous incident. This incident resulted in me breaking up with him via text. I explained I was unhappy and that we needed to separate. He did not respond to that text, but when I returned home from work, his bags were packed. I thought, he packed his bags to leave. I did say in the break up text that he does not need to leave straight away as I understood it would take him a while to find some accommodation.

He packed his bags and never left. We did have a conversation about it though. This happened after the incident with him and Ayanna's dad. He expressed that he believes I only wanted him to leave, because I want to invite Ayanna's dad into my home. (ISSUES beyond belief).

This was not the case. I wanted him to leave, because, in my head, I knew we would not work out. We were incompatible. I loved him, but after everything that happened with Ayanna's dad, I knew where his head was at and I knew, he would not fit with regards to the way I want to raise my girls.

Anyway, back to what I was originally saying. He packed his toiletries in his suitcase, and started sorting out his clothes as if he was leaving. I actually thought he was, deep down, I wanted him too. But, once again, he went nowhere and that evening, we were sleeping in the same bed as if nothing had ever happened the night before.

After this, he went back to his old ways and our evening arrangement, went out of the window. He was up at the crack of dawn again to go to work, would get home between 10 and 11, smelling of Ganja and Rum, fall asleep on the sofa and wake up to do the exact same thing the next day.

I was at home all day, every day, looking after a new born and a 2-year-old.

Now and again, I would smoke some cannabis. It helped me sleep. I was permanently tired and exhausted and the spliffs would help me to relax after my girls had gone to bed. One evening, my mum came over and she had had a spliff in the kitchen. We had no garden and all smoking took place in the kitchen, windows wide open and kitchen door closed. That night, the scent of the Ganja entered our hallway. I don't know how, but it was really bad. Aniyah's dad was visibly annoyed, but said nothing. He just kissed his teeth and slammed the front room door. I ignored this, because, I knew what his issue was, but was slightly pissed with his reaction. All he had to do was tell my mum to go and smoke outside. She would have adhered. But, as previously mentioned, this man could not communicate.

I did not say anything to him or my mum that night. I went to bed and he had an attitude all night. I was still breastfeeding Aniyah and, in the morning, he had a go at me and told me to stop breastfeeding and put her on formula. I was upset at the way he spoke to me, but I knew that I should not be smoking whilst breast feeding and that day, whilst he was at work, I went and bought the formula.

That evening, he returned home about 8.30pm. I had been at home for weeks, and I needed a break from the night shift. About 9pm, I put on my shoes, handed him the formula, picked up Ayanna and told him that I am going out for a little while. He looked at me with this strange look and asked "don't you have a baby to look after?" I responded by saying, she is with her dad. He then started having this rant about, why I didn't give him any notice and let him know he will be having the baby? Why am I only taking one child, I should take both of them.

Honestly speaking, this was a test. Yes, I needed a break, but I did not really have anywhere to go. I was just going to sit with my mum at her house for a couple of hours. He had not spent any quality time with his daughter as he was always at work, then just come home and go to bed. This was my way of helping him spend some time with her. But his reaction was really unexpected. He then put on his shoes and said that he had somewhere to go.

I let him put his trainers on, I let him step outside, then I locked the door. Within 2 minutes of him leaving, he tried the key and realised he could not enter. He then started knocking on my door telling me to let him in. I refused. I could not believe how childish this man was. When I reflect upon the whole scenario, I feel like, he was scared and felt like he would not be able to manage having the baby alone. I could be wrong, but way act in this childish way? Why not ask, where I am going? How long am I going to be? Why just go off on one. Its, because, he could not admit that he felt fearful about having the baby on his own, so he had to try and find a way to disrupt my plans, so I ended up going nowhere. Are you identifying the narcissistic traits?

If he had approached the situation in the way I have just explained, believe me, I would not have gone anywhere and he would not have got locked out. But, to say you are going out, put on your trainers and leave, only to come back 2 minutes later is childish. I do not play those games.

Whilst my door was locked, he was knocking and telling me to open up. I remember saying, I thought you had somewhere to go? He then tells me, he wants to see his daughter, I tell him, he can see her the following day. He then starts crying, telling me he wished he never met me, telling me, I am going to get the neighbours involved and all sorts. There was no response from me whilst he was behaving this way. I was silent and just sat in my sofa, watching my TV. Eventually he leaves. My daughters and I once again have a peaceful night and once again, I do not call him.

The next day, I receive a phone call from my father. He expresses that my boyfriend contacted him, letting him know what had happened the night before. Dad said he had told Aniyah's dad to return to the flat at 5pm and he will be there by 5.30pm to help us resolve this issue. I was unimpressed and I did not have any form of regret about locking my front door.

When both had arrived, we discussed everything. This includes, the incident at Ayanna's birthday, his issues with my parenting of Ayanna. He cried, I cried, dad reasoned with both of us, expressed some of the issues he had gone through with my mother and attempted to keep us together.

Though we spoke about our issues, there was no conclusion. I wanted this relationship to work, for the sake of my daughter...she was only 8 weeks at this time. Plus, regardless of his flaws and insecurities, I really loved him and I could see that he really needed me to love him, but I had to think. Can I put up with his behaviour, immaturity, lack of communication, lack of empathy, jealousy? The answer I gave myself is, I will try. After all, we have been together for two years, we have a small family that we both wanted. I always knew he wanted to be a father and I gave that to him. We cannot give up on each other so easily.

So, we stayed together and carried on living.

Within 3 weeks, we were at it again. I came home with my mother and the children about 9pm one evening. He was in the bedroom. I entered and told him that my mother was in the front room and he ignored me. I left, the room, then thought to myself, no. I was not putting up with this any longer. I went back to the room and repeated myself. His respond was "and" I thought to myself how rude can you be. I said, its common courtesy to say hello. He then went off on one and told me that my mum can enter the room and say hello to him. I did not appreciate his tone. I then mentioned the fact that I had enough manners and courtesy to get out of my bed and sit with his family 24 hours after giving birth, even though, I was tired and did not want any visitors. His response was "What is this, a mummy issue?" I had no idea what he meant and at this point, I told him to leave. He went, got a black bag, packed some clothes and left. Whilst he was packing, he was saying things like, "everything I have done for you was in vain" "This is the last time, you will see me leaving your house with a black bag". I was just quiet, once again, waiting for him to leave.

As soon as he left, I sent his mum a message asking if I can bring his belongings to her. She responded by saying, she had no space. I then messaged his sister; she told me I could bring them to her home the following Tuesday.

When Tuesday arrived, I called and she did not answer her phone. Twice. Straight away, I thought to myself, he has told her not to respond to me. I know how he thinks. In his mind, once his belongings are out of my house, we are definitely over. By keeping his belongings in my house, he is hoping, I will give him a call, maybe send a nice text asking him to come home. I am not that female. This man did not deserve a phone call to say "come back please?". He was the one who behaved in an inappropriate way, he is the one who refused to say hello to my mother. Your mother-in-law, your daughter's grandmother. Even if you have a dislike for my mother, still be respectful and say hello. I would have never disrespected his mum, the way he did mine. This man had absolutely no manners, no respect for people older than him and I was not going to upset myself anymore or allow myself to cry tears, due to his behaviour. This was it; we were finished.

A week had past and I remember sending him a message, telling him, I would be disposing of his belongings, if he did not collect them. He called and asked to come over. I let him in and he just started crying. I looked at him, feeling very sorry for him. I knew he wanted to do right by his daughter and I, but I also knew, he is set in his ways and will never change. At this point I had to decide, whether this is something I can deal with for x amount of years. I had some serious thinking to do, but let him come home that same evening.

The final incident occurred in April of 2021. Ayanna was unwell, with a severe cough and at about 1.30am, I decided to bring her to the hospital. Aniyah's dad was asleep on the sofa and I woke him, telling him I am taking Ayanna to the hospital and that I am leaving Aniyah in her crib. When we returned it was about 5am. I went into the kitchen and lit the tail of my spliff that I had left there the previous night. Ayanna was in the kitchen with me. Neither of us had any sleep, Aniyah, was due to wake up in a couple of hours and I needed to get some sleep before she did wake up, because my partner was due to go to work within the next hour or so.

He entered the kitchen and started shouting at me, because I was smoking in front of my daughter. I am fully aware of the dangers of passive smoking and am fully aware that I should not be smoking in front of my children. He had every right to be mad at me and every right to tell me I was wrong. But, once again, he started arguing and cursing me in front of my daughter. This was and had always been my main issue with him. Looking back, if he really cared, he would have removed my daughter from the kitchen and wait until I had put her to bed, to say anything to me. I had always expressed that I hated my daughter to see us argue, but he disregarded my feelings, because he always started an argument in front of her.

The reason I lit that spliff in front of her is because, as previously mentioned, I needed to sleep. My daughter was unwell and clingy. She would not go to bed unless I went to bed. Could I have put her to bed first? Yes, I could have, but, by the time, she would have fallen asleep, Aniyah would have woken up for her morning feed. I would then be running on no sleep at all. I had to do what I had to do, to ensure I got some rest. Since, he was so busy working and sleeping all the time, I only had myself to rely on. This may sound selfish and you readers are probably judging me right now, but I have no regret about lighting up that day.

I was in the kitchen, letting him cuss and rant. He was cursing for a while. I calmly opened the kitchen door and I told him to Fuck off. When I said this, he told me, "OK, I am fucking off then". He started packing, Finally, is what I was thinking. I had been up all night with a sick child, I had a 4-month-old that was due to wake up soon and I just wanted this man to leave so I could get some sleep. During the argument, he took his hand and he banged our dining room table. This really upset me. I took his mobile phone and threw it at him. It hit him on his back. He turned around, picked his phone up off the ground and carried on packing. After he was packed, he left. I remember looking for my phone after he was gone and it was nowhere to be seen. I heard my letter box opening and then I heard, your sim card is here. Mother Fucker, was my first thought. He bought me the mobile phone and thought taking it back would hurt me in some way. It did not. I just thought, you have left me here with no phone and I have your 4-month-old, plus my two-year-old. What type of father does this?

In addition to this, I was so self-reliant, everything in that flat, belonged to me. The only thing he could take was that phone, because he never brought anything else into that flat. This further validates my reasons for being a self sufficient as I am. I was so glad I did not rely on him financially, as I know his style.

I went to bed, feeling relieved that he was gone.

I was woken up by a light knock at the door. I was mad, because I thought he had returned. I looked through the spy hole and saw two female officers. I immediately opened the door as I thought something was wrong with a family member. They explained that an allegation had been made against me. They proceeded by saying, I was not being arrested, but may need a lawyer. They then asked to enter the property. They looked around then left, saying they will be in contact. I was shocked. The father of my 2nd child has called the police on me. Immediately, I thought it was because of the spliff I had smoked in front of my daughter. I could not believe it.

After waking up, from going back to bed after my visit, I went to the phone shop and took out a new contract. I am a woman of pride. If he thought, I was going to put my old sim card in a new phone, he had another thing coming. Taking my mobile phone, whilst you are leaving my house, because you bought it for me is childish and immature. He was not thinking when he did this and he did not think about the consequences this would have on his ability to be a father to his daughter, because now, you do not have my number and neither do your family members. Another classic example of a man putting his ego and pride before his daughter.

Two months had passed and we had not spoken since the day of the argument. During this time, anytime he wanted to see Aniyah, he would contact me via what's app to tell me he wants to see her on that day. Though I had changed my number, I had not changed my What's App. It was still attached to the old number. I did not like this, but I would not complain, because, I knew I would be returning to work soon and eventually, things would have to change. Meaning, he would need to decide what day of the week he would like to have his daughter. Apparently, he was unable to do this, because he had to prioritise work.

After 2 months, I was taking my daughter for a walk in the park and there he was, smoking a spliff with a friend. He approached me, we were civil and he invited me to a BBQ that same evening. He told me to bring Ayanna and I did.

We had a nice evening and he eventually came over to the flat that evening. We slept together that night. I will not lie and say I did not miss him, because I did. But after sleeping together, he left and went home. I thought this was the best thing for us, as a lot had happened and we had not spoken about any of it and I did not want to repeat our previous mistakes of getting back together when we have not resolved the issue that caused the break up in the first place.

He texts me asking if I was Ok that morning and I responded yes. For about 2 weeks, all was well. Then, one evening, I was in bed and he called me asking if could come over. I said yes. But when he arrived, he was drunk and was trying to sleep with me. I was having none of it.

Though we were seeing each other regularly and we were being civil, we still had not discussed our fall out and I felt like we needed to do this. I could not go back into a relationship with this man without, discussing our issues and what we were going to do moving forward. When I refused to sleep with him, he started acting childish and immature again. I could not believe; we were here again. I asked him to leave my home and he told me no. I really had to control myself, because, I really wanted to claw his eyes out. How dare you refuse to leave my home and you no longer live here. I left instead.

I drove to my mums where I stayed for about 2 hours. Whilst I was at my mums, I was thinking about everything that had occurred throughout our relationship. Out of nowhere, it come to me. This man feels, because we have a child together, he can appear whenever he wants and have sex with me whenever he wants. This is why, he has issues, with Ayanna's dad. In his head, he thinks whenever we see each other, we have sex. He is judging me by the standards of Jamaican relationships.

It is very common in the Caribbean for men to have children with multiple women and to be sleeping with every single one of the mothers. This is the life I refused to live with both of my children's fathers.

Ayanna's dad cut us off, because, I am his baby mother, but yet, I have a next man around his daughter. Though we were not in a relationship, he felt like he could claim me.

I returned home and Aniyah's dad was in my bed. I went to lay in the front room and eventually went to sleep. In the morning, he got dressed and left. I said nothing to him and at that moment, I knew we were done for good and that I need to move forward with my life.

Throughout the next two months, he would message me, when he wanted to see Aniyah and that was it. In August of 2021, I had the opportunity to move to a bigger and cheaper property. I informed him and his mother that I was moving and I asked for some help with Aniyah. His mum was happy to have Aniyah for me and she had her for 3 days, whilst I was at my new property, ripping up carpets and decorating. During this time, I told him that we needed to have a conversation and that I was coming to see him. He said OK.

The reason, I was there, was to inform him about the fact that I felt uncomfortable giving him my new address. Due to his behaviour, the fact that he had called the police, given them my address and refused to leave my home when I asked, whilst we were no longer in a relationship, proved to me that I had to set some boundaries. I was hoping to have a conversation about how he was to see his daughter, because at that time, he would collect her from the flat every Saturday. As I was moving, and felt uncomfortable, giving him my address, this plan would have to change, because, he would no longer be able to collect her from the flat. But he was not thinking along those lines. His ignorance got the better of him and his response was "I do not need to know where you live." I said OK. I was not going to argue or discuss this with him, in my head, I thought, he will learn the hard way.

I then went on to discuss the future. I reminded him, Aniyah will be having a 1st birthday and that I assume, he will want to be a part of it. I then reminded him, about his behaviour at Ayanna's 2nd birthday and I told him, I will not be inviting him to Aniyah's 1st birthday, because of how he reacted when her dad called her. If he believed, Ayanna's dad should not have called her on that day, there is no way, he will be calling my phone on Aniyah's birthday.

My logic is this, you did not appreciate the coparenting relationship I had with Ayanna's dad. You did not apologise for your behaviour, or acknowledge your wrongs. I will treat you, the way you wanted me to treat him. Karma is a bitch, and this man will learn this the hard way.

He did not appreciate that statement and he asked me to leave. I was just about too, then I remembered when he refused to leave my home. So, I said no. Just to see his reaction as this is something he had done to me. He threw a glass of water at me. After he did this, I left. That was definitely it. That day I decided, I will no longer communicate with him. I changed my What's app to my new number without giving him any notice.

Saturday arrived. The day he is meant to collect Aniyah. I was expecting my landline to ring, but he did not call. I called him that evening asking him why he never collected his daughter. He expressed he had been trying to call me all day and was unable to get through. I said he should have rung my house phone and he told me he did not have my landline, which was a blatant lie, but I let him go with it.

That was the day before I was moving home and that was my final attempt to rearrange the current arrangement of him seeing his daughter on Saturday's. As usual, that conversation went left and after him telling me to leave him alone, I hung up and successfully moved house.

At this point, my telephone number had changed and so had my address. I was finally free from the stress and toxicity that came from this man and his old wounds.

I had come to the realisation, co-parenting with this man is going to be more stress than it is worth. I ended up writing his mum a letter, letting her know, he must use the courts to see Aniyah.

He did not. He and his daughter had no contact for a year. We were not in contact and I would not be contacting him. As far as I am concerned, it's a fathers responsibility to ensure he keeps the contact with his child. This is the reason I respected Ayanna's dad so much. If he was waiting for me to contact him about his daughter, he had another thing coming. In order for this man to acknowledge where he went wrong, I was going to make sure, I treated him, the way he wanted me to treat Ayanna's father. Two wrongs do not make a right, but I am very tit for tat. If you are unable to acknowledge and apologise for your wrong doings, everything you did to me, will come right back at you.

Eventually, he applied to the Child Maintenance Service and his daughter was awarded £35 monthly.

Chapter 3

My Healing Process

Acceptance was the first step for me. Once I had accepted my relationship had ended, I knew I was on my own. When I say on my own, I mean, in the sense that, I only had myself to depend on. If I was to move forward in my life, I had to re prioritise myself, thoughts, feelings and all emotions.

It was not easy and healing does not take place overnight. In order to heal correctly, you need to be comfortable in your decisions.

I knew my relationship with Aniyah's father was toxic and I knew, I was not the toxic one. Now, I am not perfect and I am not saying that I made no mistakes during the course of that relationship. But, I know, I can compromise and put aside my ego's and pride for the sake of my children. None of their fathers have done this.

As a woman, you have to know your worth and what you want out of life. I know I deserve a man that will love me and my children. I know, I need a man that can communicate. I know I need a man who takes my feelings into consideration. I need a man that will not lie to me. Regardless of my reactions to what he has to say. In my opinion a real man will talk to his woman about everything and anything. A couple will never agree with one another 100% of the time. But, there must be some form of compromise, agreeing to disagree. I need a man that wants to build a life with me as we move forward as a team. I can keep going, but I am sure you get my drift.

If you are a woman reading this, ask yourself, what do you want? This question does not have to be related to romantic relationships. Maybe you are unhappy at work. You may feel like you are not getting the best out of life. The next question should be, how do I get what I want?

If you are a man reading this, the same applies to you. What do you want out of life and how can you achieve it?

At 30 years old, I knew I wanted a baby. By the time I was 35, I had 2. I knew I wanted a family, but the man I wanted to build my family with was incompatible with myself and our relationship failed.

At this stage of my life, I know, I want to be the best mother I can be for my girls. I know, I want to shield them from the experiences I experienced as a child. I am no doctor or medical professional, but I believe I have some form of

PTSD from what I witnessed growing up. I also believe in generational trauma and I think this runs deep within myself and my family.

Intergenerational trauma refers to trauma that is passed from a trauma survivor to their descendants. It can also be referred to as transgenerational or multigenerational trauma.

People experiencing intergenerational trauma may experience symptoms, reactions, patterns, and emotional and psychological effects from trauma experienced by previous generations (not limited to just parents or grandparents).

For example, someone may have grown up in a household where there were generations of yelling and shouting at their children in anger, stemming from a place of unresolved trauma and pain. In order to understand intergenerational trauma, it is important to acknowledge the impact of what the parents/grandparents/great-grandparents/ancestors/etc. survived that resulted in their yelling or shouting.

Source: www.verywellmind.com.

The above is one definition of generational trauma.

With regards to me, I believe my generational trauma stems from my personal history. I am a British woman of Caribbean descent. My DNA analysis from ancestry.com confirmed my lineage to be from Nigeria. There are a few more African countries included in my DNA analysis, but Nigeria had the most percentage.

We all know about the transatlantic slave trade. But, just knowing or learning about the slavery the Africans endured was not enough for me. I had to research my own story.

I have since discovered the women within my maternal line, were abused by men. I have managed to go back 4 generations and have discovered the names of my great grandmother and her mother.

My mother is A Smith

Her mother is E Reid

Her mother is R Price

Her mother S Martin

There are loads of records online that record a number of births from Miss R Price. She had a fair amount of children. I can not say exactly, but I know it was within the double figure mark. I have also discovered, she gave birth to a mixed race baby. This baby was not raised by her though. Her parents raised this baby.

Whilst undertaking my research I communicated with the grandson of my great aunt. He confirmed his grandmother was indeed raised by her parents and that our great grandmother bore a child to a white man, in which, she served. I am unsure if she was a paid servant or a servant who was forced to work for free.

Whilst speaking with my distant cousin, he also was unable to confirm whether the conception of his grandmother was consensual or forced. Due to the fact that our great grandmother had no involvement in raising this child, I believe it was a forced conception. I believe this man Mr C Tyson, raped my great grandmother. I think this is the reason for the baby being raised by her parents. I do not have any evidence of this and I plan to continue researching my family history from the Caribbean as I believe I have utilised all of the resources available here in the UK.

My grandmother, Miss E Reid was another child of miss R Price. My grandmother ran away from home at the age of 14. Apparently, her stepfather, whom she thought was her actual father, was an Obeah man. This is an individual who partakes in black magic or VooDoo as some call it. The family have no idea why she ran away from home. But, lets be realistic. Why do most female teenagers run away from home? Usually, to escape some form of abuse. Be it, physical or sexual.

My grandmother left home at 14 and had no contact with her parents or siblings. That side of the family was a mystery to me, but I am glad I have uncovered what I have. Discovering everything I have discovered about the females in my maternal lineage, has helped me be the person I am today.

I have to break this generational trauma for the sake of my daughters.

My parents were together for over 20 years. All they have to show for their relationship is my brothers and I. They were never married, never bought a house, or gained any assets. They were just living.

In this present day, my parents do not communicate and my mother can not stand my father. No exaggeration, she can not stand to be around him. If she is at my home and my father calls to say he is coming over to see me, she will instantly leave the house. If I mention him to her, she just curses him to me. Their relationship ended over a decade ago and she still speaks negatively of him. She has not healed from this relationship.

When I sit and analyse my parents relationship, including the current behaviours of both my parents, it helps me realise, this is not how I want to live my life. Both of my parents are miserable. I want to be happy. My mum stayed with my dad for over 20 years for the sake of the children. She put her happiness aside, so my brothers and I were raised in a family unit. But in the long run, it made her bitter.

Learning of the abuse my ancestors endured from men has made me stronger and slightly ignorant if I am being honest. I have learned from my mothers mistakes and I refuse to repeat them.

The first step of breaking this generational trauma was to leave my toxic situation and live for my daughters and I.

This is exactly what I have done.

CHAPTER 4

Moving Forward

I am now on a quest to find my happiness and my true calling. One of my aims in life is to create some generational wealth for my daughters and descendants to come.

In this western way of life, I am considered working class. My family have no assets or anything else to hand down to myself or my brothers. My grandparents had no assets and my great grandparents, I really do not know.

To earn a living, we all need to work. We go to school, then to college, some of us go to university and then we get a job. I am educated to undergrad level and the highest salary I have ever earned was £27000.

I have to be honest and say it was by choice. I used to work in a secondary school that eventually turned into an academy. I used to do learning and behaviour support. That role was considered a support role. The working hours for support staff was 8.30am-4.15pm. The working hours for teachers were, 8.30am-3.30pm.

I am a strong believer in the work life balance and I believe your professional life should be kept separate from your personal life. When the school academized, the expectations of staff drastically changed. There was less support from senior leaders and you were basically expected to fulfil your roles and duties regardless of whether you have had any training or not.
If you approached the principal with an issue, his response most of the time would be, just get it done. If a member of staff needed time off work for a personal issue such as a child graduating from uni, the answer would be, you can not attend, you have to come to work.

A few women had babies and asked for their working hours to be changed from Full to Part time. His answer was always no. If an employee needed to leave work early for any personal circumstance, the answer was no. I am an observer. I observed the behaviour of the principal to his employees and immediately decided, this academy, will not be getting any good will out of me. I used to just do my job and go home. A lot of my colleagues would work past their contracted hours to fulfil their roles.
The Head of Learning was responsible for an entire year group. Approximatley, 360 students. There was many aspects to this role, but there were never enough hours within the school day to complete them. Some HoL's started

their school day at 7am and would leav e the premises at 6pm, with no extra pay. They were expected to manage an entire year group, produce assemblies, sometimes with only 24 hours notice.

I had the opportunity to become a Head of Learning, but I did not apply for the role. Yes, the role was more money than my Learning and Curriculum Support Officer role, but, money was not my main motivator. In addition to this, I was not going to be giving up my work life balance for anybody. I was that employee that left the building 4.15pm on the dot and not a minute later. Sometimes, I would be driving out of the school at 4.15pm. Nobody could get me to stay later than my contracted hours. If we were in an after school meeting and it ran past 4.15pm, I would take my belongings and leave.

This Academy had no empathy for their employees. There was no way, I was going to go above and beyond for a school that would deduct your wages for the smallest of things. Fail to pay overtime, because the employee chose to stay late, but yet, still chastise that same employee for not completing a specific task on time, when they have other duties to fulfil.

Whilst working at that Academy, our staff turnover was through the roof. We had some members of staff have mental breakdowns, turn into alcoholics and drink alcohol whilst still at work.

Now, we all need money to survive, but, the fact is, money stays on this Earth after we die. This is my mentality. There was no way, I would allow any job to break me mentally. There was no way, I was going to put my employers before my health. Be it mental, physical or emotional. Life is too short. In the 12 years I worked for that academy, 3 members of staff had passed away. As far as I am concerned, they worked until they dropped. There was no memorial service for these deceased employees, not even an announcement. What does that tell you?

After 12 long years and having 2 children during this time, I decided to leave the corporate world and attempt to go into Business for myself. I decided enough was enough. I worked from the age of 16, I was now 35. I could not buy a house as my wages were never high enough, I had no savings, because I was always paying rent, bills, and childcare. I felt stuck and I needed more out of life. So, in April of 2022 I resigned and decided to migrate that same year. I needed a lifestyle change and I decided to move to Jamaica.

The Move

The move was not too difficult, as I had already made some preparations. After visiting the Island in 2016 I applied for my Jamaican Citizenship and passport, opened a Jamaican bank account and applied for my TRN (Tax Registration Number). I then started Saving.

After leaving work, I had to decide what I was going to do for an income. So I came up with a business idea and I am currently working on marketing this business. I wrote a business plan, registered my business with the Companies office of Jamaica, designed my website and designed my marketing materials. It felt so good to be setting up a venture that I will be bringing with me to the Caribbean. I was and still am very excited.

October 2022, I left the UK with my 2 children. It is now January of 2023 and I am 3 months into my migration journey. We moved here with nowhere permanent to stay. After living in a holiday apartment for one month, and then living in a guest house for 2 months, I have finally acquired a home for my daughters and I. Though I am renting, the aim is to eventually build or buy a home as this is something I believe is a lot more achievable in Jamaica than it is in the UK. In addition to this, when this goal is achieved, I will have something to give to my daughters.

This is just the beginning of this new chapter in my life and I am excited to see what the next 3-6 months will bring.

Why am I telling you this? Somewhere someone in this world is feeling the way I was feeling. Stuck. As I have gotten older, I have come to realise we are responsible for our destiny. Life is all about choices. I choose to be happy, drama free, at peace and I have chosen to change the narrative for my daughters and I. Whilst I am not a fan of the school system, my children are exceling here in Jamaica. I prefer the Jamaican education to the British education. In Britain, 4 and 5 year old's are being taught about homosexuality.

Please understand. I am not homophobic and if any of my children turned out to be gay, this is something, I will accept. But, I will not have the UK government expose my children to something I believe they are too young to be taught.

This was another reason I left the UK. I just hope Jamaica has no plans to add this to their curriculum any time soon. Children are innocent and their innocence does not need to be taken from them at 4 years old.

Chapter 5

Words of Wisdom!

Life is hard. Life can break you. It has broken many people. In order to stay mentally strong and focused, you need to decide what you want out of life and go for it with no apologies. Is someone or something holding you back? Do you want a new job? A career change? To leave a toxic relationship? To distance yourself from toxic people?

No matter what it is you desire all that is needed is careful planning. Sometimes in life, you need to take a few steps backwards to move forward. If this is your predicament, please, do not allow fear to stop you. Fear can sometimes create self sabotage and procrastination. Fear is a normal human emotion, but we must learn how to manage our fear and at the same time, not allow the fear we are feeling stop us from getting what we want out of life.

Before I had my children, I feared leaving my job. This paid my rent and my bills. I remember the UK recession of 2010. People lost their jobs, their homes, their cars. People were queueing in food banks, because they had no money to buy food and I am not talikg about the unemployed. A large number of people in employment are still using food banks, because currently, wages are only paying rent, bills and travel. Inflation is rising, but the wages stay the same.

Fear has resulted in people going hungry, because they are scared to get into debt with their household bills. My ignorance has replaced my fear. If I have to choose between feeding my children and paying bills, I am feeding my children. After studying my family history and studying the system, I have decided, I want my two daughters to be free of all the oppression that comes with being a working class individual. I do not want my daughters to rely on government handouts. I want my children to be independent, resilient, hard working women. This starts with me. I must set an example to my daughters, hence why I have moved abroad and have started my own business. There is no benefit system in Jamaica. I have no choice but to work for myself as the wages paid in Jamaica are very low indeed.

I hope by the time they reach working age, they will want to be apart of mums business. I plan on employing my daughters when they reach of age. Assuming my business is something they want to take part in. If not, no problem. At least I would have built a business they can maybe sell when I am no longer on this Earth.

Everything I am doing is for them.

Where am I now?

It is now February of 2023 and my daughters are settled in school and preschool.

I have set up a land and property maintenance service. I have started a YouTube channel and am in the process of finishing this book. I am enjoying being my own boss, setting my own schedules and still being able to spend time with my children.

It does get hard, being a single parent of two young children, whilst attempting to manage all of my personal projects, but, as they grow, I am sure it will get easier.

My Main goals

My main goal whilst in Jamaica is to secure financial freedom. I am working on gaining multiple streams of income, to be able to secure some assets, that will eventually create the generational wealth my daughters deserve.

This page is for you, the reader. Complete this table to start the process of finding your happiness!

What do I want from my life?	What Obstacles are in the way?	How will I remove these obstacles?	Plan of action, once obstacles are gone.	Time frame

Moving to Jamaica and starting my own business was one of the best decisions I have ever made in my life. Putting myself first allowed me to follow my dream of moving abroad. I will not say it has not been challenging, there are times where I want to tear my hair out, because I only have me, myself and I to rely on. There is nobody to call when the children are unwell, this means, I am unable to work and may lose on a job.

Travelling in route taxi's during the school run, or whilst grocery shopping is hard. I have no car, so I rely heavily on public transport. I cant go out and socialise as there is nobody to take care of the girls.

It gets hard at times, but, I focus on the end result. That will be me running a highly successful land and property maintenance business, whilst gaining an extra income from my book sales and an additional income from my YouTube channel.

Resilience, positiveness and self belief. This is what is needed.

The Update

Today is the 2nd of February 2024.

Would you believe me if I told you that I am now a mum of 3. Yes. My son, Tafari was born on the 22nd of October 2023. After being in a relationship for only a couple of months, I fell pregnant to who I thought was a wonderful individual.

This will be discussed in my next book. “Life in Jamaica”.

If you have any questions or comments, you may email me at T_gayle@aol.co.uk.

The website for my business

www.jalandandpropertyservices.com

My YouTube Channel - Me and Mine

Instagram, Personal - Me_and_mine0401

Instagram, Business - Jalandandpropertyservices

Printed in Great Britain
by Amazon

57376406R00035

La mujer fugitiva

Alicia
Giménez
Bartlett

La mujer fugitiva

Alicia
Giménez
Bartlett

Ediciones Destino
Colección Áncora y Delfín
Volumen 1627

Ediciones Destino, un sello editorial de Editorial Planeta, S. A.
Avda. Diagonal, 662-664, 08034 Barcelona (España)
www.planetadelibros.com
www.edestino.es

Primera edición: enero de 2024
ISBN: 978-84-233-6446-6
Depósito legal: B. 20.296-2023
Composición: Realización Planeta
Impresión y encuadernación: CPI Black Print
Printed in Spain - Impreso en España

Para el doctor Bismarck Abella,
un médico de verdad

I

Era un primer interrogatorio un tanto dificultoso. El tipo no paraba de llorar. Llevamos a término todos los protocolos aconsejados ante los excesos emocionales: le rogué que se serenara utilizando mi voz más dulce. Le alargué un pañuelo desechable. Garzón le ofreció café. Incluso le insinuamos que, haciendo una excepción, podía encender un cigarrillo aun estando en comisaría. No fumaba, no quiso café y llevaba su propio paquete de pañuelitos. Lo único a lo que parecía dispuesto era a seguir llorando con desconsuelo. Ni el subinspector ni yo somos dos monstruos. Nadie podrá acusarnos de no respetar la sensibilidad de los testigos. Pero de aquel hombre esperábamos algo más que un simple testimonio. Las circunstancias lo hacían en principio sospechoso. En principio, nada más, porque justo al principio del caso nos encontrábamos. Hacía sólo tres horas que se había procedido al levantamiento del cadáver.

Christophe Dufour, ciudadano francés residente en España. Treinta y ocho años. Documentación en regla. Ocupación: restaurador. A falta de informes forenses más extensos, sabíamos que había sido asesinado de un par de certeras cuchilladas con un cuchillo grande y afilado. Sucedió de madrugada, mientras dormía apaciblemente en su *food truck*.

—¿Su qué? —preguntó Garzón exagerando el tono de la curiosidad.

—Ya sabe, subinspector, esas furgonetas que elaboran y venden comida. Ahora están muy de moda, son un fenómeno mundial.

—¿Y va a escribirlo así en los informes, *fud trac*?

—Es que si lo traducimos queda fatal. ¿Furgoneta de comida, camión restaurante?

—Pues a mí lo de *fud trac* me parece una majadería.

Le prometí buscar una alternativa hispana que no ofendiera su ortodoxia lingüística. El subinspector era así, capaz de ponerse melindroso con cuestiones adyacentes cuando los problemas que nos acuciaban eran de primer orden. Y en aquel caso lo eran: no existían pistas iniciales de las que pudiéramos ir tirando ni tampoco testigos. Si estábamos intentando interrogar a aquel plañidero contumaz no era porque de entrada existiera nada en contra suya. Simplemente Eduardo Castillo era amigo y socio de la víctima —y como tal, algo debía de saber, o yendo un poco más allá, algo podía haber hecho.

—Señor Castillo, por favor. Si no se contiene un poco no podemos hablar, y está usted aquí justo para eso, para hablar.

—¿Y no podemos dejarlo para mañana? A lo mejor ya estoy un poco más entero.

—No, es importante que sea ahora.

—¿Por eso de que las primeras cuarenta y ocho horas después de un crimen son las más importantes para investigar?

—Más o menos —respondí, pero al comprobar que Castillo había abandonado el desvarío lacrimógeno y hacía preguntas de aficionado a la sección de sucesos, el subinspector perdió la paciencia.

—A ver, Eduardo, tiene usted cuarenta años. A su edad, uno ya controla los lagrimales, así que no nos haga perder más tiempo y conteste a nuestras preguntas.

—Pero si todavía no me han hecho ninguna —dijo con la inocencia de un niño de pecho. Llevaba razón. En ese momento comprendí que el tal Eduardo era un hombre bastante especial y que, entre eso y el dichoso *food truck*, también aquel caso se presentaba como algo fuera de lo corriente. No me equivoqué.

Eduardo Castillo Montes. Cuarenta años justos, lo que hoy en día se considera «un joven» y años atrás se denominaba un hombre en la madurez. Soltero. Natural de Madrigal de las Altas Torres, pero trasplantado a Barcelona desde tiempo inmemorial. Estudios de Psicología que había abandonado en segundo curso. Por fin, aquel «sospechoso» tomó la palabra, y hubo momentos en los que pensé que lo prefería llorando a perorando. Era tan caudaloso en su expresión verbal que, tras preguntarle, nos veíamos obligados a cortar sus discursos cada dos por tres.

—Éramos los mejores amigos. Uña y carne. Christophe era la uña porque aunque más joven que yo, era más duro y más resistente ante las adversidades. Yo, la carne, porque todo puede herirme con facilidad. Hace tres años que empezamos con este negocio. Nuestra sociedad hubiera podido convertirse en una olla de grillos. No sé si ustedes están familiarizados con el funcionamiento de un *food truck*, pero ya pueden hacerse una idea. El espacio para cocinar es pequeño. La mayor parte de las veces uno cocina y el otro sirve al mismo tiempo. Si no estás muy bien avenido, pueden saltar chispas a la menor ocasión. Pero entre nosotros no hubo chispas jamás. Christophe hacía las especialidades que no había acabado de preparar la noche anterior y yo servía a los clientes sin el más mínimo estrés. Nuestra gastronomía, francesa en general, pero también con toques de «fusión», gustaba muchísimo y...

—¿Vivían ustedes juntos? —fue mi primera interrupción.

—Como estaba diciéndoles, la vida en el negocio del *food truck* tiene un cariz especial en muchas cosas. Por ejemplo, en cómo nos alojamos este tipo de empresarios. En nuestro caso...

—Lo que quiero saber es si existía una relación sentimental entre la víctima y usted.

—¡No, para nada, ni hablar! Los dos somos heteros y entre nosotros sólo había amistad. Además, como iba a decirles, por nuestra especial forma de vivir, ni siquiera compartíamos el mismo techo. Nuestra furgoneta está acondicionada para que una persona pueda dormir con comodidad. Cuando llegábamos a un lugar para trabajar, uno de los dos tomaba una habitación en un hotel y el otro se quedaba en el vehículo. Nos turnábamos, un día él, otro yo. Así podíamos ducharnos y, al mismo tiempo, el que se quedaba vigilaba para que no sufriéramos robos ni vandalismos y...

—¿Es ese tipo de alojamiento lo habitual? —preguntó Garzón.

—Hay de todo, cada uno se lo monta como puede. A nosotros nos iba bien así porque...

—¿Dónde se conocieron?

—Comiendo en la barra de una cafetería. Habíamos pedido los dos el mismo plato, y como estaba infame, nos pusimos a despotricar en voz muy baja y entonces...

Mi paciencia empezó a flaquear.

—Eduardo, ¿podría ser más concreto en sus explicaciones?

—No la entiendo, pero si estoy concretando muchísimo.

—Eso está claro, concreta usted mucho y habla muy bien, con mucha propiedad. Lo que quiero decir es que no sea tan prolijo en sus explicaciones, que vaya más al grano de lo que nos interesa.

—Lo intentaré.

Talmente, parecía que estaba disfrutando del interrogatorio, que superada la fase de lágrimas, se sentía el protagonista de una representación teatral. «Individuo curioso», volví a pensar.

—Hábleme de Christophe. ¿Tiene familia?

—No creo. Era la persona más solitaria del mundo. Nunca me dijo que tuviera familia.

—¿Novias, relaciones sentimentales?

—Era más bien de ligue puntual.

—¿Usted conocía a alguno de sus ligues?

—Sí y no.

—¿Puede ser más explícito?

—¡Es que tengo miedo de pasarme, inspectora! Después del corte que acaba de pegarme...

—No es nada personal. Usted quiere que aparezca el asesino de su amigo, ¿verdad? Pues al hablar, piense en lo que puede ayudarnos a descubrirlo y en lo que no.

Suspiró resignado. Llevaba un mono tejano y un grueso jersey de lana. Desgarbado, de estatura media. Flaco, con nariz prominente, pelo lacio y pequeños ojos vivaces. Tenía una pinta divertida, un poco infantil.

—Yo conocía a los ligues que a veces hacía entre las clientas, era un hombre guapetón, tenía éxito con las mujeres. Pero cuando digo conocía quiero decir que las había visto. Él nunca me las presentó ni me hablaba de detalles. Era muy reservado.

—¿No le habló de su pasado?

—No demasiado. Había nacido en París, dio muchas vueltas por el mundo, había trabajado en un buque carguero, en una agencia china de importación y exportación.

—¿Y luego se hizo cocinero?

—No sé si era cocinero profesional con estudios y todas esas cosas, pero cocinaba muy bien.

—¿Les funcionaba su negocio desde el punto de vista económico?

—Sí, estábamos ganando bastante dinero. La historia de los *food trucks* es una moda en expansión. No nos perdíamos una feria, ni una concentración deportiva... Cada vez teníamos más contactos, nos avisaban desde los ayuntamientos por si queríamos reservar plaza en algún evento. Todo nos iba muy bien. La idea era ahorrar hasta poder poner un restaurante convencional. Al final, todos nos aburguesamos y pensamos que echar raíces y vivir como la gente corriente es lo ideal a partir de cierta edad, aunque probablemente cometemos un error.

Bajó la vista y se quedó pensativo.

—¿Tiene usted idea de quién ha podido matar a su socio, alguna sospecha, alguna teoría?

—Nadie robó nada, inspectora. Chris no tenía amigos, pero tampoco enemigos. ¿Qué le puedo decir? Un loco, un desalmado, alguien de otro planeta... No lo sé.

—Puede irse.

—¿Ya no hablamos más?

—Si el asesinato de su amigo no se resuelve en cuarenta y ocho horas, hablaremos muchas más veces, ya verá.

Garzón me comentó que aquel sujeto lo ponía de los nervios. Lanzó su teoría sobre el tipo de testigos en el que lo incluía. Según él, alguien que habla mucho e intenta dar toda clase de detalles que no se le han pedido oculta algo. El bosque verborreico tapa el hallazgo concreto. La teoría no era mala, tampoco nueva, pero presentaba dificultades para darla por buena en esta ocasión. Primero: el testigo puede ser una persona que en cualquier circunstancia se exprese a lo grande, y segundo: no todo lo que pudiera querer ocultar el testigo verboso sería necesariamente un delito. Yo siempre había sido más partidaria de pensar que aquel que mucho habla es porque tiene poco interesante que decir, y eso incluía a testigos y ciudadanos en general. A mí, de entrada, Eduardo Castillo no me causaba sospechas de culpabilidad. Parecía sincero, y sus incontenibles lágrimas iniciales mostraban, desde mi punto de vista, un auténtico dolor. Pero ¿quién puede saber? Las capacidades actorales del ser humano no están medidas ni contadas, en especial ahora que todo el mundo anda enganchado a las series de televisión y puede ponerse a remedar a los protagonistas.

No resultaba muy claro por dónde debíamos empezar. Me había dejado llevar por los impulsos que habitualmente me acometen y antes de leer los pocos informes que había dado tiempo a que me presentaran, había decidido interrogar a Castillo. Así, el primer paso en las investigaciones también vendría dado por mi intuición. Al fin y al cabo, la intuición femenina es uno de los clichés menos pestilentes sobre las mujeres que circulan por ahí.

—Vámonos a la morgue, Garzón.

—¿Usted cree?

—¿Se le ocurre algún sitio mejor?

—¡Hombre, inspectora, tratándose de ese sitio... puede apostar a que sí! ¿Y no sería mejor empezar por el dosier que nos han preparado? No sabemos si ha aparecido un testigo en los últimos momentos ni las circunstancias exactas ni...

—¡Ya lo sé, ya lo sé! Pero quiero ver físicamente a la víctima e imaginármela a dúo con Castillo.

—El dúo del *food truck*, parece un grupo musical, aunque uno de los componentes va a tener pocas oportunidades de cantar.

—Nunca se sabe, Fermín, ¿no dicen que los muertos también hablan?

—Pero nadie ha dicho nada de que canten.

A aquellas alturas de mi vida profesional, alturas que empezaban a producirme vértigo, entrar en la morgue no me causaba la misma impresión que en mis inicios. Sin embargo, un cierto respeto siempre se dejaba notar. Allí moraban los muertos en tránsito hacia su final definitivo; de modo que visitarlos era una especie de rito social. El forense encargado del difunto francés se puso muy nervioso cuando nos vio. Empezó a pergeñar excusas antes de que le pidiéramos ninguna explicación: era demasiado pronto, había otros cadáveres en lista, una autopsia no es cosa de un ratito como nosotros sabíamos muy bien... Cuando le dije que sólo pretendíamos saludar al cadáver, su nerviosismo aumentó. Aquel era un ejemplo evidente de por qué detesto relacionarme con personas sin sentido del humor. El subinspector acabó de liar la situación preguntándole de modo tajante: «Pero ¿ya lo ha rajado o no?». El galeno, que era joven y carente de experiencia en el trato policial, me miró como preguntándome quién era aquel cavernícola que me acompañaba, y luego su mirada se convirtió en una petición: «¡Por Dios, aléjelo de mí!».

—Doctor Rosselló, lo único que queremos es echarle una mirada al cuerpo para ver qué aspecto tiene, nada más. Luego esperaremos el resultado de la autopsia, que cuando llegue bienvenida será. ¿Podrá permitírnoslo, por favor?

Nos llevó con notable fastidio hasta la sala y abrió

el cajón frigorífico correspondiente con un gesto furtivo que parecía esperar alguna acción imprevisible por nuestra parte. ¿Qué temía, que secuestráramos el cuerpo? Sin separarse demasiado de nosotros, se instaló en un segundo plano para observar lo que hacíamos. Me volví serenamente hacia él:

—¿Podría dejarnos a solas, por favor? Es que necesitamos tener una charla confidencial con el muerto.

Se largó por fin. Imaginé perfectamente lo que les diría aquella noche a sus amigos o a su mujer: «Han aparecido dos de la bofia diciendo insensateces y me han hecho pasar un mal rato, de verdad». Antes de centrarme en mirar el cadáver, mi mente dio un rodeo pensando en la cantidad de tiempo que te hacen perder las relaciones humanas. Testigos charlatanes, forenses desconfiados..., si eran ciertas las predicciones de que el mundo acabaría dominado por robots, tal extremo debía considerarse como una absoluta bendición para el trabajo.

El cuerpo de Christophe Dufour era impactante: alto, fuerte, compacto, de grandes manos y pies. En su cara pálida resaltaba una barba pelirroja, color idéntico al de su abundante cabello. Los rasgos, algo alterados por la muerte, eran regulares, varoniles, casi nobles, me atrevería a decir. Debió de haber sido muy atractivo para quien gusta de los hombres tipo nórdico, tirando a vikingo. Garzón, como en el fondo tampoco comprendía qué demonio hacíamos allí, me preguntó bisbiseando:

—Y bien, inspectora, ¿qué le parecen las puñaladas?

Ni siquiera me había fijado en las heridas, pero sí, allí estaban, cárdenas y regulares junto al corazón.

—Unas puñaladas limpias y directas.

—Pues me pregunto qué especie de animal pudo pegárselas, porque este tío es un cachalote. El asesino debía tener una fuerza tremenda. Eso nos descartaría a una mujer.

—Descarte sólo a los niños, Fermín, y no porque no tengan instintos asesinos, que cada vez van a más. Hay mujeres muy fuertes.

—No se defendió.

—El asesino lo sorprendió, o se conocían o se plantó de improviso ante él. Y fue directo al corazón, con buena puntería. Pero eso ya nos lo contará la autopsia con más precisión.

—Entonces, ¿qué es lo que le interesaba ver, inspectora Delicado?

—Lo que quería ver ya lo he visto. Ahora me hago una idea perfecta de cómo era el dúo del *food truck*.

2

La furgoneta gastronómica de la víctima estaba estacionada la noche del crimen entre otras dos. En la primera, dedicada a comida alemana, no pernoctaba nadie habitualmente. La otra estaba regentada por una joven pareja que preparaba platos vegetarianos. Habían dormido ambos en el vehículo, pero no oyeron nada que perturbara su sueño. Eran en total cinco *food trucks* las que ocupaban la plaza del Nord, conocida popularmente en Barcelona como la plaza dels Lluïsos. No cabían muchas más. Paraban allí durante una semana con motivo de unas jornadas alimentarias que organizaba el ayuntamiento del barrio, una de esas iniciativas que se crean sin un motivo concreto procurando dinamizar el tejido social de la ciudad. No contábamos con testigos ni cámara de seguridad alguna grabó movimientos nocturnos. Sin testigos y sin huellas, empezábamos mal. Por la postura del cuerpo, la víctima se había despertado y, al ir a levantarse de su yacija, se lo impidieron las certeras cuchilladas. El asesino iba a por él. La puerta estaba abierta. Su socio dijo que nunca la cerraba porque sentía una cierta claustrofobia al verse confinado en un lugar tan angosto. No era un hombre miedoso.

¿Se conocían víctima y asesino? Quizá, Christophe no gritó al verse sorprendido o, dada la poca distancia entre vehículos, alguien lo hubiera oído. Sin embargo, eso no significaba gran cosa. La hipótesis del mutuo conocimiento podía fundamentarse más en el tipo de agresión. Iban a por él, seguro. ¿Por qué si no alguien abre una puerta, va directo al camastro colocado tras el asiento del conductor y apuñala a un hombre en el pecho? Garzón discutía esa posibilidad.

—No tenían por qué conocerse. Quizá no le dio tiempo a gritar. Le recuerdo que hay mucho pirado por el mundo, inspectora. Y en este ambiente...

—¿A qué ambiente se refiere?

—En fin, Petra, todos estos tíos..., ya lo ve usted. Hoy aquí y mañana allí, sin casa, sin un lugar fijo al que acudir, sin familia estructurada..., vaya a saber qué historia tienen detrás. El francés pudo haberse hecho un enemigo. Bien pudo tratarse de cualquier descerebrado al que miró mal, con quien discutió mientras le servía... Un pirado sin más.

—¡Maravilloso, Garzón! Ha lanzado usted una completa batería de prejuicios en pocas frases. A ver, cuénteme por qué la gente que no acude a una oficina en horario laboral tiene que llevar por fuerza una vida licenciosa. ¿No tener casa fija es sinónimo de disipación? En cuanto a la familia estructurada ni lo comentaré, me parece de una carcundia atroz.

—Vida licenciosa, disipación..., puede seguir con todas las palabras cultas que se le antojen, pero sabe que llevo razón. Saltimbanquis, feriantes, cómicos, artistas de circo, vendedores ambulantes... Aunque sólo sea por la cantidad de gente que frecuentan, no son ciudadanos normales y corrientes.

—Pero eso no los convierte necesariamente en carne de presidio.

—Lo son más que un padre de familia que trabaja en un banco. A ver, ¿qué padre de familia duerme en un camión con la puerta sin cerrar?

—A lo mejor el francés esperaba a alguien, una cita galante.

—¿Una cita galante a la que espera metidito en la cama y bien dormido? No me cuadra.

—¿Tiene también una teoría sobre las citas galantes de los saltimbanquis?

—¡No!, pero reconozca que si la víctima hubiera sido un padre de familia convencional, ahora estaríamos investigando en su entorno, mientras que aquí el entorno al que nos enfrentamos comprende a toda la población.

—También el francés tendría un entorno, ¿no? Por cierto, ¿cómo tenemos su búsqueda de coordenadas?

—Hemos pasado datos de pasaporte y huellas dactilares a la Europol francesa. No hemos hecho nada más.

—En cuanto hayamos acabado de interrogar a los vecinos de *truck*, investigue en el consulado y en la embajada francesa de Madrid. Yo me ocuparé del único entorno del difunto con que contamos.

—¿El socio parlanchín?

—Hagamos de su defecto virtud. Entre tantas palabras, algo dirá que sea sustancial.

Se encogió de hombros, pensando probablemente que todas nuestras elucubraciones no valían un pimiento.

Era una mañana bastante desapacible. Las jornadas gastronómicas no se abrían habitualmente al público hasta la una del mediodía, pero el asesinato había obligado a congelar su actividad. Sin embargo, mientras nuestros hombres no hubieran completado todos los interrogatorios, ningún feriante tenía permiso para marcharse. El ambiente era, pues, de evidente consternación. Aparte de lo inquietante del asesinato, una amenaza para la seguridad general, aquella pausa involuntaria les impedía tanto trabajar allí como trasladarse para hacerlo en otro lugar. Ya habíamos recibido las primeras protestas. Uno de los cocineros ambulantes nos espetó que nunca se nos ocurriría cerrar la actividad comercial de un barrio entero por un asesinato en un restaurante. ¿Por qué sus negocios debían ser considerados de modo diferente? Tenían comida comprada que podía estropearse. ¿Quién se haría cargo de las pérdidas? Ninguna de sus quejas carecía de fundamento. Las razones que Garzón había esgrimido sobre la gente que carece de ubicación inamovible pesaban también en la consideración oficial. Nunca nos habíamos enfrentado a un caso como aquel.

La pareja propietaria del *food truck* vegetariano vecino al del crimen nos recibió envuelta en gruesos abrigos y bufandas. Eran jóvenes, ninguno de los dos pasaba de los treinta. Estaban asustados, ella casi lloraba. Decidí que entráramos en un bar para librarnos del frío, también con el fin de que se tranquilizaran. Garzón y yo pedimos café. Ellos debían militar en la especialidad que cocinaban, porque ambos se inclinaron por sendas infusiones. Elisenda y Javier eran sus nombres. Les preguntamos por sus circunstancias, por su actividad. Elisenda era licenciada en Sociología. Javier, químico. Nunca habían ejercido trabajos que correspondieran a sus estudios.

—¿Y eso por qué? —quiso saber el subinspector.

—Todo está muy difícil —contestó el chico—. No hay trabajo, y si encuentras alguno, eres eventual un tiempo, luego te echan a la calle y a volver a empezar. Y que conste que no hablamos de empleos bien pagados, eso ha dejado de existir. Pensamos que intentaríamos buscarnos la vida de otra manera.

—¿Con la furgoneta de comidas?

La chica empezó a hablar, ya más serena.

—Al principio alquilamos una casa en un pueblecito pequeño medio deshabitado para abrir un restaurante con encanto, pero no funcionó. Luego se nos ocurrió lo de la furgoneta, como está tan de moda... Pedimos un crédito al banco para montarla por todo lo alto.

—¿Y les va bien a pesar de servir vegetariano? —preguntó de improviso Garzón.

Ambos se echaron a reír con cierta timidez.

—¡Bueno, yo creo que eso es justamente lo que ayuda a que nos vaya bien!

—No puedo creerlo.

Tomó la palabra el varón:

—La cultura gastronómica vegetariana está muy

extendida. Aparte de los temas obvios de salud, hay platos riquísimos, y es un modo de respetar el planeta.

—Pero no me negarán que renunciar a comer un buen jamón es un sacrificio de los gordos.

—Nosotros, por decirle toda la verdad, nos permitimos comer un poco de jamón en ocasiones señaladas —declaró la chica como admitiendo una grave culpabilidad.

Atajé un interrogatorio que tomaba caminos poco útiles a la investigación.

—Cuéntenos sobre Christophe, ¿lo conocían?

—Coincidimos con él y con Eduardo muchas veces. En este mundillo acabamos conociéndonos todos —dijo Elisenda—. Era un hombre muy callado, poco comunicativo. No hacía amistades con facilidad. Parecía antipático, hosco con la gente; pero con nosotros siempre se portó muy bien. Sabía mucho de fontanería y una vez que tuvimos un problema con el grifo de la cocina vino a echarnos una mano y lo solucionó.

—¿Y qué tal con su socio, Eduardo?

—A Eduardo todos le llamamos Bob. Es todo lo contrario de su compañero, le gusta hablar, bromea todo el tiempo, se enrolla con las piedras. Un hombre muy divertido.

—¿Se llevaban bien entre ellos?

Intercambiaron miradas sin saber qué decir:

—Suponemos que sí, nunca los oímos discutir o enfadarse; pero tampoco había entre nosotros ningún tipo de intimidad como para saber esos detalles.

—Centrémonos en el presente. El día previo a la

noche del crimen, ¿vieron a alguien hablando con los dos socios?

—No me fijé demasiado —apuntó Javier—. Tuvieron bastantes clientes, eso sí, pero no pasó nada especial.

Elisenda levantó un dedo como una niña de escuela.

—A mí me llamó la atención que Christophe estuvo hablando bastante rato con una mujer.

—¿Cómo era esa mujer?

—Alta, morena, guapa, maquillada, con buen tipo... Al principio pensé que era un ligue, pero luego vi que había comprado un montón de cosas. Christophe le dio dos bolsas grandes de papel para que se llevara todo el material. Iba cargada.

—¿Pensó que era un ligue porque era guapa o por la actitud de ambos?

—¡Ay, inspectora, en la actitud sí que no puse interés! Piense que yo estaba rellenando rollitos de pasta con coliflor escabechada y sólo miraba de vez en cuando. Creí que era un ligue porque ella era guapa y él también era atractivo.

—Sí, ya lo vi.

—¿Lo vio?

—En el depósito, cuando ya era cadáver.

Como si le hubiera lanzado un puñado de realidad infecciosa a la cara, Elisenda se la tapó con las dos manos, emitió un sollozo profundo. Su pareja le pasó un brazo por los hombros, intentó consolarla. Ella se las apañó para hablar, aunque entre lágrimas.

—Esto es horrible, espantoso, no puedo ni pensarlo. Nosotros ahí durmiendo como dos benditos y justo al lado...

—Tranquilízate, Eli, por favor. —El chico se volvió hacia nosotros—. Es horrible, y además nos hace mucho daño, una mala publicidad. La gente ya cree que este tipo de negocios lo llevamos cuatro bohemios, que somos una especie de...

Como no encontraba la palabra justa, le ayudé:

—¿Saltimbanquis?

—¡Exactamente!

El subinspector se removió con incomodidad.

—Pero la verdad es que cumplimos con los impuestos, somos honrados, respetamos las leyes, aunque ni con esas. Los bancos se lo piensan mil veces para darte créditos y las aseguradoras se hacen de rogar. Y todo por no tener domicilio fijo. Miren, nosotros compramos la mejor furgoneta del mercado, que aún estamos pagando. Tiene una pequeña habitación, tiene ducha y excusado, un rincón para comer, leer o ver la televisión. ¡Es un hogar en toda regla! Pero no, para ser respetable hace falta un pisito con salón comedor o un adosado en las afueras. Hay mucha gente que vive en el Pleistoceno, créanme.

Miré a mi compañero con divertida ironía. Él puso cara de póker y desvió la conversación. En cuanto regresamos a la furgoneta, Garzón preguntó:

—¿No les quedará por ahí ningún rollito de coliflor?

La pregunta cogió a todo el mundo a traspié. Elisenda enseguida reaccionó:

—¡Pues claro, guardé dos para nuestro almuerzo de hoy!

—En ese caso no he dicho nada.

—Se lo caliento en un pispás. Me hace ilusión que lo pruebe. Nosotros improvisaremos algo para la hora de la comida, por eso no se preocupe.

El inefable Garzón se zampó aquel bocado, que realmente olía muy bien, acompañado de una cerveza que aquellos chicos nos ofrecieron. Mientras miraba relamerse a mi compañero, no dudé de que su intención fuera contribuir a la sostenibilidad del planeta. Ahí acabó el interrogatorio. Más tarde, mientras Garzón se encaminaba a vérselas con el servicio diplomático francés, yo fui a charlar de nuevo con Eduardo. Habíamos quedado en el hotel donde se alojaba, que estaba cerca del parque Güell. Se llamaba Aparthotel Barcelona City. «¡Qué horror de nombre!», me dije. Me hacía pensar en un montón de turistas internacionales dando vueltas por la ciudad sin saber si se encontraban en España, Marruecos o Disney World. Pero el hotel no estaba mal, pequeño y muy moderno, era una casa de vecinos que había sido rehabilitada para albergar las manadas turísticas de las que disfrutaba Barcelona en los últimos tiempos. Antes de pedir que avisaran a Eduardo, me ocupé de comprobar su coartada en recepción. Me identifiqué, pregunté:

—Necesito saber a qué hora llegó el huésped Eduardo Castillo Montes a su habitación anteayer.

La chica me observó con consternación. Pensé que sería el susto habitual que sufre la gente ante una identificación policial, pero resultó bastante más complicado.

—De entrada no puedo saberlo, inspectora. A cada huésped le damos dos tarjetas llave. Una es de la puerta principal del hotel, la otra de la habitación. Para saber a qué hora llegó anteayer este señor, tendríamos que consultar las grabaciones de seguridad de la entrada y del pasillo de su habitación.

—Muy bien, de acuerdo; ¿puede darme una copia de esas grabaciones?

—Es que para eso necesito el permiso del director y hace un rato que salió.

—Pues deme la copia usted, tratándose de un requerimiento policial, su director no podría oponerse.

—Es que no sé cómo funciona lo de la grabadora.

La vi tan apurada que no me mostré todo lo despiadada que requería la ocasión.

—Llame al director y le comenta la historia, que le dé su permiso, que llame a un técnico de la NASA..., dispone de tiempo. Yo voy a hablar ahora con el señor Castillo, y nos demoraremos un rato. Por cierto, avísele de que ya estoy aquí, me espera.

No se movió. Tragaba saliva con dificultad. Al percatarse de que mi mirada empezaba a adquirir tintes de furia, dijo en voz queda:

—¿Pasa algo grave, inspectora? Es por si me lo pregunta el director.

—Nada grave. Si le pregunta, dígale que estoy haciendo una encuesta de la Dirección General de Seguridad.

Asintió de tal manera que no supe si había entendido la ironía o se disponía a pedir socorro lanzando alaridos. Por fortuna, se inclinó por llamar a Castillo mediante el teléfono interno. Lo esperé en una pequeña salita junto a recepción. Cuando llegó, miró a derecha e izquierda.

—Inspectora, ¿qué tal si nos vamos a un bar? Esto es muy poco acogedor.

—No tengo inconveniente.

Le dije a la chica que volvería al cabo de una hora para recoger la grabación. Salimos y rápidamente Eduardo me llevó a una cafetería agradable que había en la esquina. Nunca hay que caminar demasiado en Barcelona para encontrar un bar. Los dos pedimos cerveza.

—No me había dicho que su hotel no cuenta con recepcionista o vigilante por las noches.

—Ni se me ocurrió.

—Ahora tenemos que comprobar su coartada.

—No sé qué quiere decir.

—Pues es muy sencillo: las cámaras de seguridad nos dirán si estaba usted en su habitación cuando mataron a Christophe.

—¡Demonio!, ¿es que sospechan de mí?

—Eduardo, aprovecho la ocasión que se me presenta. ¿Mató usted a su colega? Si lo confiesa ahora, nos ahorraremos un montón de trámites enojosos y a usted le beneficiará legalmente.

Se irguió como un gallo picoteado.

—¡Inspectora, ni hablar, nunca, jamás de los jamases! ¿Por qué querría yo matar a mi compañero? Nos llevábamos bien, trabajábamos sin problemas. No digo que fuéramos amigos íntimos porque cada uno iba a su bola y, como él era tan reservado, nos contábamos poco. Pero jamás en la vida se me hubiera ocurrido una atrocidad semejante. Yo no soy capaz de matar a nadie. Le diré más, en toda mi vida le he dirigido un insulto a ninguna persona. ¡Ni cabrón, ni gilipollas, ni siquiera tonto! ¡Tampoco en el colegio cuando era pequeñito, fíjese bien!

—De acuerdo, de acuerdo, déjelo ya, le he entendido.

—Además, a mí, la muerte de Chris me representa un problema. ¿Qué hago yo ahora con el *food truck*? ¡Él era el cocinero principal!

—Contrate a otro.

—Pero ¿y nuestra sociedad? Todo estaba dividido entre dos, también los pagos. Además, ¿dónde encuentro yo a alguien que domine la cocina francesa?

—Oiga, Bob, lo que tenga que hacer usted con su negocio no es el tema que me ha traído hasta aquí; de modo que...

—¿Quién le ha dicho que me llaman Bob?

—Su vecina de *truck*.

—¡Ah, Elisenda! Es una chica muy agradable. Puede seguir llamándome Bob, es más corto.

—De acuerdo. Elisenda me dijo que la tarde del crimen vio a Christophe hablando bastante rato con una mujer. Una mujer alta, morena, guapa.

—No me acuerdo.

—Era una clienta porque, al parecer, les compró muchas cosas.

Sus ojos vivos, pequeños y rasgados, un tanto enloquecidos, buscaron el recuerdo con intensidad. Al final, se llevó una mano a la frente dándose un golpecillo iluminador.

—¡Sí, ya, ya lo tengo! ¡Era una señora muy distinguida, como de cincuenta años más o menos! No me fijé demasiado en los detalles, tampoco sé si habló mucho o poco con Chris, pero nos compró muchísimas cosas, como si fuera a celebrar una fiesta o algo así: *bœuf bourguignon*, *confit de canard*, paté de *campagne*...

—¿Cómo se acuerda de eso si usted no la atendió?

—No la atendí, pero le cobré.

—¿Recuerda cómo le pagó?

—Creo que con tarjeta.

—Muy bien, quiero ver ese ticket.

—Todos los papeles los tengo en la furgoneta, cuando quiera nos vamos y se los enseño.

—No corra tanto, hay que regresar al hotel.

—¿Para qué?

—Para comprobar su coartada.

—Inspectora, por favor, ¿aún sigue con eso?

—Oiga, Bob, ¿usted en qué cree que consiste una investigación policial? No se trata de tomarle manía a alguien de manera gratuita. Hay unos procedimientos, unos protocolos...

Supongo que no lo convencí, porque me miró con cara de fastidio y, cuando en el hotel me entregaron las grabaciones, él daba la impresión de lamentar la pérdida de tiempo. Fuimos caminando hasta la plaza del Nord. Oía cómo hablaba sin parar de la posibilidad de que aquella clienta misteriosa fuera la asesina. Me puso la cabeza como un bombo. Lo interrumpí:

—Dígame, ¿Christophe era muy ligón?

Miró el aire que nos rodeaba como si allí fuera a encontrar la respuesta. Cabeceó.

—Él nunca contaba nada, pero yo creo que tenía bastante éxito con las mujeres. Alguna que otra vez me había pedido cambiar el turno de dormir en la furgo. Se limitaba a decir que tenía una visita imprevista y que era más adecuado recibirla en el hotel. Luego me guiñaba un ojo.

—¿En alguna ocasión vio a esas visitas, o hubo alguna que se repitiera con cierta asiduidad?

—No, no vi nada y como no vi nada no puedo saber si las visitas eran repetidas o no.

Imitándolo sin percatarme del todo, fui yo quien husmeó el aire a nuestro alrededor.

—Hay algo que no entiendo, Bob. Usted y su socio llevaban casi dos años de convivencia. Y esa convivencia era más estrecha de la habitual entre socios de trabajo. No es lo mismo una oficina llena de empleados que su camión, donde el roce es muy intenso. Aunque no estuvieran siempre juntos, ¿cómo es posible que no hubieran desarrollado ni una mínima intimidad?

—Bueno, yo sí estaba dispuesto a entablar una relación más profunda, pero Chris era como un muerto, y que Dios me perdone por decir eso.

—¿No hablaban de nada?

—Sí, claro que hablábamos: de las recetas, de restaurantes, de las noticias del mundo, de fútbol, de la clientela, del tiempo...

—Nunca de nada personal.

—Pues no, es verdad que no intercambiábamos confidencias, pero los hombres no estamos tan inclinados a contarnos la vida como hacen ustedes las mujeres. Tenemos más pudor.

—Lleva razón, por eso se aburren tanto. En cualquier caso, alguna vez tomarían cuatro copas juntos, se sentirían desinhibidos por el alcohol, se dirían cosas más privadas...

—Yo sí, pero él no. Sólo una vez me dijo que era soltero, y eso porque se lo pregunté.

—¿No llegó a pensar que ocultaba algo de su pasado?

—¿Chris? ¡No, qué va! Era muy buena persona. Porque uno sea reservado con sus cosas no se puede concluir que se trate de un criminal.

—Yo no iba tan lejos. Si no un crimen, bien podía tener un pasado turbulento, haber cometido por ejemplo un desfalco, una estancia en la cárcel...

Dejó de caminar, se puso frente a mí.

—Inspectora Delicado, la verdad, la triste verdad, es que éramos dos fracasados totales a los que empieza a pasárseles la edad de hacer cosas importantes. A mí todo me había salido mal en la vida: los estudios, el trabajo, el amor..., y supongo que a él también. La idea del *food truck* nos salvó a los dos. ¿A quién le apetece recordar un pasado negro cuando empieza a verse un poco de luz al final del largo túnel?

—Es usted un auténtico poeta, Bob.

Al llegar abrió su camión, que ya había sido exhaustivamente analizado por nuestros hombres, sacó dos cervezas de la nevera y sobre una mesita extendió sus papeles de contabilidad. Mientras él buscaba entre facturas el pago de la mujer misteriosa, yo escudriñaba nuestro entorno. Era increíble que se pudiera vivir y trabajar en un espacio tan reducido, por bien organizado y milimetrado que estuviera. De una parte, la cocina, pertrechada con todo lo que un cocinero pudiera necesitar: armarios de almacenaje, hornos, fogones, grifos... Tras los asientos de conductor y copiloto, un lugar exiguo con la mesa y un par de banquitos. Detrás, el camastro donde una persona podía dormir. Y cuando llegaba el momento de abrir al público, bastaba con levantar uno de los laterales abatibles del camión para estar de golpe y porrazo en otro lugar: la barra de un bar, vasos y platos de papel, clientes comprando, curiosos paseando... Increíble, pensé, con la cantidad de presuntas comodidades, espacios divididos y metros cuadrados que parecen necesitarse en la vida diaria, y sin embargo, allí uno podía hacer no sólo su vida normal sino también trabajar en cuatro pasos contados.

—¡Aquí está el resguardo de la tarjeta! Es de CaixaBank —exclamó Castillo por fin.

—Muy bien, me la llevaré. Voy a pasar por el banco. De hecho, voy a llevarme toda la contabilidad.

—¿Quiere que la acompañe?

—¿Le gusta hacer de policía, Bob?

—Sólo si eso ayuda a cazar al asesino de mi compañero —respondió dignamente.

Se oyeron un par de golpes en la puerta de la camioneta. Era el subinspector.

—Llamé a comisaría y me dijeron que no estaba. Me imaginé que la encontraría aquí.

Bob le franqueó la entrada con ademanes de anfitrión.

—¡Pase, subinspector! Hay sitio suficiente si nos apretamos un poco en el banco. Aparte de la cerveza, le voy a ofrecer unas tostaditas con *foie* auténtico. Lo tengo en la nevera, aunque si seguimos sin abrir al público, igual se estropea.

Atajé la hospitalidad afirmando que debíamos irnos, pero el subinspector ya se había enganchado a la promesa de las tostaditas, prometiendo que las despacharía en un instante. Comprendí en aquel momento que la resolución de aquel caso alteraría al alza su peso corporal.

3

De todas las instituciones que velan por nuestra privacidad, la banca es quien lo hace con más ahínco y convencimiento. No fue fácil que me dieran los datos de la titular de la tarjeta con la que se pagó en la camioneta. Nunca había visto menos respeto frente a una identificación de la policía. Era como si me dijeran en las propias narices que el anonimato de un cliente está por encima de cualquier infracción, incluido un simple asesinato. Le pedí al director de la sucursal que no me obligara a ir en busca de una orden del juez. Evidenciando con ademanes circunspectos que me daba los datos por obligación ineludible, por fin los editó en su impresora y me los puso sobre la mesa. ¿Y bien? Quedé al instante sobrecogida porque el nombre que figuraba en el papel era... ¡francés! El mundo se me iluminó al tiempo que se me oscurecía la realidad más inmediata. Quizá no habíamos seguido una pista falsa. Aquella mujer, de nombre Nathalie Verbeux, debía tener alguna relación con la víctima, no podía ser un azar que ambos coincidieran en nacionalidad. La interfecta sólo hacía dos meses que era titular de la cuenta bancaria.

Aquel dato con el que ahora contábamos no aclaraba nada todavía, pero era una especie de puente tendido por el que se podía transitar. Me embolsé el papel donde también figuraba la dirección en Barcelona de la francesa y corrí en busca de Garzón.

Encontré al subinspector redactando el primer informe. Me miró como alucinado cuando le conté mi reciente hallazgo. Acto seguido, derramó un jarro de agua fría sobre mí.

—Veamos, Petra. No digo que no sea importante haber encontrado la identidad de esa mujer, pero el hecho de que sea francesa tampoco me parece tan prometedor. ¿No es bastante normal que a un francés le apetezca en un momento dado volver a comer cosas de su tierra y vaya a comprarlas a un lugar especializado?

—¿Y el tiempo extra que Christophe pasó charlando con ella?

—La testigo que nos contó eso no estaba demasiado segura, se trataba de una simple apreciación. Pero, aun así, aun contando con la charla, ¿no es normal que una ciudadana francesa se explaye un poco cuando encuentra a un compatriota?

—¡Joder, Fermín!, eso sería normal si los dos fueran de Madagascar, ¡pero Barcelona está lleno de franceses!

—Yo no me haría demasiadas ilusiones.

—¡Es usted un cenizo y no respeta para nada mi intuición! ¿Por qué no le hacemos una visita a esa señora?

—Vale, mañana por la mañana puedo recogerla en casa si le parece bien.

—Yo me refería a ahora.

—¿Sabe qué hora es? A las diez de la noche no podemos hacerle una visita a nadie. Si estuviera implicada en el caso, el que llegáramos tan tarde no haría más que ponerla en guardia.

La lógica y la prudencia del subinspector no tenían réplica posible. En todas las pegas que acababa de ponerme llevaba siempre razón. Justamente por eso lo hubiera estrangulado con mis propias manos. Yo era presa de la conocida enfermedad del detective: la pasión por saber. No era la primera vez que la padecía, y sabía perfectamente cuál era el remedio que mejora los síntomas: la paciencia. Y, sin embargo, me resultaba una medicina amarga de tragar. Mi impulso hubiera sido largarme sola a *chercher la femme*. Sin embargo, volví a casa con un elevado índice de frustración.

Marcos, mi marido, ya había cenado, pero, aun así, me preguntó si no le había traído ningún pequeño bocado del *truck*. El entorno de aquel asesinato, debido a su excepcionalidad, concitaba la curiosidad de todo el mundo, de la prensa también. Afortunadamente, el comisario Coronas nos había relevado de cualquier obligación de hablar con periodistas. Desafortunadamente, ese aligeramiento no incluía cónyuges ni familiares. Mientras me calentaba un potaje vegetariano que había preparado nuestra asistenta, Marcos quiso saber cómo era el ambiente en el grupo de *trucks*.

—No lo sé. Tenemos el recinto precintado. Al no haber clientes, no puedo decirte.

—Les habéis fastidiado el negocio.

—Nosotros no, ha sido un asesino. De todos modos, supongo que dentro de uno o dos días les permitiremos abrir de nuevo, aunque no marcharse a otro lugar.

Vino a hacerme compañía a la cocina mientras yo me zampaba el potaje. Se sirvió una copa de vino y me miró de repente con aire soñador:

—Esos tipos de los *food trucks* tienen su mérito. Se arriesgan a llevar un modo de vida diferente. Forman parte de la sociedad, pero están en otra dimensión. Supongo que encuentran muchas compensaciones en su actividad.

—¿Por ejemplo? —pregunté engullendo un garbanzo.

—Bueno, no están atrapados en una ciudad, duermen cada noche en un lugar distinto, no deben preocuparse por las pequeñas miserias de un vecindario, ven gente diferente casi cada día. Es como si su compromiso con la vida fuera menor.

—¡Bah, imagino que también tendrán sus problemas!

—Sin duda los tienen, pero gozan de más libertad.

Interrumpí la ingesta vegetal y clavé en mi marido una mirada curiosa.

—¿Te ha ido mal hoy en el despacho?

Soltó una risotada, bebió un largo sorbo.

—No, todo ha ido muy bien. Era sólo una reflexión.

—El subinspector opina que son todos unos saltimbanquis que no tienen donde caerse muertos.

Se echó a reír de buena gana.

—¡Ah, Garzón es inefable! Eso significa que está contento con su vida tal y como es.

—¿Tú no lo estás con la tuya?

—No me interpretes mal, mi vida es completa y feliz. Pero ¿sabes lo que pienso a veces, Petra? Que cuando dejemos de trabajar sería fantástico comprar una casa en un lugar apartado y marcharnos a vivir al campo. Una vida sencilla, serena, con un jardín, quizá un pequeño huerto donde plantar cuatro tomates. Tener un perro, la chimenea humeando en invierno, recibir alguna visita de mis hijos de vez en cuando...

—Sí, no estaría mal si al cuadro idílico le añades muchos libros y un copazo de buen whisky cada día al atardecer. Supongo que eso mataría un poco el aburrimiento.

Volvió a reír, cabeceó resignadamente.

—¿Por qué me casaría con una mujer tan poco romántica?

—Ya lo eres tú por mí. De todas maneras, no me hagas mucho caso, estoy cansada.

Me besó en la frente y volvió al salón. Yo me quedé un poco preocupada. ¿Qué ocultaba aquella ensoñación de Marcos? ¿Quizá se sentía abrumado por la presión del día a día, los compromisos que comportaba nuestra vida empezaban a incomodarlo? Es cierto que no debía inquietarme en exceso, ya que operaba sobre mí cierta deformación profesional. Acostumbrada como estaba a sacar conclusiones ocultas de las declaraciones de la gente que interrogaba, a cualquier frase inocente le adjudicaba significados de los que probablemente carecía. La única realidad interpretable era que mi marido ansiaba un poco de tranquilidad. Lamentablemente, yo no podía secundarlo en aquellos momentos. Llevaba un caso que me tenía en ascuas y demasiados interrogantes en la mente como para ponerme a pensar en plantar tomates. Una cosa estaba clara, aquella historia de los *food trucks* despertaba en las personas sugerencias que nunca hubieran nacido de haberse cometido el asesinato en un restaurante convencional.

El domicilio que figuraba en la ficha de la misteriosa francesa estaba en la calle Enric Granados. Y allí fuimos Garzón y yo al día siguiente, dispuestos a averiguar si tenía alguna relación con la víctima. Yo contemplaba con mimo aquella posibilidad, mientras que el subinspector estaba convencido de que no existía. Ninguno de los dos ganó la apuesta. Simplemente, nadie conocía a una tal Nathalie Verbeux en aquel lugar. El ático al que llamamos pertenecía a un fabricante de alfombras retirado y a su esposa. No daban crédito a nuestras preguntas, ¿una señora francesa?, ¿en aquel piso? Jamás, hacía más de veinte años que lo ocupaban. ¿Entre los vecinos? Les hubiera extrañado mucho porque conocían a todo el mundo. Aun así, no tuvimos más remedio que ir vivienda por vivienda, y vivienda por vivienda recolectamos negativas. A los que no estaban en casa los avalaba el vecino de rellano, que lo conocía desde tiempo inmemorial. Un fiasco, un desastre, una pérdida de tiempo. Sólo una certeza: Verbeux no había habitado jamás entre las paredes de aquel inmueble.

Regresé al banco, esta vez con mi fiel camarada.

Para empezar, le pegué una bronca muy hispana al director de la sucursal. ¿Cómo era posible que no comprobaran los datos de sus clientes? ¿Cómo es posible que ninguno de sus empleados recuerde el físico de esta señora?

—Inspectora, ahora ya no se mandan notificaciones ni extractos de cuenta a direcciones postales, todo funciona online. En realidad, sólo comprobamos los informes que nos interesan: impagos anteriores, fiscalidad adecuada...

—Es decir, lo que les interesa es que el cliente tenga dinero.

Miré a Garzón de reojo. Se divertía. Le gustaba el ensañamiento con presas obvias como el capital. Creo que monté aquel pequeño numerito innecesario sólo para proporcionarle placer.

—Inspectora, tiene toda la documentación que obra en nuestro poder.

—Menos una copia del pasaporte.

—Para eso necesitaré una orden judicial.

Pensé si debía seguir en la línea dura o dar un giro a mi actitud. Probé con un estadio intermedio.

—Mire, estamos investigando un asesinato a sangre fría. Hay un hombre a quien le han reventado el corazón a puñaladas. Una llamada al juez que instruye el caso bastará para que me gire una orden inmediatamente, sólo le pido que no me haga perder un tiempo que puede ser crucial.

Funcionó. Salimos de la sucursal con la fotocopia del pasaporte de la tal Verbeux. Garzón alabó mi estilo.

—Lo ha hecho muy bien, Petra, un poco de

caña a ese capullo y luego la estocada final. Hacía tiempo que no la oía decir eso de «a sangre fría».

—Los clásicos siempre convencen, Fermín, no pasan de moda. Encárguese de mandar fotocopia de la fotocopia a la poli francesa. Les daremos un poco más de trabajo.

En la oficina pasé revista a los elementos en nuestro poder mientras Garzón hacía sus diligencias. Un panorama devastador se presentó ante mis ojos. El teléfono que figuraba en la ficha bancaria era de prepago, una dirección equivocada, un correo electrónico que estaban investigando, pero que seguramente no correspondería a nadie. Un par de testimonios sin demasiado interés y un círculo íntimo de la víctima completamente desconocido. Llamé por el teléfono interno a mis colaboradores. Habían prácticamente acabado de ver el vídeo de seguridad del hotel y aseguraron que Eduardo Castillo entró en las instalaciones sobre las diez de la noche y salió a las nueve de la mañana, sin más movimientos. Apunté una nueva frustración en la lista. Bob tenía coartada. ¡Al infierno con todo! ¿Era posible más oscuridad? Caminábamos de noche, con niebla y con los ojos tapados por un pañuelo negro. Caer en un pozo era nuestra más probable opción. ¡Y eso que sólo estábamos al principio!

Fui a sacar un café de la máquina. El ambiente en los pasillos de la comisaría estaba animado. La gente caminaba de un lado a otro con decisión. Los envidié, realmente parecía que sabían hacia dónde se dirigían, que los esperaba algo concreto que hacer mientras yo permanecía parada dando vueltas sobre el mismo círculo cerrado. Me llevé el vasito de papel a mi despacho. ¡Cuánto tardaba el subinspector! Miré por la ventana, hacía viento. Seguramente al día siguiente la parada de *food trucks* sería desmontada. Legalmente, no se les podía inmovilizar durante más tiempo. ¡Lástima!, hubiera querido ver cómo funcionaba aquel tinglado, echar una mirada final. Todos los propietarios habían sido interrogados por nuestra gente, pero yo necesitaba comprobar el conjunto en directo, observar cómo se movía la gente en el recinto. Me dirigí a consultar con el comisario, que enseguida me recibió.

—¿Trae noticias del caso, Petra?

—Me temo que no. Está la cosa francamente peliaguda.

—Este asesinato nos ha sido confiado a la Policía Nacional porque puede haber sospechas de crimen organizado.

—Pues devuélvaselo a los Mossos, señor. Todo pinta fatal.

—¡Vaya respuesta, inspectora! ¿Ha venido para decirme eso?

—No, pero usted me pidió noticias y no las hay. Hace tres días del asesinato y seguimos en el punto inicial. El subinspector Garzón ya ha escrito los informes.

—Luego los leeré. ¿Pensaría que soy un grosero si le pregunto qué la trae por aquí?

—Quisiera que el grupo de comerciantes de comida abriera sus puertas al público por lo menos un día antes de que se deshiciera la reunión.

—¿Para qué lo necesita? Tengo entendido que todos han sido ya interrogados.

—Estoy actuando por intuición.

El comisario Coronas se arrancó las gafas de la cara y me miró con los ojos muy abiertos. Tardó unos segundos en exclamar:

—¡No me diga!

Procuré que no siguiera hablando, imaginaba el aluvión que caería sobre mí.

—Tampoco pido demasiado, señor. El alcalde de barrio no se opondrá porque tiene un contrato con los feriantes que no se ha completado. Y los comerciantes estarán encantados.

—¿Usted cree? ¿Le parece que se acercarán clientes a un lugar donde se ha cometido un crimen?

—Es justo lo contrario, señor. La gente acudirá en manada llevada por el morbo de la situación.

—Puede que esté en lo cierto. Hace tanto tiempo que no piso la calle que a veces se me olvida lo odiosa que es la gente. Está bien, veré lo que puedo hacer. Hablaré con el alcalde de barrio y le diré que necesitamos al grupo de restauradores en activo durante un día más. Añadiré que semejante decisión se debe a sus cualidades intuitivas. A ver qué me contesta.

—Lo comprenderá.

—Puede, lo que yo no consigo entender es por qué logra siempre convencerme, se lo aseguro.

—¿Quizá confía usted en mi intuición?

—Lárguese, Petra, antes de que lo piense mejor.

Regresé a mi mesa bastante contenta, aunque sin saber muy bien por qué. No tuve tiempo de darle muchas vueltas, sentado en una silla me esperaba Garzón.

—Perdone que no me levante, inspectora, pero estoy muy cansado hoy. Ayer noche asistimos a una fiesta con mi mujer y esta mañana no podía con mi alma.

—Ese es el precio de la frivolidad. ¿Qué tal con sus gestiones?

—Le traigo dos noticias.

—¿Una buena y otra mala, como suele decirse? Si es eso, empiece por la buena, se lo ruego.

—Me temo que no podré. Las dos son malas de cojones.

—Desembuche, Fermín.

—El pasaporte de la francesa es falso.

—Me lo temía. ¿Y la otra noticia?

—El pasaporte del francés asesinado, también.

—Cojonudo, ¡*vive la France*!

4

Si el camino hacia la resolución había sido oscuro hasta aquel momento, a raíz de saber que ambos documentos de identidad eran falsos, nos metíamos en un túnel del que no se veía la salida. Perseguíamos a dos fantasmas, dos fotografías, en realidad. Lo único que se aclaraba un poco era la sospecha de que ambos individuos estaban conectados de alguna manera. Resultaba demasiado casual que dos tipos con documentación falsificada, y ambos de la misma nacionalidad, hubieran charlado un ratito sobre gastronomía. Por alguna razón, la francesa había estado con la víctima justo el día antes de su asesinato. Eso la marcaba con el letrero de principal sospechosa.

Tendría que participar la policía francesa de nuevo, esta vez atendiendo a otra petición. Los nombres de los documentos falsos, incluso los mismos pasaportes, podían haber sido utilizados allí en algún delito, o podían pertenecer a un alias conocido, o quizá las fotografías figuraban en sus archivos como las de delincuentes habituales. Era necesario confiar en sus gestiones, y no sólo eso, sino hacer algo mucho peor: esperar a que llegaran los resultados.

Odio esperar. Detesto aguardar mi turno en una cola. Si me he citado con alguien, cinco minutos de retraso por su parte son suficientes para hacerme fruncir el ceño. Pero lo que llevo peor es tener que aguardar datos en una investigación, ahí sí se me llevan los diablos. Y en eso estaba, dejándome transportar por un batallón infernal, cuando Garzón me propuso ir al campamento de *food trucks*.

—No me apetece demasiado. Vaya usted.

—A ver, inspectora, se ha montado un circo monumental para que las camionetas siguieran un día en activo. Todo porque su intuición se había puesto en órbita. ¿Y ahora va a quedarse tan fresca en el despacho? ¡Ah, no!, soy capaz de ir a acusarla con el dedo frente a Coronas.

—Está bien, voy con usted, pero considerando que todos esos testigos potenciales ya fueron interrogados en su momento, tengo poca fe en que surja algo.

—¿Ya no le dice nada su intuición?

—Oiga, Fermín, ¿qué tal si deja de tocarme las pelotas con la intuición? No soy tan tonta, le recuerdo que mi intuición sobre que esos dos estaban de algún modo conectados parece que va a ser cierta.

—No hay nada contrastado todavía; lo que sí es un hecho indiscutible es que está usted de un pésimo humor.

Me endosé la gabardina sin responderle. No me hacía gracia que mis estados de ánimo fueran tan transparentes, pero luchar contra ellos para ocultarlos me cogía demasiado mayor.

Que estuviéramos en viernes, brillara un sol cálido y fuera la hora del aperitivo eran circunstancias confluyentes para que en la plaza del Nord hubiera bastante gente pululando de una furgoneta a otra. Todos estaban en plena efervescencia culinaria: sándwiches, degustaciones de jamón, montaditos variados, hasta una paella recién hecha se veía mellada por las raciones que de ella se habían servido. El aire olía a cerveza. Nadie en su sano juicio hubiera dicho que en aquel contexto pudiera pensarse en un asesinato. Comer, beber, charlar y pasear alegremente eran siempre indicativos de vida. El único camión que permanecía cerrado era el de Bob. Todavía debía andar en busca de cocinero. Garzón y yo nos dedicamos a hablar con los comerciantes. Tras identificarnos, preguntábamos de nuevo, esta vez centrándonos en la figura de la mujer francesa. Nadie la recordaba, pero el viaje no estaba resultando baldío porque el subinspector, como estaba cantado, probó un montón de aquellas delicias gastronómicas poniendo siempre los ojos en blanco de placer. Uno de los cocineros le dio un canutillo relleno de marisco que acababa de salir de la sartén. Fui testigo de que, literalmente, mi compañero se tambaleaba por la impresión.

—Es lo mejor que he comido jamás —soltó. El otro se mostró encantado con el piropo.

—Tome otro, por favor, le invito con mucho gusto.

Para disimular la inoperancia de nuestra presencia policial allí le pregunté un poco a bulto:

—¿No ha venido hoy por aquí Eduardo Castillo?

—¿Bob? No lo he visto. Debe de estar buscando cocinero, el pobre. Mejor pregunte a Elisenda y Javier, los vegetarianos, como son tan amigos sabrán por dónde anda. ¿No se anima a otro rollito, señor?

Antes de que fuera inevitable una respuesta positiva, contesté yo.

—¡No, muchas gracias! No queremos que se haga tarde, tenemos cosas que hacer.

Me encaminé hacia el camión vegetariano y Garzón me siguió.

—¡Caramba, inspectora!, ¿por qué le ha entrado tanta prisa?

—Modérese, Fermín, van a decir que somos unos gorrones.

—Yo no pido que me inviten, sale de ellos mismos.

—Sale de ellos y acaba en su tripa. ¿No ha aprendido a decir no? Cuando lleguemos al *truck* de esos chicos no se zampe nada, por favor. Aunque le pongan delante a la madre de todas las coliflores no le hinque el diente, se lo ruego.

—Para algo sano que podía comer... —protestó por lo bajo.

Allí estaban Elisenda y Javier, atareados preparando y sirviendo montaditos de verduras con queso. Los envidié, parecía un trabajo beneficioso para el equilibrio de cualquiera. Sin salir de casa, sin tomar autobuses ni metros, sin aguantar jefes ni compañeros de oficina, sin fichar, sin repetir escenarios todos los días. Ellos dos solos, dando de comer al mundo hambriento. ¡Ah, quizá la de mi marido no era una idea tan mala! Largarnos a una casa en el campo, lejos de Barcelona, lejos de la pretendida civilización que tantos quebraderos de cabeza venía dándonos. Tras la pandemia, las reacciones de los individuos se habían dividido en dos grupos. Por un lado, estaban los que ansiaban continuar con la vida anterior, si bien intensificada en los placeres prohibidos en su momento por Sanidad: viajar, comer en restaurantes, reunirse entre amigos..., un *carpe diem* con recuperación de los años perdidos. Luego, y no sé en qué porcentaje porque se les veía menos, venían aquellos que pretendían haber aprendido la lección y buscaban el aislamiento, la paz del campo, la reflexión sobre la vida, la salud y los beneficios de la naturaleza. ¿Pertenecía Marcos a aquel último apartado? Su idea de comprar una casa en un lugar solitario me había dejado un tanto mosqueada, entre otras cosas porque no tenía muy claro a qué grupo de ciudadanos pospandémicos pertenecía yo.

—¿Qué tal va eso, muchachos? —saludó Garzón a los dos jóvenes—. Necesitamos hablar con vosotros un momento.

—Es que ahora estamos a tope de trabajo. ¿No puede ser más tarde? —dijo ella.

—Bien, podemos quedar después en comisaría.

Intervino Javier, que le estaba cobrando a un señor.

—Si no es necesario que estemos juntos los dos, pueden hablar con ella y después conmigo. Con uno que esté atendiendo es suficiente. Si es sólo un rato, nos apañamos.

Me dio pena alterar su trabajo haciéndolos perder tiempo por la tarde... Accedí. Javier vino hasta donde estábamos y nos pidió separarnos un poco de la gente. Incluso sin uniforme, un policía nunca es bienvenido en un local público. La esposa siguió atendiendo a los clientes. Tampoco tardaríamos tanto, la pregunta que íbamos a plantear era muy concreta.

—¿Sabía usted que Christophe llevaba documentación falsa?

Aquel chico sereno y razonable cambió su actitud y pareció enfadado de pronto.

—A ver, inspectora, ¿cómo quiere que yo sepa eso?

—Casi siempre eran vecinos de ubicación, incluso acaban de decirme que eran amigos. ¿Nunca notó nada sospechoso en él?

—¿Sospechoso de qué tipo?

—No sé, comentarios, visitas de alguien, algún intento de ocultar datos, algún detalle en general...

—Oiga, ya se lo dijimos el otro día. El tal Christophe o como se llame era un tipo cerrado, que no hablaba, que no soltaba prenda de lo personal. ¿Le parece normal que un día viniera a decirme: «¿Sabes que yo no soy yo?, ¿sabes que mi pasaporte es falso?». ¡Por favor, un poco de seriedad!

El subinspector se tensó, hizo un intento de saltar que yo atajé tocándole el brazo.

—Está bien, prometo comportarme seriamente de ahora en adelante. Si recuerda algo, el más mínimo detalle que pueda aportar a la investigación, llámenos. En cualquier caso, como el resto de sus compañeros, tendrá que mandar un correo electrónico a nuestra comisaría con sus próximas localizaciones de trabajo.

—¿Y eso hasta cuándo?

—Hasta que se descubra al asesino que andamos buscando.

Se encogió de hombros como si lo que le estaba diciendo fuera una de las cosas más absurdas que había oído jamás. Volvió a su puesto, nos envió a su mujer con un gesto de cabeza malhumorado.

La reacción de Elisenda al saber que la identificación de Christophe era falsa nada tuvo que ver con la de su marido. Se sorprendió, se alteró, estuvo a punto de echarse a llorar.

—¡Ay, inspectora, era lo último que me faltaba por saber! ¡Qué va a ser de nosotros si empieza a apuntarse gente rara a nuestro trabajo! ¡Correrá la mala fama, los clientes pensarán que no somos de fiar! La idea de los *food trucks* ha sido muy bien recibida por la sociedad, pero no deja de ser nueva aún, en cualquier momento puede irse todo al infierno. Y nosotros nos ganamos la vida limpiamente, trabajamos a conciencia.

—Tranquilícese y responda a mi pregunta. ¿Tuvo alguna vez la impresión de que su compañero escondía algo?

—No, no, de ninguna manera. Y por supuesto no sabía que Chris tenía documentación falsa. ¿Cómo hubiera podido ni siquiera imaginármelo?

—¿Nunca vio nada sospechoso?, ¿nunca le extrañó que hablara tan poco de sí mismo?

—¡No, cada uno es como es, cada uno se toma la vida de una manera! Nunca le vi hacer nada sospechoso, nunca pensé que...

Se echó por fin a llorar. Garzón, siempre en la

tradición policial, le pasó un pañuelo de papel. La chica se sonó, hizo un esfuerzo por seguir hablando.

—¿Había hecho algo malo Christophe?, ¿lo han matado por eso?

—No lo sabemos todavía. Si recuerda algún detalle, por insignificante que parezca, llámenos enseguida.

Caminamos unos pasos en silencio, pero enseguida el subinspector saltó sobre mí:

—¿Cómo le ha consentido a ese mequetrefe vegetariano dirigirse a usted de semejante manera?

—Tranquilo, Fermín. No pasa nada. La gente anda cabreada. Durante la pandemia les han dado órdenes oficiales que muchas veces eran contradictorias: lleve esta mascarilla, lleve la otra, no lleve ninguna..., reúnanse sólo cinco, sólo siete, sólo dos..., no se reúnan en absoluto..., quédese en su casa, puede salir para trabajar, salga pero no salga...

—De acuerdo, pero ¿qué culpa tenemos nosotros de semejante desbarajuste?

—Directamente, ninguna, pero representamos una autoridad y los ciudadanos han dejado de confiar en la autoridad, sea la que sea. La hacen culpable de todo, han desmitificado la capacidad que tiene de solucionar problemas, de velar por el bien general. Se sienten con derecho a encararse contigo, a soltarte lo que han estado incubando durante dos largos años.

—Vale, de acuerdo, esa es una explicación, ¿y qué se supone que debemos hacer?

—Tener un poco de paciencia, relativizar, templar gaitas, aguantar... No hay cabreo que cien años dure.

—¡Ah, no, pues conmigo que no cuenten para eso! Le aseguro que al próximo jovenzuelo que se insolente le pego dos hostias como hay Dios. Así irán recordando lo que es la autoridad.

Iba a reírme con ganas, pero algo me lo impidió. Sin que nos hubiéramos dado cuenta, teníamos a tres metros por delante de nosotros al mismísimo Bob, su boca sonriendo con alegría, sus ojos ocultos tras unas gafas de sol. Nos saludó despreocupadamente:

—¡Muy buenas! ¿Qué tal les va por aquí? ¿Necesitan ayuda? ¡Les invito a una cervecita de celebración! Parece que las cosas van encarrilándose. ¡Por fin he encontrado cocinero! Es un chaval joven, que ha estudiado cocina y domina el estilo francés. Como se encontraba en paro, le ha venido muy bien mi oferta. Estará a sueldo, claro, no seremos socios como con Chris, pero creo que funcionará bien. Me ha caído simpático y es que...

—Bob, necesitamos hablar con usted —le interrumpí.

—¡Ah, estupendo! Pues mientras tomamos la cervecita...

—Mejor en comisaría.

Se puso serio, se acercó y bajó la voz.

—¿Han encontrado ya al asesino?

—Me temo que no.

—¿Estoy detenido?

—¿Quiere dejar de decir soplapolleces? —le soltó Garzón—. Queremos hablar con usted en comisaría. Estamos investigando, ¿comprende? No hemos venido aquí a comer.

—O sea, que es un interrogatorio oficial.

—Sí, es oficial, tratándose de nosotros todo es oficial. Nosotros mismos somos la oficialidad en persona. Así que vamos a buscar el coche, subimos, estamos en silencio absoluto durante el trayecto y, una vez en comisaría, empezamos a hablar oficialmente. ¿Lo ha entendido?

El inesperado exabrupto del subinspector surtió efecto y dejó al locuaz testigo callado como un muerto. Por una parte, fue un verdadero descanso, pero por la otra me hizo temer que Bob perdiera su talante festivo y se mostrara remiso a contestar. Para rematar la faena, cuando nos sentamos en comisaría Garzón le espetó:

—Ahora empieza el interrogatorio oficial propiamente dicho.

Aquel pobre tipo parecía bastante aterrorizado, así que intenté disminuir un poco la presión.

—Vamos a ver, Bob. Usted y Christophe eran socios, trabajaban juntos en estrecho contacto, se repartían el trabajo y las ganancias, ¿voy bien?

—Sí, claro, va bien.

—En tal caso, ¿cómo es posible que usted no supiera que su socio y compañero estaba usando una documentación falsa?

—¡¿Qué, cómo ha dicho?!

—Lo que acaba de oír. Christophe Dufour no era Christophe Dufour. Su documento de identificación es falso.

—¿Y quién demonio era entonces?

—No lo sabemos aún, pero la policía francesa dará con su nombre auténtico dentro de poco tiempo. Por eso sería conveniente para usted que nos dijera la verdad sobre la identidad real de su amigo.

—Pero yo les he dicho toda la verdad. No tenía ni idea de que Chris estuviera utilizando un pasaporte falso, ¡ni idea!

—¿Firmaron un contrato?

—¡Claro, con un abogado delante! Y no hubo el más mínimo problema, el tipo cogió el pasaporte, escribió sus datos y ya está. Y Chris pagaba sus impuestos en España, todo muy legal, con su pasaporte. A nadie se le ocurrió que pudiera estar falsificado.

—De acuerdo, nadie suele dudar de la autenticidad de un documento si está bien falsificado. Pero usted ha pasado mucho tiempo con la víctima, Bob. ¿Nunca sospechó de él, nunca vio nada raro?

—No, nada.

—No conteste tan rápido, quiero que piense. ¿Vio a gente extraña con su compañero? ¿Alguna visita de un amigo, algún cliente que se repitiera en diferentes ciudades o barrios?

Tardó en responder, parecía pensar intensamente. Negó con la cabeza. Yo seguí:

—¿Alguna vez su socio le contó algo que le pareciera extraño o que diera a entender que su pasado era borrascoso?

—¿Borrascoso? No. Ya les dije que Chris era muy callado. Nunca entrábamos en lo personal.

—¿Y eso no le pareció extraño?

—No, no especialmente. Quizá me sorprendió un poco al principio, pero después me acostumbré.

—¿Le dijo algo o le contó algún episodio que entonces no le llamara la atención, pero que con las circunstancias actuales cobre sentido?

—A bote pronto, no; pero me pondré a pensar.

—¿Su socio consumía drogas o pudo tener usted la impresión de que incluso traficaba con ellas?

—¡Qué va, pero si sólo bebía cerveza, nunca lo vi tomar nada más fuerte! Y de traficar, nada de nada. Yo me hubiera dado cuenta, ¿no le parece?

—Esa es la cuestión que nos inquieta. ¿Está usted contándonos la verdad?

—No sé qué decirles para que me crean. Es la verdad, lo aseguro, lo juro, por mi madre, por Dios, por mi honor.

—Vale, no jure por tantas cosas. Pasemos a la mujer que les hizo la compra importante el día de autos.

Me levanté y salí de la sala. Necesitaba un poco de descanso. Dejé a Garzón al frente. A partir de aquel momento sólo cabía machacar al testigo repitiéndole las mismas preguntas de modo diferente hasta que perdiera los nervios y confesara la verdad o cayera en alguna contradicción aprovechable. Sentía cierta piedad por aquel tipo. Me daba la impresión de ser un pobre hombre, pero aunque mi tan autocacareada intuición no me indicaba nada negativo sobre él, podía estar mintiendo como un bellaco.

En mi despacho pedí información interna.

—No, inspectora Delicado, todavía no han encontrado el móvil de la víctima. Pero me dicen que trabajarán a tope, que no se preocupe.

¡Que no me preocupara! ¿Qué se puede esperar de un cuerpo policial que te habla como si fuera tu hijo adolescente: «No te preocupes, mamá, que llegaré a punto para la cena»? Es cierto que la impaciencia acaba por darnos la impresión de que todo el mundo es indolente, pero lo malo es cuando en estado de calma sigues pensando igual. ¡Ah, nuestra querida y soleada España! «Un momentito, un segundo, un ratito, ya está casi, pierda cuidado, no se preocupe...» Tomé el teléfono de nuevo.

—No, inspectora. Todavía no hay datos de esa mujer, pero estamos en ello.

¡Estamos en ello!, se me había olvidado otra expresión nacional. Claro que los franceses tampoco parecían espabilarse demasiado. No sabían nada sobre dos de sus ciudadanos que se dedicaban a campar con documentación falsa por el país vecino. Había que esperar. Esperar, esperar, esperar. Teléfono.

—Los datos de la autopsia no estarán hasta mañana por la mañana. Ya la avisaré.

Nuevas expresiones bien conocidas: ya le avisaré, ya le diré algo, lo tenemos presente, será el primero a quien atienda. Teléfono.

—Garzón, estoy hasta los cojones. Cuando acabe con ese pájaro, venga a La Jarra de Oro. Le espero tomando una cerveza.

Carraspeo del subinspector y por fin:

—A sus órdenes, inspectora.

¡Eso sí sonaba bien! «A sus órdenes.» Sin dilaciones, sin excusas, sin dobles tintas o promesas falsas.

Llegó al cabo de media hora, derrengado y sediento. Pidió una cerveza. Yo ya llevaba dos, pero para no dejarlo solo me sumé a la comanda.

—¿Qué? —pregunté con gran economía retórica. Él, más económico aún, negó con la cabeza. Aprovechó la energía que le quedaba para señalar con el dedo una bandeja de chorizo frito que estaba expuesta en la barra. Indicó un dos al camarero. Dio un trago a la cerveza, empezó a comer.

—¿No piensa soltar prenda?

—Espere un momentito, inspectora. ¡Soy un ser humano!

—No me había fijado, perdón.

—Está bien, ya le cuento. A mí, el tal Bob me tiene comida la moral. No sé si miente o no. Es posible que sea verdad lo que dice. Si su socio tenía algo que ocultar, mayor motivo para que no se lo confesara a él, que podía delatarle. Pero no sé, dudo, el dichoso Bob es demasiado simpático, tiene un punto raro.

—Y su socio demasiado misterioso. ¿Le ha preguntado de nuevo por los ligues?

—Sí, la víctima quedaba a veces con algunas chicas, pero no ha sido capaz de darme ni un nombre, ni una descripción.

—Dos amigos singulares. Siempre juntos y nunca se dicen nada íntimo.

—En fin, inspectora; ya hemos hablado de eso muchas veces, el propio Bob se lo comentó. Entre hombres no es nada extraño que suceda así. Tampoco usted y yo nos contamos la vida.

—¡Hombre, Fermín! Pero si los dos trabajáramos en los pocos metros cuadrados de un camión restaurante, quizá la cosa se prestaría más a la confidencia. Cuando usted no tuviera la boca llena de comida, quiero decir.

—Muy graciosa.

—Además, lo sabemos todo el uno del otro: familia, aficiones...

—Sí, pero, vamos a ver, ¿alguna vez le he contado yo algo sobre mis novias de juventud?

—Nunca, es verdad.

Seguimos con nuestro aperitivo en riguroso silencio. Tras una larga pausa le pregunté:

—¿Cómo eran sus novias de juventud, subinspector?

—Casi todas bastante feas.

—¿Ese era el punto común entre todas ellas?

—Tampoco fueron tantas, nunca he sido un donjuán. Recuerdo a una que me gustaba de verdad. Trabajaba en una mercería en el centro de Salamanca. Era bajita y regordeta, pero alegre como un cascabel. Se reía, bromeaba, de repente se ponía a cantar cuando menos lo esperabas. A mí me encantaba pasear con ella por el parque, llevarla a bailar, ir al cine.

—¿Y en el cine también se ponía a cantar?

—Sólo si la película era musical. Me está tomando el pelo, ¿verdad, Petra?

—Estaba bromeando. ¿Qué pasó con su relación?

—La cortó ella. Tenía aspiraciones elevadas de cara al matrimonio. Le parecía poco un patán como yo. Acabó casándose con alguien más glamuroso: el director de la banda municipal.

—Sería para que la dirigiera en los cánticos.

—Por lo menos era un artista, y no un simple madero como yo.

No pude evitar echarme a reír a carcajadas. Garzón sonreía *sotto* el bigote.

—¡Qué bien se lo pasa usted con las andanzas de un paleto como yo! ¿Eh, inspectora?

—¿Quiere que le diga de corazón lo que pienso? Su novia la de los trinos era boba de nacimiento, porque usted no es un patán, ni un simple madero y mucho menos un paleto. Usted es un hombre encantador, sabio y prudente, con el que da gusto trabajar y charlar.

—Y comer chorizo —acabó él la frase entre risas, pero orgulloso de lo que acababa de oír—. Por cierto, podíamos quedarnos a almorzar aquí mismo. Allí hay una mesa libre.

—Será un placer, Fermín, un verdadero placer.

5

La conversación con Marcos me había dejado completamente mosqueada. Al día siguiente comprobé que mi marido había avanzado un paso más en sus elucubraciones, y lo que antes fue una especie de ensoñación futurible, ahora caminaba hacia la realidad inmediata.

—Petra, ¿qué te parecería si compráramos una casa en el campo, no muy lejos de Barcelona? Quizá algo ya construido que permita una rehabilitación, quizá un terreno adecuado en el que sea factible edificar. Se convertiría en un modo de salir de la ciudad los fines de semana, y cuando nos jubiláramos, fijaríamos allí nuestra residencia. ¿Qué te parece?

—¿Quieres que te conteste con sinceridad?

—Te lo ruego.

—Me parece una barbaridad.

—¿Por qué? —se extrañó.

—Demasiadas dificultades. Por ejemplo, mi trabajo. No siempre estoy libre los fines de semana. También tú tienes muchas veces cosas que hacer los sábados. ¿Cómo lo solucionarías?, ¿replicando tu estudio en la nueva casa? Y al margen de eso, están tus hijos. Ya son mayorcitos, empiezan a tener amigos con los que salen, compromisos sociales... Si les dices que los fines de semana nos retiramos a la paz del campo, estoy segura de que tendremos rebelión a bordo.

—Pero ellos sólo nos visitan cada quince días. Y no me has dicho nada sobre la jubilación en un lugar apartado pero cercano.

Salté del sillón en el que estaba sentada, perdí el control.

—A ver, Marcos, estoy empezando a investigar un caso que se presenta crudo y tú me hablas de la jubilación.

—Olvídate, olvida todo lo que te he dicho. Tus jodidos asesinatos son más importantes que nuestra vida, que nuestro futuro.

—Eso es una magna gilipollez, y además te estás poniendo grandilocuente.

Se levantó de la mesa de la cocina y dijo:

—Me voy a trabajar.

No había dado un portazo ni tampoco intentado decir la última palabra. Sin embargo, me quedé sin recibir su habitual beso de despedida. Para los estándares de cabreo de mi señor esposo, eso significaba que estaba muy pero que muy enfadado. Yo me encontraba bastante perpleja. ¿Qué coño de mosca le había picado? El retiro, el campo, una casita construida quizá según sus propios planos, la jubilación... Los periodistas que, como de costumbre, se habían pasado todo el tiempo que duró la epidemia internacional escribiendo sobre lo que no sabían habían hablado sobre el síndrome campestre, sin llamarle de esa manera, claro está. Es fácil deducir de qué se trata: algunas personas que han sufrido confinamiento en su hogar sienten la ciudad como una segunda cárcel de la que quieren escapar. Al parecer, la idea de contar con un lugar cerca de la naturaleza se convierte para ellas en una auténtica necesidad. ¿Era Marcos uno de aquellos ciudadanos para quienes calles, tiendas, semáforos, cines y bancos constituían una maldición? Me negaba a creerlo. Marcos había sido siempre un hombre equilibrado, difícilmente influenciable, ajeno a síndromes que pudieran variar su personalidad. ¿No serían otro tipo de razones las que estaban gravitando sobre él? Quizá tenía algún proyecto difícil en su estudio de arquitectura del que no quería hablar o quizá, y esta era una terrorífica posibilidad, estuviera cansado de nuestra convivencia, de manera que yo no era ya más que otra pared de su prisión. Me inquieté. No en vano aquel era mi tercer matrimonio y sabía bien que los primeros síntomas de desavenencia tomaban a veces formas caprichosas a las que había que estar muy atento para detectar su verdadera raíz: vivir en el campo, practicar un nuevo deporte en común, viajar a países lejanos.

Tenía una madalena a medio comer en la mano y la abandoné. Se me había pasado el apetito. Lo que me faltaba, pensé, volver a los problemas amorosos a aquellas alturas de mi vida. Y encima, empezando la investigación de un caso en el que no sabíamos por dónde tirar. A lo mejor estaban en lo cierto los que afirmaban que, en según qué profesiones, hay que carecer por completo de vida privada. Me interrogué prematuramente: llegado el caso extremo en que me viera obligada a escoger entre mi matrimonio y mi trabajo, ¿qué haría? No me apetecía lo más mínimo ponerme a dilucidar sobre tan dramática opción. Resultaba ridículo entrar en esos temas cuando los síntomas de crisis eran tan leves, quizá sólo producto de mi imaginación. Apuré la taza de café, fui en busca de mi gabardina y salí a toda prisa de casa. Me esperaba Garzón en el Anatómico Forense. Los informes de la autopsia ya estaban listos, y como nosotros practicábamos el método de la vieja escuela, comentarlos en vivo con el forense tenía una importancia capital.

El subinspector daba paseítos por la calle cuando llegué con cierto retraso. Enseguida me reconvino con suavidad.

—Se le han pegado las sábanas, Petra.

—¡Qué va, hace ya mucho rato que las dejé!

—Sólo se lo digo porque como siempre es tan puntual...

—Tenía cosas que hacer.

—¿Cosas relacionadas con nuestro caso?

—No, Fermín, me limitaba a pensar y estaba tan absorta en mis pensamientos que se me fue el santo al cielo.

—¿Y no podía pensar y conducir al mismo tiempo? ¡Para que luego digan que somos los hombres los incapaces de hacer dos cosas a la vez!

—Es demasiado pronto para que empecemos a discutir. ¿Entramos ya?

El doctor Rosselló no estaba presente, y nunca habíamos coincidido con el médico que le sustituía.

Era joven, rubio como un angelito de un cuadro barroco y no tenía muchas ganas de hablar. Al principio, se limitó a leernos el informe que ya conocíamos. Se veía a las claras que consideraba innecesaria nuestra presencia allí. Luego, se avino a contestar a las preguntas de cierta mala gana.

—Dice usted que la trayectoria de la puñalada que lo mató fue de abajo hacia arriba. ¿Cree que fue necesaria bastante fuerza para asestarla?

—Sin duda. Interesó la zona pericordial y provocó la muerte casi instantánea de la víctima. El segundo ataque no hubiera sido necesario.

—¿Podría usted hacerse una idea de la envergadura del atacante?

—Sinceramente, no. Piensen que la víctima estaba tumbada y se incorporó. Piensen también en lo que ustedes mismos han informado: la postura del atacante debía ser inclinada. No hablamos de personas de pie y frente a frente, eso desvirtúa mucho cualquier apreciación. La víctima se incorporó y el asesino debió por fuerza inclinarse.

—¿Pudo ser una mujer? —preguntó el subinspector.

El forense lo miró como acopiando mucha paciencia para contestarle.

—La estatura de una mujer suele ser menor que la de un hombre, cosa que aquí, como acabo de decirles, no se puede calibrar debido a las posturas de víctima y atacante. Si se refiere a la fuerza..., es algo que hace tiempo que hemos dejado de considerar. Hay mujeres enormemente fuertes, muchas acuden a gimnasios con regularidad, practican deportes duros...

El subinspector se puso nervioso.

—Oiga, doctor, no somos tontos y estamos al tanto de los avances deportivos del sexo femenino. Se lo preguntaré de otra manera: ¿hay algún detalle subjetivo que le haya llevado a sospechar que se trataba de una mujer?

—Lo que ustedes quieren desde el principio es que yo ponga adornos a mi informe, cosas subjetivas, usted mismo lo ha dicho: «me da la impresión», «podría ser que», «me ha extrañado que». Pero lo que me han enseñado a hacer en la Facultad de Medicina es justo lo contrario. Una autopsia es una autopsia, empieza y acaba en los hallazgos sobre el cadáver, no hay más.

Observé que la faz de mi compañero iba tiñéndose de rojo, por lo que decidí intervenir antes de que se produjera alguna explosión.

—En el análisis toxicológico puede leerse que la víctima había consumido marihuana. ¿No hay más que añadir, puede saberse si era consumidor habitual?

El angelito barroco sonrió con conmiseración.

—No, inspectora, no puede saberse. Simplemente pudo fumarse un porro o dos.

—Muchas gracias, doctor. Espero que siga usted siendo tan objetivo en todo. No le molestamos más.

Cuando habíamos dado tres pasos fuera del edificio, Garzón empezó a despotricar.

—¡Maldito gilipollas sabelotodo! ¿Cómo se atreve? ¡El mundo no es lo que era, Petra! Si todos los tíos jóvenes con los que nos encontremos son así, me jubilo mañana. ¡Qué a gusto le hubiera arreado un mamporro!

—Sí, ya tuve esa impresión, pero hubiera sido un poco excesivo.

—De acuerdo, pero al menos confiaba en que usted le pegara uno de sus cortes característicos, alguna ironía, una frase punzante. Pues nada, se ha limitado a escucharlo en silencio.

—¿Usted sabe cuánta energía se pierde luchando por cualquier cosa? Pues imagínese que esa «cualquier cosa» te la encuentras cada vez con más frecuencia. Estamos rodeados de gente joven, Fermín. Están bien preparados, saben mucho, son conscientes de su valía y, sobre todo, detestan el modo en que trabajamos los de más edad. Hubiera sido preferible que nos recibiera el doctor Rosselló, pero tampoco hubiera podido darnos muchos más datos.

—Rosselló ha salido hincando en cuanto supo que veníamos, y no me extraña. Después de nuestra última visita y aquel número que usted le montó con que queríamos visitar al muerto, se esperaba lo peor.

—¿Le sería posible dejar de criticarme cinco minutos?

—Perdóneme. Estoy de mal humor. No es sólo que el forense sea un capullo, es que, encima, este caso parece de los que no avanzan ni a la de tres. No hemos sacado nada en limpio, ni un detalle por su parte, ni una simple intuición.

—El capullo llevaba razón en lo que ha dicho, ya no se trabaja así. Las corazonadas policiales, los detalles que desvelaban pruebas..., todo eso se acabó. Ahora todo es más científico, por decirlo así.

—¿Y la ciencia es exacta?

—No.

—¡Pues estamos al cabo de la calle, joder!

No estábamos al cabo de ninguna calle; es más, en el fragor de nuestra discusión, habíamos caminado sin rumbo fijo. Miré el reloj. Hora de ir a comisaría. Hicimos bien en personarnos con rapidez, el comisario Coronas había estado buscándome. Por fin había tomado una decisión con respecto a todos los *food trucks* presentes en el lugar del crimen. Le resultaba imposible retenerlos más tiempo, en especial no habiendo encontrado ninguna pista que implicara al grupo de comerciantes. Sin embargo, todos y cada uno de ellos aposentarían su negocio juntos en los próximos días y se les prohibía salir de Cataluña mientras el tiempo de esa prohibición fuera razonable. Hacer que se personaran en comisaría generaría retrasos y ausencias, y no digamos nada de tener que ir a buscar a cada uno de ellos a un pueblo diferente. El comisario me aseguró que había sido una decisión difícil de tomar. La polémica estaba servida y, además, lo insólito del entorno de aquel asesinato nos ponía en el punto de mira de los periodistas, que desde el inicio habían sentido curiosidad, si bien debo decir que se olvidaron pronto, esa era otra de las características de los nuevos tiempos: la falta de persistencia en la información, el cambio rápido de un tema a otro que se presentaba más interesante, es decir, más morboso.

—¿La policía francesa ya ha dicho algo sobre las identidades auténticas de sus compatriotas? —me preguntó el comisario Coronas.

—Todavía no, señor.

—Si necesita que los apretemos, avíseme. Intervendré yo mismo.

Tanta amabilidad por parte de Coronas era indicativa de dos cosas. La primera parecía obvia, y ni el subinspector ni yo habíamos pensado demasiado en ella: la aparición de un cadáver de nacionalidad extranjera se contabilizaba siempre como una complicación añadida. La segunda podía considerarse como más subjetiva: el hecho de que los testigos estuvieran itinerando por toda Cataluña multiplicaba la posibilidad de conflicto con otros cuerpos policiales. Habría que explicarse, mostrar órdenes, identificarse cada dos por tres. La investigación no sólo se presentaba como difícil, sino como un auténtico tostón. Sería necesario esperar largamente todos los informes que pidiéramos a Francia vía Europol y, por supuesto, ir viajando de vez en cuando en busca del campamento de *food trucks*. Era un caso de los llamados de «picar piedra», y el comisario lo sabía.

Garzón no estaba contento, claro está. Tal y como me sucedía a mí, las esperas siempre lo habían sacado de quicio, y la historia de tener que ir a buscar a los testigos allá donde se celebraran los eventos, a lo largo de toda la geografía catalana, le parecía una pérdida de tiempo colosal. ¿A qué venía permitirles a aquellos tipos que se dispersaran a su placer? De ser él la máxima autoridad sólo les hubiera consentido moverse por los diferentes barrios de Barcelona, y eso como una concesión especial. Yo sabía que resultaba inútil intentar convencerlo de que estarían implicados ayuntamientos de pequeñas ciudades con los que aquellos feriantes deberían cancelar su contrato temporal, de que los camiones no podían quedarse un montón de tiempo en la plaza dels Lluïsos sin permiso municipal y, sobre todo, de que aquella gente no podía ser privada de su fuente de ingresos: no sólo daban de comer a los demás, sino que ellos comían también. Aplicando mis conocimientos sobre la psicología de Garzón que, después de tantos años, dominaba de maravilla, primero lo dejé renegar cuanto quiso. Escuché con estoicismo maldiciones, juramentos, parrafadas sobre lo mal que funciona nuestro país y alguna blasfemia de poco calado (se había pulido con el tiempo). Una vez concluida la fase eruptiva, pasé a recordarle que visitar de vez en cuando a aquellos cocineros ambulantes tenía sus ventajas: podíamos picar de sus guisos, probar nuevas especialidades, y como estarían diseminados por sitios diferentes con diferentes vecinos de *truck*, pasaríamos desapercibidos y nadie nos calificaría de gorrones. Funcionó, se tranquilizó bastante encogiéndose de hombros como rendición. Yo hubiera sido una psicóloga maravillosa con la cláusula necesaria de que mi único paciente fuera el subinspector.

Cuando llegué a mi despacho, reclamé los resultados de la búsqueda del teléfono móvil de la víctima, aun sabiendo que no estarían listos todavía, como así fue. «Un día más, inspectora, denos un día más.» Había oído aquella petición de aplazamiento muchas veces y sabía que la unidad temporal de un día se encontraba sujeta a muchas variables.

Durante la tarde me llamaron del departamento de huellas dactilares. Todas las que habían tomado en el lugar del crimen pertenecían a la víctima y a Eduardo Castillo. Sólo dos, halladas en el quicio de la puerta del camión, eran de otra persona. ¿Quizá del asesino que había puesto la mano allí para impulsarse y entrar en la cabina? ¿O era más lógico pensar que cualquier cliente de los que pasaban a montones por aquel sitio hubiera tocado distraídamente aquella parte del vehículo estando la puerta abierta? Poco importaba, en realidad, ninguna de las dos huellas estaba registrada en ninguno de los bancos policiales: ni en los Mossos ni en la Guardia Civil. Fin del capítulo, aunque la decepción fue limitada porque nunca deposité demasiada confianza en aquel hallazgo.

Otro día de espera. Otro día perdido. A las ocho en punto cerré el ordenador, me endosé la gabardina y fui a despedirme de mi subalterno. Inútilmente, no estaba, se había largado sin decirme ni adiós. «*Sic transit gloria mundi*», pensé, y como era lo único que sabía de latín, no añadí nada más. Cuando paraba en los semáforos miraba estúpidamente a los transeúntes, en especial si eran mujeres altas y morenas. ¿Alguna de ellas era Nathalie Verbeux? Aquella mujer andaba entre nosotros. ¿Dónde estaba?, ¿quién era?, ¿cómo se llamaba en realidad? Preguntas absurdas, baldía curiosidad.

Sólo al abrir la puerta recordé que los chicos de Marcos cenaban y dormían en nuestra casa aquella noche. Los gemelos jugaban a un juego electrónico en la tele del salón. En cuanto me echaron la vista encima, Teo estiró las manos hacia mí y se defendió sin haber recibido ningún ataque:

—Ya hemos acabado los deberes, hemos estudiado y ahora estamos en nuestra fase de relajación.

—Vale, muy bien. ¿Dónde está vuestra hermana?, ¿y vuestro padre?

—Marina, en su habitación. Hugo ha intentado entrar un momento y le ha pegado tal bufido que no lo ha probado otra vez. Papá está en su estudio, proyectando el Taj Mahal bis.

Ya estaba habituada al registro irónico de Teo, pero con la edad, ya tenían catorce años, la ironía devenía frecuentemente en sarcasmo y había que reprenderle. No lo hice en aquella ocasión. Hugo, que era más normalito, se limitó a preguntarme si el día había sido duro para mí.

—Hasta que he llegado a casa iba bien. Ya veremos ahora —devolví el dardo a Teo como pude.

Los dos hermanos se echaron a reír como dos tontos y se propinaron unos cuantos golpes, uno en el hombro del otro. Todavía pesaba sobre ellos la parte infantil. Luego, volvieron a hundir sus mentes en aquel juego misterioso para mí, con una concentración asombrosa.

Marina, ¡*o tempora, o mores*! (sí sabía algo más de latín), también se encontraba de pie frente a una pantalla, en este caso la del ordenador. Su concentración parecía similar a la de los gemelos, pero con una variación interesante: estaba bailando. Me miró de reojo y me paró con un gesto para que no la interrumpiera. Debía haber llegado en un momento crucial de su interpretación. Miré la pantalla y vi a un muñequito ejecutando movimientos. Ella intentaba imitarlos con fortuna desigual. Al final, se paró, apagó el ordenador y vino a darme un beso. Sudaba copiosamente.

—¿Ensayando para alguna función escolar? —aventuré.

—¡Qué va! Es un juego de ordenador. Lo hago algunas veces cuando no he podido practicar deporte. Sirve para la coordinación corporal y tonifica los músculos.

—¡Caray, quién diría que se pueden hacer tantas cosas sin salir de una habitación!

—Ya sé lo que me vas a decir.

—¿Qué?

—Lo que un día me dijo el subinspector Garzón, que cuando él era pequeño salía a la calle para jugar a la pelota con otros niños, y que se lo pasaban pipa corriendo y haciendo el burro. Yo le contesté que si sales a la calle en Barcelona haciendo el burro, o te ponen una multa o te atropella cualquier coche que te pase por al lado sin prestar atención.

—¡Ah!, ¿y qué dijo él?

—Que los tiempos habían cambiado y que ahora todo era una mierda.

—¿Y piensas que yo iba a decirte lo mismo que el subinspector? Te recuerdo que es bastante mayor que yo.

—Sí, pero piensas lo mismo que él.

Marina tenía la habilidad, natural o adquirida, no lo sé, de mirar en el interior de las personas con una lupa. Como era inocente aún, te soltaba lo que veía sin pensarlo dos veces.

—Pues a ver si adivinas lo que voy a decirte a continuación.

Hizo como si buscara en sus pensamientos.

—A ver..., pueden ser dos preguntas: una, si ya he hecho los deberes del colegio. Otra, qué ha dejado preparado la asistenta para cenar.

—Ni la una ni la otra, listilla. Además, no es ninguna pregunta, es una orden: ¡corre a ducharte inmediatamente, y echa el chándal a lavar, estás sudando como un pollo!

Salió corriendo hacia el cuarto de baño como si yo fuera a perseguirla. La llamé:

—¡Por cierto, Marina! ¿Qué hay esta noche para cenar?

—¡No pienso decírtelo! —gritó, muerta de risa.

«¡Cielo santo!», pensé. En realidad, daba igual que estuviéramos en la actualidad o en la Edad de Piedra, los niños siempre han tenido la capacidad de derivarlo todo hacia la ligereza y el juego. Es lo que ahora se denomina resiliencia y antes se llamaba felicidad.

Subí a comprobar qué tal iba mi marido con el Taj Mahal. Estaba, en efecto, inclinado sobre su mesa de dibujo mientras iba mirando la pantalla del ordenador.

—¿Con el lápiz en la mano? ¡Qué raro!

—El cliente quiere que algunos detalles no sean virtuales. Por lo visto así se da una idea más clara.

—¡Bueno, eso está muy bien!

—Es un gilipollas integral. Se hace una casa fuera de la ciudad para vivir todo el año. Estuve con él viendo el terreno. Me asegura que quiere un proyecto tradicional, una casa de campo tal cual la pintaría un crío. Vale, le presento los planos y me suelta que dónde están los elementos geométricos. Le contesto que una edificación clásica no lleva elementos geométricos. Y el tío se descuelga con que lo geométrico se lleva mucho, que si no puedo hacerle un *mix* entre tradición y modernidad.

—A mí me parece que estás de suerte, en el fondo eso ha sido siempre una aspiración de los arquitectos.

—¡Déjate de coñas, Petra! En una casa de ese tamaño no puedes ponerte en plan creativo, y menos con esas premisas.

—Esperará que le presentes el Taj Mahal bis —probé fortuna por si le hacía gracia.

—Algo por el estilo. De momento, aquí me tienes pergeñando monstruitos. —No le hizo gracia.

—Cenamos dentro de media hora.

Dio un mugido como signo de aceptación. No había levantado la vista de su trabajo ni una sola vez. No me había mirado. Estaba de mal humor. Ya en la mesa, riñó a Marina porque se había sentado a cenar con el pelo mojado. Los gemelos también recibieron correctivo verbal por decir que las croquetas estaban demasiado pastosas. Cuando el ambiente estuvo lo suficientemente enrarecido como para que nadie osara hablar, Marcos rompió el silencio con la siguiente pregunta:

—¿Os gustaría que compráramos una casa en el campo?

Seguía con la misma canción. No podía creerlo. Noté que sus hijos tampoco supieron a qué atenerse. Teo preguntó:

—¿Para qué?

—¿Para qué son las casas, Teo? ¡Para vivir! Buscaríamos un lugar cercano a Barcelona y nos trasladaríamos allí. Cuando os tocara visitarnos, contrataríamos a alguien que os llevara en un coche en caso de que no hubiera autobús. Al día siguiente yo mismo os dejaría en la escuela de camino a mi estudio.

—Sería un follón —se atrevió a comentar Hugo.

—¿Un follón? Lo que sí es un follón es vivir en una ciudad llena de tráfico, contaminada, donde todo el mundo está de los nervios, una ciudad con una densidad de población que parece la de Bombay. En el campo se respira mejor, hay más tranquilidad, ¡hay pajaritos que puedes oír nada más levantarte por la mañana!

—¿Y a qué hora tendríamos que levantarnos para oír los pajaritos? —incidió Hugo.

—No es momento de entrar en detalles —arguyó Marcos.

—¿A Petra le parece bien? —puso, como de costumbre, el dedo en la llaga Marina.

Todos, incluido su padre, miraron hacia mí. Tardé un instante en contestar. Por fin dije con una sonrisa forzada:

—No es momento de entrar en detalles.

Los chicos se rieron. Marcos se tensó. Comimos el postre en silencio. En cuanto hubo apurado la última cucharada de yogur, el causante de tanto desconcierto se levantó de la mesa y se fue. Debía continuar trabajando un buen rato.

—¡Cómo está el patio! —mascculló Teo.

—¿Tú tenías idea de esa historia del campo, Petra? —preguntó Hugo.

—Alguna vez lo ha comentado últimamente, pero se refería a nuestra jubilación, no hablaba de hacerlo ahora mismo.

—¿Por qué está de tan mal humor? —quiso saber Hugo.

—En fin, chicos, el trabajo de vuestro padre no es fácil y en estos tiempos en los que todo el mundo andamos exigiendo...

—¿Tú quieres irte al campo, Petra? —dijo Marina en tono preocupado.

Di una palmada en el aire. Miré el reloj.

—Muchachos, dejémoslo. El tema no da para más. Ayudadme a recoger la mesa. Ya se le olvidará la idea a vuestro padre cuando se le pase el mal humor.

Obedecieron sin estar muy convencidos de mi afirmación. Al terminar, dieron las buenas noches y cada uno se metió en su habitación. Yo tampoco estaba muy convencida de lo que acababa de decir.

6

Miré detenidamente las fotografías de los dos pasaportes falsos que obraban en nuestro poder. Allí estaban sobre la mesa de mi despacho, inertes como el pescado en la cesta de un pescador. Eran una captura, pero no se movían, yacían sin vida. Nathalie tenía unos ojos grandes, maquillados con profusión. Christophe no miraba a la cámara directamente, sino de soslayo. Ninguno de los dos sonreía. Como España es el único país europeo que permite sonreír en los documentos acreditativos de identidad, una posible deducción lógica era que no habían sido falsificados aquí. Sin embargo, era una conclusión sesgada, cualquiera de aquellos dos franceses había podido decidir permanecer serio para la foto por cualquier motivo o por casualidad. Estaba harta de esperar noticias de Francia que no llegaban. Llamé a Garzón, que se presentó casi inmediatamente.

—Subinspector, ¿qué le parece si vamos a hacerle una visita a Manolito?

—¿Usted cree? Lo más razonable es pensar que esos documentos se falsificaron en Francia. La ciencia de Manolito no creo que llegue tan lejos.

—Subestimar a Manolito me parece un tremendo error.

En eso, Garzón estuvo de acuerdo conmigo. Manuel Cercedilla, cuyo alias era en sus malos tiempos Manolito, empezó su carrera como falsificador allá por el lejano año 1998. Era el mejor. Le daba a todo: carnets de socio de algún club, firmas en documentos oficiales, autorizaciones, cambios estratégicos en testamentos, títulos universitarios, declaraciones juradas, pasaportes, salvoconductos..., un auténtico crack. Él solía decir con orgullo que sus primeros trabajos los realizó de pequeñito, cuando alteraba sus calificaciones escolares para presentarlas ante sus padres dándoles un cariz más brillante. Como suele suceder en muchos casos, lo trincaron por una estupidez. Aceptó falsificar un título nobiliario, no recuerdo si de conde o de marqués, para un amiguete suyo que era estafador y lo necesitaba a fin de hacerse pasar por noble. Detuvieron a su amigo intentando venderle a un particular un palacete vacío del que consiguió las llaves ligándose a la agente inmobiliaria que lo gestionaba. Tirando del hilo, la Policía Judicial descubrió que la obra de arte del título nobiliario había sido perpetrada por Manolito. Por si se requería más seguridad, el amigo, ya enchironado, cantó su identidad. Manolito pasó unos años a la sombra y aprovechando su habilidad hizo unos cursos de restaurador de papel. Cuando hubo cumplido su condena, puso un negocio absolutamente legal. Restauraba cualquier cosa que estuviera escrita o dibujada. En una palabra, se rehabilitó, y tanto fue así que colaboraba con nosotros cuando se necesitaba la labor de un experto en falsificación. No había entre las filas de la poli ningún especialista que fuera mejor que él.

Garzón se mostraba remiso a pedir su cooperación. No le gustaban los confidentes policiales.

—Últimamente ha pedido dinero por sus informes —arguyó.

—Somos una comisaría rica.

—Cuénteselo a Coronas y ya verá lo que le dice.

—¡Estoy harta de esperar la respuesta de los colegas franceses! Y también estoy harta de hacerlo todo según las normas. Abríguese un poco y vámonos.

—Habrá que pedir autorización al comisario, ¿o quiere pagarle a Manolito de su bolsillo?

—Nos ayudará desinteresadamente, ya verá.

Hacía frío en la calle. Aquel otoño se había presentado desapacible en Barcelona: viento, lluvia y temperatura por debajo de lo habitual. Fuimos a pie hasta el barrio antiguo. Entre las secuelas de la pandemia y el aire helado, pudimos transitar sin que manadas de turistas nos cortaran el paso. Manolito tenía su pequeña tienda en los aledaños de la calle Petritxol. No sonrió al vernos entrar, debía dar buena imagen porque se encontraba hablando con una clienta, una señora mayor que quería restaurar una acuarela vieja, probablemente sin otro valor que el sentimental. Él la trataba con gran amabilidad, atendió a todas sus dudas y demostró tener una paciencia envidiable. Cuando al fin la maldita señora se largó, Manolito, que no había olvidado el lenguaje carcelario, se dirigió hacia nosotros con menos miramientos.

—¿Qué demonio le pica a la pasma hoy?

—Digamos que la curiosidad —respondí, y puse sobre el mostrador ambos pasaportes falsificados.

Les echó una ojeada superficial.

—Pasaportes franceses, no está mal. Supongo que traéis una orden del juez.

—No te pases, Manolito. Tú no eres un perito autorizado —contraatacó Garzón.

—El caso es que no me gusta que os presentéis en mi tienda por las buenas, sin ni siquiera avisar. Ya se lo he dicho mil veces a otros colegas vuestros. Tengo una reputación y quiero conservarla intacta.

—Vayamos al grano —le conminé—. Ambos documentos son falsificados y queremos saber quién lo hizo.

—El grano consiste en que, si doy en el clavo, la mitad se paga por adelantado. Si no sé quién es el autor, sólo cobro una pequeña cantidad por el tiempo perdido.

—No tenemos permiso del comisario para pagarte —le espeté.

—Entonces ya podéis marcharos por donde habéis venido.

El subinspector se tensó a mi lado. Yo fingí perder los nervios.

—¡Basta, ya está bien! Estamos investigando la desaparición de un niño. Cada minuto que pasa es crucial. De tener pistas sobre esos documentos depende que lo encontremos con vida. Si quieres, te pagaré yo misma de mis ahorros. ¿Estás más contento así?

Garzón me transmitió su reacción con una simple mirada: estupefacción, alarma, incredulidad..., ni una gota de admiración iba disuelta en la mezcla. También Manolito quedó un poco desconcertado.

—¿Un niño? No he visto nada de eso en las noticias.

—¡Porque no lo hemos hecho público, joder! Es cuestión de vida o muerte, ¿necesitas que lo repita?

Algo se movió en la sensibilidad de aquel rufián, rehabilitado hasta cierto punto. Cabeceó, se pasó una mano por la cara y fue a buscar una serie de lupas diferentes en forma y tamaño. Luego, se puso a la labor y empezó a escrutar los dos pasaportes desde todos los ángulos, completamente enfrascado. Alternaba uno u otro, medía, ampliaba, cambiaba de ángulo. Tardó más de una hora en darnos su dictamen, pero parecía muy seguro de sus palabras.

—El del tal Christophe está elaborado aquí, en Barcelona, y sé casi seguro quién lo ha hecho. El de la mujer, no tengo ni puta idea. Lo habrán falsificado en Francia, quizá. Ni idea, ya os digo.

—Muy bien. Pues danos las señas del autor del que sospechas y le haremos una visita.

—Pero ¿tú estás loca o qué? No es ese el acuerdo que tengo con la bofia. Soy yo quien habla con el interesado. No soy un soplón, ¿comprendes?, entre otras cosas porque ya estaría criando malvas si lo hiciera como tú dices.

—Manolito, pero el niño...

—Ni por ese niño ni por una docena de niños recién paridos. Si queréis saber algo, volved mañana a esta misma hora.

—¿Mañana? ¡Ni lo sueñes, necesitamos los datos hoy mismo!

—Tendré que cerrar la tienda una hora antes. Vale que no me paguéis el peritaje, pero ¿quién me compensa por los clientes que puedo perder?

Eché mano a mi bolso, busqué el monedero y dejé un billete de cincuenta euros sobre la mesa.

—¿Es suficiente?

Lo cogió con cara de resignación.

—Supongo que a las ocho ya sabré algo. ¿Dónde quedamos?

—¿En La Jarra de Oro?

—¿Ese bar que está lleno de maderos? Ni lo sueñes. En el bar Lupita del Raval, a las ocho en punto.

Garzón salió bufando de la tienda.

—¡Joder, inspectora!, quizá lo del niño no era necesario, una buena hostia lo hubiera convencido sin mentiras.

—Un niño siempre da un toque de dramatismo, y encima nos hemos ahorrado una buena pasta. Además, le recuerdo que Manolito colabora extraoficialmente con la poli, no es cuestión de liarse con él a mamporros.

A las ocho de la tarde en punto estábamos en el Lupita. Llegamos veinte minutos antes, en realidad. Según mi compañero, anticiparse era bueno para observar posibles movimientos previos en el lugar de la cita, aunque yo estaba segura de que Garzón, muerto de hambre, aspiraba a algún aperitivo sustancioso antes de cenar. Acodados en la barra, provistos de una cerveza helada, lo vi pasando revista silenciosa a las tapas exhibidas tras un cristal. Le señaló al camarero una bandeja de boquerones en vinagre y estiró cuatro dedos de la mano derecha.

—Yo no voy a comer —dije.

—Por eso pido sólo cuatro.

Se rio en tono bajo y yo lo miré con el rabillo del ojo.

—¿De verdad le gusta tanto comer, Fermín?

—Se lo juro.

—Ahora dicen que los que escogen la comida como placer principal es porque tienen carencias psicológicas.

—¡Bah!, teorías, estudios que hacen los americanos cuando se aburren o quieren vender algo en concreto. Ahora todas las noticias que recogen los periódicos van dirigidas a joder al personal. Antes estaba la religión para eso, pero como ahora nadie hace caso de los preceptos de la santa madre Iglesia, alguien tiene que meterte la mala conciencia en el cuerpo. El caso es joderle la vida a la gente.

Sonreí vagamente. La filosofía casera de aquel hombre siempre contenía un punto de razón. Puede que el subinspector fuera un tanto primitivo, pero sin duda resultaba fácil tratar con él. Se me ocurrió una idea repentina.

—¿Quiere que nos vayamos luego a cenar por ahí, o le espera Beatriz en casa?

—¿Mi mujer? ¡No está, se ha ido con un grupo de amigas pijas a Nueva York!

—¡Demonio!, ¿y usted no la ha acompañado?, podía haber pedido unos días libres.

—Que el diablo me libre de todo mal. Van de tiendas. ¿Se imagina el coñazo? Hacen algún viaje de ese tipo de vez en cuando. Yo siempre le digo a Beatriz que cuando me jubile ya iré con ella, pero no tengo la menor intención. ¿Usted está hoy sola también?

—No, pero le mando un wasap a mi cónyuge y ya está.

—¡Cojonudo! Hace tiempo que no salimos usted y yo mano a mano. Así nos quitamos las carencias psicológicas los dos a la vez.

Se concentró en los boquerones, blanquecinos como la lengua de un ángel. Tal que si hubiera estado planeado, cuando hubo acabado con el último, Manolito apareció por la puerta del bar. Se sentó a nuestro lado en la barra, si bien con la distancia necesaria para preservar su reputación.

—Bueno, ya está —dijo levantando la voz. Garzón enseguida le señaló su torpeza.

—¡Coño, Manolito! ¡Si te pones tan lejos tendrás que gritar y se va a enterar todo dios! Acércate un poquito, que nadie te va a ver. Venga, te invitamos a una cerveza.

—Es lo menos que podéis hacer —exclamó, corriendo su taburete hacia nosotros.

—¿Resultados, muchacho? —pregunté, imitando a Sam Spade.

Me alargó una nota manuscrita. En ella sólo figuraba un nombre: Pierre Laurent.

—Así se llama en realidad vuestro hombre. Mi contacto pudo saberlo porque le pidió su pasaporte real para copiarlo. Es una garantía que tiene; así se asegura de que no es un asesino muy conocido, un yihadista o cualquier otra cosa que lo comprometa demasiado si se descubre el pastel. Le pareció que su pasado de delincuente no era de los importantes. Le preguntó, y el tipo le dijo que había estado metido en drogas. Estuvieron a punto de cazarlo y se hartó de andar huyendo. Salió del país pasando la frontera en coche. No lo cogieron. Llegó a Barcelona con la intención de no andar nunca más en trapicheos, pero para eso necesitaba un pasaporte nuevo. Le contó a mi contacto que buscaría un trabajo como cocinero, ese sería su empleo-tapadera.

—¿Algo más?

—Nada más.

—¿De eso cuánto tiempo hace?

—Unos tres años.

—¿Sabía tu contacto si el individuo tenía amigos o familia en Barcelona, alguna novia quizá?

—¡Carajo, inspectora, ya es mucho lo que le contó! Hay tipos que no abren la boca. Este se enrolló mucho porque sabía que volvería a necesitar los servicios de mi contacto para las renovaciones del documento. Eso indica que decía la verdad.

—¿La verdad sobre qué?

—¡Sobre que había dejado los malos rollos! Pensaba establecerse en Barcelona. Se había rehabilitado.

—¡Joder con la rehabilitación! —exclamó el subinspector—. Se rehabilita con todas las cuentas pendientes en su país. Así cualquiera.

—No todo el mundo es como yo —respondió Manolito orgullosamente.

—Sí, Manolito, tú eres un santo de altar. San Manolito virgen y mártir. Pero si tu rehabilitación es de las buenas, ¿por qué no nos pasas el nombre de tu contacto, eh? Estás encubriendo a un falsificador, a unos cuantos, sería mejor decir.

—Oye, Garzón. Yo he cumplido las condiciones del trato, así que no me toques los cojones.

El subinspector se cabreó de pronto, subió el tono.

—Así que esas tenemos, ¿no? ¡Encima que le soplas a la inspectora cincuenta euros por una mierda de información! Tú te fías de nosotros, ¿verdad? Pues nosotros no nos fiamos de ti. ¿Quién me dice que es verdad lo que has contado?

Manolito miró a mi compañero con estupefacción. Levantó ambas manos sin comprender nada.

—Pero ¿a qué viene esto? Yo siempre colaboro con la poli.

—¡Pero cobras, muchacho! Y a eso no se le llama colaboración. ¡Y encima te habíamos advertido de que era un caso especial y no contábamos con presupuesto! ¡Devuélvele enseguida la pasta a la inspectora!

Manolito resopló de indignación. Metió la mano en su bolsillo y sacó un billete arrugado, lo dejó sobre la barra.

—Aquí tienes, pero la próxima vez no vengáis a buscarme.

Salió, digno y altivo, no sin antes haber deglutido de un trago hasta la última gota de su cerveza. Me volví hacia el subinspector.

—¿Y si cumple la amenaza?

—Si volvemos a necesitarlo, mandaremos a un compañero en nuestro lugar.

—No estoy segura de que haya sido prudente por su parte, Fermín. Total, no era tanto dinero.

—Usted sabe que me fastidian los confidentes, los soplones y los colaboradores con la poli. Hay que aguantarlos, vale, son una institución que a veces necesitamos. Pero de eso a soportar que se nos insubordinen, que encima nos estafen y nos cueste dinero de nuestro bolsillo... ¡ni hablar! Coja sus cincuenta euros, van a venirnos muy bien para la cena.

—Tendríamos que pasar antes por comisaría para dar inmediatamente la información a la policía francesa.

—Llame al comisario y que la pase él. Dígale que así estaremos más seguros de que los gabachos se ponen las pilas. Dígale lo que se le ocurra, pero esta cena no nos la van a joder, y es tarde ya.

Sin pensarlo demasiado, le obedecí. Coronas no puso ningún inconveniente. Apuntó todo lo que le dije, incluido el nombre de Pierre Laurent. Le escribí también a Marcos para decirle que no cenaría en casa. Enseguida contestó: «OK». Estábamos por fin libres para asuntos tan poco profesionales como sentarse a la mesa.

El lugar que elegimos era sencillo y funcional. Garzón no podía soportar ningún restaurante que oliera a diseño, fusión o cualquier otra novedad culinaria. Opinaba que eran una tomadura de pelo. Según él, se comía poco y mal. Le parecía que las inspiraciones de los cocineros de nueva generación estaban bien siempre que las experimentaran en su propia casa, pero ofrecer esos platos a la clientela cobrándolos a millón era un abuso difícil de perdonar. Por eso siempre parábamos en figones animados y tradicionales, donde servir tomate frito por encima de la tortilla de patatas ya se consideraba el colmo de la innovación. Yo a veces discutía con él, diciéndole que era un inmovilista y un tabernario, aunque muy en el fondo pensaba igual. Aquella noche no le llevé la contraria, me daba exactamente lo mismo dónde discurriera la velada, lo que de verdad me interesaba era, cosa inaudita, comentarle mi vida sentimental.

El subinspector pidió sopa de menudillos. Yo me limité a una ensalada, y de segundo compartimos un chuletón. Enseguida se le fue la cabeza a nuestro asesinato.

—¿Usted de verdad se cree que Bob no sabía nada de que su colega no era trigo limpio? A mí me cuesta tragarme esa píldora. Mañana mismo hay que apretarle las tuercas a ver por dónde sale.

—Sí, localizaremos al tal Bob y habrá que interrogarlo de nuevo.

—Vale que los hombres no somos muy comunicativos entre nosotros, pero...

Lo interrumpí suavemente.

—Garzón, ¿usted es feliz en su matrimonio?

La acción de llevarse a la boca una cucharada de sopa quedó interrumpida.

—¡Coño! —exclamó por lo bajo.

—No quiero darle la tabarra con asuntos personales, pero me gustaría saber su opinión sobre algo en concreto y es imprescindible que sepa eso, si es usted feliz en su matrimonio.

La cuchara volvió intacta al plato.

—Pues sí, claro. Bueno, usted que se ha casado tantas veces ya sabe lo que es el matrimonio. Algún día puede haber una trifulca, otro tú piensas de una manera y ella de otra..., pero en general estoy muy a gusto con Beatriz. Nadie daba un chavo por nuestra convivencia y ya ve usted, va como una seda. ¿Le ocurre algo, Petra?

—No sé, me ha entrado la manía de que Marcos ya no está enamorado de mí.

—¿Hay otra mujer, sospecha usted algo?

Sonreí, negué con la cabeza.

—No, no se trata de eso.

—¿Y entonces?

—Quiere que nos vayamos a vivir al campo, aunque sabe perfectamente que yo me opongo. Desde el confinamiento ha venido dándole vueltas a la idea: una casa en un pueblo cercano a Barcelona, un sitio donde descansar. Tal y como estamos aquí en la ciudad se siente oprimido.

Garzón continuó dando cuenta de su plato. Dijo con despreocupación:

—¡Bah!, ¿y por esa historia piensa usted que ya no la quiere? ¡Si estuviéramos en una investigación nunca hubiera sacado una conclusión semejante! Esta coña de la pandemia, el confinamiento y la madre que lo parió nos ha puesto a todos un poco de los nervios. ¿No ha hablado con alguien de ese tema? Resulta que hay personas que todavía no se atreven a salir a la calle por miedo a contagiarse. ¡La gente no quiere morirse, Petra, y menos cuanto más viejos son! No lo entiendo, piensan que van a quedarse en el mundo hasta la hecatombe final. Y no digo que sea el caso de su marido, no. Para mí es normal que Marcos tenga ganas de campo, es un hombre con muchas responsabilidades. Ya se le pasará.

—Todo lo que me cuenta es muy razonable, pero en algunas ocasiones atribuimos nuestros sentimientos y deseos de cambio a algunos motivos que no son los causantes en realidad. Él se siente oprimido y eso me escama mucho, me preocupa.

—¡Joder, inspectora, que usted se preocupe y sea pesimista no es ninguna noticia! Mujer complicada, de mente retorcida y siempre llena de dudas. Así la describiría yo si me pidieran hacerlo en un informe. ¡Olvídese de segundas intenciones! Y en el caso de que Marcos insistiera mucho con lo del campo, pues tampoco es tan grave. No se irían a Toledo, digo yo, sino cerca de Barcelona. Algún fin de semana les visitaríamos Beatriz y yo para que nos invitaran a una barbacoa.

—Tiene usted unas ideas demasiado literales, subinspector.

—¡Lo que faltaba! Cuando ha empezado a hablar sobre Marcos me ha asustado un poco, pero ya veo que no son más que sus neuras normales y corrientes.

Para demostrar que no se encontraba inquieto en absoluto, hincó el diente en la carne que nos trajeron a continuación, demostrando su infinito placer. Ojalá en su cerebro de lógica simplista hubiera existido un pequeño rincón para mí. Pero no, no me había tranquilizado con sus palabras. Las personas sencillas sólo conciben una ruptura sentimental si hay de por medio infidelidades o nuevos amores. ¡Con lo frágil que es la fina telaraña del amor!, ¡como si no hubiera más razones para rasgarla!

Cuando llegué a casa, Marcos ya dormía. Con

cuidado de no despertarlo, me cambié y me acosté a su lado. Su cuerpo despedía un agradable calor.

Un prófugo de la policía francesa. Todo empezaba a encajar, aunque sería más correcto decir que, al menos, empezábamos a tener una matriz en la que meter las piezas. No era demasiado, pero auguraba más hallazgos.

Los franceses pronto contrastaron nuestros nuevos datos. Eran correctos. Christophe y Pierre Laurent eran el mismo individuo. Llegó desde Marsella una documentación completa que incluía un par de fotografías del muerto, bastante más joven de como lo habíamos visto en el depósito. Y bien, ¿todo se resumía en esto: un pequeño traficante que se hace matar por alguna pequeña deuda? Una pequeña muerte, un pequeño caso. Daba igual, había que descubrir quién lo había matado y por qué. Me dieron ganas de mandar todo el asunto a Francia, metido en una maleta, que ellos se apañaran con sus delincuentes, pero la hipótesis de que la mujer misteriosa había sido la asesina sólo seguía siendo eso, una hipótesis, una incógnita que había que despejar.

Conducida la investigación hacia las drogas, contactamos con la Guardia Civil. Pierre Laurent no estaba en sus archivos bajo ningún nombre. Si nuestro falsificador rehabilitado había calculado bien, en los tres años que llevaba en España no había cometido ningún delito por el que hubiera sufrido detención. La fotografía de la tal Nathalie no les sonó de nada a los de la Benemérita. Aun así, nos vimos obligados a meter los pies en el mundo de los traficantes. El teniente Cuevas, quien teóricamente más sabía sobre estupefacientes, nos asesoró: nombres, lugares, contactos... El caso continuaría en nuestras manos, pero necesitaríamos cooperación. Le pedí a Coronas que hablara con los mandos policiales de la autonómica. Si nos topábamos con los Mossos, estos debían saber que andábamos tras un asesino. Necesitábamos vía libre.

7

Garzón detestaba aún más que yo los asuntos de drogas. Si una de esas implicaciones surgía en una investigación, se daba a todos los demonios. Teníamos nuestros motivos para que fuera así. Todo solía resultar sórdido, todos los comprometidos exhibían habitualmente rasgos de carácter limítrofes con la enfermedad mental, con la marginación, con la vileza de un comercio clandestino que no tenía piedad de nadie. Cualquier cosa podía suceder en ese ámbito. Pero por mucho que protestara mi compañero, debíamos organizarnos para seguir la estela del asesino, y esa estela señalaba las drogas.

La primera dificultad era la itinerancia de nuestra víctima. Nada daba a entender que Barcelona hubiera sido el lugar donde se generara el asesinato. El mundo de la droga no se limita a las capitales ni a ciudades importantes, más aún, en torno a esas poblaciones que centran los acontecimientos delictivos suele florecer un tejido social en el que se vulnera la ley. La cosa pintaba cruda en el caso de Barcelona. Un cinturón de poblaciones crecidas a rebufo de la importancia de la capital contenía colectivos marginales que no habían sido capaces de aguantar el ritmo del éxito y vegetaban en las cunetas, con pocas esperanzas de recuperar la carretera principal.

En primer lugar, hablamos con Bob. Debía darnos una lista de los eventos que había visitado su furgón, al menos en el último año. Por supuesto, aprovechamos la ocasión que se nos brindaba y volvimos a apretarle las clavijas sobre su relación con Christophe-Pierre. No se apeó ni un instante de su versión oficial, si bien añadió juramentos relativos a su inocencia. Desconocía la posible pertenencia de su socio al mundo del tráfico de estupefacientes y él mismo no había probado las drogas jamás. Nada, ni una pastilla, ni una esnifada, ni siquiera un mal porro para probar. Siempre había detestado los paraísos artificiales porque era, casi siempre, un hombre feliz, alguien que se conformaba con su suerte y que, para mejorarla, sólo confiaba en el esfuerzo personal. Garzón acabó por hartarse de tanta exhibición de virtud y le recordó que, aunque no hubiera nada contra él, seguía en el punto de mira de la investigación.

Cuando se fue, un tanto asustado, había dejado sobre mi mesa una lista de lugares y la correspondiente celebración que los condujo a ellos con su camión restaurante. Le eché una ojeada, más desesperada a medida que iba avanzando: Badalona, Mollet, Mataró, Cerdanyola, Sant Cugat, Sitges... Un montón. Feria de la diversidad, fiestas del pueblo, exposiciones de productos típicos, muestra de artesanía local... Me quedé perpleja al comprobar la cantidad de eventos que sucedían cerca de mí sin que me hubiera enterado ni me hubiera sentido tentada de asistir. Le pasé la lista al subinspector. Quedó descorazonado al momento.

—¡Joder, Petra, a ver si me aclaro! Se supone que hemos de visitar todos estos pueblos, dar con su círculo drogota, investigar si un tío que pasó por allí hace tiempo estuvo en contacto con ellos, compró material o lo vendió, en fin, traficó... Pero ¿usted ha mirado bien la lista que nos ha pasado este gachó?

—La he dejado a mitad de la lectura.

—¿Síntomas de depresión?

—De agobio, más bien. Porque no podemos olvidar que también hemos de ir controlando a la caravana de furgonetas en su estado actual, moviéndose de pueblo en pueblo.

—Oiga, inspectora, ¿y no podríamos dimitir?

—¿Dejar la policía?

—Sólo me refiero al caso que nos ocupa. No me veo con ánimos, la verdad. Hay en el Cuerpo gente más joven, con muy buena preparación, con ganas de sobresalir, de demostrar lo que valen, de que les cuelguen medallas. ¿Por qué no dar un paso al lado y dejarlos actuar?

—En serio, no le reconozco, Fermín. ¿Estaría usted dispuesto a hacer eso?

—Bueno, si fuera un caso muy lucido, si se hubieran cargado al presidente, al rey, a un obispo, a un empresario de tronío..., pero a un feriante que siempre estaba moviéndose de un lado a otro vendiendo bocatas y haciendo de camello...

—Dimita usted, yo continúo.

—¿Por sentido del deber?

—No, pero me imagino a mí misma diciéndole al comisario que hay otros más jóvenes y más preparados que yo para un trabajo y me entra una furia asesina. No cuente conmigo, dimita usted.

—¿Y que pongan a otro en mi lugar, a uno de esos jovenzuelos sin ni puta idea de nada y que lo único que aportan es la informática y el inglés? No insista, yo me quedo donde estoy, alguien tiene que protegerla. He cambiado de parecer. —Me eché a reír. Garzón me miraba con cara de pitorreo. Añadió a sus palabras—: Aprenderé geografía de Cataluña, eso nunca está de más.

Tuvimos una larga reunión con el teniente Montilla. Sí, era evidente que existían puntos neurálgicos de venta de drogas en los pueblos cercanos a Barcelona. Mirando la lista que nos había dado Bob, él se centró en tres: un bar en Badalona, una casa okupada en L'Hospitalet y una tienda de ultramarinos de Mataró.

—¿Una tienda de ultramarinos? —pregunté con sorpresa.

—Acumula una serie de denuncias e investigaciones por nuestra parte, sabemos que todavía tiene actividad, pero nunca hemos podido cazarlos. Es una tapadera perfecta. De todos modos, inspectora, cuando vayan con los okupas me gustaría acompañarlos. No espere cooperación de esos tipos en ninguno de los tres sitios, pero los de L'Hospitalet son peligrosos. Yo los he interrogado varias veces, creo que mi presencia les impondrá.

—Estaremos encantados, siempre que sus superiores le den permiso.

—Pida a su comisario que me reclame.

—Lo haré sin ninguna duda.

Cuando se hubo marchado, el subinspector exclamó:

—¡Ya llueve menos! La ayuda de este chico me da esperanza.

—¡Y eso que es joven! ¿Cree que tendrá puta idea de algo?

—Algo sabrá. De momento, nos ha dado tres lugares y tres nombres por quienes preguntar: Carlitos en Badalona, el Tiras en L'Hospitalet y Dámaso en Mataró.

—Parecen tres alias.

—No creo que se sientan ofendidos si, de entrada, los llamamos así.

—Pero hay que guardar las formas.

—De acuerdo, usted guarda las formas y yo paso a la acción.

Empezamos por Badalona. A lo mejor frente al mar el panorama se veía más despejado. Garzón conducía mirando de vez en cuando el GPS para orientarse. Canturreaba. Su mente podía estar centrada en cualquier cosa, pensé, cerca o lejos de allí. La mía no quería centrarse en nada. Creo que evitaba profundizar, enlazar los indicios de crisis que aparecían en mi vida: un trabajo en el que la relajación y el sosiego eran imposibles, un marido que quería marcharse al campo, un cierto extrañamiento del mundo en general. Miré a mi compañero.

—¿Lleva usted las fotos, Fermín?

—Sí, claro, claro.

Noté que había contestado mecánicamente, sin pensarlo siquiera. Sonreí.

—¿En qué está pensando?

Me dio la impresión de que se sonrojaba.

—¿Yo? Nada. La cabeza me va dando tumbos de aquí para allá. Nada importante.

Hubo un silencio que sólo se interrumpía por el ruido del tráfico a nuestro alrededor. De repente, Garzón añadió:

—Pero le aseguro que soy muy feliz.

Me eché a reír.

—Yo no le he preguntado eso.

—Ya lo sé, pero con las mujeres siempre me pasa igual, también con Beatriz. Tengo la impresión de que continuamente me cogen en falta. Ustedes van más allá de las cosas que se dicen de boca para afuera, sacan conclusiones sobre uno que ni yo mismo sería capaz de pensar.

—Entramos en la mente de los hombres como cazadoras furtivas.

—Búrlese todo lo que quiera, yo sé lo que me digo.

—Nunca lo he dudado. Lo que le ocurre a usted debería llamarse «el síndrome de la madre» y supongo que todos los hombres llegan a sufrirlo un poco. Desde la niñez saben que los consejos y las reglas que su madre les daba eran de lo más justo y prudente, lo que más les convenía en cada ocasión. Por eso, ya en su vida adulta, siempre contrastan sus actos con aquellas enseñanzas maternas cuando están en presencia de cualquier mujer. Y lo hacen de manera inconsciente, claro está.

Mi subalterno aceleró un poco, elevó la voz.

—Oiga, inspectora. Estamos llevando un caso complicado. Nos dirigimos a hacer una gestión que no tendrá nada de agradable. ¿Y qué se le ocurre a usted? ¡Analizar mis pensamientos más ocultos y ponerse a hacer teorías extrañas! De verdad le digo, de lo que no existe la más mínima posibilidad es de que alguien acierte en qué coño está pensando usted.

En el fondo, mi compañero llevaba razón. Me callé prudentemente, forzándome a pensar en el caso. Una mujer se planta en otro país para matar a un hombre. Ese hombre tiene un pasado delictivo en drogas, quizá un presente también. La mujer lleva documentación falsa, de lo que se deduce que tampoco ella es una ciudadana normal. El móvil pasional queda descartado casi por completo. ¿Qué móviles puede tener esa mujer para cometer un asesinato? Pues los clásicos: ajuste de cuentas, venganza. Pierre se metió dinero en el bolsillo durante su época en Francia y la organización a la que estafó manda a una sicaria o a otro miembro de la tribu a cargárselo. Cuando lo localiza, tiempo después, la suerte está echada. No quedaba nada claro el hecho de que la dama encuentre la puerta de la furgoneta abierta, pero el socio de Bob asegura que solía dejarla así. ¿Creemos a Bob, nuestro gentil testigo intermitente? No hay nada contra él, pero creer, lo que se dice creer..., yo seguía teniendo la impresión de que si no mentía, al menos ocultaba.

—Si recapacitamos con lentitud y seriedad... —le dije al subinspector—. Ya todo está resuelto.

—¿Hablamos del caso? —quiso saber él con bastante retranca.

—Del caso, sí. Sólo nos falta probar la única hipótesis posible: ajuste de cuentas en asunto de drogas.

—También nos falta capturar a la asesina.

—Sí, es un detalle que debemos considerar. A lo mejor esa tipa está bien escondida esperando que la tormenta amaine o quizá partió de vuelta a Francia.

—Y quedan flecos por aclarar. ¿Dónde tenía la pasta escondida Pierre, si es que se la llevó? Quedan más flecos que en un mantón de Manila.

—Eso del mantón es antiguo, Fermín.

—Como yo.

El buscador nos había llevado hasta un polígono industrial formado por inmensas naves de almacenaje. Estábamos cerca del mar, cerca de las tres chimeneas, un vestigio de una época en que nadie sabe si el barrio era peor o mejor. La mayor parte de las naves tenían letreros en chino escritos con grandes signos. En principio, parecía dudoso que allí se encontrara un bar, pero al descender del coche lo descubrimos en un recodo. Era un local pequeño de aspecto harto miserable, pero por sus ventanas se filtraba un delicioso olor a café. Me volví hacia el subinspector.

—Ahí está el único bar. A por ellos, Garzón, que son pocos y cobardes.

—Mientras no sean chinos que no hablen español...

Lo eran, al menos la joven que nos atendió. No había ni un cliente a aquella hora. Pedimos café, y mientras la chica lo preparaba, le pregunté:

—¿Podemos ver al dueño?

Ella se volvió hacia mí, me observó con desconfianza. Garzón le enseñó la placa. Siguió sin hablar, porque ni una sola palabra había pronunciado todavía. Sólo cuando hubo servido las dos tazas, hizo una inclinación de cabeza y desapareció por la puerta que daba a la cocina. Al cabo de un momento, salió un hombre de unos cincuenta años, corpulento, de rasgos europeos. Cuando habló supimos que era español.

—¿Se les ofrece algo?

—Como le hemos dicho a su empleada, queríamos hablar un momento con usted.

—No es mi empleada, es mi mujer. Y ustedes son policías, ¿no?

Le enseñamos ambas placas. Tenía una nariz superlativa e informe, que destacaba como un tubérculo, quizá patata, quizá boniato, en un rostro ya de por sí espeluznante.

—Pues vale... —dijo—, antes de empezar a hablar, que sepan que en mi local no hay nada que rascar. De vez en cuando vienen sus compañeros a meter las narices y nunca han encontrado un carajo, así que...

—Muy bien —le interrumpí—. Ahora empecemos a hablar. ¿Alguna vez ha visto a este hombre?

Se quedó mirando la foto de la víctima con cara de asco.

—No, nunca lo había visto.

Saqué la foto de Nathalie. Se la mostré.

—¿Y a ella?

—No, tampoco me suena de nada.

—¿Puede llamar a su esposa?

—¿Para qué la quiere?

—Pudo ver a una de estas dos personas un día en que no estaba usted.

—¿Y eso qué cambiaría?

—¡Llámela! —gritó el subinspector perdiendo la paciencia.

Con un gesto violento, el hombre se acercó a la cortina que cubría la puerta y la llamó.

—Liu Ci, ven, por favor.

Nada atemorizada, o sería mejor decir sin ninguna expresión detectable, la camarera esposa llegó hasta nosotros. El dueño del bar intentó coger las fotografías que estaban en las manos de Garzón para enseñárselas él mismo. Se lo impedimos. Las tomé yo en mi mano y se las mostré a la chica.

—¿Los reconoce, alguno de los dos ha venido por aquí?

Negó con la cabeza. Nos miró. Su marido la tomó suavemente de un brazo y le dijo:

—¿Estás segura, mi amor?

—Sí —pronunció su primera palabra, añadiendo después con un acento extraño—: ¿Puedo irme? Tengo trabajo que hacer.

—Puede irse, sí.

Nos quedamos frente a frente con el hombre.

—¿Y usted está seguro de no haberlos visto? Voy a contarle una cosa: a este hombre, un francés que se llamaba Pierre Laurent, lo han asesinado. Creemos que la asesina puede haber sido la mujer de la foto. Los dos estaban en el mundo de la droga. La cosa es seria, como ve. Volveré a preguntarle.

—No hace falta —soltó de repente—. No los he visto en mi vida. Puede que yo haya tenido mis cuentas con la justicia, puede que estuviera metido en embrollos con drogas, pero eso se acabó, ¿comprenden? Se acabó. Hace un año que me he casado con Liu Ci. Es lo mejor que me ha pasado en la vida, lo único bueno, quizá. ¿De verdad cree que voy a arriesgarlo todo por encubrir a un delincuente? Les juro que no. Ahora soy un hombre honrado y vivo exclusivamente de este bar. No me hace falta mucho más. Tengo tranquilidad y tengo amor.

Asentí varias veces. Saqué una tarjeta, se la tendí.

—De acuerdo, pero si llegara a saber algo, si la mujer se presentara por aquí, llámenos. Si de verdad quiere preservar lo que tiene, llámenos.

Volvimos al espacio fantasmal que dejaban las naves entre sí. Intercambiamos una mirada, yo elevé los ojos al cielo.

—El amor hizo en mí maravillas, ¡gloria al amor!

—¿No le cree?

Me encogí de hombros.

—¿Y usted?

Se encogió él.

—Nunca digas «no sirvió de nada» —sentencié. Y Garzón completó la máxima con una ordinariez.

Pero el día no había acabado. Según nuestros planes de investigación binaria, teníamos que visitar a los feriantes que aquel día se encontraban en Sant Cugat con motivo de una exposición municipal.

—¿Por qué hacen tantos eventos en la puta calle? —preguntó él retomando el volante y la conducción.

—Porque en España hace sol.

—¡La madre que los parió a todos!

—Al mal tiempo, buena cara, Fermín, aunque viéndolo a usted, creo que es justo al revés. Al buen tiempo, mala cara.

8

El asesinato de Pierre Laurent había tenido como resultado no deseado el cambio de ubicación de muchos de los feriantes. Ahora iban siempre todos juntos. No hubo demasiadas protestas, pero se vieron obligados a ponerse de acuerdo. Al llegar a Sant Cugat comprobamos que todos ellos se habían colocado en la misma posición que ocupaban el día del crimen. La pareja vegetariana estaba al lado del *food truck* de Bob Castillo. Elisenda vino enseguida a preguntarnos cómo iba la investigación. No me había fijado demasiado bien en su aspecto. Rubia, de piel muy blanca, ojos azules... Era como una mujer renacentista: dulce, lánguida, con un aire de fragilidad.

—Todo va avanzando poco a poco —le respondí.

—Pero aún no saben quién ha sido, ¿verdad?

—No, aún no lo sabemos.

—Es horrible, inspectora. Yo que siempre duermo como un tronco, desde que sucedió la desgracia me despierto cada noche sobresaltada.

—No fue una desgracia... —repliqué—, fue un asesinato. Si decimos una desgracia da la impresión de que ponemos la historia al mismo nivel que un accidente de tráfico, y no es así. Aquí hubo un asesino que fríamente quitó la vida a un hombre, lo mató.

La chica me miraba con cara de horror. Masculló:

—Es verdad, es verdad.

Su marido vino a buscarla enseguida. Se dirigió a mí:

—Inspectora, si no es urgente... Es que se nos está acumulando la clientela.

Era verdad, varios clientes esperaban frente a la barra de su camioneta. Asentí, Javier tomó a su mujer del brazo y, comprobando que estaba afectada por algo, le dio un beso en la cabeza. «Tranquila, ¿pasa algo?», oí que le susurraba. Inopinadamente, había dado con una veta de maridos que eran enormemente dulces con sus esposas: el dueño del bar y la china, ahora el par de vegetarianos... Y, sin embargo, el mío sólo pensaba en largarse al campo, por más en contra que estuviera yo. La vida es misteriosa, misteriosa y cabrona de verdad.

En la caravana de Bob encontramos en acción a su joven cocinero. Garzón y yo estuvimos observando cómo se las componía con unas crepes. Lo hacía muy bien: movimientos precisos y calculados, rostro impasible. Al terminar se las ofreció, en una bandejita de cartón, a dos chicas que aguardaban. Sólo cuando les hubo cobrado nos acercamos a él.

—¿No está Bob?

—Sí, ha ido un momento al colmado. Hemos hecho corto de cebollas.

—Somos policías. Le supongo enterado de la situación. ¿Alguna novedad por aquí? ¿No ha visto a nadie ni ha venido nadie que nos dé alguna pista en la investigación?

—Nada especial: gente, trabajo..., lo de cada día.

—¿Usted se queda a dormir aquí?

—Sí, me resulta más barato y la cama es cómoda de verdad.

—No tiene usted manías.

—No la entiendo.

—Quiero decir que otra persona quizá sintiera un poco de reparo quedándose en el lugar donde han asesinado a un hombre.

—¡Bah, no es mi caso! Cuando la policía se largó lo limpiamos todo bien a fondo.

—Al menos cerrará la puerta por las noches —intervino Garzón.

—¡Qué va! Aunque quisiera no podría. Está estropeada.

—¿Qué ha dicho?

—Sí, vengan, lo verán.

Nos llevó hasta la puerta, estuvo accionando la palanca de cierre, que, en efecto, no funcionaba. Luego se volvió hacia nosotros.

—Pero no tengo ningún miedo, ¿o debería tenerlo?

—No, en principio, no; pero sería preferible que le diga a su jefe que la haga arreglar.

Una pareja se había acercado al *truck* y nos miraba. El cocinero se excusó.

—Parece que me esperan clientes. ¿Puedo atenderlos?

—Vaya, por supuesto que sí.

El subinspector y yo nos miramos fijamente. Le pregunté:

—¿Quién de la Científica hizo la inspección?

—Gamero. Tengo su número de móvil.

—Pásemelo.

Tecleó, y cuando el número apareció en mi pantalla, tecleé yo.

—¿Gamero? Soy Petra Delicado.

—¡Hola, Petra! ¿Qué tal vas?

—No muy bien. Tengo una pregunta que hacerte: cuando hicisteis la inspección del furgón de comida en el caso Laurent, ¿no visteis que la cerradura estaba estropeada?

Hubo un momento de silencio, después respondió.

—Sí, sí que lo vimos, lo recuerdo perfectamente. Había una palanquita de seguridad que no podía bajarse, estaba averiada.

—¿Y por qué ese detalle no figura en tu informe?

—No pensé que tuviera importancia. Vimos que la cerradura no había sido manipulada recientemente, no había arañazos ni muescas. Tomamos las huellas dactilares, ¿qué más podíamos hacer?

—Informar de ese detalle.

—¿Ese detalle es importante para la investigación? El cierre podía estar estropeado desde hacía meses, años quizá.

—Ni aunque fuera desde el Diluvio, Gamero. Tu deber era informar.

—¿Y qué quieres que haga ahora, Petra, llorar de arrepentimiento?

—Llora lágrimas de cocodrilo, pero te aseguro que hasta un cocodrilo lo hubiera hecho mejor.

Colgué. Garzón ponía cara de circunstancias.

—¿No ha estado un poco dura, inspectora? En realidad no sé si el detalle es importante.

En ese momento vimos llegar a Bob Castillo con una bolsa de supermercado en la mano. Vino directo hacia nosotros. Me anticipé a los prolegómenos de bienvenida, interpelándolo con brusquedad.

—¿Usted sabía que la cerradura de su furgoneta estaba estropeada?

Se quedó un momento en suspenso, captó la onda, cabeceó.

—Sí, claro que lo sé. Se cascó al poco de comprarla. Al principio pensé en mandarla reparar, pero después con el trabajo y el estrés, y como encima Christophe no quería dormir encerrado, no me pareció urgente, se me pasó.

—Ya le dije que debía contarme cualquier detalle, ¿me oye?, cualquiera. Y espero que lo haga a partir de ahora. Me ha entendido, ¿verdad? ¡Y deje de llamarle Christophe! Su nombre era Pierre, Pierre Laurent.

—Lo siento, inspectora, lo siento. Le aseguro que he intentado hacerlo todo correctamente. Pero no se vayan todavía, tomen una crep, una cervecita a cuenta de la casa...

No aceptamos su invitación. En el coche yo estaba preparada para las preguntas de Garzón, y la primera dio en el blanco.

—¿Es importante el detalle de la cerradura o simplemente está de mal humor?

—Ambas cosas, subinspector. El detalle es importante. Ahora sabemos que el asesino estaba seguro de encontrar la puerta abierta. La deducción primera fue que víctima y asesino se conocían lo suficiente como para que el segundo estuviera al corriente de los hábitos del primero. Pero no necesariamente era así, alguien que lo supiera pudo informar al atacante de que la cerradura estaba averiada desde tiempo atrás.

—Es un detalle significativo, sí.

—De ahí viene mi mal humor. Ni siquiera los compañeros son capaces de estar alerta. No me fío del tal Bob, ni un pelo me fío. Que le intervengan el teléfono, que lo sigan. Veremos qué hay detrás de su apariencia tranquila.

—A la orden. Pero para no ponerlo sobre aviso sería conveniente que se mostrara más amable con él.

—¿Más amable?

—Sí, por ejemplo, no rechazando sus invitaciones. Esa crep con cerveza...

Di un golpe de cabeza como dejándolo por imposible. El subinspector no conseguía que mis malos humores se disiparan, pero siempre se las apañaba para, al menos, hacerme sonreír.

A pesar de que aquel caso era un auténtico quebradero de cabeza, por las noches conseguía dormir a pierna suelta. Durante toda mi vida ha sido así, pueden ocurrir de día montones de incidencias, pero por la noche el sueño me abre los brazos amorosamente. Mejor para mí, me esperaba un día fino aquella mañana. Aparentemente, todo estaba en orden. Llegué a comisaría, saludé a diestra y siniestra, me serví un café, y cuando iba a sentarme a mi mesa, apareció Garzón enarbolando unos papeles. Saltaba, literalmente saltaba. ¡Por todos los demonios, eran las ocho de la mañana, el subinspector ya tenía una edad, el día estaba lluvioso! ¿De dónde sacaba semejante energía? Lo observé con el aire más escéptico que pude simular.

—¿Ejercicios matutinos, Fermín?

—¡Por fin, inspectora, por fin! Acaba de llegar el informe de la pasma francesa.

Lejos de soltar de una vez por todas alguna información, seguía dando manotazos en el aire aferrado a los folios.

—¡Siéntese, por favor!

—Tiene los datos también en su ordenador, pero lo he impreso porque sé que es usted una antigua y le gusta el papel.

Dio un par de histriónicas carcajadas y continuó con aquella absurda perorata.

—Si quiere se lo leo, que también conozco cómo le gusta tener sirvientes. Está todo escrito en perfecto español, seguro que hay algún Martínez o algún López que trabaja con ellos.

—Está bien, empiece, lacayo, pero deje de moverse, se lo ruego.

—Le haré un resumen de lo importante. Nuestra querida Nathalie Verbeux se llama en realidad Martine Marchand. Cincuenta y dos años. Amplio historial delictivo siempre en tráfico de drogas. Buscada por la Interpol. Piensan que actualmente se halla al frente de la red de narcos más importante al sur de Europa. Paradero desconocido.

—Pues para ser una prófuga tan destacada han tardado un montón en dar con su identidad.

—Tiene muchos alias, muchos documentos falsificados. Si abre el informe de los gendarmes, verá que han incluido fotografías.

Abrí el informe. Lo leí. La última fotografía de la mujer misteriosa la mostraba con toda claridad. No coincidía con la de su pasaporte falsificado. Ojos grandes, mirada desafiante, abundante pelo negro recogido en una coleta lateral. Era hermosa, no joven pero hermosa.

—El informe también dice que es muy peligrosa. Se le atribuyen dos asesinatos por ajuste de cuentas. La justicia no ha conseguido encausarla jamás. No la encuentran, parece que se escabulle como una anguila.

—Pues por Barcelona se ha paseado con toda naturalidad.

—Desde luego, ¡vaya pájara! ¿Sabe lo que pasará ahora? Pues que nos quitarán el caso de las manos: Brigada de Narcóticos, Guardia Civil, Mossos d'Esquadra, Interpol..., y eso que íbamos bien encaminados.

—Seguiremos yendo igual. Nosotros estamos investigando el asesinato de Pierre Laurent y esa mujer ha aparecido en nuestras gestiones. Muy bien, pero está por averiguar si fue ella quien lo mató. No mezclemos churras con merinas. ¿Ha informado al comisario de todo esto?

—No ha llegado todavía, pero no creo que tarde. Bien, supongo que ya tiene toda esta información en su ordenador, se la envié hace un rato.

—Entonces la tiene, por supuesto. Bien, ahora voy a redactar el informe de ayer, incluiré las acciones que tenemos planeadas para hoy.

—¿Cuáles son?

Improvisé porque no existía ningún orden del día.

—Iremos con el teniente Montilla a la casa okupada de L'Hospitalet. Por cierto, dele un toque a ver si puede acompañarnos. Si no le va bien, lo haremos solos. No creo que Coronas le llame a usted personalmente, pero si así fuera, avíseme enseguida. Yo me las compondré con él para explicarle qué estamos haciendo.

Salió de estampida. Yo suspiré a fondo para disipar la tensión que había empezado a atenazarme las cervicales. Empecé a redactar el informe del día anterior. Tres páginas que incluían detalles. Al final, puse una *nota bene* dirigida al comisario:

> Esperamos de verdad que el caso del asesinato de Pierre Laurent siga a cargo del subinspector y mío. Estamos en vías de su esclarecimiento y la derivación a otros cuerpos de seguridad no haría sino entorpecer el resultado de las pesquisas.

Sólo cinco minutos después de haberlo enviado, mi pantalla relucía con la respuesta de Coronas. El texto era limitado en extensión:

> Muy bien, inspectora, muy bien. Continúen.

Era obvio que no le había dado tiempo a leer la totalidad del informe, pero la *nota bene* sí había sido objeto de su atención. El comisario nos secundaría, era lógico que así fuera, tampoco él quería que le birlaran el caso a la Policía Nacional.

Llamé a Garzón. Me sentía eufórica. ¿Por qué razón? Ni yo misma lo sabía. Todo seguía igual de negro. Quizá no, ¿un poco gris? Los otros cuerpos policiales buscarían también a Nathalie-Martine y eso sería una ayuda, ¿o no? Ahora pienso que lo único que me animaba era la fuerza resolutiva que había mostrado frente a los demás.

Los riesgos que pudiéramos correr acudiendo solos a la casa okupada eran muy relativos. El ofrecimiento de Montilla contenía la sana intención de protegernos, pero también pretendía meter las narices en nuestro caso. Dirigiéndonos hacia L'Hospitalet, le comenté eso mismo a Garzón.

—Es usted como una loba para con sus lobeznos —dijo, divertido.

—Esta camada no me la tocará nadie —respondí—. Por cierto, Fermín, ¿usted ha entrado alguna vez en una casa okupada en plan oficial?

—Ni en plan oficial ni en ningún otro. He estado informándome, esta es uno de esos edificios medio ruinosos que aún existen en el extrarradio y está okupada por un pretendido movimiento juvenil que organiza actividades culturales. Puede imaginarse lo que quiera.

En efecto, L'Hospitalet tenía su propio ayuntamiento, pero estaba tan pegado a Barcelona que no dejaba de ser una especie de extrarradio. Algunas de sus calles conservaban edificios antiguos que la presión inmobiliaria de la capital no había destruido todavía. El que buscábamos era uno de ellos: esquinero, dos plantas, en un estado bastante ruinoso. Una pancarta desvencijada y medio despintada rezaba: «Okupación es vida y cultura». La puerta principal estaba abierta y daba a una escalera de madera podrida. Circulando por ella vimos a varios jóvenes con la típica pinta alternativa: rastas, ropa *hippiosa* y sandalias con calcetines. Ni siquiera nos miraron. En la planta superior se extendía una gran sala en la que se acumulaban libros usados y posters pacifistas. Unas cuatro o cinco personas charlaban en un rincón, sentadas en sillas hechas trizas y un enorme sofá que había conocido días mejores. En el aire, el polvo danzaba con total libertad. El olor a grifa era tan potente como si lo hubieran extendido con un espray. Oí cómo Garzón soltaba un taco. El grupo de conversadores se volvió hacia nosotros sin mostrar demasiada curiosidad. La única chica entre ellos nos saludó.

—Paz y amor. ¿Buscáis a alguien?

—Buscamos al Tiras, para hablar un momento con él —soltó el subinspector sin pensárselo dos veces.

Todos se echaron a reír.

—¡Hostia, el Tiras! Sois de la poli, ¿verdad?

Nos acercamos hasta donde estaban. No hicieron nada por ocultar los canutos que estaban fumando. Sonreían como bobos. La chica parecía la más despejada y fue ella quien aclaró.

—Es que lo del Tiras es como le llama la Guardia Civil, la poli..., las autoridades. —Sus compañeros de tertulia estallaron en risas—. Pero él se llama César, como el romano que mandaba tanto. —Nuevas carcajadas.

Garzón empezó a incomodarse.

—Aquí la inspectora Delicado, yo soy el subinspector Garzón. Los dos de la Policía Nacional. Sabemos que somos muy graciosos, pero no hemos venido a haceros reír. ¿Dónde está César, alias el Tiras?

Uno de aquellos tipos, gruesa boina de lana sobre sus cuatro pelos, señaló el porro que tenía en la mano y dijo:

—Consumo propio.

Vi que mi compañero caminaba amenazadoramente dos pasos hacia él y lo sujeté por el brazo. La chica se dio cuenta del cariz que estaba tomando la situación y se puso de pie.

—Venid, que yo os llevo.

No fue necesario. Se abrió una puerta que había al fondo y por ella salió un hombre bajito y muy delgado. Su atuendo era parecido al del resto. Llevaba el pelo largo recogido en una coleta. Junto a él aparecieron dos tipos más, de su edad aproximadamente: unos cuarenta. Lo flanquearon por ambos lados cuando se puso frente a nosotros.

—Creo que me buscan a mí —dijo.

—Somos...

—Sí, ya sé quiénes sois. Os he estado escuchando, pero esperaba que contarais qué queréis de mí antes de salir.

Sonreía aviesamente. Le correspondí con otra sonrisa no menos desagradable.

—Queremos hablar con usted, en privado, por supuesto.

Hizo una reverencia teatral indicándonos la puerta por la que había salido.

—Pasemos a la salita. Lo malo es que no tengo té para ofreceros —dijo con ironía.

Dudé un momento. El subinspector tampoco dio un paso al frente. Si nos metíamos en «la salita» estaríamos en la boca del lobo. El Tiras notó nuestra renuencia.

—¿Prefieren los señores que vayamos a un bar? Aquí al lado hay uno de lo más distinguido.

Hice una afirmación con la cabeza. Luego señalé a sus dos acompañantes.

—Pero solos, ¿eh?

—Claro, claro. Síganme, por favor.

Le obedecimos. El sarcasmo, claro al pasar del tú al usted, no se despintaba de su cara.

El bar estaba justo en la esquina. Era un ejemplo perfecto de la larga tradición de bares cutres de nuestro país: cristales sucios, pizarra garabateada con las «especialidades gastronómicas», sillas y mesas de plástico rojo, con el logo de una conocida marca de cerveza. Saludó a la patrona y nos sentamos lejos de la barra, donde nadie pudiera oírnos. Unos vejetes jugaban al dominó metiendo una bulla considerable. Pedí un té para Garzón y para mí, en plan de seguirle la broma del refinamiento al okupa. Él se inclinó por la cerveza. Cuando estuvimos servidos, y antes de que pudiéramos empezar a hablar, el Tiras preguntó:

—¿Tienen algo en mi contra, una orden de detención, quizá?

—No, mejor demos comienzo de otra manera, ¿le parece? Estamos aquí para solicitar su colaboración.

—Vale, pero han tenido miedo de entrar conmigo en la salita. Alguien les ha cantado que el centro cultural es como la cueva de Alí Babá y que yo soy más peligroso que Escobar cuando estaba vivo.

Se rio de su propia gracia. Lo atajé sin miramientos.

—Oiga, Tiras o César, o como coño se llame. Vamos a dejarnos de chorradas y no nos haga perder el tiempo. A mí me importa tres cojones si es usted Escobar redivivo o el alcalde de Kuala Lumpur. Y le aseguro que le tengo tanto miedo como a mi abuelita, que está tan muerta como Escobar.

—¡Vaya, es usted muy chistosa, inspectora!

—Me pongo a su altura. ¿Conoce usted a este hombre?

Le había plantificado la fotografía de Pierre Laurent delante de las narices. Tuvo que separarme un poco el brazo para poder verla bien. La escudriñó con bastante interés. Negó.

—No, no tengo la más mínima idea de quién es ese tipo. No lo había visto jamás.

—¿Está seguro?

—¿Quieren que les diga una cosa, aquí en la intimidad? Se la voy a decir quieran o no: el teniente Montilla es un imbécil, un imbécil de primera división. Hace unos cuatro años me detuvo y..., bueno, historias. Estuve un poco, muy poco tiempo a la sombra. Pero a partir de aquello se quedó con la copla y, cada vez que pasa algo, viene a darme el coñazo. Pues bueno, quiero que sepan que nada de nada. Yo dejé el rollo de las drogas hace tiempo ya.

Garzón y yo no abrimos la boca. Confieso que sentí cierta curiosidad por saber cómo acabó la pendencia entre él y Montilla. Nuestro silencio lo animó a continuar.

—Sí, de acuerdo, ustedes han estado ahí al lado y han visto a cuatro chicos fumando porros, han notado la peste que echa el local. ¿Y qué es eso, es tráfico de drogas? ¡Venga ya! ¿Ustedes no han visto las drogas chungas de verdad y los montajes que hay? Fumaderos de opio que dan grima, salas para pincharse caballo, tíos que venden mil dosis de coca al día, lo más bestia del mundo mundial. Eso sí es el sector de la droga de verdad, lo de la marihuana es un juego infantil, pronto las darán en las escuelas para que los críos se porten bien.

—No voy a ponerme a discutir con usted sobre drogas en plan problema social. Usted sabrá cómo se empieza con ellas y cómo se acaba.

—¡Yo hago chapuzas de fontanería en las casas para poder vivir! ¡Yo ya no...!

Había elevado tanto la voz que casi gritaba. Lo atajé poniéndole la fotografía de Martine Marchand frente a la cara con el mismo estilo que había utilizado para la anterior. Centró la mirada y dio un respingo. Su larga perorata autoexculpatoria quedó abortada al instante. Miraba la imagen sin parpadear. Se puso serio como la muerte.

—¿Conoce a esta mujer?

En una reacción impensada, dirigió la mirada en todas direcciones como si temiera verse acorralado.

—¿Qué pasa con ella? —preguntó en un susurro.

—¿La conoce?

—Sé quién es.

—Nosotros también lo sabemos: Martine Marchand, ciudadana francesa. Narcotraficante.

—¿Están buscándola?

—Es sospechosa de asesinato.

—No sé a quién se ha cargado, pero seguro que ha sido ella. ¿Está en Barcelona?

—Se ha cargado al hombre de la foto anterior. ¿Sigue estando seguro de no conocerlo?

—No lo he visto en mi vida, de verdad. ¿Ella está en Barcelona?

—Es posible.

—Oigan, yo aquí no voy a continuar hablando. Si quieren saber algo más, vamos a la salita del local. ¿O aún tienen pánico de mí?

—Parece que el pánico le haya entrado a usted.

—¿Vienen o no?

Fuimos tras él. Era fácil darse cuenta de cómo había desaparecido la actitud tranquila y desafiante que exhibía al llegar. Hasta a los vejetes miraba con desconfianza.

Una vez en el local okupado, los dos tipos que lo habían flanqueado cuando se presentó ante nosotros se acercaron en modo interrogativo. El Tiras se limitó a soltarles un desabrido:

—Dejadme en paz.

La salita no era menos destartalada que el resto del «club cultural». Nos indicó un par de sillas de madera desgastada. Se sentó delante de nosotros.

—Esa tipa sí es peligrosa de verdad. Una bestia. En mis tiempos de..., bueno, cuando yo iba por el mal camino, o como le quieran llamar, tuve tratos con ella.

—¿Tratos digamos... profesionales? —quiso saber Garzón.

Cabeceó sin decidirse a dar el visto bueno a aquella expresión. Finalmente asintió.

—Bueno, sí. Ya les he dicho que yo hace cuatro años que no ando en nada feo. Lo dejé. Era demasiado riesgo, demasiado estrés. Además me he vuelto un hombre religioso, se lo digo de corazón, y si no lo había dicho antes es por si me tomaban a cachondeo, como muchos suelen hacer. Pero les aseguro que voy a misa, colaboro con la parroquia, este mismo centro en el que nos encontramos...

Lo interrumpí:

—César, continuemos por su mal camino, del bueno ya nos hablará en otra ocasión.

—Vale, vale, ya lo entiendo. Eso no les interesa, ¿no?

—Como policías, no.

—Pues bueno, la cosa es que cuando estaba en la droga, yo llevaba con esa mujer un asunto relativo a un envío que se hizo desde Montpellier a Barcelona..., un envío de material, quiero decir. Faltó algún kilo que otro en las sacas. No viene al caso entrar en detalles. La tía tenía a sus hombres repartidos por aquí en Barcelona, pero no los envió, fue ella misma la que vino en persona a buscarme. Sospechaba que era yo quien había aligerado las sacas y sin decir ni una palabra... me marcó. Se lo llevó todo de mi almacén, hasta lo que no le correspondía y... me marcó.

El subinspector y yo nos miramos sin comprender. Entonces el Tiras se levantó de su silla, nos dio la espalda y se arremangó la camiseta que la cubría. Un enorme costurón se mostró a nuestros ojos.

—Veinte puntos de sutura. Los ven, ¿no? Me rajó bien rajado. Dos de sus gorilas me sujetaron por los brazos, pero lo hizo ella personalmente, con sus manitas maravillosas de señora elegante. Luego me dijo: «Esto no es para que no vuelvas a trabajar más, que no vas a hacerlo aunque quieras, sino sólo para que te acuerdes de mí. Para que sepas que conmigo no se juega, y el que se atreve pierde». Se llama Martine no sé qué más y se la conoce como la Leoparda.

Esperó un momento para volver a su postura normal. Obviamente, quería que pudiéramos ver bien aquel desaguisado. Y así era, ni el subinspector ni yo éramos capaces de apartar la vista de la terrible cicatriz. Prosiguió su relato.

—Luego me dejaron tirado en la calle. Cuando un señor que pasaba avisó a la ambulancia, ya había perdido mucha sangre porque la herida era profunda. No me quedé frito de milagro.

—A lo mejor fue ese milagro y no los milagros de la religión lo que le hizo abandonar el negocio —disparó certeramente Garzón.

—Piense lo que quiera, pero sepan que si hay que testificar contra esa mujer yo estaré dispuesto, porque capaz de matar sí lo es, bien seguro estoy. Pero mientras no la hayan cazado, tomaré mis precauciones.

—Le dejaré nuestros teléfonos —dije—. Llámenos a mí o al subinspector si se entera de algo, si la ve, si le llega alguna noticia. Seremos discretos.

—Sobre todo no le digan nada de nuestra conversación al capullo del teniente Montilla. Es capaz de venir a tocarme las pelotas otra vez, y si los hombres de la Leoparda andan cerca...

9

¿Necesitábamos más evidencias de lo que parecía la única verdad? Pierre-Christophe estaba metido en drogas hasta el cuello y estafó de algún modo a la organización con la que trabajaba. Por desgracia para él, la jefa suprema era Martine-Nathalie. Sentencia de muerte. Su desfalco, o lo que fuere, debió ser mayor que el del Tiras, porque la dama no se limitó a dejarle una advertencia a modo de costurón en la espalda, sino que se lo cargó. Aviso para navegantes, un aviso definitivo y fatal. Sin embargo, Garzón y yo seguíamos dándole vueltas a la historia. Faltaban piezas para que el rompecabezas encajara bien. La principal era el móvil detallado. La estafa de Pierre sólo podía consistir en dos cosas: o se había quedado dinero de una transacción, o una parte de droga pura y dura, heroína, pastillas, coca, cualquiera que fuera el material. Y bien, si era dinero, ¿dónde lo había guardado? La misma pregunta servía para la segunda opción. ¿Dónde estaba la droga? Lo más sorprendente era que la terrible dama justiciera no se hubiera interesado por encontrar ninguna de las dos cosas. No había signos de que nadie hubiera estado hurgando en la caravana en busca del botín, ni tampoco de que el atacante de Pierre hubiera intentado sonsacarlo con algún tipo de tortura. La sucesión de los hechos indicaba claramente que la víctima tuvo el tiempo justo de incorporarse en su yacija cuando su atacante lo acuchilló y desapareció.

—A lo mejor Pierre ya le había dicho dónde estaba el dinero, o la droga, mientras estuvo comprando en el camión —apuntó el subinspector.

—Sí, claro, póngame dos raciones de suflé y de paso me cuenta dónde ha escondido la cocaína.

—Hablaba por hablar.

—Tampoco encaja que Martine se dejara ver de aquella manera tan gratuita. Si había localizado su paradero y pensaba matarlo como venganza y escarmiento general, ¿para qué diablos se presenta como clienta y, encima, hace una gran compra que hasta llama la atención de los vecinos de camioneta?

—¡Exacto! Y si se desplaza desde Francia, con riesgo de que la cace la poli, ¿para qué coño abre una cuenta en el banco?

Cabeceamos los dos, con cierta tristeza.

—Hay casos tan enrevesados que dan asco, ¿verdad, inspectora?

—Los que son demasiado simples dan asco también.

Me miró con cara de policía *simplicissimus*, sonrió.

—Los asesinatos deberían tener un grado medio de complicación, ¿no le parece, Petra?

—En ese caso podría esclarecerlos cualquier aficionado.

—Eso sí. ¿Quiere que vayamos a comer?

—He quedado con mi marido en un restaurante vegetariano.

—¡Joder!, ¿la han convencido los chicos del *truck* de la importancia de lo verde?

—Lo propuso el propio Marcos. ¿Usted se va a casa?

—No, voy a matar dos pájaros de un tiro. La feria de caravanas está hoy en Sabadell. Les hago una visitita a ver si hay alguna novedad, investigo un poco, y de paso me tomo algunas consumiciones.

—No se pase.

—¿De investigar o de consumiciones?

—Un exceso de ambas cosas mezcladas puede sentarle muy mal.

—Seré comedido y prudente. No me enteraré de nada nuevo y me quedaré con hambre.

—Desgraciadamente, eso es lo más probable, Fermín.

Había quedado con Marcos en un nuevo local de Gràcia, un barrio que era uno de mis predilectos en la ciudad. Se llamaba Aire. Cuando llegué, él ya estaba sentado en la terraza. Inspeccionaba la carta y bebía una cerveza. Se levantó y me besó como si hiciera un mes que no nos hubiéramos visto.

—Como hace tan buen día, he pensado que aquí estaríamos bien, pero si tienes frío...

—Sentados al aire libre, un sitio que se llama Aire, espero que no nos hagan pasar del aire también.

—¡Qué va, se come de maravilla! Estuve anteayer con un cliente. Me invitó. Voy a hacerle una casa en el Empordà. En la cima de una pequeña colina. Desde donde se alzará la casa hay una vista magnífica. Los campos de labor, las carreteras que cruzan en la lejanía... ¡Una pasada! ¿Y sabes a qué se dedica mi cliente?

—Vengo cansada de investigar, pero dame una pista.

—¡Es creativo de publicidad! Uno pensaría que en un trabajo semejante hay que estar todo el tiempo de un lado a otro moviéndose por la ciudad, con intensidad, con estrés. Pues nada de eso, resulta que este tipo, que ya tiene un nombre y una reputación, ha descubierto a partir de la pandemia que puede permitirse el lujo de trabajar desde su casa de campo. Sistemas sofisticados online, reuniones por Skype, teléfono, pantallas, y de vez en cuando un desplazamiento a Barcelona para cosas puntuales.

—Entonces, ¿por qué os encontrasteis personalmente anteayer?

Soltó una risotada.

—¡Petra, porque todavía no le han construido la casa! Pareces tonta, con perdón.

—Pero si no os hubierais reunido, no estaríamos comiendo aquí.

—Estaríamos comiendo vegetales de su huerto, o del mío, *chi lo sa*.

La intención de «llevarme al huerto» era tan evidente que decidí practicar la resistencia pasiva. Miré la carta.

—Vamos a ver...: patatas rellenas de pesto, berenjenas al horno, humus, ravioli de queso... Todo tiene muy buena pinta, la verdad. ¡Y además hay alcohol: cerveza, vino, sidra...! No creo que tengamos problemas para escoger.

No los tuvimos. Yo me incliné por las berenjenas acompañadas por una ensalada y Marcos pidió pasta. Un buen vino blanco regaría aquel plantel. Pensé que las nubes rurales ya habrían escampado, pero me equivoqué. A mitad de la comida mi querido esposo volvió a la carga indirecta.

—A este cliente del que te hablaba le voy a instalar en la casa un nuevo sistema de calefacción que aprovecha el calor que la tierra alcanza a cierta profundidad. Vamos a intentar que la vivienda sea cien por cien sostenible. He proyectado unos ventanales en la sala principal con unas persianas, aún en periodo de experimentación, que acumulan calor durante el día y lo irradian por la noche.

—¡Caramba, con tanto calor se van a asar!

—En el campo hace frío, no es como en la ciudad donde los coches atufan el aire con gases calientes y los edificios impiden la circulación de las brisas.

—Sí, sí, es horrible, ya me había fijado.

Continuó cantándome las bellezas del campo, entreveradas con explicaciones técnicas de los planos que estaba realizando para el publicista. En ningún momento caí en la trampa fácil de darme por aludida en cuanto a sus verdaderas intenciones. Sólo al final contraataqué.

—Estoy segura de que ese hombre estará encantado con su nueva casa despacho. Trabajará cómodamente desde allí. ¡Vaya suerte!, ¿no? Lástima que mi labor no pueda hacerse online. ¿Te imaginas el follón? Una rueda de reconocimiento de un sospechoso por plataforma, una inspección ocular sólo con cámaras, un interrogatorio sin ver la jeta del individuo... No puedo imaginármelo, de verdad.

Esta vez fue él quien encajó la andanada sin dar señales de haber captado el mensaje subyacente.

—¡Quién sabe! Con el tiempo...

¿Hasta cuándo íbamos a seguir con aquel juego de sobreentendidos pretendidamente no entendidos? Afortunadamente, el tira y afloja subterráneo no duró toda la comida. Hablamos de los chicos, de la actualidad política, de nuestros planes para el fin de semana. En ningún momento me preguntó acerca de mi trabajo como tenía por costumbre. Quizá, después de tantos años juntos sin que mi ocupación constituyera un problema, un brote de conflicto acababa de surgir. Pensé que teniendo paciencia y buena educación todo volvería a la normalidad. Marcos se olvidaría de sus deseos de cambio ambiental y la vida fluiría como siempre, cada uno a lo suyo y coexistencia pacífica.

Justo al inicio del postre, me llamó el subinspector.

—Petra, ¿ha acabado ya de comer? No es urgente, pero en vez de volver a comisaría, tendría que pasarse por aquí.

—¿Dónde está?

—Sigo en Sabadell.

—¿Lleva coche?

—Claro.

—Espere un momento. —Tapé el teléfono con la mano y me dirigí a Marcos—: ¿Tú puedes acercarme a Sabadell?

Asintió, comiendo una cucharada de helado.

—Páseme la dirección.

—Muy fácil, estoy en la plaza Major. Los camioncitos están todos aquí, una feria o algo parecido.

Casi no hablamos mientras íbamos en el coche. Mi marido sólo me preguntó:

—¿Es algo grave?

—No creo.

A un costado de la plaza estaba, en efecto, montado aquel tinglado de chiringuitos multicolores. No contribuía a potenciar la belleza del lugar. Garzón me hizo señas desde lejos. Bajé del coche no sin antes haber besado a Marcos en los labios. Me sonrió. Se olvidaría de nuestra casa en el campo, estaba convencida, se olvidaría de cualquier cosa que lo alejara de mí.

—Siento haberla molestado, inspectora, pero es que los chicos del camión de salchichas dicen que ayer vieron a Martine por aquí.

—¡No joda! ¿Y por qué no avisaron?

—Dicen que no estaban seguros, que no recordaban bien la cara...

—Pero se les dio una copia de la fotografía auténtica, ¿no?

—Ya sabe que sí, pero estos tíos están como medio empanados.

Eran dos varones jóvenes, y estaban empanados del todo, según comprobé. Sólo con dificultad pude recomponer su testimonio. Antes no habían estado seguros de haber visto a la francesa, pero al hablar con el subinspector se les habían activado las neuronas y ahora estaban seguros de que era ella. Apareció al anochecer, ya prácticamente a la hora del cierre. Se fijaron en ella porque miraba insistentemente hacia los vehículos y porque daba la sensación de que quería esconderse. Dio un par de vueltas por los alrededores y se fue sin más.

Comprendí que era necesario reunir a todos los propietarios de las furgonetas. Me resultaba diáfanamente claro que aquellos dos chicos no habían avisado a la policía en un principio para no complicarse la vida, por pereza, por negligencia, para no implicarse en algo de lo que se sentían muy distantes.

—Dentro de una hora tienen que estar todos en este punto de la plaza, Fermín.

—Pero tendrán que cerrar.

—Me da igual. Será breve. Comuníqueselo a todos. Y que nadie se quede de guardia.

Al cabo de un tiempo vi cómo las persianas iban cerrándose y, un poco después, los comerciantes estaban todos a mi alrededor, con cara de pocos amigos. Primero conté que aquellos chicos creyeron ver a la mujer y ya era extraño que fueran los únicos, pero no nos avisaron en ningún momento. Después los arengué apelando a su conciencia ciudadana. Luego les pegué una bronca en toda regla y por último los amenacé: si no cooperaban adecuadamente con la policía, podían ser acusados de complicidad en el asesinato. Hubo murmullos. Una señora ataviada de cocinera tradicional levantó un dedo.

—Porque esos rapaces no se hayan acordado de llamarlos a ustedes no puede cortarnos a todos por el mismo patrón.

—Sólo les pido que abran los ojos y si ven algo, avisen enseguida, a nosotros o a la Policía Local. Espero que me hayan entendido.

Se dispersaron todos menos la señora de los «rapaces», que lógicamente regentaba una camioneta de platos gallegos. Se acercó a nosotros. Creí que vendría a protestar. Me miró con apuro.

—El caso es, inspectora..., el caso es que a mí también me pareció ver a esa mujer el otro día.

Me puse en tensión.

—¿Cuándo y dónde?

—Una tarde casi noche, cuando estábamos en Sant Cugat. Dio una vueltecita por los alrededores, miró y se marchó sin más. ¡Pero no vaya a reñirme porque no les llamé! Tienen que darse cuenta de que uno no tiene la seguridad de reconocer a alguien partiendo de una foto tan pequeña. Te dices a ti misma que estás tonta, que estás obsesionada por lo que pasó y no ves más que visiones.

En parte llevaba razón. La dejé marchar.

—Esa tipa anda merodeando por las ferias.

—Eso no lo habíamos previsto.

—¡¿Quién iba a prever algo parecido?! ¿Qué es: estúpida o temeraria? Y si quiere algo de aquí, ¿por qué no manda a alguno de sus hombres? ¿No se ha traído a ningún gorila?

—¿Ponemos vigilancia?

—Me fastidia tomar esa decisión. Estamos ante una miembro destacado del hampa, si ponemos vigilancia, aunque sea de paisano, se dará cuenta enseguida.

—Pero no hay otro remedio.

—Puede que no. Con dos policías de paisano, bastará.

Nos fuimos a un bar. Después de la filípica que les había echado a los feriantes, no era cuestión de quedarse por allí. Dos cervezas nos ayudaron a recapitular, y como ya estaba convirtiéndose en costumbre, la recapitulación se limitaba a un montón de preguntas. ¿Por qué Martine se arriesgaba a ser detenida? ¿Qué o a quién buscaba? ¿Por qué permanecía en el país? Como no había pruebas claras de que fuera la asesina, no habíamos previsto ningún operativo en las fronteras. Hubiera podido largarse adonde fuera. Estaba señalada por la policía francesa, pero por nuestra parte seguía libre como un pájaro, sin cargos.

—Busca el dinero que Laurent le birló —conjeturó mi compañero.

—Un poco tarde, ¿no? Además, no es esa la manera de proceder que le corresponde, una jefa de organización del narcotráfico no actúa sola como ella lo está haciendo.

—Sabemos que era jefa de una organización, pero ¿lo es todavía? Si actúa por su cuenta es que quizá ya no forma parte de ningún grupo. Puede que lo dejara porque los gendarmes andan tras sus pasos, puede que esté desesperada y aislada en España, de modo que necesita dinero. Se lo exigió a Laurent, este se negó a dárselo y ella se presentó por la noche en su caravana y lo asesinó.

—No tiene sentido, Fermín.

—No lo tiene, no. ¡Por todos los demonios coronados, por todas las putas del mundo! A no ser que... —Enarboló una mano, la bajó con delicadeza—. A no ser que el móvil del crimen no tenga nada que ver con las drogas.

Me miraba como si fuera Arsenio Lupin ideando una fechoría. Guardaba silencio para enfatizar su final de frase.

—¿Quiere acabar de una vez, Garzón? No me gustan las adivinanzas.

—¿Y si se trata de un crimen pasional? Esos dos estaban liados, él decide cortar la relación y la mujer, despechada...

Eché un trago de mi cerveza. Que el móvil de un asesinato resultara no ser el obvio, el evidente, había ocurrido más de una vez en la historia policial. Pero es un error dejarse seducir por los antiguos casos resueltos. Saqué la racionalidad que me caracteriza y respondí:

—En fin, dos tipos están funcionando en España con documentación falsa. Los dos tienen, en mayor o menor grado, antecedentes delictivos. Los dos son de la misma nacionalidad extranjera. Ella es una cruel vengadora. Sabemos que si se han visto lo lógico es que fuera por motivo de una transacción comercial. ¿Y qué se nos ocurre pensar?: que son amantes y han roto su lazo pasional. Forzado, muy forzado, Fermín.

—Bueno, piense en Bonnie and Clyde.

—¿Bonnie and Clyde?

—En Romeo y Julieta también.

—¡Pero ¿qué demonio dice?!

—¿A qué se dedicaban Romeo y Julieta?

—Ninguno de los dos había trabajado en su vida.

—Por eso pasó lo que pasó. Si no se trabaja, una acaba cayendo en el delito —dijo con una risotada.

No me dio tiempo a embromarlo o simplemente mandarlo al infierno. Por la puerta del bar estaba entrando Bob. Su llegada no era ni mucho menos casual. Se había fijado en dónde nos metíamos al salir de la plaza y venía a saludarnos. Ese era el contenido de su mensaje verbal y tuvimos que entresacarlo de entre un cuarto de hora de explicaciones. Pensé que no era tan extraño que Laurent nunca se hubiera comunicado demasiado con su socio, simplemente no le había dado la ocasión de abrir la boca porque siempre hablaba él.

—¿Hay algo nuevo, Bob?

—Nada, inspectora. ¡Vaya filípica que ha echado!

—Tengo modelos de filípica aún más destacados.

—No se lo tome a pecho. La gente es como es, tienen miedo de verse demasiado implicados en este asunto terrible.

—Este asunto terrible les concierne a todos.

—En el fondo ellos piensan que yo debo ser el único interesado porque perdí a mi socio, los demás...

Garzón debió compadecerse de él, porque salió en su ayuda.

—¿Qué tal el nuevo cocinero?

—Bien, es buen chaval y tiene buenas manos para los platos, pero nunca será igual que con Christophe. Ya llevábamos tiempo trabajando juntos y nos entendíamos sin ni siquiera intercambiar palabra.

—Sí, ya sé que hablaban poco. Y diga, ¿ya ha hecho arreglar la cerradura de la camioneta?

—Lo hice a toda velocidad, y no porque a mi joven cocinero le importara demasiado dormir con la puerta abierta. Dice que no tiene ningún miedo. Es joven, inmaduro. Puede que él no tenga miedo, pero yo sí. Si asesinan a alguien más en mi negocio, me tiro por la ventana.

—¿Y por qué iban a asesinar a alguien más? —salté al instante.

Se parapetó tras los brazos estirados hacia mí, las manos muy abiertas.

—¡Era una manera de hablar, inspectora, sólo eso! Pero reconozca que, mientras ustedes no descubran al asesino, las cosas no están claras y existe un riesgo.

—¿Piensa que usted mismo puede correr peligro?

—¿Yo? No, para nada, era otra manera de hablar. Me voy al hotel, ha sido un placer charlar con ustedes.

Se marchó por donde había venido, con aire derrotado. El subinspector me sonrió.

—A este pobre lo tiene aterrorizado, Petra.

—Sabe que una sombra de sospecha se cierne sobre él.

—¡Joder, se expresa usted como en una novela policiaca de las malas!

—¡Quién sabe si no acabaremos así, querido colega!, escribiendo noveluchas donde los policías siempre aciertan.

—Sí, y atrapan al asesino antes de que se cebe con

su última víctima. ¿Ya ha decidido si les ponemos seguridad a esa panda de saltimbanquis?

—Habrá que hacerlo, supongo. No podemos esperar mucho de sus avisos o testimonios.

—Sobre todo si sigue merodeando esa mujer. ¿Usted cree que la han visto de verdad?

—¡Y yo qué sé, Fermín! Empiezo a dudar hasta de que esa mujer exista.

—¡Bah, eso es porque está usted de bajón! ¿Quiere que nos arreemos otra cervecita?

—¿En este bar tan horrible?

—¡Y qué más da!, mientras la cerveza esté bien helada... no nos hará ningún mal.

No nos hizo ningún mal.

10

Al día siguiente fui a ver al comisario Coronas. Tenía que autorizar que un par de hombres vigilaran a los feriantes. Tal y como imaginé, se puso como un basilisco e hizo las preguntas retóricas de rigor: «¿Acaso yo no sabía lo mal que andábamos de efectivos? ¿Se me había pasado por las mientes lo mucho que podía durar la permanencia de ese operativo? ¿Es que en los pueblos cercanos a Barcelona no había Guardia Urbana?». Las preguntas clamaban al cielo, pero las recibía yo. Por fortuna sabía cómo reaccionar: cara seria como si se me hubiera muerto un tío abuelo (un parentesco más cercano hubiera sido exagerado), cabezazos de asentimiento compungido y contraataque humilde con adversativas de baja intensidad: «Pero, comisario, han visto a una sospechosa merodeando por el lugar». «Pero es que parece que los posibles testigos no están muy dispuestos a cooperar.» «Pero es que puede existir un peligro real para esa gente reunida allí.» Habíamos agotado escrupulosamente todas las líneas del guion; ahora sólo faltaba el desenlace, que tampoco fue sorprendente.

—Veré lo que puedo hacer —sentenció Coronas con magnanimidad.

Ya estaba la obra teatral representada, y como llevaba muchos años en cartel, en cuanto Garzón me vio, adelantó cómo se resolvía el final.

—¿Veré lo que puedo hacer? —aventuró.

—¡Exacto!, pero no espere que le felicite por llegar a esa conclusión.

—No, claro. Estaba cantado. ¿Cree que autorizará la vigilancia?

—Sí, como de costumbre, pero con la rebaja pertinente: nada de dos hombres, sólo uno y sólo por la noche. Es todo lo que podemos esperar.

—Algo es algo, hay cosas de las que ya no cabe esperar nada.

—¿Por ejemplo, Fermín? No me ponga nerviosa.

—Ya tengo el informe sobre el móvil de la víctima.

—¿Y?

—Nada es nada. Han dejado de buscarlo ya. Obviamente, se lo llevó el asesino.

—¿Y para eso han tardado tanto tiempo en hacer el informe?

—Los muchachos dicen que cada vez las búsquedas son más difíciles, como ahora hasta los niños de tres años tienen teléfono...

—Una excusa infantil.

—¡Y nunca mejor dicho! —rio el subinspector su propia gracia.

Consulté en el calendario de los feriantes. Según nuestra lista, hoy dejaban Sabadell y se encaminaban a Sitges. Perfecto, nos vendrá bien un poco de aire marino.

—¡Todo es tan absurdo, Garzón! Cada vez nos dejan menos responsabilidades a los policías nacionales, y cada vez tenemos menos medios para afrontarlas.

—Le advierto que a este muerto lo están codiciando todos: Mossos, Guardia Civil..., usted verá si quiere que les pidamos ayuda.

—¡Ni de coña! Ya se está endosando una prenda de abrigo. Vamos a ponernos en movimiento.

No fue posible tanta precipitación. Desde la centralita de comisaría me pasaron un aviso. Me llamaban de la comisaría de Sant Adrià. Escuché, me estremecí y colgué.

—¿Me quito la prenda de abrigo? —preguntó mi subalterno.

—No, con la que se nos cae encima, mejor póngase dos.

Salimos de la oficina a toda prisa.

Estaba hecho una furia, una hidra, un Júpiter tronante. Su cara se había metamorfoseado a causa del intenso rubor y el rictus de rabia, resultando más feo aún. No lo hubiera reconocido en un principio, pero obviamente era él, Carlitos, clamando en la puerta de su bar cutre. El objetivo de sus denuestos: dos policías nacionales bastante jóvenes, que asistían a la regañina con cara de buenos chicos.

En cuanto el energúmeno nos vio aparecer, dio unos pasos hacia nosotros blandiendo un dedo acusador. Uno de nuestros chicos le cortó el paso. El otro se nos acercó.

—¿Inspectora Delicado? Somos de la comisaría de Sant Adrià. La comisaria Margarita Gandía...

—Lo sé, lo sé. Pueden retirarse. Díganle a su comisaria que luego me paso a verla.

—Pero ese hombre está fuera de sí. Ha insistido en que viniera usted. A lo mejor hace falta nuestra protección.

—No se preocupe, nosotros nos encargamos. Si no atiende a razones, con un par de sopapos se calmará.

Se quedó muy sorprendido por mi estilo tabernario, pero pareció que dejaba de inquietarse por nuestra integridad. Nos acercamos a Carlitos, que reemprendió sus diatribas.

—¡A ustedes quería verlos! Supongo que ya se han enterado, si es que se enteran de algo. Mi mujer está en el hospital. Dos salvajes hijos de la gran puta le han dado una paliza.

Me volví hacia uno de los policías con aire interrogativo.

—La están curando, inspectora. Un parte de lesiones menores.

—Pueden marcharse.

Miré a Carlitos. Esta vez el dedo amenazante lo exhibía yo.

—Pasa dentro del local, aquí estamos escandalizando. Y como vuelvas a chillarme a mí o al subinspector, te va a caer un puro de la hostia. ¿Me has entendido? ¡La madre de todos los puros te va a caer, me encargaré personalmente!

Obedeció y entramos en el bar, que, naturalmente, estaba vacío.

—Cierra la puerta —le ordené—. Y ahora, sin gritos y sin histerias, nos cuentas qué coño ha pasado.

Tragándose la indignación que aún sentía, empezó a hablar.

—Ha sido esta misma mañana. Yo estaba en el mercado y Liu Ci se quedó aquí limpiando el local. Al volver me la encontré en el suelo llorando, con la cara hecha un mapa, con sangre en el suelo...

—¿Sabes quién fue?

—Fueron dos hombres.

—¿Tu esposa los conocía?

—No, de nada.

—¿Le dijeron algo?

—¡Y yo qué sé qué cojones le dijeron! ¡Enseguida me la llevé para el hospital! Sean quienes sean, la han apalizado porque ustedes los guiaron hasta aquí. ¿Cómo se han atrevido a plantarse en la casa de un hombre honrado? ¿Por qué sacan ahora historias de drogas de hace mil años que ya se han acabado? ¿Con qué derecho?

—¡Eh, un momento, a lo mejor vinieron a robar! —intervino Garzón.

—¡Y una mierda vinieron a robar! Si se busca dinero, es al final del día, cuando está la caja llena con la recaudación. Por la mañana hay que ser gilipollas para venir a buscar algo aquí.

—Pero algo buscaban, ¿no?

—Le repito que no eran ladrones, sólo querían hacer daño.

—¿Tienes alguna cámara de seguridad?

—Eso ya me lo han preguntado los nenes esos que acaban de irse y no, no tengo cámaras. Miren, no sé nada, no estoy metido en nada. Si a mi mujer le pasa algo... —Se le quebró la voz. Se desplomó en una silla. Con las manos tapándose la cara, empezó a sollozar. El subinspector dio dos pasos hacia él y le tocó el hombro.

—Tranquilízate, hombre. Tu mujer está bien. ¡Vamos, Carlitos, no te vengas abajo!

Nada más oírse llamar Carlitos se puso en pie como catapultado por una fuerza mayor.

—¡No me llamo Carlitos! ¿Es que nunca podré tener una vida normal? No es justo, no es humano.

Le hice una seña de salida a Garzón.

—Nos vamos. Denuncia la agresión inmediatamente. Ya tienes mi teléfono. Llama si ves algo raro, ¿de acuerdo?

Con la cabeza baja, musitó.

—No vuelvan, no vuelvan más por aquí.

No había sido plato de gusto, pero ¿qué otra cosa podíamos hacer? Puse rumbo a la comisaría de Sant Adrià. Garzón me preguntó:

—¿Conoce a la inspectora Gandía?

—Sí, mucho. Fuimos compañeras de estudios en la Academia, pero hace tiempo que no nos vemos.

—¿Compañeras de curso? Pues ella ya es comisaria, ¿y usted?

—Yo estoy muy bien donde estoy. Si me ascendieran a comisaria tendría que dejar la calle y dejarlo a usted. Es más de lo que puedo soportar. Lo nuestro ya es un asunto pasional, subinspector, un nudo eterno, me atrevería a decir.

—Un nudo en el cuello, bien apretado.

—Gracias, Fermín. No esperaba menos de su sensibilidad.

Margarita había cambiado muy poco. Estaba tal

y como la recordaba: alta, fuerte, morena y muy bella. Saltamos la una a los brazos de la otra nada más vernos. Los policías a nuestro alrededor se quedaron un tanto anonadados ante las exclamaciones y grititos de placer. «¡Qué guapa estás!», «¡Qué alegría de verte!». Nos extendimos un poco más en los lugares comunes de la amistad, si bien estos expresaban un afecto auténtico.

—He pensado en llamarte desde que me destinaron a Barcelona, Petra; pero he tenido más trabajo del que pensaba.

—No estás en una comisaría fácil, no.

Le presenté al subinspector, que se cuadró ante ella.

—Descanse, subinspector. Ya sé lo que os trae por aquí.

—La paliza a la chica china. Su marido estaba hecho una furia. ¿Qué ha pasado?

—Un testigo vio entrar a dos hombres en el bar. No supo describirlos, pero no eran chinos. Salieron al cabo de un rato, aparentemente después de agredir a la chica. Nos avisó el marido, que se la encontró hecha un cristo al llegar. Dos de mis hombres la trasladaron al hospital. Nada grave, contusiones sin más. Ya debe estar de vuelta en su casa.

—¿La habéis interrogado?

—No, cuando el marido mencionó que lo habíais visitado hace unos días, te hice llamar enseguida.

—¿Sabes que el marido...?

—Sí, estoy al tanto de sus antecedentes, pero está limpio.

—Eso dice él.

—Y creo que es verdad. De ella no estoy tan segura.

—¿Cómo?

—No la conocéis, claro. Liu Ci Chung. Con antecedentes por tráfico de drogas. Creemos que entró hace unos tres años en el país, mafia china mediante. La detuvimos en una redada. Le cayó poco tiempo en la trena. Al salir conoció a Carlitos. Viven juntos desde entonces.

—¡Con la pinta angelical que tiene!

—Ya ves, los orientales son así. Acuérdate de Fu Manchú, cualquier día se pone de moda otra vez, con eso del *vintage*...

Nos reímos como dos tontas. Garzón nos observaba, sorprendido por el tono de nuestra conversación.

—¿La interrogas tú o la interrogo yo? —inquirí.

—Como quieras; de todos modos va a dar lo mismo...

—No te entiendo.

—Los chinos no hablan, Petra. Nunca saben nada, nunca han visto nada, nunca conocen a nadie. Ni a su padre conocen, es así. Ya pueden haberlos golpeado, robado o intentado asesinarlos, aunque sepan perfectamente quién ha sido el autor, no lo dirán. Sonríen con una sonrisa que nosotros no sabemos interpretar, se encogen un poco de hombros y se acabó. Vosotros no estáis acostumbrados, pero yo sí. Este barrio es Chinatown.

—Lo intentaré para cubrir el expediente. ¿Tus hombres aún están en el bar? Les dije que se alejaran.

—Mientras yo no se lo ordene, allí seguirán. ¿Qué hago?

—Cuando hayamos terminado, te aviso. Déjalos de momento para que Carlitos no ande dando el coñazo.

—Llámame y quedamos a comer.

—¿En un chino?

Volvimos a reír, nos besamos. No me había preguntado por el caso que estábamos llevando, debía de haberse informado ya.

De regreso al bar de Carlitos, comprobamos que sus ánimos se habían aplacado bastante. Ni siquiera protestó cuando los policías lo hicieron salir a la calle. Entramos y allí estaba la frágil Liu Ci, con algunos apósitos en la cara. Impasible y con la vista baja, contestó a todas mis preguntas: ¿quién te pegó?, ¿sabes por qué?, ¿te dijeron qué querían? Sus respuestas oscilaban entre varias posibilidades: no lo sé, no lo vi, no me fijé. Sólo cuando quise saber si había visto antes a aquellos dos hombres, me pareció que sus bonitos ojos rasgados centelleaban mínimamente, pero ¿de qué servía aquella fugaz impresión? Imposible levantar sobre ella una sospecha, de una certeza no cabía ni hablar. Nos fuimos. El subinspector no había participado para nada en el interrogatorio. Yo no le había prestado mucha atención, pero entreví que estaba inspeccionando el bar. Antes de subir al coche no hizo falta preguntarle qué había hecho.

—¿Sabe, Petra? En el bar alguien había arreglado las cosas. En la primera visita me fijé en que todas las tazas de café limpias las ponían amontonadas en unos grupitos muy curiosos que no eran una pirámide. Hasta pensé que se trataría de una costumbre china. Pues bueno, ahora estaban todas alineadas. Y le diré más: he visto cristalitos en el suelo, alguien ha barrido los restos de una botella o un vaso roto después de la agresión. Eso significa que no piensan denunciar.

Las observaciones del subinspector habían resultado más fructíferas que mis preguntas. Una limpieza exprés del local, sin duda llevada a cabo por Carlitos cuando encontró a su mujer, significaba que aparte de la violencia ejercida sobre Liu Ci, los atacantes habían causado algún destrozo. Preguntamos a los hombres de Margarita si habían realizado un registro. Sí, lo habían hecho, sin resultado aparente. No había nada fuera de lugar.

—Si los intrusos rompieron enseres, a lo mejor es que estaban buscando algo. Si el objetivo hubiese sido destruir el local como venganza, tenían las manos libres y no lo hicieron, ¿no? Cuando Carlitos se encuentra a su chica hecha unos zorros, arregla los desperfectos antes de avisar a la poli. No quiere que la impliquen en nada, la protege. Algo buscaban esos dos tipos.

Me encogí de hombros con ademán de auténtica desesperación. Miré al subinspector.

—En este momento, Fermín, tengo el cerebro a punto de explotar. No me diga nada más.

—De acuerdo, ¿y usted tampoco dice nada?

—Si quiere puedo cantar.

—No creo que sea necesario.

Sin duda, la rehabilitación de un preso es posible en las cárceles de países avanzados. Cuando el sujeto rehabilitado abandona la prisión, una nueva vida le espera en la sociedad. Supongo que haber estado internado nunca es una buena carta de presentación para reubicarse en la organización general del mundo. Supongo que los malos recuerdos surgirán en los exreos sin avisar, ensombreciéndolos. Todo eso es fácil de deducir, aunque no estoy segura. Hay algo, sin embargo, sobre lo que no albergo ninguna duda: quien ha estado en chirona huye de la policía como del demonio, convirtiéndose en una presa fácil para los malhechores. Quizá sólo el asesinato de Liu Ci hubiera sido espoleta suficiente para que aquel hombre colaborara con nosotros. Sabía algo y callaba. En ningún momento pensé que ignorara por completo la identidad de los que habían agredido a su mujer.

Aquella noche llegué a casa realmente cansada. Mi cuerpo estaba bien, pero no había manera de que mi mente consiguiera reaccionar: embotamiento y hartazgo eran lo único que sentía. Traspasando la cancela del jardín, recordé lo que Marcos me había advertido por la mañana: «Esta noche llegaré tarde, tengo una cena en el Colegio de Arquitectos». «Mejor —pensé—, tomaré cualquier cosa y me iré a la cama.»

Al abrir la puerta una vocecita me llamó.

—Petra, ¿eres tú?

Descubrí los pies de Marina bajando por la escalera. Iba en pijama.

—Ya me había acostado, pero te he oído entrar.

—¿Tus hermanos también se han ido a dormir?

—¡No, qué va! Hoy no han podido venir por no sé qué. Están en casa de su madre.

—¿Estabas sola entonces?

—Sí, papá se fue hace un ratito.

—¿Y él sabía que te quedabas sola?

—Dijo que sería solo un momento porque enseguida estarías aquí.

Di unos pasos airados hacia el salón, tiré violentamente la gabardina sobre un sofá. Empecé a despotricar en voz bien alta.

—¡Esto es el colmo! Lo que me faltaba justo hoy.

—Pero no pasa nada, Petra, ya sabes que yo no tengo ningún miedo.

—No tienes miedo, ¿eh?, puede que tú no, pero hay motivos para tenerlo. No puedes quedarte sola en casa y menos por la noche, ¿comprendes? Puede pasar cualquier cosa, encontrarte mal... ¡Yo qué sé! Pero aquí parece que todo el mundo va a la suya y adiós muy buenas a la mínima prudencia.

—Me encuentro bien y no ha pasado ninguna cosa. A una niña nadie le va a hacer daño, ¿verdad?

Puse un índice muy estirado delante de su cara asustada.

—¿Sabes por qué yo no he tenido hijos, Marina? Te lo diré: justamente para no tener que contestar a ese tipo de preguntas.

Se echó a llorar.

—Yo no he tenido la culpa, yo...

Creo que fue entonces cuando mi mente empezó a funcionar con normalidad después del largo día. Me incliné para estar a su altura, la abracé.

—Perdóname, querida. Lo siento, estoy nerviosa, estoy tonta o, mejor dicho, ¡soy tonta! No quería gritarte ni hablarte así. Lo siento, de verdad.

La niña aún hipaba entre mis brazos. La aparté para mirarla a la cara.

—¿Ya has cenado?

—Sí. Papá me dio la cena.

—Bueno, da igual, ¿sabes lo que vamos a hacer? Nos meteremos en la cocina las dos. Yo me prepararé un sándwich y a ti te haré una taza de leche con cacao bien caliente. Luego... ¡al catre y hasta mañana! ¿Te parece bien?

Asintió, limpiándose los ojos. La fórmula del consuelo había sido simple, pero triunfó. Me encaminé a cumplir lo prometido con alegría impostada, porque en el fondo sólo sentía terror por mi comportamiento anterior. A medio camino Marina me hizo parar.

—Petra, no vas a enfadarte con papá porque me haya dejado sola, ¿verdad? No merece la pena.

—¿Yo enfadarme con tu padre? ¡Ni hablar, por nada del mundo, pero si es un ángel divino y un santo varón! —Como Marina estaba acostumbrada a mis ironías, sonrió—. No me enfadaré con él. Cuando lo vea le daré un par de besos, un abrazo, y cuando ya lo tenga completamente confiado, ¿sabes qué haré? Le arrearé tal puñetazo en la nariz que las gafas le saldrán volando.

La niña se reía abiertamente. Me dio la mano y entramos en la cocina. Mientras disolvía el cacao en su tazón, pensé que la vida del policía es paradójica. En un mismo día tienes que ocuparte de los temas más escabrosos y luego sacar del bolsillo tu lado tierno y maternal. Aunque me daba la clara impresión de que ese tipo de contrastes sólo te sucede si eres mujer.

11

La primera conversación de la mañana hubiera debido tener formato de bronca. De hecho, así comenzó, pero fue derivando civilizadamente hacia el contraste de pareceres. Mi marido no estaba por la labor de discutir y se limitó a ir contestando a mis preguntas, que estaban formuladas en tono inquisitivo. Para empezar, había dejado sola a Marina porque en casa había suficientes sistemas de seguridad. Para seguir, sólo se ausentó durante tres horas. Para finalizar, tanto la niña como yo teníamos en nuestros móviles sendos wasaps enviados por él en los que nos decía que si en una hora y media yo no había llegado o no podía llegar hasta más tarde, le avisáramos inmediatamente porque abandonaría la cena y se plantaría rápidamente en el hogar. Marina le había contestado en cuanto yo hice acto de presencia. Yo ni siquiera lo había abierto.

—Aun así, Marcos, te agradecería muchísimo que no vuelvas a hacerlo. Habría sido diferente si los gemelos hubieran estado con la peque, pero sola...

—Ningún problema. Siendo tú policía, te conciernen por completo los temas de seguridad. No volverá a quedarse sola ni un minuto.

Mi cabreo se había disipado bastante. Debía reconocer que Marcos hacía gala con su respuesta de un aceptable sentido común. Pero, un segundo después de la última frase, añadió:

—Si viviéramos en el campo no pasarían estas cosas.

Yo estaba enfundándome la gabardina y ante semejante sentencia dejé a medias la operación.

—¿Cómo? Pues según yo lo entiendo, sería mucho peor.

—En absoluto, yo tendría la excusa perfecta para no ir a esas cenas de compromiso.

—Es decir, que te quedarías todas las noches en casa y renunciarías a tu vida sociolaboral.

Me miró con un punto de retranca.

—¡Me encanta eso de la vida sociolaboral!

—Oye, Marcos, voy a llegar tarde a comisaría. Yo creo que queda todo claro, ¿no?

—Por supuesto, querida, por supuesto. Nos vemos por la tarde.

Se acercó y me besó en los labios con suavidad. O definitivamente estaba volviéndome imbécil, o hubiera jurado que aquel beso tenía un punto irónico.

Garzón llegó tarde aquella mañana. Se plantó en mi despacho bufando como un bisonte.

—¿Ha preguntado el jefe por mí?

—No, que yo sepa. ¿Qué le ha pasado?

—Tonterías, bobadas...

—¿Puede ser más explícito?

—Pues nada, que Beatriz me ha montado una escena. Resulta que va a cambiar las cortinas del salón y, según ella, lleva dos semanas persiguiéndome para que le ayude a escogerlas en un catálogo que le han prestado en la tienda. Hoy se me ha ocurrido contestarle que lo miraría al llegar a casa por la noche y no vea, Petra, ha organizado la de Dios: que si no me importan nada nuestros asuntos domésticos, que si ella es siempre el último plato del menú, que si nuestro matrimonio me trae al pairo, que si ya no la quiero... ¡Una escena en toda regla! ¡Si hasta se ha puesto a llorar! Total, que ya me tiene a mí observando las telas de las putas cortinas de los cojones con más paciencia que el santo Job. Luego, naturalmente, hemos escogido la que a ella le ha pasado por las narices... En fin, ¿qué le puedo decir?

—El matrimonio es un coñazo, ¿verdad, Fermín?

—Usted me perdonará, pero yo creo que el coñazo son ustedes las señoras. ¿Cómo se puede sacar la conclusión de que uno ya no quiere a su esposa porque no se interesa por unas putas cortinas? Es un poco excesivo, ¿no?

Se me erizó el vello de los antebrazos. Intenté no gritar.

—Beatriz pasa más tiempo que usted en casa, ¿sí o no?

—Pero es que...

—Sólo responda sí o no.

—Sí, de acuerdo.

—Es Beatriz quien se ocupa de todos los temas de la casa, ¿sí o no?

—Sí.

—Y de esos temas de la casa se aprovecha usted también. Por ejemplo, las cortinas, ¿no le taparán a usted también el sol y la visión del espacio exterior?

—Inspectora, va usted demasiado lejos.

—Sólo pretendo hacerle ver que la generalización de cómo somos las señoras es una injusticia y una banalidad. Porque si yo generalizo también, lo primero que me viene a la cabeza es que ustedes, los señores, pasan de todo aquello que no sea su tarea profesional, pasan de todo aquello que sus esposas se ven en la tesitura de solucionar, se la trae floja la sensibilidad y los detalles y, encima, van de víctimas abnegadas. Ahí tiene una generalización, pero tengo más ejemplos, no crea.

Oí que el subinspector musitaba.

—¡Vaya día que llevo! —Después, en voz más alta, preguntó—: ¿Puedo retirarme a mi ordenador?

—Por mí, como si se retira a un convento.

Se cuadró frente a mí, cosa que sólo hacía cuando deseaba marcar la distancia entre los dos, y salió con aire digno de la estancia. En otras circunstancias lo que acababa de suceder me hubiera divertido, pero en aquel momento no me encontraba muy contenta de mi actuación. Resultaba evidente que mi subalterno había pagado el mal humor que yo llevaba acumulado. Aunque, si lo analizaba bien, sus deleznables comentarios no habían hecho más que echar leña al fuego que momentos antes mi marido había prendido en mi interior. «¡Ay, Petra, el análisis!», me autosermoneé. El análisis había sido siempre mi punto flaco. Un exceso continuo en mí. No se puede analizar todo, es imposible, enloquecedor. Un hallazgo analítico te lleva a otro, que puede contradecirlo, hasta que los temas se van imbricando de tal manera que acabas con la picha hecho un lío, como dicen los clásicos. Tenía la picha liada en el asesinato de Laurent y ahora se añadía sin venir a cuento el conflicto matrimonial, la lucha eterna entre sexos, el modo diverso de gestionar los cabreos... Me veía como en la escultura de Laocoonte, acosada por los hijos, las serpientes y el subinspector Garzón. No, basta, ya era suficiente. Llamé a mi compañero por el teléfono interno.

—Subinspector, ¿puede escribir usted el informe de ayer? Yo tengo que salir. Avíseme si hay algo importante.

—A sus órdenes —oí. Continuaba todavía en plan ofendido-oficial.

Tomé el coche y me fui a Sitges. La panda de saltimbanquis gastronómicos, según la descripción de mi compañero de fatigas, estaría todavía allí. No había tenido ninguna iluminación que me llevara en busca de testimonios o pruebas, pero en Sitges había mar, y el Mediterráneo siempre me calma los nervios.

No había actividad en el lugar. Casi todos los furgones estaban cerrados. Me acerqué al de Bob, donde tampoco había nadie. De modo instintivo comprobé que la manecilla de la puerta del copiloto estaba cerrada. En ese momento una voz detrás de mí me sobresaltó.

—¿Es usted, inspectora?

Giré la cabeza a toda velocidad. Era Elisenda, la dulce chica del camión contiguo. Me sonrió.

—No quería asustarla, sólo pretendía asegurarme de que era usted. Como las cosas están como están... ¿Le apetece un café?

—Si me sirve un café se lo agradeceré eternamente.

—Ya iba a abrir la persiana, venga.

Nos desplazamos hasta su carromato. Abrió la persiana con cierto estrépito. La observé mientras armaba la cafetera. Era delicada en sus ademanes, hermosa sin estridencias.

—¿Hoy no está su marido?

—Ha ido a comprar. Hay que abastecerse todos los días. Es complicado porque como no siempre estamos en el mismo sitio, los proveedores van cambiando.

—Es verdad, no lo había pensado.

Sacó un taburete y lo acercó a la barra para que pudiera sentarme. Luego regresó al interior y se sentó frente a mí. Bebimos en silencio.

—¿Le gusta esta vida, Elisenda?

—Sí, sí que me gusta, le aseguro que es una vida normal.

Temí que me hubiera malinterpretado.

—Ya sé que es una vida normal, pero tiene cosas especiales con respecto a la vida de otras personas. Es más original, por ejemplo.

Sonrió desvaídamente.

—Eso es lo que parece desde fuera, pero al final es lo mismo: se trabaja, se come, se duerme...

—Pero siempre trata con clientes que están de fiesta, eso dará alegría, ¿no?

—Buena falta nos hace. Desde que pasó lo que pasó, todos andamos bastante deprimidos.

—¿Qué dicen sus compañeros?

—Bueno, protestan: que si hemos tenido que alterar nuestros itinerarios ya contratados, que si es una imposición el tener que estar siempre juntos...

—Es una medida consensuada con el juez que instruye el caso.

—A mí me parece bien, inspectora, pero ya sabe cómo se las gasta la gente. Han matado a un compañero y parece que no les importa nada, sólo se preocupan del negocio, de sus intereses. Pero a mí sí que me ha afectado. Era un hombre joven, muy amable, muy encantador.

Se le habían llenado los ojos de lágrimas. Intenté distraerla.

—La entiendo. Me imagino que a sus colegas tampoco les habrá gustado que el otro día me pusiera dura con todos ustedes.

—No, no les gustó. Pero en eso tiene usted que comprenderles: reconocer a alguien por una foto no es fácil con la cantidad de personas que pasan por aquí. Yo que vi a esa mujer cuando estaba comprando..., pues como estoy alterada, me da la impresión de que la descubro a cada rato. ¡Hasta esta mañana me pareció verla merodeando! Y claro, nunca es verdad, seguro que no. ¿Y qué puedo hacer, llamarlos cada dos por tres para dar una falsa alerta?

—¿Le pareció verla esta mañana?

—No me haga caso, inspectora. No estoy bien, ya le digo que no estoy bien.

Sus ojos se anegaron de nuevo. En ese momento apareció su marido, empujando una carretilla llena de paquetes y bolsas. Su sorpresa al descubrir nuestra improvisada reunión no fue de las agradables. Dejó la carretilla, vino hasta nosotras.

—¿Pasa algo?

Intenté tranquilizarlo, me levanté.

—Nada nuevo, no se inquiete. Su mujer me ha invitado a un cafelito, pero ya estaba a punto de irme.

—Me había asustado.

Me despedí de ellos. Elisenda permanecía callada, me dijo adiós con un gesto. Cuando ya estaba a unos quinientos metros de las caravanas, oí la voz de Javier, llamándome. Caminaba casi corriendo en dirección a mí.

—Perdone que la moleste, inspectora, pero es que, verá, Elisenda es una chica muy sensible y todo este asunto la tiene completamente trastornada. Ella no vio nada el día de la muerte ni sabe nada, así que...

—¿Me está pidiendo que no hable con ella?

Pareció escandalizarse, alzó la voz.

—¡No, no, en absoluto! No quiero que me entienda mal, sólo era advertirla de que, si habla con ella, lo haga con delicadeza, comprendiendo que...

—Los policías no somos unas bestias salvajes,

Javier, estamos dotados de sentimientos y también somos capaces de cierta comprensión hacia los demás. Ya he visto que su esposa se encuentra un poco inquieta y lo he tenido en cuenta al charlar con ella. Puede quedarse tranquilo.

—Perdóneme, quizá soy demasiado protector con ella, pero la quiero mucho. ¿Me disculpará?

—Por supuesto, por supuesto que sí.

¡Ah, los enamorados que protegen a sus enamoradas! ¿Y quién puede ser el enemigo principal del que cualquiera necesita protección? ¡La policía, naturalmente! Estoy convencida de que todos los españoles piensan lo mismo: «Si ves a un policía, guárdate de él. Eso de que vela por tu seguridad es un camelo». Con sinceridad, siempre me ha parecido algo lacerante. Nunca he aspirado a ser la Caperucita inocente que trisca por el bosque, pero tampoco me siento el lobo feroz que la espera en un recodo para zampársela.

Comí sola en un pequeño restaurante de menú a quince euros. Actualmente, mucha gente te escribe contándote sus buenas noticias y siempre añade al final: «Quería compartirlo contigo». Nadie manda un correo que ponga: «Estoy de una mala hostia insufrible. Quería compartirlo contigo». La vida moderna sólo admite mostrar lo mejor de uno mismo, cuando vienen mal dadas, mejor te lo aguantas tú.

Pasé la tarde en comisaría, encerrada en mi despacho. Garzón debía estar aún enfadado conmigo, porque no se dignó a aparecer. No trabajé en el caso, ni revisé el informe que, con toda seguridad, el subinspector ya habría acabado de redactar. Fue una tarde budista, de meditación muy auténtica: mente en blanco y ver cómo pasan las horas sin sentir ni pensar. A las siete de la tarde estaba hasta las narices de Buda. Me puse la gabardina y salí al pasillo. La fortuna no me acompañó: casi me di de bruces con el comisario. Nada más verme, en vez de saludar amablemente, se puso a la defensiva.

—Ya lo sé, Petra, ya lo sé. No me he olvidado, pero no ha sido posible, de verdad. Ustedes no tienen ni idea de las carencias de nuestra policía en Cataluña. Algo habrá que hacer al respecto o nos vamos al carajo. Aun así, le he conseguido vigilancia a partir de mañana. Un hombre solo y sólo por la noche, pero algo es algo, ¿no? ¿Sabe si los feriantes han contratado seguridad privada?, no vayamos a liarla con confusiones.

—Creo que, de momento, no han contratado a nadie. No parece que se sientan muy amenazados.

—Le diré francamente que no creo que lo estén.

—Pero...

—¡No, no me diga nada! Para cuatro gatos que somos, no nos vamos a pelear. Mañana noche tendrá a su hombre, ¿de acuerdo? Las instrucciones concretas se las da usted.

Salió zumbando pasillo adentro y yo hice lo mismo hacia la salida. La sesión meditativa me había sentado bien porque no me indigné, ni me pregunté a mí misma qué coño pintaba allí si nadie me hacía caso, ni me embargó la sensación de caos que siempre me atenaza cuando hablo con los mandos, ni juré dimitir al día siguiente. ¡Adiós muy buenas, ya os apañaréis! Tomé el coche y me planté en casa mucho antes de lo que solía. No había llegado nadie todavía. Miré el calendario de visitas de los hijos de Marcos que colgaba de una chincheta en la cocina. No, aquella noche no les tocaba venir. Abrí el horno y, como si fuera un cofre maravilloso de *Las mil y una noches*, descubrí un tesoro en el interior. Nuestra mágica asistenta nos había preparado una lasaña reluciente y apetitosa. Bendita fuera. Descorché una botella de vino blanco, me serví una copa y fui a tomármela al salón. Cuando iba por la tercera, me dormí arrellanada en el sofá.

Me despertó Marcos, riendo.

—Petra, ¿has sufrido un desmayo o es un simple colocón de vino blanco?

—Te estaba esperando.

—Obviamente, no me has esperado para empezar a beber.

—No, para eso no necesito compañía. Me las apaño sola perfectamente.

Marcos me estiró de la mano hasta que estuve de pie. Fuimos a la cocina y allí él se encargó de todo: calentó la lasaña, puso la mesa, sirvió vino de nuevo... Estuvo tan encantador que ni siquiera repitió la monserga de irnos a vivir al campo. Yo lo miraba con aire soñador.

—¿Has tenido un día muy duro, Petra?

—Al contrario, no he pegado ni golpe.

—Eso es raro, muy raro.

—No, siempre me sucede cuando investigamos un caso imposible, un caso que no vamos a resolver.

—¡Bah, bobadas! Lo que pasa es que estás agotada.

—Pero no quiero irme a vivir al campo —balbucí.

Se echó a reír de buena gana. Me miró dulcemente.

—Petra Delicado, la mujer que pelea hasta dormida. ¿Te acompaño a la cama?

—¿Y quién recoge los restos de la cena?

—Yo lo hago, no te preocupes. Vete a dormir. Mañana verás las cosas menos negras.

—Sí, marrón oscuro, quizá.

Se quedó trasteando en la cocina mientras yo subía las escaleras, derrotada. Hice mis abluciones, me enfundé el pijama y, ya acostada, una imagen me sobresaltó. Veía claramente al subinspector Garzón en mi cabeza. Yacía muerto en una especie de monumento funerario, rodeado de flores. Lo habían amortajado con unas cortinas de salón color magenta. Siniestro. Sacudí la cabeza varias veces hasta que el espectro desapareció. ¿Había sido demasiado brusca con él? ¿Había sobrepasado algún límite con mi soflama feminista? ¿No llevaría él un poco de razón y las mujeres éramos pesadísimas en lo que a cortinajes se refiere? Y si al día siguiente me decían que había muerto como en mi sueño, ¿qué tal me sentiría?

Por fin, aparté todos aquellos pensamientos ridículos de un plumazo. Basta, Petra, me dije, sigue meditando como has hecho esta tarde: nada en el cerebro, nada en el corazón. Veremos quién tiene más fuerza, si los malos augurios oníricos o las simples ganas de dormir.

Llegó el sueño. Apartados los trasgos, venció la realidad. Lo que yo no sabía en aquel instante era que la realidad, con toda su magnitud inapelable, iba a parecerse a una pesadilla poco rato después.

12

En mi primer atisbo de conciencia alguien me zarandeaba por un brazo. En el segundo, oí una voz. Sólo en el tercero comprendí. Marcos estaba de pie junto a mi lado de la cama, casi gritándome.

—¡Petra, despierta! Tu móvil está sonando a todo trapo.

Me senté y no tuve tiempo ni de restregarme los ojos. Me llamaban desde comisaría, uno de los policías de guardia. Eran las cinco de la mañana.

—Inspectora, tiene que personarse en las coordenadas que voy a pasarle por email, cuanto antes, mejor.

—¿De qué se trata?

—No tengo ni idea. A mí sólo me han dicho que la llame.

—¿Han avisado al subinspector Garzón?

—Un momento, por favor.

La voz potente del policía se dirigió a otra parte.

—¿Habéis avisado a Garzón? —aulló. Y desde una distancia indeterminada, alguien contestó al berrido berreando a su vez: «Sí, Garzón va para allá. Y hay ya una dotación de hombres».

—Inspectora...

—Ya lo he oído, mándeme la dirección. Voy enseguida.

Salté de la cama y empecé a barajar opciones: ¿ducharme, desayunar, no hacer ninguna de las dos cosas? Marcos salió del lavabo.

—¿Qué pasa, Petra, te vas?

—No sé qué demonio ha pasado, pero no te preocupes, volveré.

Las indicaciones me llevaron hasta un descampado en las inmediaciones de Castelldefels. Desde lejos vi varios vehículos policiales de los nuestros y de los Mossos, también a unos cuantos hombres de uniforme. El resto de las imágenes que vislumbré a medida que iba acercándome me resultó mucho más difícil de identificar. Bajé del coche y caminé. Sí, no había ninguna duda, el centro de atracción de todo el mundo era una furgoneta; mirándola con más atención, descubrí que estaba medio despedazada: puertas arrancadas, tapicería destripada, cristales rotos..., un montón de chatarra, un caos.

Al saludo marcial de los polis, contesté con la típica pregunta.

—¿Qué ha pasado aquí?

—Es una de las caravanas de la feria gastronómica. Nos han informado de que está relacionado con un caso que lleva usted, inspectora.

Fui escudriñando de cerca el desastre. ¡Cielos, sin duda alguna reconocí la furgoneta de Bob! La habían destrozado a conciencia. En ese momento llegó Garzón. El policía le repitió lo que me había contado a mí.

—¿Y esto?, ¿qué carajo ha pasado? —se limitó a inquirir mi compañero mientras yo continuaba con mi inspección.

—Forzaron la puerta a lo bruto, un solo golpe. Maniataron al chico que dormía dentro y le taparon los ojos. También le ataron las piernas.

Oír aquello me hizo saltar hasta donde se encontraban los hombres.

—¿El chico?, ¿y dónde está el chico?

—Allí al lado, inspectora. No ha sufrido ningún daño. Lo encontraron aquí mismo unos señores que iban paseando al perro. Estaba tan asustado que ni intentó librarse de las cuerdas para ir a pedir ayuda. Los del perro nos avisaron.

Al joven cocinero los policías lo habían cubierto con una manta. Estaba sentado en el tocón de un árbol. Se sostenía la cabeza entre las manos, mirando al suelo. No se puso en pie cuando el subinspector y yo llegamos a su altura.

—¿Se encuentra bien?

Me miró, encogiéndose de hombros. Estaba lívido, le temblaban las manos.

—¿Usted qué cree?

—Cuéntenos qué ha pasado.

—Pero, inspectora, no me han dado ni un café. Tengo frío, me encuentro fatal.

—¿Le han hecho daño?

—A mí no, pero a la furgoneta..., ¿ha visto el destrozo? ¡No queda nada que no esté roto!

Hablé con uno de los hombres para que trajeran café desde algún bar, pero los *mossos*, que ya habían informado y estaban retirándose al ver que el caso era nuestro, llevaban un termo lleno de café. Nos lo brindaron enseguida.

—¿Y cómo les devolvemos el termo?

—Quédeselo, inspectora, da igual.

Después de beber un par de tragos, el cocinero recuperó algo de forma. Garzón volvió a preguntarle por lo ocurrido.

—Yo estaba durmiendo tranquilamente. Había cerrado la puerta, me acuerdo muy bien. Y de pronto, noto un golpazo casi en la cabeza y algo que salta por los aires y me da en el pecho. Entonces me cogen por los sobacos y me arrastran fuera del camión. Eran dos tíos con pasamontañas negro. Uno me pone la manaza, que era como un martillo, en la boca y me la precinta con algo pegajoso. El otro me inmoviliza por detrás y me sube al camión otra vez. El primero, el de la manaza, se sienta al volante y arranca.

—¿Tuvo que hacer un puente para ponerse en marcha o le quitó las llaves a usted?

—Las llaves estaban puestas —musitó cabizbajo—. El otro cabrón me ata de pies y manos y, lo más horrible, va y me pone una especie de antifaz de esos que te dan en el avión para los viajes largos. El muy bestia me tira al suelo del pasillo y ahí me deja. Como no estaba previsto circular, pues los cacharros no estaban guardados ni fijados y empezaron a caerme encima cacerolas y todo tipo de cosas de la cocina. Caían cuchillos también, pero nadie se ocupó de eso. Iban los dos en la cabina del conductor. Yo en ese momento pensé que ya se me había acabado la vida, que me mataban sí o sí.

—¿Hablaban entre ellos?

—No, ni una palabra, ni tampoco se dirigieron a mí. En las películas siempre se dicen frases, ¿no?: «Si gritas, te corto el cuello», «Como intentes algo, te mataré». Pues aquí nada, ni mu. Claro que, tal y como me dejaron, a ver cómo iba a gritar ni cómo coño iba a intentar algo.

—Siga. ¿Qué pasó entonces?

—Pararon al cabo de un rato y me sacaron del furgón. Por el aire fresco me imaginé que estaba al aire libre. Olía a tierra, además, había mucha humedad. Creí que me tirarían otra vez al suelo, pero no, dimos malamente unos pasos, porque yo no podía andar, y me sentaron en una piedra. Luego oí golpes en el metal y cristales rotos y ruidos de estropicio. «Se están cargando el vehículo», pensé. ¿Y saben el temor que me entró en ese rato y en el que no podía dejar de pensar? Ahora me parece una chorrada, pero entonces, créanme, lo veía, lo veía venir. Me repetía: ahora le pegarán fuego a la furgona y el fuego se extenderá y vendrá hasta donde estoy y no podré huir y...

Se estremeció visiblemente, las manos le temblaron con fuerza. Bebió como pudo otro sorbo de café.

—¿Los oyó marcharse?

—No, pero debieron de hacerlo a pie porque no oí ningún coche, a no ser que estuviera lejos, claro.

—Descríbanos a los asaltantes.

—¿Está de coña, inspectora? ¡Pero si ya les he contado cómo fue! Se me echaron encima, iban tapados...

—Cuente los detalles en los que se fijó.

—¡Joder, estaba yo para detalles! Uno era una bestia, ya se lo he dicho, con una fuerza de la hostia y el otro..., en fin, no puedo asegurarlo, pero me pareció...

—¿Qué le pareció?

—Me pareció que era una mujer. Cuando me ataba..., bueno, hubiera jurado que me llegó olor a perfume. Pero ¡vaya usted a saber!, igual era un tío con colonia o..., no estoy seguro, no lo sé. ¿Y ahora qué hago, inspectora?

—Lo llevarán a comisaría para que preste declaración y la firme.

—¿Otra vez tendré que contar lo mismo? Estoy muy cansado, tengo hambre.

—Le darán comida caliente, no se preocupe.

Garzón y yo nos acercamos a la furgoneta devastada. Miramos someramente sin tocar nada.

—Buscaban algo —dijo el subinspector.

—El dinero que no pudieron recuperar la noche del asesinato de Laurent —apunté.

—¡Pero nosotros registramos la caravana el día del asesinato!

—No hasta el punto en que lo han hecho ellos, ¿verdad?

—No, desde luego que no.

—Organice este cirio, Fermín, el atestado, la Científica..., seguramente querrán llevarse el vehículo a su depósito para un examen pericial. Yo voy a avisar a Bob. Quiero que vea su furgoneta antes de que se la lleven. ¿Sabe si por aquí hay algún bar? No he podido tomar nada al salir de casa.

—Hay una gasolinera a un kilómetro más o menos. Le da tiempo de ir, comer algo y volver hasta que llegue el interfecto.

—Avíseme si llega antes.

En el bar de la gasolinera la oferta gastronómica era tétrica. Unas tristes madalenas industriales compartían espacio con varios bocadillos de beicon parecidos a los que les ponían en el zurrón a los soldados de la Segunda Guerra Mundial. Me incliné por las madalenas, que no ante ellas. Estaban horribles. Sin embargo, el café fluyó por mis venas como una droga vivificante.

Había pasado más de una vez por el trance de anunciar un asesinato a los familiares del muerto. No es una situación fácil ni agradable. No tenía que hacer lo mismo en esta ocasión, pero aun sin fallecimientos, seguía siendo un trago amargo. Dile a un tipo que el negocio del que vive se lo han reducido a un montón de chatarra. Incluso suponiendo que tuviera un seguro a todo riesgo, era una auténtica faena. Llamé y cité a Bob.

Se iban ajustando las piezas de nuestro rompecabezas. Martine irrumpe en la caravana de Laurent por la noche y se lo carga. Espera a que pase un poco de tiempo para que todo se calme y se lleva el vehículo en pleno para poder buscar con tranquilidad. ¿Qué es lo que buscan ella y sus secuaces? ¡El dinero que Laurent les ha birlado en alguna operación de droga! Le pegué un mordisco a la madalena con más rabia que hambre o placer. Aquella hipótesis era una auténtica mierda y no ajustaba ninguna maldita pieza. ¿No es más lógico buscar y luego matar, o buscar inmediatamente después de haber matado? Igual que habían secuestrado al pobre cocinero y se lo habían llevado a un descampado para registrar el vehículo, ¿no podían haber hecho lo mismo con Laurent? ¿Para qué soliviantar a la policía y los vecinos de *truck* con una muerte? ¿Para qué merodear por las ferias y arriesgarse a que te reconozcan tal y como había ocurrido con la Leoparda? No, la jugada correcta era la que habían ejecutado la noche anterior, sólo que unos días antes y con Laurent amordazado e inmovilizado en el suelo del camión. Es más, si lo hubieran tenido trincado y amenazado de muerte, quizá les hubiera dicho dónde estaba el dinero y se hubieran ahorrado aquel vandalismo monumental.

Cogí el resto de la madalena y la lancé sobre el plato. Rebotó. El camarero vino enseguida hasta mi sitio en la barra.

—No está buena, ¿verdad? ¿Quiere que le haga una tostada con mantequilla o aceite?

Era un chico joven que me miraba con consternación. Me arrepentí de haber mostrado tan groseramente mi mal humor. El chico siguió hablando.

—Ya le digo a mi jefe que no compre esas pastas, no valen nada. Yo sé de otras marcas que están mejor. Pero no me hace ni caso. Ya sabe usted cómo son los jefes, no hay manera con ellos.

—Perdone, sólo la he tirado porque estoy de mal humor.

Silbó apreciativamente, sacudió la cabeza.

—¡Joder, pues si se pone de mal humor ya a estas horas de la mañana, mal va!

Le sonreí. Pagué la cuenta y le dejé siete euros de más. Una multa que me autoimpuse por haber sido desagradable. Me miró con sorpresa.

—Es demasiado.

Hice un gesto con la mano para quitar importancia al asunto. Al llegar a la puerta de salida, me llamó.

—¡Señora! ¿Cuánta propina me hubiera dejado si hubiera estado de buen humor?

Solté una pequeña carcajada y me fui. «Al final me ha hecho reír, y es que los camareros españoles son una auténtica institución nacional», pensé. Deberían condecorarlos a todos, hacerles un monumento, declararlos de interés general. Son más útiles que el gremio de psiquiatras en su integridad. Solucionan los problemas en menos tiempo y los productos que sirven no son tan tóxicos como una medicación, si bien mi madalena estaba cerca de un bote de psicotrópicos.

Ordené que una pequeña dotación fuera al campamento de Sitges e inspeccionara el lugar donde aparcaba la caravana en busca de pruebas. Volví al circo. Los de la Científica todavía estaban haciendo fotos de la furgoneta destruida y Bob, por desgracia, no había llegado. Había concebido la esperanza de que Garzón lo hubiera recibido en mi ausencia. Llegó al cabo de diez minutos y, como la zona estaba acordonada, se dirigió hacia nosotros a pie. Lo observé intensamente. A medida que se avecinaba, sus ojos miraban a un lado y a otro hasta que la descubrió. Se plantó a cierta distancia de su furgoneta. No decía ni una palabra, sólo miraba. ¿Quizá no la había reconocido? Se llevó las manos a las sienes, se las apretó. Sí, sabía perfectamente que era la suya. Se volvió hacia mí.

—Secuestraron a su cocinero, no le hicieron daño. Acaba de irse para declarar en comisaría. Se encuentra bien. ¿Tiene usted asegurada la camioneta? —inquirí.

Afirmó varias veces con la cabeza. Siguió sin hablar. Tras un lapso prolongado, acertó a preguntar.

—Pero ¿quién...?

—No lo sabemos. —Me anticipé a más preguntas—. ¿Lo sabe usted?

Se volvió enloquecido hacia mí.

—¿Yo? ¿Qué quiere que sepa, inspectora?, ¿qué?

—No grite. Vamos a aquel rincón.

Le hice una seña al subinspector para que viniera, y regresamos al tocón del árbol donde antes habíamos estado. Era un buen lugar para un interrogatorio.

—Siéntese.

—No quiero sentarme.

—¡Siéntese, Bob!

Obedeció. Como mi intención era intimidarlo, nosotros permanecimos de pie.

—¿Puede contarnos qué ha pasado aquí?

—Pero, inspectora, de verdad que no la entiendo, yo...

—Los tipos que se llevaron su vehículo y lo destrozaron iban buscando algo. No pretenderá que nos creamos que no sabe qué es. Es su furgoneta, trabaja en ella todo el día, conoce sus rincones y sus piezas. En esa misma furgoneta mataron a su socio. ¿Qué buscaban, Bob? ¿Qué había en el interior?

—No lo sé, inspectora, no lo sé. ¿Cómo quiere que...? Ayer trabajé como siempre y luego volví al hotel.

—Eso ya lo sabemos. ¿Qué buscaban esos hombres?

Se levantó de golpe, empezó a chillar.

—¡Me machacan mi medio de vida y encima usted...!

Garzón le dio un ligero empellón en el hombro que lo sentó de nuevo. El hombre empezó a llorar.

—¿Qué va a ser de mí ahora?, ¿qué voy a hacer?

—¡Suéltelo ya! Es imposible que siempre haya estado tan en Babia. Tiene usted un socio con documentación falsa y antecedentes por drogas y no se entera. Se lo cargan en su propia furgoneta y no tiene ni remota idea de quién ha podido ser. Ahora le vandalizan el cacharro buscando quizá dinero y tampoco le suena de nada. ¿Qué es usted, un espíritu puro, pasa por encima de las cosas sin verlas? ¡Por favor, es ridículo!

—Inspectora Delicado, no sé de qué me habla, ¡se lo juro por Dios! Mi socio era quien pasaba más tiempo en la furgoneta. Nunca vi nada raro, nunca encontré dinero ni ninguna otra cosa. Créame, no estoy mintiendo, créame.

—Le cargamos las culpas al muerto. Más cómodo, ¿no?

—¿Cree que le mentiría en estas circunstancias? Después de este desastre, ¿de qué voy a vivir? El seguro me pagará lo que me pague, pero ¿cuándo? No soy un hombre rico y estaré sin ingresos. No sólo eso, el hotel vale una pasta, ¿hasta cuándo podré pagarlo? ¿Dónde dormiré después? ¿Cree que si supiera quién me ha jodido la vida no se lo diría?

—¿Qué buscaba el cabrón que le ha jodido la vida, Bob?

Se echó a llorar con total desconsuelo. Garzón y yo intercambiamos una mirada. Él negó. Llevaba razón, no íbamos a sacarle nada. O era inocente o no era el momento adecuado para interrogarlo. La conmoción que mostraba era completamente auténtica. Le dejamos marchar.

Garzón abrió ampliamente los brazos a modo de conclusión.

—¿Se da cuenta de que la vida de estos tíos no es la que todos llevamos, Petra? Normalmente, si a uno se le prende fuego en el local de su negocio, pues tiene su casa para vivir. Pero ya ha oído a este hombre, ¿dónde va a dar con sus huesos?

—Bueno, eso es como decir que una mujer tiene que tener necesariamente un amante por si se queda viuda, ¿no?

—No me líe, inspectora. Usted sabe lo que quiero decir.

El siguiente paso obligado era volver al lugar de los hechos. Sitges se despertaba. Sobre el mar flotaba una suave calima que producía impresión de irrealidad. Garzón miraba la lista mientras íbamos en tránsito.

—Mañana estarán en Caldes de Montbui. Podemos tomar un baño de aguas termales.

—Me conformaría con que hubiera algún bar cerca de donde acampen.

El cuadro que componían las caravanas por la mañana lo conocíamos ya. Los propietarios iban y venían de un lado a otro, salían a comprar víveres, desayunaban al aire libre porque hacía buen tiempo aún. El lugar donde había estado la furgoneta de Bob lo custodiaban dos policías.

—¿Han encontrado algo los compañeros de la Científica?

—Parece que no había nada. De todos modos, han recogido un par de colillas y una huella de zapato. Poco es. Hace un rato que se fueron.

—Ustedes pueden volver a comisaría.

—¿No deja a nadie de guardia, inspectora?

—No es necesario.

Dimos un par de vueltecitas tontas mirando al suelo. Se acercó a nosotros Javier.

—Buenos días, inspectores. ¿Quieren tomar un café?

—Eso me suena a música divina —exclamó Garzón.

—También puedo ofrecerles un bizcocho que hicimos anoche.

Fuimos con él hasta su caravana. Preparó el café y cortó un bizcocho que tenía una pinta maravillosa y unas galletitas, según dijo, de zanahoria. Me lancé sobre las viandas sin ni pizca de educación. El subinspector, por una vez menos hambriento que yo, preguntó por su esposa.

—Hoy ha ido ella a comprar. Quería salir de aquí. Todo esto la tiene muy nerviosa. En realidad, todo el mundo empieza a estar alterado. Sus compañeros han estado inspeccionando el sitio donde estaba Bob. Les hemos preguntado y no han querido decir nada. ¿Qué está pasando? ¿Dónde está Bob? ¿Corremos algún peligro? No pueden tenernos sin saber, no es justo.

Llevaba razón. Me limpié cuidadosamente los labios con una servilleta de papel.

—Hemos venido para interrogarlos a todos. Luego los reuniremos, pero empezaremos por usted, Javier, ya que estamos aquí. ¿No oyó nada anoche mientras dormía?

—Sí, en fin, medio en sueños, me pareció que se ponía en marcha la furgoneta de Bob. Me extrañó.

—¿Y qué hizo?

—Nada, seguir durmiendo.

—¿Le extrañó oír la furgoneta y no se levantó a ver qué pasaba?

—Inspectora, estaba calentito, bien abrigado, en lo mejor del sueño. Ni siquiera pensé en levantarme. Remoloneé, y me dije medio inconsciente que alguna explicación habría. En realidad no me dije nada, seguí durmiendo.

—¿Oyó algo más?, ¿algún golpe, alguna voz?

—No, sólo el motor arrancando, nada más.

—¿Tiene idea de qué hora era?

—No estoy seguro, estaba muy zombi. No miré el reloj, pero más o menos atendiendo a mi reloj interior debían ser las dos o las tres de la mañana, aunque puedo equivocarme, desde luego.

—¿Elisenda oyó algo?

—No, ya lo hemos comentado, no oyó nada. Inspectora, ¿se puede saber qué pasa?

—Unos desconocidos encapuchados irrumpieron en la caravana, maniataron al cocinero y se llevaron el vehículo con el chico dentro. Cuando nos avisaron esta mañana la camioneta estaba hecha pedazos. El cocinero está bien.

Su semblante pasó a tener una seriedad preocupada, nos miró fijamente.

—Es algo de drogas, ¿verdad, inspectores?

—¿Eso le parece?

—¡A mí no me parece nada y ustedes no abren la boca! Pero yo no soy tonto, ¡ni yo ni ninguno de los colegas! ¡Todos pensamos lo mismo, es un asunto de drogas! ¿Qué otra cosa puede ser? Y si eso es verdad, todos corremos peligro.

Aquel hombre empezaba a ponerse pesado. Lo atajé.

—No sé qué demonio de peligro ve usted.

—¿A usted le gustaría que unos encapuchados estuvieran rondando su cama?

—¡A mí lo que me gustaría es que se tranquilizara de una vez!

El subinspector medió con calma y buen criterio.

—Oiga, Javier, ¿por qué no va a avisar a sus colegas de que deben reunirse para hablar con nosotros? Les cuenta lo que tenga que contarles y luego los esperamos aquí mismo. ¿Usted tiene influencia sobre ellos?

Se había serenado por fin. Miró a mi compañero, un tanto cabizbajo.

—No, yo no tengo influencia. Eso el gallego, al gallego la gente le hace caso.

—¿Al de la comida gallega que trabaja con su esposa?

—Sí, pero anda muy cabreado, les advierto. Hemos estado hablando esta misma mañana.

—Haga un aparte con él antes de convocar al resto. Dígale que nosotros estamos muy muy cabreados, que queremos saber si han visto u oído algo esta madrugada, que si alguien se guarda algo por prudencia, de un modo u otro nos enteraremos y el cabreo aumentará.

Su mirada estaba preñada de indignación y desprecio mientras me escuchaba. Se levantó y fue en busca de sus congéneres. Garzón aprovechó para recriminarme la actuación.

—¡Caramba, inspectora, ha estado muy dura con él! El pobre nos ha invitado a desayunar.

—¡Ni desayunos ni pollas en vinagre! Estoy harta, tal parece que los delincuentes fuéramos nosotros. ¿De qué nos echan las culpas, eh? ¿Somos nosotros quienes violamos la ley, quienes cometemos las fechorías?

—No, pero es verdad que si esta noche hubiera habido vigilancia...

—¡Eso se lo cuenta usted a Coronas, que yo ya lo intenté!

—No pienso contarle nada, y si usted lo hace en ese tono, me la veo dentro de cuatro días en el departamento de los carnets de identidad.

—¡Bah, vaya mierda de trabajo hemos escogido, Fermín!

—Yo quería ser torero, pero ya ve...

—No estoy para bromas. Voy a ver si me aclaro con la cafetera y me arreo otro café, aunque ese tío es capaz de denunciarme por entrar en una propiedad privada sin permiso.

—Me parece que no le da tiempo, mire, ya vienen todos hacia aquí. ¿Quiere que hable yo? Me parece que hoy no está usted muy dialogante.

Tuve la sensación de que se aproximaba un pelotón de fusilamiento. Apenas saludaron entre dientes al llegar. Garzón los interrogó con santa paciencia: ¿qué han visto?, ¿qué han oído, ¿alguien se despertó? Ninguna respuesta, todo el mundo dormía apaciblemente. Cuando todas las negativas habían salido a la luz, el gallego dio un paso al frente indicando que deseaba tomar la palabra. Lo hizo con voz alta y clara que indicaba una firme determinación.

—Señores policías, es evidente que nuestro grupo ha aceptado todas sus órdenes al pie de la letra y sin protestar: nos hemos mantenido juntos, aun cuando eso nos ha creado problemas de contratos y cancelaciones, hemos estado todos ojo avizor por si podíamos servir de testigos, les hemos facilitado una lista de los pueblos por donde nos movemos. En una palabra: hemos cumplido. Pero después de lo que nos ha contado el subinspector: encapuchados que se acercan por la noche, un secuestro, una caravana en ruinas..., pues, en fin, creemos que corremos peligro y tenemos la sensación de que nadie vela por nuestra seguridad.

—Todos los problemas han estado centrados en una sola camioneta que ya no estará presente —respondí.

—En ese caso, supongo que ya somos libres y podemos ir cada uno por su lado.

—No, eso es prematuro. Tendrán que seguir los planes trazados unos días más.

—Entonces, inspectora, hemos decidido y estamos todos de acuerdo en contratar a un vigilante privado que pase las noches aquí. Supongo que eso es legal, ¿no?

—Si es una empresa homologada y con los permisos en regla, es legal. Hemos estado escasos de efectivos en la policía, pero yo creo que esta misma noche está previsto que uno de nuestros hombres haga guardia en sus locales.

—No se ofenda, inspectora, pero ya que no les sobra gente, preferimos tener nuestra propia seguridad.

Sentí que se me arrebolaban las mejillas, pero ni se me ocurrió contestarle mal. El hombre era respetuoso, se había expresado correctamente y me fastidiaba reconocerlo, pero llevaba una parte importante de razón. Sabía muy bien lo que iba a decirme mi compañero en el viaje a comisaría.

—El tipo ha estado muy en su papel, ¿verdad, inspectora? A lo mejor, si yo estuviera en la piel de esa gente, tomaría la determinación que ellos han tomado.

—¿Contrataría a un segurata?

—En fin, no estoy afirmando que lo hiciera, pero están asustados, no saben de dónde les llueven las hostias. Con un vigilante tienen la sensación de llevar ellos las riendas, aunque les cueste una pasta la solución.

—No hemos sido capaces ni de ponerles un puto poli.

—Ya sabemos que eso ha sido culpa del comisario, pero él es un hombre razonable y lo reconocerá.

Pronto lo sabríamos. El policía de recepción me dijo que Coronas me reclamaba en su despacho. Garzón, que me tenía más miedo que a un nublado, me hizo las consabidas recomendaciones de prudencia antes de entrar.

—No se desmande, inspectora. No se le ocurra recriminarle nada al jefe. No hable demasiado. ¡Ojalá pudiera estar yo presente para controlarla un poco!

Todos aquellos consejos resultaron inútiles, Coronas no me dejó prácticamente abrir la boca. Al verme, se lanzó.

—No me diga que esto no hubiera pasado si... Que a ese tipo le hayan vandalizado la camioneta ha sido providencial. Una bendición del cielo, diría yo. Ahora tenemos una prueba más, una prueba importante de que la asesina iba buscando la droga o el dinero que le había estafado el muerto. Siga ese rastro y acabará cerrando el caso de una maldita vez, que ya va siendo hora. ¿Tiene algo que decir?

—No mucho, lo que ocurre es que le han hundido el negocio a un ciudadano contra el que no tenemos ningún cargo legal.

—¿Y eso qué importa? ¿Sabe, Petra?, a la policía no nos pagan por ser empáticos ni por sentir piedad. En el grupo de Homicidios nuestro deber es resolver asesinatos a cualquier precio, lo paguemos nosotros o no. Y si lo pagan otros, miel sobre hojuelas. ¿Algo más?

—Los comerciantes van a contratar seguridad privada.

—¡Fantástica noticia! Me ahorro poner en servicio a un hombre por el qué dirán. Que se lo solucionen a lo Juan Palomo me parece una inmejorable decisión.

Garzón atisbaba el final del pasillo para verme salir. Vino hacia mí con semblante preocupado.

—La audiencia ha sido muy corta. ¿Le ha dicho usted algo chungo?

—¿Yo, qué le iba a decir? No se le dice nada chungo a un hombre razonable, justo y preocupado por el bien común. Me entiende, ¿verdad?

—Me temo que sí.

13

En esta investigación no caminábamos en línea recta y hacia delante, sino que íbamos dibujando pronunciados meandros en un río del que ni siquiera estábamos seguros de que iba a dar a la mar. Afortunadamente, la prensa había perdido el interés por nosotros al cabo de unos días. En el ejercicio de la profesión había advertido cómo los periodistas se habían vuelto progresivamente menos insistentes. La sección de «sucesos» seguía siendo uno de los apartados preferidos del público, pero para concitar verdadera atención, el asesinato debía ser verdaderamente truculento. Si había miembros cercenados, descuartizamientos completos o el crimen llevaba aparejados ultrajes sexuales, los plumillas sí rondaban a la poli intentando recabar información. También el grado de parentesco de los sospechosos o culpables confesos con la víctima desataba bastante curiosidad. Por el contrario, muertes escasamente violentas, resultantes de peleas multitudinarias o enfrentamientos fortuitos, no atraían a nadie. Ese era el caso de Laurent. Al principio, resultaba atractivo que lo hubieran matado en un *food truck*, pero después nos habían dejado en paz sin el menor deseo de saber. Mejor así, porque poco habíamos avanzado y poco podíamos contar.

Había que continuar indagando donde habíamos dejado el caso antes del desgraciado episodio de la furgoneta de Bob. Garzón echó mano de la libretilla donde todo estaba apuntado. Él confiaba en la informática, pero solía decir que todo se le quedaba mejor fijado en la mente cuando utilizaba papel.

—Nos falta visitar a Dámaso, de Mataró.

—¿Quién es ese tipo?

—¡Joder, inspectora! ¿Ya no se acuerda de la lista del teniente Montilla?

—Es verdad, había cerrado el capítulo con el lío de la china.

—No cierre nada, vamos de lío en lío.

—¿Y ahora hay que largarse a Mataró? De verdad le digo que estoy de viajecitos hasta el moño. Al tal Dámaso, ¿dónde se supone que lo encontramos?

—En su tienda de ultramarinos. El teniente está seguro de que anda todavía traficando, de que se mantiene en activo. ¿Quiere que le pidamos que nos acompañe por lo que pueda pasar?

—¿Está loco? Nada ha cambiado, Fermín. En cuanto pidamos ayuda a otro cuerpo, nos quitan el caso en un santiamén. Oiga, ¿usted cree que es normal tener un garito de estupefacientes en una tienda de ultramarinos? ¿El tendero es el «capo»? Todo me parece un poco cutre a primera vista.

—Cuanto más inofensiva sea la tapadera, mejores prestaciones puede dar. Además, en una tienda entra y sale mucha gente.

Afirmé varias veces, puse cara de pena.

—¿Desde cuándo se ha vuelto tan perezosa?

—A lo mejor debería jubilarme anticipadamente.

—¡Bah, déjese de hostias! ¿Y a qué se iba a dedicar: trabajos manuales, voluntariado, al cuidado del hogar?

—¡A follar como una loca, Garzón, a eso iba a dedicarme!

Me miró, intentando no reírse.

—Desde luego, Petra, ¡qué bruta es usted!

Era cierto que estaba volviéndome perezosa, pero yo lo atribuía al caso que llevábamos. Nuestras pesquisas resultaban siempre baldías y los acontecimientos que iban sucediéndose lo hacían al margen de cualquier previsión por nuestra parte. ¿Para qué, pues, esforzarse tanto? Quizá todo consistía en cruzarse de brazos y esperar a que pasara el siguiente episodio.

—¿Nos vamos? —preguntó Garzón contradiciendo mis pensamientos.

—¡Vamos allá! —dije con un ímpetu tan excesivo que resultó paródico.

La red de carreteras que rodea Barcelona estaba siempre atestada de tráfico. Sin quererlo, se me fue la cabeza a los planes de mi marido. No me ubicaba a mí misma levantándome cada día a las seis de la mañana para llegar a tiempo a trabajar, por muchos pajaritos que trinaran a aquellas horas. Y, sin embargo, había un montón de gente que lo hacía. ¿De verdad les compensaba? ¿Qué demonio tenía Marcos en el imaginario mental? Vivíamos en una casa de planta con un pequeño jardín, Poblenou era un barrio tranquilo. ¿Qué más necesitaba?, ¿a qué venía aquella añoranza de naturaleza y vida contemplativa? Yo seguía pensando que sus aspiraciones radicaban en dar un salto en el aire, forzar un cambio total. Quizá lo que deseaba en el fondo era librarse de nuestra vida doméstica y quizá, mucho más en el fondo aún, lo que ansiaba era librarse de mí.

—¿En qué piensa, inspectora? —preguntó súbitamente Garzón.

Me sobresalté un poco. Volví la cara hacia él.

—¿Por qué quiere saberlo?

Se encogió de hombros.

—No sé, me pareció que estaba muy concentrada.

—¿Y qué cara ponía?

—¿Quién?

—¿Quién va a ser?, ¡yo!

—No la entiendo.

—Pues es muy fácil de entender: ¿se me veía preocupada, triste, angustiada?

—¡Y yo qué coño sé! ¡Voy conduciendo, Petra!

—Desde luego, Fermín, la simplicidad de los hombres me pone enferma. Son ustedes incapaces de estar en los detalles, inútiles para captar cualquier matiz.

—¡Hala, chúpate esa! Sin haberlo sospechado, una bronca me han echado.

Guardé silencio, él también, pero como no se había quedado satisfecho ni yo le había ofrecido reparación por la ofensa, enseguida se arrancó.

—Me gustaría que supiera que hay algo en lo que todos los hombres estamos de acuerdo y que, ciertamente, no admite ningún matiz. A ustedes las mujeres no hay manera humana de entenderlas. Nada, es imposible, es inviable, nunca aciertas ni por aproximación. Es como si te pusieran delante de un periódico chino y te dijeran: «Venga, cuéntame qué pasó ayer».

Me eché a reír. Él apartó la vista de la carretera y me miró fugazmente.

—¿Ahora se ríe?, pues todavía la entiendo menos.

—No me haga caso, subinspector. Lo único que debe entender es la investigación de este maldito asesinato.

—A buenas horas, mangas verdes —dijo en voz muy baja, y lo repitió varias veces antes de llegar a nuestro destino.

El lugar donde nos dejó nuestro GPS demostraba que el teniente Montilla estaba anticuado a pesar de ser joven. Nadie hoy en día hubiera calificado aquel negocio como una tienda de ultramarinos. En la jerga actual todo el mundo lo hubiera llamado «un paki». Se trataba de un pequeño autoservicio de los que suelen estar regentados por uno o varios pakistaníes y que abundan hoy en día en todas las ciudades españolas.

Una chica, en efecto de rasgos indios, atendía la caja. El local se encontraba vacío en aquel momento. Le enseñamos nuestras placas acreditativas al informarla de que éramos policías.

—Queremos hablar con el señor Dámaso.

Los maravillosos ojos negros de la dependienta se abrieron y cerraron en señal de asentimiento. Desapareció y volvió a aparecer al cabo de un instante. Se puso a quitar el polvo de unas latas de conserva con energía. En ese momento Dámaso salió de la trastienda. Era un individuo enormemente alto y corpulento, de unos sesenta años, que exhibía en el rostro rufianesco un gesto agrio. No es que tuviera cara de pocos amigos, sino que se hubiera podido afirmar que desconocía el significado de la palabra *amistad*. Su saludo fue un desplante hacia nosotros.

—¿Qué quieren?

Le plantifiqué mi placa a dos centímetros de la nariz.

—En primer lugar, queremos que nos hable correctamente —solté.

—Esto es un supermercado, no una biblioteca.

—Seguro que no, pero también estoy segura de que aquí hay libros. Libros de contabilidad, por ejemplo, ¿no?

No respondió, me miró con los ojos encendidos de odio.

—Verá, Dámaso, si no quiere que entremos a saco en sus cuentas y empecemos a tocarle los cojones hasta que se le queden calvos, será mejor que responda a nuestras preguntas y colabore con nosotros.

Siguió sin hablar.

—Piense que nosotros tenemos tiempo, mucho tiempo, todo el tiempo del mundo.

Hizo un gesto brusco con la cabeza indicándonos paso libre.

La trastienda era una sala más grande de lo que hubiera podido parecer desde fuera. Contenía varias estanterías que almacenaban diferentes botes y productos de limpieza. Vimos a un lado una mesa de despacho con su silloncito correspondiente y un ordenador de última generación en el que obviamente había estado Dámaso trabajando.

—¿Qué tal van los negocios? —dijo el subinspector a modo retórico.

—Van como tienen que ir. Estoy esperando que me pregunten, ¿qué quieren saber?

—Le informo antes de nada. No somos de la brigada de drogas, ni tenemos nada que ver con la Guardia Civil. Nosotros vamos de otro palo y en este momento no nos interesa a lo que se dedique usted.

—¿Delitos económicos?

—Homicidios.

Noté la sorpresa en él. La espalda, que tenía algo encorvada, se estiró, haciendo aún mayor su envergadura.

—¿Me acusan de algo?

—No. Le voy a enseñar una fotografía. Es de una mujer. Quiero que la mire detenidamente antes de contestar. Piense que estamos investigando un asesinato del que ella podría ser culpable. Si la conoce y decide mentir, podríamos acusarlo de ocultación o incluso de complicidad.

Garzón sacó de su bolsillo la fotografía y se la mostró.

—¿La conoce?

Localizar cualquier reacción significativa en aquella cara de bruto no era tarea fácil. Sin embargo, me esforcé y quise ver, más que vi, un parpadeo ligeramente descontrolado. El tipo dijo por fin:

—Es posible que la haya visto alguna vez, pero quién sabe, por aquí pasa mucha gente.

—Haga memoria, puede mirarla todo el tiempo que necesite.

En ese momento oímos un ruido extraño en el exterior, después estrépito de vidrios rotos. Por más prisa que nos dimos, el primero en salir fue el tal Dámaso, rápido como un guepardo. La cajera se había agachado tras su mostrador. Se tapaba la boca con ambas manos, presa del terror. En el pequeño escaparate con que contaba la tienda era fácil de descubrir un impacto bastante grande que había roto el cristal. Me precipité hacia la calle. Una anciana miraba la escena con gesto de pasmo. Le grité.

—¿Ha visto qué ha pasado, señora?

—Ha sido un hombre bajito. Se ha ido corriendo por allí.

Señalaba la estrecha calle, que estaba desierta. Aun sabiendo que mis posibilidades eran escasas, salí pitando en la dirección que la mujer indicaba. Llegué hasta el final, donde se abría una avenida mucho más transitada por coches y gente a pie. Miré a derecha e izquierda y no vi nada. Llevaba la pistola metida en el bolsillo. Me quedé allí plantada un par de minutos, como un monumento a la inutilidad. Algunos paseantes me miraban, sorprendidos por mi demasiado evidente actitud de alarma. Di media vuelta y regresé.

En la puerta se habían reunido un par de curiosos, no más. La testigo estaba hablando con Garzón. Cuando me acerqué, uno de los curiosos dijo:

—Si son ustedes policías a ver si le avisan al ayuntamiento de que esto no puede ser. Mataró se ha llenado de gamberros y pandilleros, pero es que encima les damos munición. —Señaló un pequeño socavón que había en la calzada en cuyo perímetro se veían descarnadas algunas piedras de basalto—. En cuanto no vives en pleno centro o cerca de la zona comercial, parece que ya no importas un carajo.

—¿Han visto ustedes a alguien?

—No, yo acabo de llegar.

—Entonces circulen, por favor.

Garzón apuntaba cosas en su libretita habitual. La anciana se mostraba más nerviosa que hacía unos minutos.

—La señora asegura que no puede describir al hombre que vio, tampoco se acuerda de si llevaba la cara tapada o no. Sólo está segura de que era bajito.

—Es que todo pasó tan deprisa. Yo oí el ruido, miré, pero... ya se estaba marchando.

Se encontraba al borde del llanto. Le toqué el brazo al subinspector para que abandonara el interrogatorio. De aquella buena mujer no sacaríamos más. Le pedimos sus datos por si debía testificar en caso de presentarse una denuncia. Antes de volver a la tienda, Garzón me soltó casi al oído.

—Esto ha sido un aviso, ¿no? La pregunta es: ¿para él o para nosotros?

—Supongo que es compartido.

Dámaso estaba acuclillado junto a su cajera, aún en estado de shock.

—¿Puede irse la chica a casa? —preguntó.

—Si no ha visto nada...

—¡Qué coño va a ver! En cuanto sonó la pedrada, se protegió.

—Puede marcharse, sí. ¿Dónde ha caído la piedra?

El hombre señaló hacia un rincón donde el canto había caído, llevándose por delante varias bolsas de patatas fritas. Sin duda pertenecía al bache de la calzada que acababan de ver.

—No voy a presentar denuncia —declaró Dámaso de sopetón.

—¿Y cómo explica esto?

—Por el barrio circulan pandas de jóvenes, hacen de las suyas de vez en cuando.

—Y ha dado la casualidad de que nosotros estábamos aquí para interrogarlo, ¿no es eso?

—Eso será.

—Aunque no presente denuncia, nosotros daremos parte de lo que acaba de ocurrir.

—No servirá de nada.

Después de ese breve intercambio de intenciones, cambió completamente de actitud. Se dirigió a una gran nevera y sacó tres cervezas. Las puso sobre su mesa de despacho. Luego fue hacia un armario y añadió a la mesa unos vasos de papel. Se tocó la frente con un dedo como alertando de una idea genial y, al cabo de un instante, las bolsas despachurradas de patatas completaron un aperitivo improvisado. Garzón y yo observábamos sus maniobras sin abrir boca. Al final trajo unas sillas.

—Con el cristo que se ha montado, un poco de calma nos irá bien.

Tras el primer sorbo, comenté:

—Apreciamos mucho su hospitalidad, pero la calma sin charla suele ser aburrida.

—Ya lo sé. Yo conozco a la mujer de la fotografía, inspectora. Puedo decirles quién es ahora mismo si quieren, pero con la condición de que no den parte de la pedrada. Ya ven qué fácil va a resultar.

—¿Hay alguna razón de peso para que no demos parte?

—¡Bah, son tonterías en realidad! Si dan parte, se presentarán aquí sus colegas de drogas y me pondrán la cabeza como un bombo. Están empeñados en cerrarme el local. ¡Como si yo tuviera algo que ver en esos asuntos! No encontrarían nada, ya lo han intentado más de una vez y se han quedado sin bola que rascar. Pero entre que se presentan aquí, preguntan, inspeccionan y todo lo demás, mis clientes se mosquearán y no quiero que mi negocio se desprestigie.

—¿Es usted consciente de que podríamos detenerlo por entorpecer la labor policial?

—No diga chorradas, inspectora. Yo conozco muy bien las leyes; si hay algo que me sé de memoria son las leyes. Si me detuvieran por eso que dice y sin la orden de un juez, me soltarían a los diez minutos. ¿Acepta el pacto sí o no?

—Usted gana. ¿Quién es esa mujer?

—Se llama Martine y es francesa. Jefa de un cártel potente. Es una mala bestia.

—Todo eso ya lo sabemos. ¿Qué más?

—He oído rumores de que está en Barcelona.

—¿Para qué?

—Para cobrarse una deuda de una pirula que le hicieron.

—¿Quién se la hizo?

—Le juro que no tengo ni idea. Los rumores tampoco lo cuentan.

—¿Conoce a un hombre llamado Pierre Laurent, quizá su otro nombre es Christophe?

—No, no me suena de nada.

—¿Sabe en qué lugar de Barcelona puede estar esa mujer o alguno de los hombres que la acompañan?

—Ni idea, se lo juro, ni idea.

—Y supongo que si lo supiera se guardaría el dato para usted solo.

—Está metiendo la pata, con perdón. Miren, yo soy muy radical y a esa tía, si pudiera joderla, la jodería sin pensarlo dos veces. Y, sobre todo, si anda con jueguecitos de tirar piedras y tocarme las pelotas. Todo lo que le he dicho es la verdad y, además, es lo único que sé.

—De acuerdo, Dámaso, le creo. Otro tema: si nosotros no damos parte de la pedrada no podemos brindarle protección y, visto lo visto, quizá la necesite.

—Por eso no padezca, tengo dos hermanos que son buenos chicos y vendrán a hacerme compañía.

—¡Ah, estupendo!, ¿y sus hermanos llevan armas, quizá?

—No sé si son aficionados a la caza, se lo preguntaré.

—Tenga cuidado con la chica de la caja, sería una pena que la frieran sin comerlo ni beberlo. Y con sus hermanos tenga cuidado también.

—Eso es lo primero, desde luego. Jesucristo dijo

que todos somos hermanos y si dijo eso es porque un hermano es lo más importante que hay.

—Contando con que Jesucristo era hijo único, no sé qué pensar.

Sonrió vagamente, por primera vez. Nos acompañó hasta la salida y, al alejarnos, vimos cómo inspeccionaba los daños en el cristal del escaparate.

Nos dejamos caer con pesadez en los asientos del coche. Garzón bufaba.

—¡Qué estrés, por todos los santos! ¿Desde cuándo peligrosos traficantes internacionales se dedican a arrear pedradas a los escaparates como si fueran delincuentes de barrio? ¿No tienen para comprarse una pistola como Dios manda?

—Era un simple aviso, Fermín. Nos están siguiendo los pasos y quieren que lo sepamos.

—¿Para qué? No tiene sentido.

—No lo tiene, es verdad. Pero ¿quién más está metido en este embrollo?

—Ni siquiera sabemos cuántos hombres se ha traído Martine para que le echen una mano.

—Si se trata de los mismos que le rompieron la caravana a Bob, son por lo menos dos.

Puso el coche en marcha y empezamos a circular. El silencio que guardábamos se volvía clamoroso a medida que íbamos acercándonos a Barcelona. Después de lo que acababa de pasar, lo normal habría sido que floreciera entre nosotros una conversación vibrante llena de hipótesis. No se produjo. Nuestra moral de combate estaba por los suelos. Me llevé las manos a los ojos y me los froté varias veces. A mi subalterno debió parecerle un ademán desesperado porque, sin duda para animarme, decidió bromear.

—De verdad, Petra, usted siempre me tacha de basto y vulgar, pero lo que es hoy quien se ha lucido ha sido usted. No doy crédito a lo que le soltó a ese tío: «Empecemos a tocarle los cojones hasta que se le queden calvos». ¡Eso sí que es basto y vulgar! ¡Si lo hubiera dicho yo me habría puesto a caer de un burro!

Dibujé en mis labios una falsa sonrisa. No estaba para bromas. De pronto y contra todo pronóstico, noté que brotaba en mí un géiser de energía y optimismo. Me volví hacia Garzón.

—Y, sin embargo, Fermín, vamos bien. Todas nuestras sospechas han dado en el clavo. Martine está en Barcelona, y fue ella quien despachó a Laurent por una cuenta pendiente. No hay más cáscaras. Ahora andan buscando el dinero que el muerto debió de esconder en alguna parte. Vamos bien, ¿comprende?, vamos bien.

—¡Pues claro que sí, inspectora! —contestó él con firmeza.

Un segundo más tarde vi que en su boca surgía la misma sonrisa falsa que un segundo antes había esbozado yo.

14

Hugo y Teo, los gemelos de mi marido, cenaban solos conmigo aquella noche. Marina había salido de excursión con su colegio y Marcos estaba en Madrid por trabajo. Frente a un plato de verduras al horno, obra de nuestra magnífica asistenta, comprobaba una vez más que aquellos muchachos quinceañeros no se comportaban igual en ausencia del padre. Curiosamente, se mostraban más solícitos y caballerosos conmigo, incluso un poco coquetos, como si recayera sobre ellos la responsabilidad del pabellón masculino. Aquella noche pusieron ellos la mesa sin que yo se lo pidiera, también calentaron el horno y llevaron a la mesa la humeante bandeja.

—Me parece que no hay nada preparado para el segundo plato —comentó Hugo.

—Eso del segundo plato es una vieja tradición española completamente desfasada —respondí.

Teo empezó a partirse de risa y aprovechó para lanzar invectivas irónicas a su hermano.

—Estás pasado de moda, tío, cualquier día volverás a contar en pesetas o hasta en maravedíes.

—¡Eres imbécil! Si digo eso es porque la asistenta

cada vez pasa más de nosotros. Como últimamente Petra no está en casa, hace lo que le pasa por las narices.

Sin aviso previo, la ventolera había girado hacia mí.

—¿Cómo que no estoy en casa?

—¡Bueno, Petra! Tienes que reconocer que paras poco por aquí —remató Teo.

—¿Vais a hacerme reproches machistas?

Saltaron los dos a la vez.

—Noooo. Para nada.

—Estamos investigando un caso complicado. No es la primera vez que se me acumula el trabajo. No debería sorprenderos.

—Supongo que, aunque papá no esté, no querrás contarnos nada del caso.

—¿Cuántos años hace que estoy casada con vuestro padre y, por tanto, soy vuestra madrastra?

—No sé, muchos —contestó Hugo.

—Pues bueno, durante todos esos años que ni siquiera sabéis cuántos son lleváis dándome la misma vara.

—Y tú contestas siempre lo mismo: de los casos no se habla.

—Oye, madrastra, cuéntanos por lo menos qué demonio le pasa a papá —terció Teo el Temible.

—No tengo ni idea de a qué te refieres.

—Sí, todo ese rollo de que nos vayamos a vivir al campo porque la civilización es una mierda. Lleva un montón de tiempo con la misma historia.

—¡Ah, eso! No sé, me imagino que está un poco agobiado en su trabajo. Ya se le pasará.

—O sea, que a ti tampoco te emociona eso de

comprar una casita y todo el copón. Que sepas que nosotros estamos contigo, vivir en el campo debe de ser un coñazo terrible.

—Teo, el hecho de que tu padre esté ausente no significa que hables como un puto delincuente común.

Esta vez fue Hugo quien estalló en carcajadas, y Teo quien le atacó.

—Eres tonto del alma, tío.

Atajé aquella conversación que sin duda se dirigía hacia algún precipicio.

—Hay queso en la nevera como complemento nutricional. Lo he comprado en la tienda de la esquina. Aunque nunca esté en casa y no me preocupe por el bienestar hogareño, de vez en cuando vuelvo al redil.

Rieron ambos entre dientes y tuve la fortuna de que no me insultaran. Al contrario, ambos se pelearon por ir en busca del queso y, acabada la cena, lo recogieron todo y llenaron el lavaplatos.

Aquella velada aparentemente inocua no hizo sino acrecentar mi inquietud sobre el estado de ánimo de Marcos. De las palabras de los chicos se deducía que también ellos interpretaban los deseos bucólicos de su padre como una alteración de la normalidad. Su primera pregunta había sido: «¿Qué le pasa a papá?». Estaba claro, a papá le pasaba algo oculto que hacía aflorar en él una necesidad de cambio, quizá de huida. De todos modos, no iba a ponerme a pensarlo en aquel momento. Al día siguiente me esperaba una nueva jornada de incertidumbre y turbulencias laborales. El trabajo duro impide a veces las reflexiones sobre la vida privada; por eso hay gente que trabaja sin parar. Ese era mi caso en aquella ocasión. Me despedí de los chicos y me fui a dormir.

Debo reconocer que estaba preocupada por cuál sería el paso siguiente que debíamos dar en el caso del francés. Sin embargo, como ya venía siendo costumbre en aquella investigación maldita, fueron los hechos imprevistos los que marcaron la continuación.

Acababa de saludar a Garzón cuando recibimos el aviso. La policía municipal de L'Hospitalet había sido alertada de buena mañana. Una casa okupada presentaba todos los síntomas de un asalto vandálico. Cuando los agentes localizaron al que parecía ser el responsable de aquel lugar destrozado, este dio nuestro número de teléfono y pidió que fuéramos localizados.

Creo que ni los propios vándalos saqueadores de Roma se hubieran empleado tan a fondo destrozando aquel sitio. Estanterías esparcidas por el suelo, pósteres y otros adornos de la pared desgarrados, muebles partidos, sofás y sillas con la tapicería despanzurrada... Escenario de guerra total. A pesar del estropicio, los guardias municipales nos dijeron que, según sus apreciaciones, los asaltantes habían sido enormemente sigilosos. La cerradura había sido vulnerada con profesionalidad y para romper los cristales que les interesaba quitar de en medio habían puesto algún retal textil envolviendo el objeto contundente empleado. El oficial de la urbana comentó:

—Para mí, inspectora, que esto debe ser algún ajuste de cuentas entre ellos.

—¿Entre quiénes?

—Los propios okupas. Alguna facción enfrentada, alguna enemistad...

—Pero nunca habían dado problemas hasta el momento.

—No, eso es cierto. La alcaldesa les permitía quedarse aquí porque se portaban bien y no alteraban la paz del vecindario. Por lo menos mantenían el local, pero después de esto... Y además, piense, inspectora, que esta gente nunca es fiable del todo: hoy son todos muy amigos, pero al día siguiente igual se matan.

—Para ser un ajuste de cuentas han ido a por todas.

—Quizá buscaban algo. No es muy normal que hayan rajado los asientos y sacado el relleno también.

—Sí, quizá sí. ¿Dónde está el que usted llamó el responsable?

—En el bar de enfrente con uno de mis agentes. Se ha puesto como loco cuando ha visto este cuadro y lo he mandado para allá. Debo informarla de que le llaman el Tiras, tiene antecedentes por drogas y...

—Lo sé, oficial, lo sé. Es como un viejo conocido.

—¿Quiere que mis hombres hagan la inspección ocular?

—Se lo agradezco, pero viene en camino una dotación de la Científica. Esto tiene relación con un caso nuestro.

—Me lo imaginé, el Tiras insistía en hablar con usted.

—Luego se hacen cargo del operativo y precintan ustedes, ¿de acuerdo?

—Siempre a sus órdenes.

Mientras Garzón se quedaba departiendo con los municipales a la espera de la Científica, yo pasé al bar donde el Tiras se encontraba retenido. Al verme, dio un salto hacia mí parecido al de un jaguar. El agente que lo custodiaba tuvo que volar para interceptarlo. Gritaba como una bestia de raza indefinida.

—¿Ha visto, inspectora, ha visto la consecuencia de su visita tan amable del otro día?

Le hice señal al policía para que lo soltara y saliera del bar.

—Pero, inspectora... —replicó el agente.

—Puede irse. Este caballero y yo vamos a tomar un café. —Después me dirigí al alterado caballero y le señalé la silla desde la que acababa de proyectarse—. ¡Siéntate!

Me obedeció. Pedí dos cafés al propietario, que observaba la escena desde la barra con cara de «a mí que me registren». Cuando estuvimos servidos le pregunté al Tiras, que milagrosamente aguardaba en silencio:

—Ahora muy tranquilito, sin chillar ni armar follón, vas a contarme lo que ha pasado.

La picadura de la furia lo hizo gritar de nuevo.

—¿Yo?, ¿que le cuente yo lo que ha pasado?

—Si vuelves a levantar la voz, te mando veinticuatro horas a un calabozo por resistencia a la autoridad. Y no voy de farol.

Echó el azucarillo en su taza y revolvió la cucharilla con tal fuerza que derramó casi todo el líquido sobre el platillo y la mesa. Yo, aparentando una calma que no sentía, ordené que le trajeran un nuevo café. El camarero pasó un paño húmedo para enjugar el pequeño desastre y colocó la consumición frente a él. Aquella maniobra del segundo café lo desconcertó y le dio tiempo para tranquilizarse. Al volver a hablar, el tono de desesperación había sustituido al de cólera.

—Inspectora, si me pregunta qué ha pasado es como si se cachondeara de mí. ¡Usted ha visto lo mismo que yo: me han destrozado el local!

—¿Alguna idea de quién ha podido ser?

—¡Pues claro que tengo una idea! Ha sido esa maldita zorra de la francesa.

—Muy seguro te veo. Me dijiste que no tenías nada pendiente con ella.

—Yo no, pero usted sí. Vinieron usted y el otro poli con su foto y días después me mandan el garito al carajo. No es casualidad, ¿o le parece que sí?

—De acuerdo contigo, no es casualidad. ¿Qué ha pasado?, ¿por qué han destrozado el garito?, ¿por qué deduces que ha sido la francesa?, ¿es que tienes información de que anda por aquí?

Negaba una y otra vez con la cabeza. Parecía sinceramente abatido. Decidí cambiar de estrategia, era posible que no estuviera mintiendo.

—De acuerdo, está bien. Nadie te ha avisado de que la francesa anda por aquí. No sabes quién ha hecho trizas la casa. No sabes nada de nada. Te creo. Vamos a enfocarlo de otro modo. ¿A ti qué te parece que ha podido pasar?

—¡Y yo qué sé lo que andan ustedes buscando!

—Olvídate de eso. Imagínate que aún estás en activo.

—¿En activo?

—En activo en el mundo de la droga.

—Pues empezamos mal porque...

—¡Basta ya, contesta de una vez! Estoy perdiendo demasiado tiempo.

—Vale, de acuerdo, siga, pero todo son suposiciones suyas, ¿eh?

—Suposiciones, sí. Estás en el mundo de la droga y una buena mañana te encuentras la casa en las condiciones que hemos visto. ¿Qué pensarías que ha pasado?

—Pensaría que algún hijoputa anda buscando algo.

—No se te ocurriría pensar que ha sido una venganza, ni un ajuste de cuentas ni un aviso. ¿Es así?

—El descojono que han montado es más bien de buscar algo. Los sofás reventados, los cuadros por el suelo para ver si había algo detrás..., como si esperaran encontrar alijos o pasta. La venganza o el aviso van de otro rollo, no hace falta destruirlo todo. A veces escribiendo en una pared con tinta roja: «Vamos a por ti» o «Esto les pasa a los traidores» ya te han dicho lo que tenían que decirte.

—Comprendo.

—Para mí que los siguieron a usted y a su ayudante. Y ustedes les señalaron el sitio donde debían buscar. A lo mejor es que ustedes y ellos buscan lo mismo, ¿no?

—Eso es algo que no te interesa.

—De acuerdo, a mí lo que me interesa es que me han liquidado la casa y en esa casa hemos hecho una gran labor social.

—Cierto, y habéis fumado vuestros buenos porros y habéis tenido un club privado donde reuniros a placer sin pagar un euro. Pero yo que tú no sufriría, puedes apuntarte al voluntariado y te darán otra labor social que llevar a cabo: comedores de gente sin recursos, albergues para los sin techo, plantas envasadoras para el Banco de Alimentos, visitas a ancianos solitarios..., hasta podrás escoger.

—Muy graciosa, inspectora, muy graciosa. ¡Y todo por culpa del jodido teniente Montilla, que no tiene ni puta idea de nada y los mandó a mí como podía haberlos enviado al Colón de la estatua!

—Vete ya, Tiras. Tienes mi teléfono. Si te enteras de algo, me llamas, y si me ocultas algo y me entero, te aseguro que te joderé vivo. Irás a parar a manos del teniente Montilla, no te digo más.

Enfiló la puerta del bar rezongando y con la cabeza baja. Lo llamé. Giró la cabeza.

—Espera un momento, ¿por qué te llaman el Tiras? Tengo curiosidad.

—Porque siempre decía: «Te quitaré la piel a tiras si no haces lo que digo». Pero eran otros tiempos, cuando yo tenía poder y era malo de verdad. Desde que soy buena gente todo me va como el culo. Ganas me dan de hacerme delincuente otra vez.

—Recuerda, Tiras: ancianos solitarios, hombres sin techo..., ahí está tu futuro.

—¡Y la madre que lo parió!

Salió del bar con gesto de mal humor. Yo fui a pagar los cafés y salí también. La calle parecía un desfile de uniformes. Nuestros hombres ya habían llegado y los de la Local no se habían marchado todavía, incluso me pareció que se habían unido unos cuantos más al grupo. Me acerqué al subinspector.

—¿Todo en orden, Garzón?

—Todo en orden.

—En ese caso ya podemos largarnos.

Como la casa estaba en el centro de la ciudad, habíamos aparcado nuestro coche en una de las calles no peatonales, a unos diez minutos de allí. Caminando, le expliqué detalladamente a mi subalterno la conversación con el Tiras. De pronto, Garzón me interrumpió de un modo insólito.

—¡Hostia! —exclamó.

Nos hallábamos al inicio de la calle donde esperaba nuestro coche. Miré hacia donde estaban fijos los ojos de Garzón y distinguí perfectamente de dónde venía su sobresalto. El cristal de una de las ventanillas laterales del vehículo estaba hecho añicos. Apretamos el paso y, al llegar, descubrimos a dos colegialas que estaban apoyadas en la pared. Abrí el coche y lo inspeccioné detenidamente mientras Garzón se dirigía a las chicas.

—¿Qué ha pasado aquí?

—Vimos a un hombre que corría y cuando pasamos al lado del coche, la ventana estaba rota. Supongo que ha sido él.

La otra intervino enseguida.

—Yo he llamado por mi móvil a la policía y me han dicho que todas las patrullas estaban ocupadas, pero que vendrían en cuanto pudieran.

—¿Cómo era el hombre que visteis?

Se miraron entre ellas, encogiéndose de hombros.

—Estábamos lejos, yo no lo vi bien.

—Yo tampoco, pero creo que era rubio.

—¡Qué va, tía, era moreno!

—¿Era joven, viejo, alto, bajo?

—Bajito —dijo una. La otra no la contradijo, pero añadió:

—No sé si era viejo, pero muy joven seguro que no era porque llevaba zapatos y no deportivas.

—Yo no me fijé.

—¿Y cuándo ha pasado eso?

—Hace veinte minutos o así.

—Una hora por lo menos, tía. No sé cómo cuentas el tiempo.

Parecía casi imposible que se pusieran de acuerdo, por lo que su voluntarioso testimonio carecía de cualquier valor. Dejamos que se fueran y Garzón anuló por teléfono la alerta que la chica había dado.

—¿A usted le parece lógico que un tío vaya arreándonos pedradas sin ton ni son? ¿Qué son estos traficantes, una panda de tarados tan imbéciles como para arriesgarse a que los cacen con tal de jodernos un rato?

—No sé qué decirle, inspectora, pero si lo que quieren es jodernos, lo han conseguido a base de bien. Verá la cara que se le pone al comisario cuando se entere de que nos han roto el coche.

El comisario no nos abroncó en exceso por el vidrio. Creo que su benevolencia se debía a que no lograba entender nada, con lo cual formábamos un trío perfecto en materia de incomprensión. Alguien se dedicaba a apedrearnos. Muy bien, con la primera piedra podía esgrimirse un argumento bíblico: quien la tiró estaba libre de pecado. Pero la segunda ya era otra historia. Habían escogido nuestro coche no por obra del azar; allí había pecado y no venial.

Coronas renunció a hacernos preguntas. Me dio la impresión de que nuestro caso empezaba a incordiarlo, siempre le sucedía con los casos que se enquistan y no avanzan claramente hacia una solución. Pero no todo fue fácil en aquella conversación. No nos hizo reproches, pero lo que nos anunció fue muy poco gracioso.

—El juez dice que no puede mantener más tiempo vigente la orden de que todos los feriantes del día del crimen permanczcan juntos. Ya no existe justificación.

—Pues es una contrariedad —encontré rápidamente el sinónimo aceptable de *putada*.

Aun siendo políticamente correcta, la réplica impacientó al comisario.

—¿Han encontrado alguna prueba en alguna de las caravanas, hay algún sospechoso? No, ¿verdad? Si se ven obligados a hacer algún interrogatorio a uno de los feriantes, convocan al interesado y en paz. Ya no más interrogatorios en comandita.

—Era práctico tenerlos a todos juntos —se atrevió a soltar Garzón.

—Era cómodo, querrá decir, pero también es práctico el teléfono móvil, que por eso se inventó. Tienen los teléfonos de toda esa gente, ¿no? Pues les llaman y santas pascuas. ¡Ah, y de paso a ver si les cuentan quién anda pegándoles cantazos por las esquinas!

Responder con un «sí, señor» a aquello no tenía mucho sentido, de modo que emprendimos una prudente retirada antes de que aumentara la turbulencia de las aguas.

15

Nuestra asistenta cogió la gripe. «En mala hora —pensé—, con todo lo que está cayéndome encima.» Después me di cuenta de que cualquier hora hubiera sido mala y de que sobre mí caía sólo lo habitual: trabajo y vida privada. Había que llenar la despensa con urgencia, esa había sido la inspiración de todos mis malos humores. Si se lo decía a Marcos corría el riesgo de una respuesta ambigua: «¿No podemos resistir ni unos días más?», o claramente negativa: «Pues yo ando muy liado, pide las cosas por internet», o quizá tan voluntariosa como inútil: «Espera sólo un poco y vamos los dos juntos». No, ni hablar. Para ir a un supermercado con Marcos había que pensárselo más que para enrolarse en una expedición antártica del siglo pasado. Íbamos provistos de dos carritos. Él se paseaba por todas las estanterías del local y sólo iba cargando las pijadas que más le apetecían: cerveza de importación, latas de aperitivos, quesos franceses, frutos secos exóticos... De vez en cuando le daba un ramalazo de responsabilidad hogareña y venía hasta mi carrito para preguntarme si había comprado vinagre, como si el vinagre fuera un producto básico sin el que una familia normal no puede celebrar ni un solo ágape. No, mejor iría yo sola. Salí a la calle y descubrí que Marcos no había cogido su coche. Perfecto, lo emplearía yo usando mi juego de llaves.

Un supermercado es un lugar donde no iría a pasar mis últimos años, donde no invitaría a mis amigos para una celebración, donde no me quedaría acurrucada en un rincón ronroneando de placer. Más bien, al contrario, me parece un espacio siniestro del que tengo ganas de salir segundos después de haber entrado. Todo es complicado: escoger la marca de un producto entre los miles que existen y todas en envases que se parecen entre sí. ¡Y leer más que en una biblioteca!, esas malditas etiquetas por las que te enteras de que unas simples sardinas en su lata pueden estar embutidas en tomate, en escabeche, en aceite, llevar o no llevar picante, estar o no estar aderezadas con limón. Por no hablar de la nueva moda de las intolerancias, que añaden un montón de paquetes «sin». Sin lactosa, sin fructosa, sin gluten, sin azúcares añadidos, sin sal, sin aditivos, sin alérgenos. ¡Sin nada, desnudos como su fabricante los trajo al mundo! Para mí es una odisea no equivocarse.

Al final, fui metiendo lo que recordaba haber visto por casa sin demasiado cuidado ni discernimiento. Pedí en la caja que lo enviaran a mi domicilio y me dirigí al parking abierto con el que contaba el establecimiento. Se me cayeron las llaves al suelo. Alguien había rayado el capó de mi coche, es decir, el de Marcos. Era un arañazo profundo y largo, sin duda producido por un destornillador u otro elemento metálico parecido, esgrimido con fuerza y decisión por una mano bien firme.

Miré alrededor, no estaba muy concurrido. Varias filas de coches más lejos, una señora mayor metía paquetes en el portaequipajes de su pequeño coche. Inútil preguntarle. Me encontraba estupefacta, incapaz de pensar nada con claridad. ¿Qué era aquello, una gamberrada recurrente? De ningún modo podía estar relacionado con el caso, absurdo pensarlo, pero lo intrigante y preocupante es que nadie hubiera debido conocer o identificar el coche de Marcos como mío, de modo que alguien rondaba mi casa y me había seguido. Como los descerebrados reincidentes no suelen perseguir a sus víctimas, no resultaba extemporáneo pensar que quizá aquellos ataques *quasi* infantiles contra mi parque móvil sí estaban relacionados con el caso.

Llamé a Marcos para advertirlo del siniestro. No se inmutó demasiado, probablemente porque ni siquiera se enteró. Había salido de una reunión para responder al teléfono y yo notaba sus respuestas flotando en una nube de vaguedad. Mejor para mí, hubiera sido difícil explicarle algo que yo misma no llegaba a entender.

En comisaría se lo conté a Garzón, que se puso frenético. Empezó a hacer aspavientos frente a mí.

—¡Tiene que dar parte inmediatamente a la superioridad!

—No veo por qué.

—En primer lugar, porque tendrán que ponerle vigilancia en su casa. Y en segundo, para que la comisaría se haga cargo de la reparación del capó. Si quiere, aviso yo mismo.

—¡Ni hablar! Usé un coche privado para atender un asunto privado. Además, Marcos tiene seguro a todo riesgo. Y en cuanto a poner vigilancia en mi casa... ¡olvídese, Fermín! Aunque me hubiera amenazado el propio Satanás, preferiría correr el riesgo. Paso de que anden dándome el coñazo todo el día.

—Es usted cabezota como una mula. ¿Para qué sirve entonces el servicio policial?

—Cuanto menos acudamos al servicio policial, más tranquilos viviremos. Y hablando de servicios, necesito que pase usted notificación al grupo de feriantes: ya pueden irse cada uno adonde les pase por las narices. Tenemos los teléfonos de todos ellos, ¿cierto?

—Sí, no falta ninguno. ¿Deben informar de sus diferentes destinos?

—No será necesario.

—Entonces, inspectora...

Se quedó mirándome como una atenta lechuza.

—Entonces, ¿qué?

—¿No doy aviso de que le pongan vigilancia por si están siguiéndola?

Hice un gesto bastante brusco con la mano. No estaba segura de si mi subalterno se preocupaba seriamente por mí o si se limitaba a intentar sacarme de mis casillas. Creo que era lo segundo, porque cuando abandonaba el despacho observé una sonrisilla bajo su bigote.

Pregunté a mi colega el inspector Nogales si tenía noticia de algún grupo u organización que se dedicara a tirar piedras por ahí a policías, funcionarios o ciudadanos en general. Mi interés no le sorprendió en absoluto. Podía ser un grupo de cualquier inspiración: ecologistas, antiabortistas en acción, bandas latinas para dar avisos, Incívicos sin Fronteras... Pero no hubo suerte, no sabía nada de acciones vandálicas puntuales. A pesar de ser el hombre más informado de la comisaría sobre temas de desórdenes públicos, quiso cerciorarse del todo y me llevó a su ordenador. Buscamos durante casi una hora. Nadie había denunciado rotura de cristales en su casa o negocio ni tampoco siniestros en su vehículo.

—Gracias, Pablo. Te invito a tomar un café en La Jarra de Oro.

Allá fuimos. Nogales era agradable y, normalmente, me gustaba charlar con él. No se quejaba de los abusos de los superiores, ni de la escasez del sueldo, ni de lo complicado que se presenta el trabajo en la actualidad. Empleaba siempre un tono neutro y huía de los tópicos profesionales.

—Lamento no haber podido ayudarte en lo de las piedras.

—Parece puro cachondeo, ¿verdad? Estamos llegando al mundo futuro, al ciberespacio, el metaverso y todo el copón, pero hay gente que sigue pegando pedradas como en las cavernas.

—La gente está cabreada, Petra, y en el fondo no sabe muy bien contra qué. ¿Los políticos, la dureza de la vida, las desigualdades? Es posible, pero yo creo que estamos cabreados contra nosotros mismos por no saber reaccionar. Tenemos la sensación de que todo lo que sabíamos ya no vale, y de que no tenemos ni puta idea de qué es lo que debemos aprender. Así que vamos dando tumbos por el mundo y cuando el cabreo se hace más intenso: pedrada al de al lado y en paz.

Me eché a reír. Bebimos nuestro café un poco más reconfortados por tener al menos un diagnóstico del desastre general. Al salir a la calle, a Nogales se le ocurrió preguntar:

—¿Cómo vuelves a casa esta noche, quieres que te preste mi coche? Hoy ya no lo necesito para el trabajo.

—Iré en taxi o en metro, no te preocupes.

—Yo voy a ir al cine con mi mujer. Llévate el mío. Mañana lo traes a comisaría y ya está, problema solucionado.

Al final me dejé tentar. Pensaba pasar toda la jornada en el despacho, redactando los informes de aquel maldito caso que Garzón y yo habíamos empezado a llamar «el berenjenal», y como saldría tarde, asegurarme un coche oficial era una garantía de llegar a casa con tiempo de preparar la cena. Nos acercamos hasta donde había aparcado y abrió con el mando a distancia, de modo que las luces destellaron. Volvió a cerrar y depositó las llaves en mi mano con una reverencia humorística.

Me encerré en comisaría con siete llaves y empecé aquel trabajo burocrático que nunca me había gustado, mucho menos si entre los hechos que reseñar no había ni uno solo a favor de una próxima resolución final. Cerca de las nueve de la noche, exhausta y deprimida, cerré el ordenador. Bajé a la calle y recordé la oferta de Nogales con respecto a su coche. Sí, allí estaba, muy cerca de la esquina. Cuando me disponía a ir hacia él, me di cuenta de que las llaves se habían quedado encima de mi mesa. Intenté no enfadarme demasiado conmigo misma, regresé, tomé las dichosas llaves y volví a bajar. El policía de guardia sonrió:

—¿Ahora sí lo tiene todo, inspectora?

—Ahora sí.

Mientras me acercaba al coche, que se encontraba a una cierta distancia, fui distinguiendo un bulto inconcreto en la bruma nocturna. El bulto se acercó al vehículo y quedó de pie en uno de los lados. Me paré en seco. Era un hombre y estaba manipulando algo en la portezuela. Eché a correr a toda la velocidad que me fue posible. El hombre se alertó y huyó, cogió la calle perpendicular a la de la comisaría. Lo seguí a grandes zancadas y, afortunadamente, las del hombre no tenían la misma envergadura. Al cabo de unos metros, lo alcancé, tomándolo por un hombro. No se volvió contra mí, no hizo nada por escapar. La fuerza de mi impacto contra su cuerpo nos desplazó a ambos con varios pasos inseguros. Lo miré a la cara. Era Bob.

—¡Levanta las manos! —le grité—. Ponte contra la pared con las piernas abiertas.

En vez de obedecerme, Bob repetía:

—¡Inspectora, inspectora, soy yo! ¡No me haga nada, por favor!

Ante mi desconcierto por aquella reacción, tiró a mis pies un objeto pequeño que llevaba en la mano. Era un destornillador.

—Perdóneme, inspectora, por favor, se lo ruego. Yo sólo soy un pobre hombre, sólo eso.

Llegó el policía de guardia que me había oído gritar.

—¿Me llevo a este hombre, inspectora?

—No, creo que ha sido un malentendido. Puede volver a su lugar.

Se marchó sin tenerlas todas consigo. Mientras tanto, Bob me daba las gracias casi de rodillas.

—¡Gracias, inspectora, gracias! Es usted buena y comprensiva.

—¡Para de decir gilipolleces! Ahora mismo vamos a ver qué coño le has hecho al coche.

—Nada, ni lo he tocado, Petra, se lo juro por Dios.

Lo llevé hasta el coche, cogido fuertemente por el brazo y comprobé que decía la verdad. La portezuela estaba intacta.

—¿Lo ve, inspectora, lo ve? Yo no he hecho nada malo.

—Hoy no te ha dado tiempo, pero lo has hecho otras veces y quiero saber por qué.

—Estaba loco, inspectora. Mi vida ya no vale nada, créame. ¿Puedo marcharme?

—Loco estás ahora si piensas que voy a dejarte ir. Vamos a mi despacho, tendremos una larga conversación.

—No, inspectora, no me detenga, se lo suplico.

—No voy a detenerte de momento.

—Pero la comisaría... Yo lo he hecho mal, inspectora, eso lo sé.

Cuando el policía me vio entrar con mi acompañante, pareció quedarse más tranquilo, no había acabado de tragarse aquello del malentendido. Recorrimos los pasillos en silencio y cerré mi puerta tras él.

—¿Ves, Bob? Aquí podemos hablar tranquilamente. Ya no queda casi nadie en el edificio. Puedes tranquilizarte. Voy a traerte un té de la máquina, así te da tiempo a serenarte un poco.

Mi nuevo tono conciliador hizo que aflojara un poco la visible tensión que lo atenazaba.

Probó el vasito de té, cerró los ojos e inmediatamente se echó a llorar sin hacer ruido. Recordé las circunstancias en las que lo habíamos conocido, aquel larguísimo interrogatorio en el que Bob hizo de plañidera casi hasta el final. Tendría que armarme de paciencia. Intenté consolarlo con las expresiones habituales, pero ninguna de ellas funcionó. Después de veinte minutos de desconsuelo, decidí abrir el ordenador y ponerme a trabajar. Aquel detalle de insensibilidad por mi parte fue apaciguando su llanto. Por fin, se sonó la nariz y dijo:

—Perdóneme, inspectora. No he podido evitarlo. Es que estoy muy mal, y soy un hombre que llevo el corazón en la mano y a quien es muy fácil lastimar.

Recordé también que, después de la tendencia al lloriqueo, la segunda característica de Bob era su desenfrenada capacidad oratoria, y como no me veía con ánimos de soportar veinte minutos más en silencio, lo interrumpí.

—Bob, dejemos los temas personales y pasemos a la acción inmediata. ¿Qué pretendía hacer en el coche con un destornillador?

—Rayarle la puerta a base de bien; pero como últimamente va cambiando usted de coche, no estaba muy seguro, dudé y por eso me pescó. Un segundo más y ya me hubiera largado.

Me quedé de una pieza. ¿Quería más concreción? Hice esfuerzos por contenerme, pero no lo conseguí.

—¿Y se puede saber por qué coño anda jodiéndome los coches? Porque supongo que del resto de los ataques también es usted el responsable.

Su cara, un tanto descompuesta, se tensó, y envalentonado como un niño alzó la voz.

—¡Pues sí, he sido yo! He estado siguiéndolos, sobre todo a usted, y he hecho todas las burradas que he podido.

—¿Incluyendo la luna rota del escaparate?

—¡Sí, también fui yo, estoy hasta las pelotas!

—¡Ah, muy bien, maravilloso! ¡La sociedad en pleno se lo agradece! Y dígame, ¿a qué se debe que sea yo la beneficiaria de su conducta delictiva?

Por primera vez vi reflejada en su rostro una actitud grave, adulta.

—Me han destrozado la caravana, que es mi medio de vida. El seguro se ha desentendido y sólo me paga una pequeña parte de los destrozos. Imposible arrancar de nuevo. No puedo pedir un préstamo porque no tengo nada para garantizarlo. Estoy en la ruina.

—¿Y de eso tengo yo la culpa?

—El subinspector y usted han ido siguiendo los pasos del asesino de Christophe, sin encontrarlo, por cierto. ¿Y yo qué? ¿Les ha importado algo mi desgracia, que perdiera a mi socio, que perdiera mi querida caravana? Nada, ni se han ocupado en saber quién me ha jodido la vida. Siento mucha rabia, mucha, y la he descargado contra ustedes.

—¿Tirando piedras y estropeando carrocerías? Pero ¿no se da cuenta de que lo que dice es absurdo?

—Puede que sí, pero lo hecho hecho está. No he tenido fortuna en la vida, inspectora, aunque me reciclé tuve dificultades: letras que pagar, ninguna novia, un buen socio pero que siempre estaba metido en líos con mujeres. Y ahora, la traca final.

—La traca final es la denuncia que le va a caer por sus actividades de delincuente.

Me miró, sereno y triste.

—¿Va a denunciarme, inspectora?

Me cogió desprevenida. No lo sabía en realidad.

—¿Y usted va a seguir haciendo gilipolleces?

—No, ya no. Ni siquiera veo que a usted le importen demasiado los coches, ¿para qué seguir? ¿Va a detenerme o me puedo marchar?

—Ya pensaré si lo denuncio o no.

—Ya sabe dónde puede encontrarme. No me he movido del hotel al que usted vino a interrogarme, parece que de eso hace un siglo ya. Me quedaré ahí hasta que se me acabe el dinero que tengo en el banco. Después, dormiré en algún albergue o en la calle, lo mismo me da. Ahora sí que he perdido toda la rabia, y de paso, las ganas de luchar. Ahora estoy bien.

Le dejé marchar, observando su pequeña figura derrotada. Una víctima colateral de la historia, como tantas veces sucede en los aledaños de un asesinato: alguien muere y esa muerte rompe el equilibrio de su entorno humano, en pocas ocasiones para bien. ¿Por qué no lo detenía cuando era evidente que debía hacerlo? No lo sé ni siquiera ahora. Supongo que me inspiraría piedad, aunque a medida que voy envejeciendo tiendo a pensar que algunas vidas no tienen remedio y es inútil sentir pena por ellas.

Naturalmente, cuando al día siguiente le conté al subinspector lo que había pasado se echó las manos a la cabeza y me puso de hoja de perejil. No se recató: ¿me había vuelto Teresa de Calcuta, se me había licuado el cerebro, estaba en vías de lograr la santidad? ¿Un medio loco se lía a pedradas contra nosotros para perpetrar una absurda venganza y lo único que se me ocurría era dejar que se fuera de rositas? Intenté inútilmente hacerle comprender mis razones.

—Piense en ese pobre desgraciado al que la suerte siempre le enseñó la popa. Un primer gran fracaso y logra reiniciar una segunda oportunidad. De acuerdo, pero no se come una rosca amorosa. Mientras su socio liga hasta con las piedras, él lleva la responsabilidad del negocio, se esfuerza, se desmelena y un buen día, sin comerlo ni beberlo, se cargan a su francés y, encima, le revientan su adorada caravana. Me da pena, qué quiere que le diga. Yo no tengo un corazón de esparto como tiene usted.

—No, usted lo tiene de oro, por eso le toca pagar.

—No voy a pagar ni un euro. Usted tampoco, de manera que ya podemos dejar el tema.

—¿Y la ley?, ¿dónde queda la ley? El que la hace la paga, ¿no, inspectora?

—Yo creo que este tío la ha pagado con anticipación.

Hice la compra de víveres aquella misma tarde. Me esforcé, intentando pensar qué hacía falta en nuestra casa. Una vez más constaté las dificultades de hacer dos cosas al mismo tiempo con un solo cerebro. Quizá alguien con gran capacidad..., pero no era mi caso. El trabajo de investigación es absorbente. Claro que a Marcos le ocurría igual cuando llegaba su turno. En realidad había que cargarles aquel enfadoso asunto de la intendencia a las imperfecciones del ser humano. ¿Para qué tanto comer? Hubiera sido mejor necesitar menos para vivir. Somos una máquina diseñada con fallos garrafales.

Suspiré, hacía tiempo que no me sentía tan deprimida con respecto a mi trabajo. Quizá por eso intentaba llenar mis pensamientos con protestas domésticas. ¿Había llegado el día en que no fuéramos capaces de resolver un caso? Había muchas probabilidades de que así fuera.

Marcos, por el contrario, parecía trabajar a todo tren y plena satisfacción. Salía de casa temprano por la mañana y no le veía el pelo hasta la noche, si es que algún asunto no lo retenía más allá de la hora de cenar. Ya que me encontraba en un momento de reflexiones negativas en el campo laboral, aproveché para extender ese talante hacia lo privado. A lo mejor el anhelo súbito de mi marido por vivir en el campo tenía más lecturas que la literal, pensé. Quizá, sabiendo que yo no compartía sus deseos de cambio, lo que pretendía era librarse de mí. No, demasiado grosera como interpretación; algo más sofisticado podía ser: le apretaba el traje del matrimonio, se le había quedado pequeño de tanto usarlo, o grande, eso da igual. El caso era que el patrón actual ya no era de su talla.

Sin duda lo indicado pasaba por una conversación seria con él. Sin embargo, me había prometido a mí misma no hacer nunca ñoñas protestas de amor al estilo clásico y ramplón: «Ya no me quieres», «Te noto distanciado de mí», «¿Qué nos ha pasado?». Me parecía una indignidad, un papel que no estaba dispuesta a representar. En un matrimonio de media-larga duración es absolutamente necesario que, aparte de la evolución amorosa, se haya desarrollado una amistad. Y bien, ¿a qué amigo le haces reproches íntimos sobre sus sentimientos?

Aquella misma noche, aunque estaba muerta de sueño, esperé a que Marcos llegara, con la intención de charlar. Di varios cabezazos sobre el libro que leía, de modo que no tuve prácticamente tiempo de elaborar una estrategia para abordar la conversación. Sobre las once, tal y como había avisado por teléfono con anterioridad, apareció mi señor esposo como si fuera el mismísimo Miguel Strogoff después de hacer los recados. Se lanzó de espaldas sobre el sofá, a riesgo de desnucarse, y expiró, por poco no definitivamente.

—¿Listo para ser enterrado? —le pregunté.

—Siempre que sea en un panteón...

—¿Has cenado?

—Sí, han traído unos sándwiches a la reunión.

—Estás trabajando con más intensidad que nunca.

—Proyectar una urbanización entera es complicado. Y no te digo nada de las reuniones que me veo obligado a mantener con el ingeniero, los propietarios, el ayuntamiento..., un condenado follón. Por otra parte, es estimulante. Lo difícil estimula, siempre ha sido así.

—Pues vivir conmigo debe de estar chupado.

Al principio, no lo cogió. Necesitó unos segundos para bajar la vista hacia mí desde el techo donde la tenía posada desmayadamente.

—No sé si te he entendido bien. ¿Podrías bajar un par de grados el termostato de la ironía?

—Lo apagaré del todo. Lo que quiero decir es que a veces tengo la impresión de que estás harto de nuestra vida en común.

Sintió la picadura de una avispa. Se enderezó.

—¡Coño!, ¿y qué te lleva a pensar una cosa así?

Intenté que mi voz sonara neutra y casual.

—Bueno, ya sabes, tus proyectos de vivir en el campo... A veces la aspiración de cambiar la forma esconde las ganas de cambiar el fondo.

—Ahora te diría que bajaras un par de grados la filosofía.

—A ver, Marcos, tan tonto no eres. Quieres largarte a vivir fuera de la ciudad, aunque a mí me repatee la idea. Eso me hace pensar que quizá no suspires por estar entre árboles y pajaritos, sino que estás deseando librarte de mí.

—¡Pero, Petra!, te he explicado cien veces los porqués de...

—¡A mí nunca me explica nadie las cosas cien veces! ¿Y sabes por qué? Porque suelo entenderlas a la primera.

—¡Ah, sí, fantástico, genial! Me inclino ante tu clarividencia. Eres capaz de interpretar los más ocultos pensamientos de una mente.

—Si esa mente es la tuya, sí.

—¿Te das cuenta de lo poco que nos aporta esta conversación?

—Si aporta poco es porque tú no hablas con claridad. ¿Por qué no pruebas a hacerlo?

—Muy bien, lo intentaré: la vida en la ciudad me agobia. Punto final.

—Antes no te agobiaba, ¿por qué ahora sí?

—Porque me hago mayor, porque evoluciono, porque soy permeable a los cambios sociales y las ciudades cada vez son más agobiantes. En fin, Petra, por un montón de razones, todas de bastante solidez intelectual.

Notaba cómo luchaba contra el enfado que sin duda estaba sintiendo, cómo se esforzaba en sonar sereno. Yo no me esforcé lo más mínimo para contestar con evidente tensión.

—Sí, eres un prodigio de sensatez y tu proyecto de vivir en el campo no puede ser más ajustado a tus virtudes naturales y a tu lógica evolución existencial. Sin embargo, te comunico que mi inmovilismo aberrante no pasa por ese plan.

En ese momento Marcos dejó de mirarme. Fijó la vista en sus manos y declaró:

—Pues es una pena. Ya he comprado un terreno con casa incluida cerca de la urbanización en la que estoy trabajando.

—¿Se trata de algo definitivo?

Su tono fue entonces más suave, menos tajante.

—No, por supuesto que no. Es simplemente una inversión. Si no te gusta la localización, se puede vender y buscar otro lugar. Además, hay que renovar la casa de arriba abajo y ahí puedes intervenir tú. De momento se trata de una simple inversión que no nos compromete a nada.

—Gracias por darme tantas opciones.

Sin añadir ni una palabra más, me fui a la cama, aunque no pude dormir.

16

Di vueltas por el despacho, recorrí la comisaría por todas partes sin seguir ningún rumbo y acabé en la máquina de café, donde a los cinco minutos apareció Garzón.

—En busca de un poco de energía, ¿eh?

—Falta me hace.

—Pues a mí no. Hoy tengo uno de esos días en los que podría enfrentarme a un león.

—No creo que encuentre ninguno por aquí.

Sopló el líquido caliente de su vasito.

—Estos putos vasos te queman los dedos al cabo de tres segundos de sostenerlos. Están mal diseñados. Cuando yo empecé de policía no había máquinas para el café. Teníamos una señora que se paseaba con un carrito por todas las mesas. En el carrito llevaba café y té, y tacitas de loza, de las de verdad. Era la misma señora que hacía la limpieza. ¡Ah, una mujer maravillosa! El café que nos servía era tan malo como este, pero nos trataba con mucho cariño, con toda dedicación, como una auténtica madre.

—Seguro que le pagaban una miseria.

—Sí, pero como a nosotros nos pagaban otra,

todo quedaba en tablas. Además, a la señora seguro que le daban un plus por el trabajo de los cafés, mientras que si siguiera aquí, por culpa de la máquina, cobraría el sueldo tasado y en paz.

Observé a mi compañero. ¿De verdad le preocupaban aquellas cosas? Lo dudaba mucho, eran simples comentarios sin más. A Garzón no había nada que le preocupara en exceso: ni el trabajo, ni el dinero, ni el amor, ni siquiera la salud. Era como si tuviera un pozo secreto de felicidad del que iba sacando remanentes. Supongo que en el fondo del pozo había conformidad, ausencia de ambiciones, paz interior y un pasado siempre peor que el presente. Garzón era un budista con una pátina castiza. Sí, pero aunque hubiera vivido una época de pobreza material, su tiempo fue menos complicado que el mío. En su vida las posibilidades de elección eran pocas, no había tenido que enfrentarse a decisiones como el divorcio, la filosofía vital, la presión laboral y, además, no era una mujer. Yo desde joven tuve la sensación de ser libre para poder elegir: los estudios, el amor, la forma en la que quería vivir. Eso genera siempre contradicciones, y de las contradicciones nacen las dudas y, en último término, la frustración. Yo había deseado ser una mujer emancipada, ganarme la vida por mí misma y, al mismo tiempo, no quería renunciar a los deleites amorosos, a la vida en pareja, a ocupar un lugar reconocible en la sociedad. Lo había conseguido, mal que bien, durante un largo tiempo. Había rectificado aquí y allá a lo largo de los años, dos divorcios son testigos de ello. Pero ahora, cuando todo parecía remansado y colocado en su sitio, volvía a surgir la incertidumbre, la vacilación. ¿Debía plegarme a las aspiraciones de Marcos, irme con él a vivir al campo, aun sabiendo que ese no era mi deseo?, ¿aun estando segura de que eso perjudicaría mi trabajo? ¿Cuál era si no la alternativa?, ¿abandonarlo, poner punto final a nuestra relación? Y en el fondo, ¿era aquella cuestión tan importante, no estaba en realidad reaccionando con una enorme dosis de narcisismo y lo único que me preocupaba era que mi marido pusiera por delante de mí esa paz que teóricamente sólo le brindaba el campo? Volví a mirar a Garzón, que ahora bebía su café a sorbitos cortos y apurados.

—¿Usted sigue enamorado de Beatriz?

Pegó un resoplido que le llevó casi al atragantamiento. Me miró como si tuviera en llamas la cabellera y soltó muy seguro:

—¿Yo?, del todo, total, pues claro. Nos llevamos muy bien.

—¿Qué haría usted si de repente ella le dijera que quiere que se vayan a vivir al campo?

—¿A qué campo?

—¡Coño, Garzón, al campo en general, fuera de Barcelona, dejar su piso y comprar una casa fuera de la ciudad!

—¡Uy, no sé yo! Beatriz es muy urbanita. Ya sabe las cosas que le gustan para su tiempo libre: merendar con sus amigas, irse de compras, a una exposición, al Liceo...

—No le estoy hablando de su caso en concreto. Le pido que se plantee la hipótesis, la posibilidad.

—¿Y por qué voy a plantearme algo que sé que no va a ocurrir?

—Porque yo se lo pido. Como una adivinanza, como un juego.

Arrugó el vasito de papel, se rascó la barbilla, negó varias veces.

—Pues... le diría que recapacitase, que en el campo se iba a aburrir como una ostra, que en invierno se hace pronto de noche y en verano hay un montón de moscas y hace calor.

—De acuerdo, pero entonces va ella y le contesta que ya ha recapacitado mucho y que se da cuenta de que la ciudad le resulta insoportable. ¿Qué haría usted, se plegaría a sus deseos, la dejaría marchar con sus trastos a otra parte y usted se quedaría en su lugar?

—¡Joder, inspectora, y yo qué coño sé! Le diría que nos mudáramos a una camioneta como esas de los feriantes, y una semana en el campo y otra en la ciudad.

—¡Es usted imposible, Fermín!

—¿Imposible, imposible yo? ¿Encima que me avengo a pensar en posibilidades imposibles para hacerla feliz?

Sonó mi teléfono móvil. Mientras contestaba, vi al subinspector alejándose. Hacía ostentosos gestos de adiós con la mano, quería librarse cuanto antes de nuestra conversación.

—¿La inspectora Petra Delicado? No sé si se acuerda de mí. Soy el gerente del hotel donde se aloja el señor Eduardo Castillo.

—Le recuerdo perfectamente. Dígame.

—Verá, no sabía a quién llamar y me he decidido a avisarla a usted. Como me dio su teléfono... El caso es que el señor Castillo falta de su habitación desde hace tres días. Nos hemos alarmado un poco porque todos los enseres de su propiedad los ha dejado en la habitación. Su ropa, colgada en el armario, sus zapatos en su sitio. En fin, nunca nos había ocurrido algo así.

—¿Quiere decir que el señor Castillo no había avisado de que iba a ausentarse?

—Exacto. Tampoco ha hecho el *check out* definitivo. Le diré que este cliente está al corriente de pagos. Como la suya es una larga estancia, nos paga cada semana. Bueno, en realidad debe dos días, pero sinceramente, este señor no me parece de los que huye dejando una cuenta pendiente, y menos abandonando todas sus cosas en la habitación. Temo que le haya pasado algo.

—¿Notó algo destacable la última vez que lo vio?

—¿Destacable?

—Sí, ¿lo encontró usted nervioso, deprimido?

—Yo no lo veía con mucha frecuencia, pero he preguntado a los servicios del hotel y nadie ha comentado nada raro.

—De acuerdo. Muchas gracias por llamar.

—Inspectora, ¿debo llamar a «personas desaparecidas» o algo así?

—No, no haga nada. Yo me encargo, no se preocupe. No toquen nada de su habitación.

—¿Podrá tenerme al corriente?

—Por supuesto. Yo contactaré con usted.

Una desaparición, ¡lo último que nos faltaba en aquel maldito asunto! ¿Bob era finalmente culpable de algo? ¿De verdad lo habíamos tenido todo el tiempo ante nuestras narices sin determinar qué grado de implicación podía imputársele en el asesinato de su socio? Llamé al subinspector y lo puse al corriente de la nueva situación. Parpadeó varias veces sin comprender. Cuando pudo atar los mínimos cabos, me miró con cara de asombro.

—¿Y eso?

—Ni idea. No lo tengo metido en el bolso, se lo aseguro.

—Voy a ponerme en acción.

—Sólo pregunte si han encontrado a alguien con su descripción.

—¿Sigo por los detenidos o en los hospitales?

—Todavía no. Quiero que me acompañe al hotel.

Mientras Garzón se hacía cargo de las primeras indagaciones, yo me senté en mi despacho. Me apreté las sienes, intentando pensar. Demasiado pronto para preocuparse, Bob era un hombre muy tocado anímicamente, resultaba perfectamente verosímil que se hubiera pasado con el alcohol y anduviera por la calle como un zombi. Quizá lo tenían detenido durmiendo la mona en cualquier comisaría. De ser así, pronto lo localizaríamos. Entró mi compañero como una bala.

—Ya está la alarma dada, inspectora.

—Muy bien, Fermín.

Al darse cuenta de mi talante contemplativo, preguntó:

—¿Ha elaborado alguna hipótesis durante este ratito?

—Bien sabemos que poner en pie teorías está contraindicado en cualquier caso. Y, sin embargo, no sabe cuánto daría por tener una a mano, cualquiera que fuera, por más disparatada que pudiera parecer. Estoy en un desierto, créame.

El director del hotel nos esperaba en recepción. Noté enseguida que se encontraba bastante afectado por la desaparición de su cliente. La primera diligencia era inspeccionar la habitación. Nos siguió y él mismo abrió la puerta. Era un espacio de lo más convencional, sin adornos ni muebles extra: una cama, un pequeño escritorio y el armario empotrado ocupando una pared.

—Todas las pertenencias del señor Castillo están en el armario, donde él las dejó.

Garzón descubrió el interior. No había mucha ropa, pero la que se veía estaba perfectamente ordenada. Dos pares de zapatos yacían bajo las camisas y los pantalones.

—¿Han tocado algo? —preguntó el subinspector.

—Lo justo para hacer la limpieza y ordenar. La asistenta me ha dicho que le trajeron un par de pantalones limpios y planchados de la lavandería.

—¿Y su maleta?

El director se quedó en suspenso, miró en todas direcciones, inspeccionó el armario.

—No está.

—¿Pudo haberla dejado en recepción?

—No, seguro que no, la hubiéramos visto.

—Me temo que tendremos que revisar de nuevo sus grabaciones de seguridad.

—Ningún inconveniente. Eso lo hacemos rápido.

—Necesitamos hablar con el personal de limpieza que atendió esta habitación el día que faltó el señor Castillo.

—Sólo hay dos chicas que se turnan, somos un hotel pequeño. Voy a preguntar a quién le tocaba.

—Bajamos con usted.

La recepcionista, que estaba ausente cuando habíamos llegado, nos miró con cara de susto. El director iba a pasarnos a su despacho para ver las cintas, pero tuve un pálpito extraño. Me acerqué hacia la chica y le pregunté:

—El señor Castillo no dejaría su maleta por aquí, ¿verdad?

—No, no, me acordaría. Justamente me dijo que la quería cambiar.

Nuestra comitiva dio un frenazo. Desanduvimos los tres pasos dados.

—¿Cómo es eso?

—Pues un día me preguntó dónde vendían maletas porque la suya estaba muy vieja y quería comprarse otra.

—¿Cuándo fue eso?

—No sabría decirle, unos días antes de que este señor se marchara.

Su jefe la miró con enorme severidad.

—¿Y eso, no podrías haberlo advertido antes?

La tez de la chica se volvió rojo pasión. Tituboó.

—Pero es que nadie me preguntó y lo que me preguntaron no era eso y...

Interrumpí, no me interesaba que se pusiera más nerviosa.

—¿Te comentó algo más el señor Castillo?

Negó con la cabeza, empezando a aterrorizarse tal y como imaginaba.

—¿Qué comercio le aconsejaste?

—Un bazar chino que hay cerca de aquí —articuló en voz casi inaudible.

El director, metamorfoseado a ojos vistas en un ogro que a duras penas se contenía, le pegó una mirada de láser y volvió a dirigirnos a su despacho. Una vez allí y mientras manipulaba las grabaciones, dio rienda suelta a un discurso que yo no oía por primera vez.

—Ustedes ya saben lo que pasa. Contratas gente joven y teóricamente bien preparada, pero a la hora de la verdad no dan pie con bola. Es desesperante.

Guardamos silencio hasta que encontró la imagen de Bob saliendo del hotel. En efecto, allí estaba y portaba claramente en la mano una maleta, probablemente vacía por la ligereza con que la cargaba. Era la una de la madrugada en la grabación. Tomé la palabra con cierto placer.

—¿Usted no había mirado esta grabación cuando echó en falta al cliente?

—No, le confieso que no, ni siquiera se me ocurrió.

—Pues eso sí es un fallo muy serio y, considerando que es usted joven y seguramente bien preparado, cabe pensar que quizá sí vio a ese hombre con la maleta y tras comprobar que sus enseres estaban en su sitio, pensó que había algo raro en el asunto y prefirió no meterse en problemas. ¿Me estoy equivocando demasiado?

—Inspectora, piense lo que quiera, yo he hecho las cosas lo mejor que he sabido.

Nos levantamos, incautamos la grabación y salimos dando una orden.

—Sigan sin tocar nada de esa habitación. Si es preciso, mandaremos a un equipo de la policía científica.

Al pasar por delante de la recepción, vi que la chica tenía los ojos arrasados en lágrimas. En la calle mi compañero comentó:

—Ha querido darle una pequeña lección a ese tipo, pero no sé si a la chica va a servirle de mucho.

—La chica me pareció tonta desde el primer día, pero yo no la he contratado, él sí.

Nada de aquello tenía mucho sentido. ¿Para qué había cargado Bob con una maleta vacía? ¿Lo había justificado frente a la recepcionista para que no pensara que se iba sin pagar? Miré a Garzón con desaliento.

—¿Adónde coño vamos ahora?

Cabeceó tristemente. Miró en todas direcciones.

—¡Hostia, inspectora! Estoy de este caso hasta los mismísimos. Vamos al bazar ese de la calle de al lado.

—Bueno, a alguna parte habrá que ir.

Los bazares chinos siempre me llenan de sorpresa. ¡Tanta variedad de objetos, tal abarrotamiento de estanterías! Como no tenía la más mínima esperanza de que surgiera ninguna luz de aquella gestión, vagué por la tienda y me paré en la sección de cosas decorativas. Me fascinaba el hiriente mal gusto de aquellas lamparitas, cajas, figuras... Era un misterio pensar en quién las compraba, pero más misterioso aún pensar en quién las fabricaba. Tomé en la mano una fuentecita orlada de ángeles que pesaba un quintal. La observé con repugnancia y embeleso, una auténtica maravilla del *kitsch*. Pensé en comprarla para regalarla a algún amigo que apreciara lo excesivo, pero antes de que cometiera despilfarro alguno, la cabeza del subinspector se asomó al final del pasillo. Venía con el móvil en la mano y las facciones alteradas.

—Vámonos, inspectora —me dijo.

—¿Pasa algo?

—Vámonos.

Me cogió del brazo y, sin ningún miramiento, me impulsó hacia la salida del comercio. Una vez fuera, me desprendí de la tenaza que era su mano.

—¿Se puede saber qué...?

—Han encontrado a Bob Castillo. Se ha ahorcado. Al levantar el cadáver han visto que llevaba una carta dirigida a usted. Si nos damos prisa todavía llegaremos al lugar de los hechos con los colegas allí. Es una zona poco transitada de Collserola. Topó con el cuerpo colgado de un árbol un ciclista de cross.

Me temblaban las manos cuando íbamos en el coche. Enfrentarse a un cadáver asesinado no era lo mismo que a uno suicidado. La voluntad de esa muerte me espantaba, pensar en el momento final, en el último acto consciente de cortar con la vida, desaparecer. Desconocía cuáles eran los pensamientos de mi subalterno, pero permanecía callado, con gesto grave, sólo atento a la conducción. Una calima de culpabilidad empezaba a empañarme la mente. Ahora veía con nitidez que Bob había estado perdiendo el juicio a ojos vistas, y esos ojos eran los nuestros. Un hombre desesperado por su situación que empieza a ejecutar acciones absurdas, infantiles: venganzas de rayar coches y tirar piedras. Hubiéramos debido darnos cuenta, quizá tomar cartas en el asunto, recomendándole ayuda psicológica o incluso deteniéndolo para asegurarnos de que no iba a seguir haciendo tonterías. Me dirigí a Garzón.

—¿Usted cree que con Bob hubiéramos debido...?

Me interrumpió. Sabía perfectamente lo que me disponía a preguntar.

—¿Quién es capaz de anticipar un suicidio?, ¿quién? Desde luego que usted y yo no tenemos esa capacidad de anticipación y menos tratándose de un tipo al que no conocemos de nada.

—Pero se notaba que no estaba en sus cabales. La mirada perdida, la voz, las bobadas que llegó a hacer...

—Déjese de cábalas, Petra, que un tío haga gilipolleces debido a su desgracia no significa que esté tan mal como para quitarse de en medio. Además, ¿estamos seguros de que ha sido un suicidio? En este jodido caso cualquier cosa puede pasar.

—¿Está insinuando que...?

—No estoy insinuando nada porque no tenemos

ni puta idea de nada. ¿Para qué sirve hacer conjeturas? Mejor callar, llegar y ver.

—A sus órdenes, subinspector.

—Perdone que le hable así, pero es que me la conozco como si la hubiera parido. Empezará a atormentarse con este pobre hombre y a sentirse culpable y a hacerse reproches... ¿Y sabe qué le digo? A lo mejor ese pobre hombre es el asesino que buscamos.

—Prometo no atormentarme, pero le ruego que tampoco me atormente usted.

17

Cuando llegamos, nuestros compañeros ya habían acabado prácticamente con todas las diligencias. El forense opinaba que Eduardo Castillo se había suicidado. Tenía pocas dudas al respecto, el cuerpo no presentaba signos de violencia. Se había colgado de una rama de pino no demasiado alta y había utilizado dos maletas apiladas para encaramarse. Sentí una punzada en el pecho al oírlo. Para eso quería las maletas aquel pobre diablo. Una solución un tanto infantil, en consonancia con su modo de ser. El juez había permitido el levantamiento del cadáver, que se encontraba ya embutido en su funda. Me alegré de no haberlo visto. Cuando lo descolgaron, había caído de su bolsillo un sobre con mi nombre. Se lo pedí a los colegas de la Científica, pero mi ilusión de leer inmediatamente la carta que contenía enseguida se desvaneció.

—Ni hablar, Petra. Tiene que pasar por el análisis de huellas dactilares. Ya te la haremos llegar.

—¿Y si me pongo guantes?

—Sabes perfectamente que no puede ser.

—De acuerdo, pero eso de que «me la haréis llegar» no cuela. Avísame cuando hagáis la prueba porque quiero estar delante. Y cuanto antes sea eso, tanto mejor.

—Siempre hay prisa para todo, ¡joder!

—En este caso, la prisa se multiplica por dos.

No pensaba transigir. Me plantaría frente al laboratorio de mi compañero enarbolando una pancarta si fuera necesario. Lo sometería a una presión continuada. Necesitábamos leer aquella carta. En ella quizá estaba la solución de nuestro caso. Lo mismo haría con la autopsia, nada de aguardar turno pacíficamente, presión. Mandaría al subinspector para que se atrincherara frente al Anatómico Forense. Esperaba que el comisario nos echara una mano en las maniobras de aceleración. Sin embargo, debió ser tan visible mi empeño, tan evidente mi determinación, que no hizo falta llegar a demasías. Al día siguiente del hallazgo del cuerpo, Luis Sotomayor, a quien conocía bien, me avisó desde la central de la Científica.

Llegamos Garzón y yo a las diez en punto de la mañana. Encontramos a Sotomayor delante de uno de los ordenadores colocados en batería. Afortunadamente, nadie más consultaba datos en aquel momento. Nos miró de reojo.

—¡Hombre, cuánto bueno por aquí! ¡Petra la acelerada y el rápido de Garzón! Has visto que hemos cumplido, ¿sí o no?

—Déjate de coñas, Luis.

—Acercaos, aquí tengo lo vuestro.

Manipuló las teclas del ordenador y empezó a comparar frente a nosotros las huellas del muerto y las que figuraban en el papel. Eran idénticas. Había encontrado alguna más que sin duda databa de unos días atrás.

—¿Estás seguro de eso?

—Casi completamente. Utilizamos la tecnología más puntera. Hemos aplicado un método descubierto en Israel en el que...

—Sotomayor, no es que no me importe lo que me cuentas, pero voy como una moto, compréndelo. Hazme un resumen, te lo ruego.

—Lo que se deduce del análisis es que las huellas ajenas al interesado pueden ser de quienes le vendieron el sobre o los folios o vaya usted a saber. Resumiendo al máximo: es casi seguro que fue él mismo quien escribió esa carta y quien se la metió en el bolsillo. Si alguien le obligó a ello o no, eso ya es otro cantar.

—¿Tú has leído la carta?

—He visto la grafía, es confusa, nerviosa, como si hubiera bebido alcohol o estuviera muy nervioso. Claro que para un hombre que planea suicidarse, podría considerarse incluso normal. Habrá que hacer estudio grafológico, si es que quieres saber más y si es que tenéis muestras escritas de ese hombre.

—Las tenemos, sí. ¿Puedo aspirar a que me des la carta ya?, ¿me has hecho copia?

Sonrió mirándome despacio, para hacerme rabiar. Contestó alargando cada sílaba.

—Pues claro que la he hecho, y si me acompañas, te la daré. ¿O te quedaba alguna duda que preguntar?

—¡Joder, Sotomayor, ni que fuera un incunable de gran valor, dámela de una puta vez!

Se levantó riendo y Garzón y yo fuimos tras él. Canturreaba algo así como: «Petra tiene prisa y habla como un carretero». Los de la Científica eran así, bromistas, teóricos y despreocupados. Se notaba que no llevaban un caso desde principio a fin.

La caligrafía de Bob no era fácil de leer. Los rasgos se alargaban y contraían caprichosamente y las líneas escapaban a cualquier horizontalidad. Unas letras se engarabitaban sobre sí mismas alcanzando gran tamaño y otras se reducían a minúsculas hormigas. Era como si la carta hubiera estado escrita por un niño o por un borracho, por un niño borracho quizá. Desentrañé el contenido con esfuerzo, decía así:

> Inspectora Delicado: Quiero despedirme de usted porque me voy a marchar de este mundo. Es una decisión mía y de nadie más. ¿Qué voy a hacer en la vida si ya no tengo nada? Mejor quitarme de en medio y en paz. Usted y su colega son buena gente y me arrepiento mucho de las burradas que les hice en los últimos tiempos. Me siento culpable de eso, de lo demás no. ¿Qué podía hacer yo? Aunque le digo que hasta en una de las burradas les señalé el camino, para que vea hasta qué punto intenté obrar de buena fe. Aunque ahora ya da lo mismo. Mil perdones y adiós.

Mi cerebro entró en ebullición. Le pasé el papel a mi compañero. Vi de reojo cómo lo leía con avidez.

—¡La madre que parió a este maldito hijo de puta! —estalló al acabar.

—¡Garzón, que todavía está de cuerpo presente, modérese!

—¿Que me modere? Y toda esa mierda que ha escrito, ¿qué coño quiere decir? Si el cabrón sabía algo, como parece, ¿por qué no lo suelta todo de una jodida vez? ¿Qué pretendía, jugar a las adivinanzas después de muerto? ¿Tan poco le importaba cazar al asesino de su socio?

—Supongo que cuando escribió esto estaba fuera de sí.

—Fuera de sí lo hubiera puesto yo a base de hostias. ¡Se lo dije, inspectora, este zángano no era de fiar! ¿Y nosotros qué hemos hecho? Compadecerlo y dejar que se vaya de rositas al más allá.

—¿Está reprochándome algo?

—No me interprete mal, Petra, usted no tiene ninguna responsabilidad.

—Castillo tenía coartada, no pudimos reunir la más mínima prueba en su contra, no incurrió en ninguna contradicción cuando lo interrogamos. No se benefició de la muerte de su socio, sino más bien al contrario. Dígame qué podíamos hacer.

—Ya lo sé, inspectora, ya lo sé, pero es que esa carta me ha puesto de los nervios.

—Lo había notado, Garzón. Sin embargo, en el momento actual esa carta es lo único que tenemos. Comprobarán la autoría, pero mientras tanto vamos a ponernos a pensar. Le propongo ir a comisaría, allí se piensa mejor.

Sin duda mi subalterno estaba impresionado por

mi reacción tranquila y ponderada, pero no lo estaba menos yo misma. Yo, por alguna razón que no tenía clara, había decidido fingir. En realidad, hubiera soltado de buena gana todos los tacos que soltó él y sus aseveraciones hubieran sido las mías. Como la española cuando besa, cuando un caso se complica, se complica de verdad. Castillo había llevado su infantilismo, su extraña manera de reaccionar hasta el último extremo: la tumba. Pero, a pesar de ser tan pueril, había tenido la valentía de ahorcarse, de acabar de una vez. Los hombres apocados se vuelven imprevisibles cuando se atreven a entrar en acción.

Salimos escapados de la guarida científica y nos atrincheramos en nuestra gruta habitual. Una vez allí, ordené que fueran a buscar todas las pertenencias de Bob al Barcelona City. Mi segunda orden fue que intentaran encontrar a cualquier pariente o allegado del suicida. Luego, empezaríamos a leer aquella carta póstuma una y otra vez hasta que consiguiéramos sacar de ella algún sentido, alguna directriz.

Cuando iba a cerrar la puerta del despacho, sonó mi móvil. Era Marcos.

—Petra, ¿qué te parece si hoy cenamos fuera? Así podemos charlar un rato tranquilos.

—Marcos, me coges en un momento muy malo.

—Te hablo de la cena, faltan horas para que se haga de noche.

—Ya sé, pero es que el momento malo se extiende a todo el día. No sé a qué hora llegaré a casa, probablemente tarde. ¿Es algo urgente?

—No es urgente, no. Habrá tiempo para hablar. Un beso.

Colgué. Charlar tranquilamente durante la cena en un restaurante. ¿Sobre qué? ¿De nuevo la casa en el campo? ¿Quería decirme que ya todo estaba listo para que nos trasladáramos a un nidito de paz? Nunca hubiera imaginado que Marcos llegara a convertirse en un problema para mí. Me había equivocado pensando que lo del campo se trataría de una manía puntual que desaparecería con rapidez. No, seguro que seguía encastillado en su decisión. ¡Todos al campo! Nos levantaríamos por la mañana oyendo el trino de los pajarillos, comeríamos los frutos de los árboles plantados en el jardín y si no nos topábamos con Adán y Eva despelotados en el paraíso, sería de pura casualidad. ¡Maldición! La teoría de que la vida matrimonial de una policía siempre se complicaba había llegado a parecerme un tópico, un manido lugar común y, sin embargo, cuando todo seguía una rutina tranquilizadora que desmentía complicaciones, ¡aquí las tenía, las mismísimas complicaciones! Agité varias veces la cabeza como si saliera de un baño en el mar. No era oportuno ponerme a cavilar sobre mi destino, ya lo haría más tarde. Sólo me faltaba añadir incógnitas a todas las que presentaba la investigación. En mi vida privada no había ningún asesinato impune, en la profesional, sí. Garzón me miró con curiosidad.

—¿Pasa algo, inspectora?

—¿Algo? A veces parece que pasa todo, y todo a la vez, Fermín. Encárguese de que comprueben si el móvil de Bob estaba entre sus pertenencias, y si es así, que lo escruten inmediatamente.

—Pero, inspectora, el cadáver lo llevaba en el bolsillo y esa orden ya se dio. ¿No se acuerda?

—No me acordaba, es verdad.

—¿Se encuentra bien? La veo un poco perturbada.

—Unas nubes, un aguacero, pero ninguna tormenta, ningún ciclón. Perturbaciones pasajeras. Nunca me había encontrado mejor, estoy acostumbrada a luchar contra la adversidad.

Me observaba como si fuera una loca furiosa; cuando en el fondo lo que yo estaba haciendo era representar una especie de función escolar, probablemente para infundirme ánimos.

—Antes de sentarnos a dilucidar, ¿puede hacerme un favor importantísimo? Traiga todo el café que pueda, no vamos a estar levantándonos cada dos por tres para ir a buscarlo a la jodida máquina, eso nos distraerá demasiado.

—En la sala de interrogatorios vi el otro día un termo. Alguien debió dejárselo allí. Voy a ver si arramblo con él. ¿Pido que nos traigan unos bocadillos?

—De momento, no. A no ser que sean imprescindibles para su inspiración.

—No se preocupe, yo también sé luchar contra la adversidad.

Media hora más tarde, nuestro exiguo equipo de dos jugadores estaba listo para empezar el partido. Cogí la carta de Bob el suicida, la sujeté con dos dedos y la hice oscilar en el aire frente a los ojos del subinspector.

—¿Ve esto, Garzón? Pues en este trozo de papel inmundo puede estar nuestra solución.

Cada uno con su copia, empezamos a leer intentando desmenuzar el texto palabra a palabra.

—En el encabezamiento nada, ¿no, inspectora?

—Yo diría en un principio que esta nota la ha escrito Bob sin coacción de nadie. Es fiel a su modo de hablar, y la decisión de matarse porque «ya no tiene nada» está en sintonía con las razones que nos dio la última vez que hablamos con él.

—Aquí pone que nos consideraba «buena gente».

—Eso no aporta gran cosa, Garzón.

—Por lo menos sabemos que no nos culpa de nada.

—Es un dato valioso, lleva razón, pero creo que deberíamos centrarnos en las «burradas» que menciona, ahí está el quid de la cuestión.

—Se arrepiente «mucho de las burradas». Las burradas son los ataques al coche, ¿no?

—Vamos a ver, recordemos las burradas. Una fue el ataque a nuestro coche el día que estuvimos en L'Hospitalet y también tenemos el último intento que hizo, justo cuando yo lo cacé antes de rayar la carrocería.

—Entonces hay que pensar que cuando dice que nos señaló «el camino» fue en L'Hospitalet. ¿El Tiras y la casa okupada? ¿Va la cosa por ahí?

Me estrujé la frente intentando llegar al cerebro, masajearlo a fondo para que trabajara más intensamente, a más velocidad. Serví una primera ronda de café, quizá prematuramente. Garzón dijo:

—Pero ¿y si a lo que él llama las burradas son todas las agresiones que sufrieron los testigos que fuimos a visitar? Me refiero a la mujer china del bar, los destrozos en la casa okupada...

—No, no, eso es imposible. El perfil de Castillo no concuerda con ese tipo de acciones. Además, ¿qué pretendía señalarnos, qué camino era ese, todos están implicados en la muerte de Laurent? Estábamos siguiendo una estela que nos indicó la Guardia Civil, es imposible pensar que Bob anduviera en ello. Además, una persona sola no es capaz de tanta devastación.

—Sí, pero es obvio que nos siguió. ¿Para qué?, ¿por qué?

—Eso ya son preguntas de gran calado, volvamos sobre las más simples.

—De acuerdo, ¿por qué nos señala el camino arreándole al coche cerca de la casa okupada?

—Esa es una buena pregunta. Me parece una manera estúpida de señalar el camino.

—Y encima repite el método o intenta repetirlo frente a comisaría, ¿qué pretende señalarnos ahí? Nada, son acciones contra nosotros.

—No nos consideraba buena gente, pongamos que incluso nos odiaba, pero ¿por qué nos odiaba como para pretender hacernos daño?

—Él sabía algo, quizá no la identidad del asesino, pero sí algo que podía conducirnos hasta él, algo evidente, algo que saltaba a la vista, pero que nosotros éramos incapaces de averiguar.

—¿Y por qué no nos lo decía directamente?

—¡Qué sé yo! Quizá tenía algún grado de implicación, quizá pretendía proteger a alguien. Deberíamos partir de la base de que Bob no era un tipo normal: carencias afectivas, sensación de fracaso, comportamiento a veces infantiloide...

—Entrar ahora en psicologías no va a servirnos de ayuda, inspectora. Bob está muerto.

—De acuerdo, volvamos a la carta. La única burrada que Bob hizo frente a nuestras narices, pero que no nos tenía como objetivo directo, fue la pedrada en la tienda de Mataró. La señora que testificó vio a un hombre bajito huyendo del lugar. Sin duda debemos conjeturar que era él.

—¿Con la pedrada estaba señalándonos el sitio o queriendo apartarnos de él?

—En cualquiera de los dos casos se trata de una señal.

—¿Que indica el camino, como él dice?

—¡Ojalá!

—Pues ya sabe lo que debemos hacer.

—Seguir la estrella, como los Reyes Magos.

—Los Reyes Magos de Oriente irán a Mataró.

18

Todas las órdenes de investigación paralela que yo había dado resultaron absolutamente infructuosas. Ni las unidades móviles, que teóricamente podían avistar y reconocer a la sospechosa principal, dieron con ella, ni los pequeños retenes temporales que habíamos solicitado en Badalona, L'Hospitalet y Mataró habían detectado movimientos inusuales en el entorno del dueño del bar, la casa okupada o la tienda de ultramarinos. Eso no significaba necesariamente que no se hubieran producido. En las novelas y los films de género los detectives siempre cuentan con equipos de condición casi divina; es decir, capaces de estar en todas partes al mismo tiempo y verlo todo a la vez. La realidad no es así. ¿A cuántos hombres y durante cuánto tiempo puedes tener dedicados a tareas complementarias? Pocos y durante un periodo mínimo, ese es el rostro que presenta la verdadera realidad. Muchas veces, quienes investigamos un crimen tendemos a cargar la culpa del enlentecimiento de las pesquisas a esa falta de ayuda general. No pensaba caer en semejante error. Quizá no era un error, sino una verdad como la copa de un pino, pero a cierta edad (que yo ya tenía) llegas a comprender que la verdad y la realidad no son siempre lo mismo, y que siempre debes contentarte con la realidad. Ese es tu sitio, tu camino, el lugar donde moras, lo demás está fuera de tu alcance y, por tanto, añorarlo es una estupidez.

El tal Dámaso estaba sirviendo alpiste a granel a una señora muy mayor. Lo sacaba de un saco de dimensiones medias y lo metía en una bolsita ayudándose de una pala pequeña. Me impresionó. Había creído que ese modo de vender ya no existía, que todo venía desde la fábrica en su propio embalaje y con un código de barras, pero no. Junto al saco de alpiste había otro con lo que parecía ser pienso de gato, y un tercero con bolitas un poco mayores que, sin duda, eran comida para perros. ¿Quién seguía practicando aquel menudeo en el panorama del comercio nacional? Muy pocos, sin duda alguna. No quedaban muchas tiendas como aquella. Ultramarinos, tal y como la denominó el teniente Montilla, hasta el nombre se había convertido en una excentricidad. Si me llamaban la atención todos esos detalles no era por un tema únicamente sociológico, sino porque a nosotros nos proporcionaban una pequeña pista inicial. ¿Quién puede vivir con lo que produce un comercio como aquel? ¿Medio kilo de pienso canino, doscientos gramos de alpiste? Según la lista que nos había facilitado días atrás el teniente de la Guardia Civil, Dámaso no era millonario, pero tenía ingresos que probablemente blanqueaba en aquel pequeño negocio. Poseía un piso en el Eixample y un Golf de primera mano. ¡Mucho alpiste tenía que vender para financiar sus gastos! Sin embargo, según el teniente, no había modo de meterle mano en la parte económica, lo tenía bien montado, probablemente contaba con un buen asesor.

Nuestro desplazamiento a Mataró había sido un tanto improvisado. No habíamos previsto ningún tipo de estrategia para interrogar a Dámaso, algo se nos ocurriría. La reacción de aquel tipo al vernos determinaría, en parte, nuestro modo de obrar. Curiosamente, no pareció alterarse demasiado cuando entramos en su tienda. Nos miró con fastidio y siguió atendiendo a su clienta sin el menor atisbo de nerviosismo. La anciana se demoró tras el alpiste comprando galletas, chocolate, café. Cuando hubo pagado, salió mirándonos de reojo. Garzón se acercó a Dámaso y le ordenó:

—Eche el pestillo a la puerta. Queremos hablar con usted.

—Pues vuelvan cuando la tienda esté cerrada —contestó secamente.

Mi compañero se dirigió a la entrada y él mismo accionó el cerrojo. El tipo lo miró de través y arrancó con pasos firmes en su dirección. Me interpuse enseguida.

—¿Adónde cree que va?

Se puso a gritar como una bestia.

—¡Estoy en mi negocio y no tenéis derecho a entrar aquí sólo para molestarme!

Le di un empujón que lo hizo retroceder, aunque me doblaba en robustez y en altura.

—Hemos venido para hablar contigo y eso es lo que vamos a hacer, te guste o no.

—No tengo nada que decir.

—Eso ya lo veremos.

Garzón permanecía inmóvil junto a la puerta, atento a cualquier movimiento que ejecutara Dámaso. De pronto, este volvió sobre sus pasos y se colocó detrás del mostrador. Me abalancé hacia él para cerciorarme de que no tenía un arma escondida. Levantó los brazos, hizo sonar de nuevo su vozarrón.

—¡Quieta, leona!

—Sal del mostrador, enséñame las manos.

Se rio con falsas carcajadas. Me enseñó las manos vacías. Inspeccioné la parte trasera del mostrador. No había ningún arma.

—¿Te gustan mis manos? No me ha dado tiempo de hacerme la manicura.

Saqué la pistola y la mantuve en la mano, sin apuntarle. Empezó a tomar en serio la situación.

—Tranquila, ¿eh?, tranquila. Si habéis venido a hablar, hablamos y cuando acabemos os largáis y santas pascuas.

—Siéntate. —Le señalé un pequeño escabel que había en un rincón. Me obedeció enseguida. Intenté serenarme, todo aquello me había alterado la respiración.

—¿Sabe quién es Eduardo Castillo, también llamado Bob?

—No me suena de nada —respondió.

—De Martine sí se acuerda, ¿verdad?

No respondió. Sus ojos se clavaron en el suelo y allí concentró la mirada.

—Sí, pero ya les dije todo lo que sabía. ¿Les parece poco?

—¿Dónde está, Dámaso?, ¿dónde podemos encontrarla? Es tu última oportunidad de decir la verdad.

—Les conté que había oído rumores de que estaba en Barcelona. No me ha llegado ninguna onda más. Ya no estoy en esos rollos, estoy limpio y, por lo tanto, es cierto que me llega algún rumor, pero no frecuento a ningún delincuente.

—Sabemos quién te rompió el escaparate de una pedrada.

Una sombra furtiva atravesó su rostro de piedra. Continué en el mismo tono de voz.

—Ahora queremos saber por qué lo hizo.

—Pues pregúntenselo a él.

—Imposible, está muerto.

La sombra se convirtió en un ramalazo de sorpresa, de inquietud. Procuró sobreponerse, y dijo en tono falsamente casual:

—¡Vaya, qué pena!, ¿se lo han cargado? ¿Era ese tal Bob por quien me han preguntado?

—Quizá.

—A mí eso ni me va ni me viene. Si era un hijoputa que andaba rompiendo cosas de una propiedad privada, se habrá encontrado con alguien que le ha dado su merecido.

—Nadie mata por una luna rota, ¿o sí, Dámaso?

—¡Y yo qué coño sé! Están intentando liarme, pero no van a salirse con la suya. Me hablan de cosas de las que ni siquiera entiendo nada, ¡Bob, la francesa, el escaparate roto! No tengo que ver con ninguno de ellos. ¿Traen una orden del juez para poder interrogarme, eh, la traen?

—Olvídate del juez. ¿Por qué no está aquí tu dependienta?

—Hoy es su día libre. ¿Eso es ilegal? Además, ya

se me han inflado las pelotas, o me traen una orden del juez o se largan por donde han venido.

—Ya nos vamos, Dámaso, no sufra. Tampoco se preocupe por la orden del juez, se la traeremos, por si acaso hace usted colección.

Le di la espalda, llegué hasta donde estaba Garzón. Tenía la mano en el bolsillo, probablemente colocada en su pistola, dispuesto para disparar. Ya teníamos lo que habíamos ido a buscar: ponerlo en acción si tenía algo que ocultar. Salimos a la calle. Nuestro coche estaba a una distancia prudencial. Entramos y esperamos, sin decir ni una palabra. El honesto comerciante tardó casi una hora en salir de su local. Echó el cierre y se metió en un aparcamiento privado que había justo enfrente. Esperamos con el motor ya en marcha. Tras unos minutos apareció, conduciendo su coche. Lo seguimos evitando ponernos demasiado cerca. Entró en Barcelona por la Diagonal, enfiló el centro urbano, se desvió hacia el Eixample.

—Parece que va a su casa —dijo Garzón.

Así fue. Paró frente a un portal que coincidía con su dirección, metió el coche en un garaje y ya no lo vimos más.

—¿Sabemos su número de teléfono?

—Me temo que no.

—No pasa nada. Llame al teniente Montilla, él lo tiene localizado por todos lados. Ya sabe, Fermín: intervención del teléfono y seguimiento integral. Verá lo contento que se pone el teniente, podrá hincarle el diente a uno de sus favoritos.

Garzón cogió su móvil y empezó a marcar. Le di un toque en el brazo.

—Dígale a Montilla que necesitamos discreción total, y subraye lo de total. Este es capaz de presentarse aquí a caballo y con tricornio.

—¡Y lanzando vivas a la patrona de la Guardia Civil! —soltó mi compañero con una risotada.

¿Al final aquel asesinato, que tan de cráneo estaba llevándonos, iba a resumirse en un asunto de drogas? En tal caso me preguntaba si había valido la pena pugnar para que nadie nos lo quitara de las manos. Con la Guardia Civil al frente desde un primer momento, quizá las averiguaciones hubieran avanzado con más claridad y rapidez. Y, sin embargo, aunque se pensara sólo en drogas como *leitmotiv* del crimen, había cosas extrañas que seguían siendo inexplicables, que salían del cauce habitual. No había un motivo claro para que Martine Marchand, con riesgo alto de ser detenida, enemiga pública número uno, se lanzara a cruzar la frontera franco-española para vengarse o cobrarse una deuda con un pequeño feriante que vive mayormente de la cocina. Encima, no está sola, sino que viene con algunos hombres de su guardia personal. Y bien, ¿por qué se exhibe yendo a comprar a la furgoneta donde cualquiera puede verla en vez de enviar a algunos de sus muchachos para hacer el trabajito de cargarse a Laurent? ¿Por qué ronda sola las ferias? Y Bob Castillo, ¿qué pinta en todo esto Bob Castillo?: la destrucción de su vehículo, el reciente suicidio... Por no hablar de los destrozos que se fueron produciendo a nuestro paso por los interrogados... Existía un rompecabezas, pero a todas las piezas les faltaba una masilla de unión con la que no éramos capaces de dar.

Hacía días, yo tenía la impresión de que eran meses, que aparecía por casa sólo para dormir. Y cuando llegaba, Marcos ya estaba como un tronco. Si a los niños les tocaba el turno de visitas con nosotros, los encontraba en sus habitaciones, fritos también. Me había convertido en una especie de libélula que sobrevolaba a la familia, sin llegar a posarse nunca a su lado con tiempo y comodidad. Sin embargo, no podía hacer otra cosa, se trataba de un caso que requería atención total, prioridad absoluta. Lo malo de descuidar las relaciones humanas es que el tiempo que no les consagras nunca se puede recuperar después. ¿Cómo hacerlo?, ¿dedicando más espacio a las personas parcialmente abandonadas como compensación posterior? Es absurdo sólo pensarlo, por no hablar de los consejos que los psicólogos suelen dar para la ocasión: «Convierta los periodos que pasa con sus seres queridos en momentos de calidad». ¿Qué coño significa eso? ¡Vaya época que me estaba tocando vivir, en la que todo se etiqueta con vocabulario comercial!: calidad de vida, inversión en el propio bienestar, ahorrar energía vital, «comprar» una opinión para decir que estás de acuerdo con ella. Una tendencia vomitiva. No, lo único sensato que podía hacer pasaba por ser consciente de que el caso del francés ocupaba mi vida aquellos días, por encima de todos y de todo.

Aquella misma tarde llegó el informe forense del malogrado Bob. Tanto Garzón como yo habíamos desarrollado la habilidad, compartida por muchos colegas, de entresacar de los informes aquello que nos interesaba específicamente, obviando toda la jerga médica que no podía ayudarnos. Eso nos evitaba tener que acudir al Anatómico para interrogar a un médico que, habitualmente, no tenía tiempo ni ganas de reunirse con nadie. A no ser que surgiera alguna intuición original, como el deseo que yo experimenté por ver el cadáver de Laurent, ya nos habíamos plegado a otro nuevo uso social: no verse nunca las caras.

Lo que buscábamos en aquella ocasión era despejar definitivamente la duda de si Castillo se había suicidado libremente o no. Según aquellas líneas, nada daba a entender que aquel hombre hubiera sido forzado a cometer su acción. No tenía signos de violencia ni había hallazgos anatómicos que denotaran que lo hubieran colgado del árbol ya muerto. La postura que presentaba el cuerpo demostraba también que él solo había subido a las maletas colocadas en equilibrio y, también solo, había anudado la cuerda a su cuello, dejándose ir después. En su estómago no se encontró ningún rastro de alimento, pero sí una más que considerable cantidad de alcohol.

—Sin duda bebió para darse ánimos —comenté.

—Entre los objetos que la Científica encontró a dos metros de distancia del cuerpo, había una botella de vodka medio vacía —me recordó el subinspector—. En ella estaban las huellas dactilares de Bob. Llegó al lugar, preparó su propio cadalso sin beber nada para no cometer errores, abrió la botella y se empapuzó de vodka, luego la tiró entre los matojos. Dos metros son fáciles de alcanzar.

—¡Qué horrible, Fermín!

—Es horrible, sí. Tenemos un oficio tan raro que

nos impresiona más un suicidio que un asesinato. ¿Usted lo entiende, Petra?

—Sí lo entiendo, sí. Ser capaz de acabar con uno mismo es una decisión desgarradora.

—Vale, pero al que lo asesinan no quiere morir, mientras que el suicida es voluntario, incluso puede tener sus buenas razones.

—¿Cuáles eran las razones de Bob?

—No lo sé, ¿cree que fue él quien se cargó a su socio? Porque si fue él, nos ha jodido vivos quitándose de en medio.

—No tiene sentido. Pudo matarse por su sensación de fracaso vital, por miedo, porque sabía cosas peligrosas o porque estaba mal de la cabeza y tenía un perfil suicida.

—Muy normal no era. Nunca sabremos por qué lo hizo, nunca. ¿Se da cuenta de la magnitud de la tragedia, como usted misma diría?

—Este caso va a acabar con mi salud mental, con mi matrimonio, con mi vida como la he vivido hasta ahora.

—Y si no lo resolvemos, a lo mejor también con nuestro trabajo. ¡Y pensar que montamos un pollo para que no interfirieran otros cuerpos policiales!

—Eso no es exactamente así, de hecho, hemos pedido ayuda.

—Más vale «no meneallo», inspectora. Le propongo algo para recuperar su salud mental. Crucemos a La Jarra de Oro y nos arreamos un copazo. ¿Qué le parece?

—Bien, lo haremos a la salud del pobre Bob.

—¿Y si era el asesino?

—Igualmente brindaremos por él.

—Si se cargó a su socio lo merece, era un fenómeno: asesinato, suicidio..., todas las variedades mortuorias, ¡joder!, ¿alguien da más?

—No sea usted bestia, Fermín.

—Así que bestia, ¿eh? Eso le va a costar una invitación. Pagará usted el copazo.

—¡Pero si ha sido idea suya!

—¡Tomarla, no pagarla!, hablemos con propiedad.

Salimos riendo y bromeando sin mucha convicción. La comisaría estaba tranquila a aquella hora, y La Jarra de Oro la encontramos medio vacía también. Demasiado pronto para que la gente hubiera acabado de trabajar. Nos acodamos en la barra, según solíamos hacer, y un camarero a quien no conocíamos, probablemente novato, nos preguntó:

—¿Qué os pongo, chicos?

—Un par de gin-tonics, zagal.

El joven se quedó un tanto atónito por la palabra con que mi compañero lo interpeló, ¿zagal?, era evidente que no la había oído jamás. Se alejó para preparar las bebidas.

—No ha entendido lo de «zagal».

—Lo he dicho a propósito. ¿Qué coño es eso de llamarnos «chicos»? Ya tenemos una edad, ¿no? Me parece una falta de respeto.

—No se entera usted, Fermín. Es todo lo contrario, hoy en día los camareros jóvenes tratan así a la gente mayor. Es como un detalle positivo, saben muy bien que ahora a todo el mundo le gusta sentirse un chavalín.

—¿Saben muy bien? ¡Esos tíos no saben ni dónde tienen la polla!

—¡Garzón, baje la voz, que va a oírle!

—Tres cojones me importa que me oiga.

Cuando el chico se acercó con ambas copas servidas, me temí lo peor.

—Bueno, chicos, a ver qué tal me ha salido la combinación.

—Pues seguro que de puta madre, chaval, muchacho, tío, colega, rapaz.

—¿Perdona? —preguntó de buena fe el camarero con los ojos muy abiertos.

—No, nada, son maneras de llamar a la gente, pero hay otras, ¿sabes?, como por ejemplo: señor, caballero, vuecencia, su majestad, su alteza, su excelentísimo y todo el copón bendito.

Sin entender de dónde venían los tiros, el jovenzuelo se echó a reír. Pensó que Garzón tenía ganas de hacerse el gracioso.

—Pues venga, chicos, a ver qué tal el copón bendito —dijo sin dar en el clavo.

Fue a atender a otro cliente que acababa de entrar. Intenté disimular el ataque de risa que me dio.

—Lo que yo le diga, Petra, ¡ni dónde tienen la polla!

Fui consciente en aquel instante de que yo también había pasado a formar parte de la nómina de dinosaurios aún en activo. Encontraba excesivas las reacciones de mi compañero, pero le concedía un punto de razón. A mí también me repateaba que un joven camarero nos llamara «chicos». No atribuía el apelativo a una falta de respeto, sino a las ridículas costumbres de la época que estábamos viviendo. Todo se infantilizaba, todo se convertía en una farsa. En la publicidad de televisión, los personajes que aparecían reían y daban saltitos sin ninguna razón. Los posibles clientes éramos considerados como seres pueriles que se dejaban engañar con respecto a la vida real. En el fondo, resultaba mucho más alarmante mi visión que la del subinspector. Él se rebelaba contra la falta de consideración hacia la edad, mientras yo pensaba que casi todo en los nuevos tiempos era pura decadencia y desintegración. A ver quién era más dinosaurio de los dos. Procuré llevar por otro camino nuestra conversación.

—¿Qué tal está Beatriz?

—Anda mosqueada.

—¿Más problemas con las cortinas?

—¡Qué va! Aunque el fondo de la cuestión es el mismo: me dedico sólo a mi trabajo y cada vez me ve menos el pelo.

—Lleva toda la razón. Últimamente, no hacemos más que trabajar. Yo también tengo abandonados a Marcos y los chicos.

—¡Nuestros dos cónyuges sabían que se casaban con policías!

—La dedicación obsesiva a un trabajo nadie la puede comprender.

Levantó el índice con energía como pidiendo la palabra en una grave sesión de debate.

—¡Un momento, un momento! Hay montones de profesionales que dedican horas y horas a su trabajo. Montones de gente que se levantan de madrugada, curran todo el día y no llegan a su casa hasta las diez. Y muchos hacen viajes frecuentes al extranjero o sostienen reuniones a deshora. De eso nadie se extraña y a todo el mundo le parece bien. Pero fíjese, exceptuando el currante puro y duro, todas esas personas absolutamente centradas en su labor suelen ocupar puestos importantes donde ganan muchísima pasta: financieros, médicos famosos, empresarios, políticos... Aunque existe otra variedad, los hay que hacen cosas de prestigio en las que se pasan jornadas larguísimas, aun sin llenarse los bolsillos a tope: artistas, escritores, investigadores científicos... Eso también le parece normal a la gente, no importa las horas que pasen en su cometido. Lo que a nadie le cabe en la cabeza es que unos pringados como somos los policías, que cobramos un sueldo justito y ya está, nos quememos las pestañas currelando como bestias. ¡Ah, no!, ahí ya empiezan las protestas y el crujir de dientes, cuando lo único que hacemos es un bien a la sociedad y esforzarnos por mantener a nuestras familias.

—¡Carajo, Fermín, debería usted dedicarse a la oratoria!

—¡Seguro que me iba mejor!

—Voy a hacerle un par de preguntas.

—Adelante, estoy en vena.

—¿Usted emplea todo este tiempo en el trabajo para hacer un bien a la sociedad?

Se quedó aparentemente estupefacto. Bajó la vista para mirar en el interior de su gin-tonic. Tomó la copa en su mano e hizo girar el líquido. Por fin me miró a la cara y dijo muy claramente:

—No.

—Segunda pregunta: ¿trabaja usted tantas horas exclusivamente para mantener a su familia?

Una sonrisilla cínica se le insinuó debajo del bigote.

—No —dijo de nuevo, y añadió—: Me casé con una mujer con posibles.

—Hasta ahí quería yo llegar. Lo que nos ocurre es que estamos bajo los efectos de la maldición del detective, mi querido colega. Cuando nos ocupamos de un caso complejo como el que ahora llevamos entre manos, no hay nada ni nadie que nos importe más que meternos en cuerpo y alma en él. Y cuando digo «nada ni nadie» quiero decir «nada ni nadie»: ni amor, ni familia, ni dinero, ni nuestra propia seguridad. ¿No es eso una maldición?

—Es duro de admitir, Petra.

—Sí que lo es.

Nos miramos y nos echamos a reír. Apuré el gin-tonic y continué:

—Si bien hay algo que contradice la parrafada que acabo de soltarle. ¿Adivina qué es?

—Pues que estemos aquí soplándonos una copa cuando tenemos tantísimo que hacer.

—¡Acertó!

Reímos tan fuerte que el camarero de «los chicos» nos miró desde su sitio con cierta prevención. Animados por nuestras propias cavilaciones declaradas en voz alta y, qué duda cabe, por la ginebra que habíamos pimplado, nos dispusimos a volver a comisaría, no sin antes pelearnos porque ambos queríamos pagar la cuenta, tradición española pleistocénica que igual un día de estos acaba por perderse.

19

Las pertenencias de Bob que pudimos revisar eran por completo decepcionantes. Tampoco habíamos puesto demasiadas esperanzas en encontrar alguna clave en ellas, pero a veces un objeto, una anotación, un pequeño detalle, pueden ayudar si no al esclarecimiento del caso, sí a comprender la personalidad del sujeto. Y bien, la personalidad del sujeto ya no nos importaba demasiado, la conocíamos además: perfil suicida. No hallamos objetos, anotaciones o detalles que nos hicieran avanzar. Todo lo que había conservado aquel hombre en su maleta era lo lógico y habitual en alguien que llevaba una vida nómada: enseres de aseo personal y ropa de uso diario. Nada más. Me pregunté, cuando Bob se suicidó, por qué una persona capaz de ir siempre «ligera de equipaje» y asumir todo lo que esa filosofía comporta un día decide morir. Supongo que al fin lo entendí mirando aquellas camisas, el espray de crema para el afeitado, los calcetines de varios colores. Cuatro cosas vulgares y corrientes propias de una existencia anodina. Lo único que hacía a Bob especial era su caravana restaurante. Gracias a su vehículo había soslayado el fracaso, había encontrado un lugar en el mundo. Si lo perdía, lo único que quedaría de él sería lo que justamente estaba frente a nosotros: unas piezas de ropa y un bote de espuma para afeitar.

A los tres días de haber solicitado la ayuda de la Guardia Civil, el teniente Montilla tuvo la amabilidad de venir a reportarse personalmente a comisaría. No me había fijado en lo apuesto que era, probablemente él tampoco, porque traía barba de tres días y sus gafas de montura fina tenían el cristal polvoriento.

—¿Hay alguna novedad, teniente? —le preguntó Garzón.

—Ninguna. Ya saben que si hubiera habido algo se lo hubiera hecho saber enseguida, pero hoy quería que nos viéramos las caras, que pudiéramos charlar un momento, por eso he querido personarme aquí.

—Se lo agradecemos muchísimo, siéntese.

A pesar de ser joven, Montilla utilizaba un lenguaje repleto de elementos policiales clásicos casi en desuso. «La gente siempre sorprende», pensé.

—Pues verán —continuó—. El sospechoso no ha realizado más movimientos que los que suele hacer. Por las mañanas se dirige a su tienda, la abre, recibe a su dependienta, que suele llegar una hora después. Pasa el día entero allí, aunque cierra al mediodía. Cuando aparece por la mañana lleva siempre una bolsa colgando de la mano, supongo que son sus provisiones ya cocinadas para comer a la hora del almuerzo. Abre por la tarde y cumple con el horario comercial, después se dirige a su casa y no sale a ningún sitio más.

—¿Tiene información sobre la clientela que acude a comprar?

—Nada que sea relevante, varias señoras de edad, algún trabajador que compra latas de cerveza antes del mediodía, chavales del instituto cercano que se acercan entre clases...

—Ninguno parece que levante sospechas.

—¿Cómo que no? ¡Esa tienda es una tapadera, inspectora! Llevo años tras esa escoria, tras ese malhechor y nunca he podido emplumarlo, pero esta vez no se me escapará, esta vez no.

—Teniente, yo entiendo que tenga una cuenta pendiente con el tal Dámaso, pero le recuerdo que nosotros...

—Ya lo sé, Petra, ya lo sé. Nuestros intereses se cruzan y el objetivo final no es el mismo: yo lo busco por tráfico de drogas y ustedes por un asesinato. Pero no tiene que preocuparse, ya conocen el celo profesional que pone la Benemérita en todo y su caso es como si fuera el nuestro también.

—Estoy convencida de eso, y dígame, ¿cree que Dámaso se muestra tan cauteloso porque intuye que lo estamos vigilando?

—Es muy probable que sea así, pero Dámaso es un depredador y los depredadores no se quedan quietos en un sitio, tienen que salir a cazar. Hará algo, Petra, ya verá.

—Pero el tiempo...

—Hay que esperar un poco.

Cuando se hubo marchado, Garzón rezongó.

—¿Y para decirnos eso viene aquí a darnos la tabarra?

—Hace lo que puede, Fermín, viene para ayudarnos y ni siquiera le hemos dicho claramente lo que estamos buscando.

—Esperamos que nos lleve hasta la asesina, ¿no es eso lo que buscamos, inspectora, o es que estoy volviéndome tarumba sin enterarme?

—Es eso, es eso, pero no le hemos dado detalles. Lo que me pregunto tras esta visita es si nuestros colegas de la Guardia Civil están haciéndolo bien.

—¿Qué quiere decir?

—Los horarios y los itinerarios de Dámaso son los esperables, muy bien, de acuerdo. No ha realizado ninguna llamada telefónica, correcto. Sin embargo, ¿se está sometiendo a la misma vigilancia a su dependienta?

—Sí, Montilla lo mencionó cuando iniciamos el proceso. Están siguiéndola.

—Bien, no lo recordaba, pero voy a ir más allá, ¿se llevan a cabo vigilancias sobre los clientes de la tienda de ultramarinos?

—Usted sabe que eso es imposible, inspectora.

—¿Y quién le dice que una de esas ancianitas que compran alpiste no le ha llevado algún mensaje a Martine Marchand de parte de su compinche Dámaso? Un aviso para que se desplace, para que huya, para que esté alerta ante nuestra intervención.

Garzón se quedó en suspenso un minuto. Luego, empezó a cabecear mirando al suelo.

—No sé, inspectora, ¡es tan improbable! No han visto a nadie sospechoso entrando en la tienda y las ancianitas...

—¿Cómo sería un sospechoso de tráfico de drogas?, ¿llevaría tatuajes visibles en la frente?, ¿olería a grifa a un kilómetro de distancia?

—Claro que no, pero pensar en un cártel de viejecitas...

—No necesariamente, piense en una clienta habitual a la que Dámaso engaña o camela: ¿podría usted, señora Pura, mandar este mensaje por mí, que tengo el móvil escacharrado?

Garzón se quedó suspendido de mis palabras. Seguramente empezaba a pensar que mis tonterías podían albergar un punto de verdad. Aun así, buscó un razonamiento para contradecirme.

—Siguiendo ese patrón también podríamos sospechar que le hiciera esa misma petición a un vecino de su inmueble.

—Sería raro. Un tipo que se dedica al narcotráfico no suele confraternizar con el vecindario, demasiado arriesgado. Además, mi querido subinspector, una intuición es una intuición, y usted sabe que las mías valen un potosí.

—Me alegra que su autoestima esté por las nubes.

—Si mi autoestima dependiera de los resultados de esta investigación la tendría subterránea.

Tomé el teléfono y llamé a Montilla. Acababa de llegar a su despacho y lógicamente pensaría que se me había olvidado hacerle alguna pregunta, pero no esperaba que fuera la siguiente.

—¿Estáis filmando o fotografiando a los clientes que acuden a la tienda de Dámaso?

—Sí, pero ya le dije que no hay presencias sospechosas.

—¿Filmando o fotografiando?

—Hay filmaciones de todos al entrar y al salir. ¿Qué pretende hacer?

—Quiero verlas, sólo para no dejar ningún cabo suelto. Pensamos que quizá Dámaso pudo mandar algún mensaje a la francesa por medio de algún cliente.

Comprendí que el bufido que me llegó a través del móvil significaba escepticismo, pero por las palabras del teniente era obvio que él añadía otra acepción.

—¡Ponerse a revisar todos los vídeos es una matada, Petra!, y con muy pocas perspectivas de que resulte útil. Si Dámaso le da un mensaje a alguien será verbal, o un papel que puede meterse en un bolsillo o en la cesta de la compra, con lo cual es imposible de detectar. En el caso de que alguien hubiera salido con un paquete o hubiera hecho un movimiento extraño, mis hombres lo hubieran captado *de visu*. ¿No le parece?

—Lo del «visu» me ha llegado al alma, teniente.

—Ya ve, cultura que atesora la Guardia Civil. Entonces, ¿qué hago, le mando las filmaciones?

—Con toda *celeritas*, por favor.

Oí una carcajada y después su despedida. Me había abstenido de entrar a discutir si la opción de pasar el tiempo viendo filmaciones era más o menos útil que pasarlo esperando a que Dámaso hiciera un movimiento, cometiera un error, como él planteaba.

Con todo, Montilla llevaba razón, mirar una a una todas las filmaciones de los clientes de la tienda ultramarina era una matada de mucho cuidado. Los compradores carecían además del más mínimo glamur. Por fortuna no había demasiados y los que acudían solían repetirse. El gran pelotón lo formaban las ancianas y es verdad que tenían poco de sospechosas. Me conmovía verlas, mujeres humildes que probablemente llevaban toda la vida yendo a comprar, realizando las mismas tareas en casa, algunas con trabajos externos también. Vestidas con ropa barata, sin prestar atención a la coordinación de colores o la elegancia. Y, sin embargo, todas y cada una de ellas mostraban el cabello bien cortado, el tinte reciente. «Si los bares son el alma democrática de este país —pensé—, las peluquerías femeninas ocupan el segundo lugar en importancia.» Por muy escasos que sean los recursos económicos o muy provecta la edad, las mujeres españolas nunca descuidan su cabello. Siempre hay algún salón económico en sus barrios o alguna vecina que sabe peinar.

El segundo colectivo que aparecía con más frecuencia en las grabaciones era de índole casi opuesta al senado femenino. Tal y como nos había advertido el teniente Montilla, se trataba de jóvenes, todos provenientes del cercano instituto de enseñanza media. En la pantalla fuimos viendo cómo llegaban en pequeños grupos de tres o cuatro, se quedaban un rato corto en la tienda y volvían a salir con latas de refresco en la mano, alguna barrita de chocolate o una bolsa de patatas fritas. Por último, teníamos a los clientes aislados, aquellos que hacían escasas repeticiones o que era evidente que sólo pasaban por allí y aprovechaban para hacer una compra.

—Bueno... —exclamó Garzón—, no creo que

esta empresa vaya a entrar en bolsa. ¿Ha servido de algo el coñazo que nos hemos arreado?

—Déjeme mirar.

Había estado tomando notas a mano. Las consulté.

—Necesito seguir con el coñazo un poco más. Vuelva a pasar las tomas 38 y 49.

Mi compañero se abstuvo de hacer preguntas y buscó en el ordenador. La primera imagen correspondía a tres de los estudiantes: una chica rubia que lucía *leggins* negros, un muchacho con marcas de acné y un tercero, muy alto y muy delgado, que salía de la tienda un poco después. Los otros dos lo esperaban fuera y cuando salió el terceto emprendían todos la retirada chupeteando como lelos sus latas de Coca-Cola.

—¿Hay algo que le parezca interesante? —preguntó el subinspector.

—Pasemos a la filmación 49 —respondí como única aclaración.

En la pantalla apareció de nuevo el chico alto y delgado. Entraba en la tienda y volvía a salir escasos segundos después. Tomé el ratón del ordenador en la mano y lo manejé yo, yendo adelante y atrás varias veces.

—¿Se da cuenta, Fermín? Toma 38: entran los tres chavales, el alto y delgado se rezaga y sale casi dos minutos después. Son las once de la mañana de ayer, la hora del recreo en la que, probablemente, sólo los mayores pueden abandonar el instituto. Perfecto, está claro, ¿no? Ahora pasemos a la 49. El chico vuelve solo a la tienda. Estamos en la misma mañana, pero son las trece cuarenta y cinco. Dámaso cierra a las catorce en punto. El chico no lleva nada en las manos cuando abandona la tienda. La pregunta es: ¿por qué regresa antes del cierre?, ¿qué ha ido a comprar? Improvíseme alguna explicación creíble.

Se rascó el bigote mientras estaba absorto en la imagen congelada del estudiante. Buscaba con intensidad en su caletre. Al fin, empezó a hablar.

—Posibilidad uno: ha comprado cualquier chuchería que olvidó y que cabe en su bolsillo. Posibilidad dos: se da cuenta de que Dámaso le ha devuelto mal el cambio y quiere reclamarlo. Posibilidad tres: es un pequeño consumidor de droga a quien Dámaso le ha vendido en alguna ocasión y vuelve a por más. Y con eso se acaba mi capacidad de repentización.

—Veamos, la primera es improbable. Resulta extraño que haya olvidado comprar una bobada. De hecho, en ninguna otra filmación se le ve volviendo a esa hora, no parece que tenga la costumbre de consumir nada hacia el mediodía. La segunda es poco creíble por una cuestión de tiempo: si hubiera ido a reclamar un cambio, eso habría dado lugar a un poco de discusión, mientras que el chico sale casi inmediatamente. En cuanto al consumo de droga... Dámaso se mueve en esferas más altas, y además, ¿cómo va a atreverse a menudear droga en el lugar que es su tapadera legal, y venderle a un muchacho tan joven al que puede darle por cantar en cualquier momento?

—Sí, la tercera era la más floja. Ahora le toca a usted, Petra. ¿Cuántas hipótesis ha elaborado?

—Ninguna.
—Pero ¿qué me dice?
—Le digo que el regreso del chico alto es lo único destacable que he podido entresacar de todo este coñazo, como usted dice. Y aunque sólo sea para que el teniente no piense que somos gilipollas viendo filmaciones porque sí, vamos a investigar la opción.
—¿Mañana a qué hora la espero en el instituto?
—Pongamos a las diez. De todas maneras, cuando llegue a casa esta noche estará todo el mundo durmiendo. Por lo menos mañana no me haga madrugar.

No madrugué, de modo que tampoco vi a nadie de la familia en esa ocasión. «Es como si volviera a vivir sola», pensé. Sin embargo, no me sentía culpable en absoluto. El trabajo es una parte de la vida, y el mío era como era, no había más cáscaras.

Garzón estaba puntualmente en el instituto a la hora acordada. Como siempre se levantaba muy temprano, deduje que ya había pasado por comisaría. Acerté plenamente. Había ido a buscar las fotos fijas del chico alto y delgado y las había cargado en su móvil, todo ello a las ocho de la mañana. No le dije que yo también había tomado esa esencial precaución justo el día antes para no agraviarlo. Los madrugadores están convencidos de que su costumbre ayuda a solucionar problemas y que además los ayuda Dios, como dice el refrán.

Al entrar en el edificio del instituto me di cuenta de que el olor que flotaba en el aire no era el mismo que yo recordaba de mi época escolar. De hecho, le faltaba el matiz principal: el lápiz. Ahora había una mezcla extraña, como de ambientador barato y efluvios de comida de vez en cuando.

Nos dirigimos a una recepcionista bastante cascada, que ocupaba un garito acristalado junto a la puerta principal.

—Queremos hablar con el director. Somos policías.

Creí que iba a sorprenderse al menos un poco, pero se comportaba como quien ya lo ha visto todo en el mundo y nada le puede alterar.

—El director no está. Ha ido a hacer recados.

—Pues entonces hablaremos con la máxima autoridad del centro que se encuentre presente. ¿Quién es?

La recepcionista cercana a la jubilación se quedó un instante en suspenso, como si no supiera qué significaba aquello de la máxima autoridad.

—El jefe de estudios —dijo por fin como si todo aquello le importara un carajo—. Pero está en clase de segundo.

—¿Puede decirle que venga, por favor?

Se levantó y salió de su chiquero, pero lejos de desplazarse en busca de la autoridad, lo que hizo fue coger del brazo a una estudiante que pasaba en aquel momento.

—Oye, Olga. Vete a la clase de segundo B y dile al profesor Llop que baje. La poli quiere hablar con él.

Garzón me lanzó una mirada escandalizada, quizá por el estilo poco formal de la señora, pero yo me había fijado en algo interesante.

—Por mera curiosidad, ¿se sabe los nombres de algunos alumnos del instituto?

—Sólo de los mayores. Como son los que llevan más tiempo...

Busqué la fotografía del chico en mi teléfono, se la mostré a la recepcionista.

—¿Este chico es alumno del centro?

Lo observó un instante con la misma indiferencia con la que todo lo hacía.

—Sí, es Jordi Dolcet, de segundo. ¿Qué ha hecho?

—Nada en especial, sólo queríamos hacerle unas preguntas.

—¡Ah! —exclamó desvaídamente.

Su fogonazo de curiosidad había prescrito. Regresó a su pecera y nos dejó solos en medio del lugar. Rápidamente, llegó el jefe de estudios, un hombre de cuarenta y tantos vestido de modo completamente informal: un jersey enorme y deformado que le colgaba por los flancos y botas camperas. Nos presentamos y le enseñamos la placa.

—¿Ha pasado algo? —preguntó.

—¿Hay algún sitio donde podamos hablar más tranquilamente?

—Sí, vengan a mi despacho.

Su despacho era una minúscula estancia con sólo una ventana que daba a un patio interior. Le enseñé la fotografía del chico.

—Al parecer este es uno de los alumnos del centro. Se llama Jordi Dolcet. ¿Cierto?

—Sí, así es. Estudia segundo de bachillerato. ¿Hay algún problema con él?

—¿Se encuentra en estos momentos en el centro? Queríamos hacerle unas preguntas.

—Sí, debe de encontrarse en clase. Puedo ir a buscarlo yo mismo, el aula está aquí cerca.

Se levantó y salió del cuchitril, dejando la puerta abierta. Al cabo volvió con el chico. Resultaba aún más espigado que en las imágenes, pero una fea mueca quizá de desprecio o suficiencia anulaba cualquier atractivo de su cara. No había asientos suficientes, de manera que nos quedamos todos de pie.

—Bueno, pues aquí está Jordi.

—¿Puede dejarnos a solas, profesor?

—¿A solas, para qué?

—Ya se lo he dicho, sólo queremos hacerle algunas preguntas.

—Pero, señores, Jordi es menor. No pueden ustedes interrogarlo. Voy a llamar a sus padres.

—No hemos dicho que haya nada en contra suya, simplemente se trata de hablar cinco minutos.

—Si les parece bien, concertamos una cita para mañana a esta hora, después de que yo haya hablado con los padres del alumno y...

—No hace falta, muchas gracias. Traeremos una orden judicial.

Arrastré al subinspector y salimos. En la boca del alumno se había pintado una ligerísima sonrisa torcida. No hicieron falta demasiados argumentos cruzados para que llegáramos a un acuerdo.

—Lo esperamos a la salida, ¿no, Fermín?

—¡Nos ha jodido, eso está cantado, aunque tengamos que apalancarnos en una esquina hasta la madrugada!

Al pasar por delante de la recepcionista, vimos que había intensificado su postura de indiferencia ante el mundo mascando un chicle con toda desfachatez. Le pregunté:

—¿Salen todos los alumnos al mismo tiempo?

Sin levantar la vista de su mesa negó ostensiblemente.

—¡Qué va! Hay grupos, subgrupos, especializaciones..., aquí cada uno sale a una hora distinta. Yo no, yo a las tres de la tarde me voy a casita y ya se apañarán.

No fue fácil buscar una ubicación desde donde pudiéramos vigilar en qué momento salía Jordi Dolcet. Existía el peligro, además, de que tomara un autobús en la parada que se encontraba justo enfrente del instituto, no podíamos alejarnos demasiado. Al final, nos decidimos por quedarnos de pie en una esquina, aproximadamente a cien metros de la puerta principal.

A partir de las doce y media esa puerta empezó a escupir grupos de alumnos, si bien la gran hégira se produjo a la una y cuarto. Desde donde estábamos se podía oír una música estridente que salía del edificio. Al espíritu crítico de Garzón no le pasó por alto ese detalle.

—¡Les ponen música a tope a la hora de la salida! ¡Vaya tela, inspectora! Y luego se quejarán de cómo se comporta la juventud. La recepcionista, una mujer mayor más pasota que un don Tancredo. El jefe de estudios, vestido como si se fuera de excursión, y la guinda: música a toda castaña a la hora de salir.

—Yo sé más cosas por los gemelos de Marcos: a la hora del recreo también ponen música en el patio, a todo trapo. Para indicar el cambio de clases no suena un timbre, sino una melodía y a los profesores, incluido el director, todos los alumnos les hablan de tú.

—¡Lo que me faltaba por oír! Si en mis tiempos yo hubiera tuteado a un profesor, me hubieran llovido las hostias hasta en el carnet de identidad.

—No sea antiguo, Fermín.

—Pero ¿a usted todo esto le parece bien?

—No, pero como justamente no son mis tiempos, me abstengo de opinar.

—Por puro miedo a hacer el ridículo, inspectora, no se engañe, sólo por el qué dirán.

Me fue imposible contestar a ese reproche, tan cargado de razón, porque avisté a Dolcet cruzando la puerta en compañía de tres chicos más. Le di un codazo a mi compañero. Reaccionó diciendo: «Déjemelo a mí». Eran las dos menos cuarto. El pequeño grupo charló en la calle durante un breve espacio de tiempo y se dispersó después. Dolcet, loado sea el cielo, vino solo en nuestra dirección. Nos retrepamos contra la pared y le salimos al paso. Se llevó un susto morrocotudo. Oímos su voz por primera vez.

—¡Joder!

Garzón hubiera querido acercarse a su cara, pero la diferencia de estatura era excesiva para ese gesto de intimidación. Lo sustituyó por un índice amenazante apuntándole sin pausa.

—¡Hombre, pero si el niño sabe hablar! A ver, criaturita, ¿qué asuntos te traes con Dámaso el de la tienda de ultramarinos?

El chico estaba visiblemente asustado.

—No podéis hablar conmigo. Soy menor.

Garzón compuso unas carcajadas teatrales.

—Tú te crees todo lo que dicen los profes, ¿verdad? Y seguro que también todo lo que dice tu mamá. Pues vas equivocado, monín. Podemos hablar contigo, podemos detenerte, llevarte a un juzgado de menores... Lo único que no puedo hacer es lo que más me apetece: soltarte un par de hostias ahora mismo.

—Yo no he hecho nada.

—¿Qué te pidió Dámaso? —intervine.

—No sé de qué me habla.

—¿A qué hora sales los martes de clase?

—A la una y cuarto.

—¿Por qué este martes estuviste esperando hasta las dos para ir a la tienda de Dámaso?

—Me quedé en la biblioteca, estudiando.

—¡Y una mierda! —soltó Garzón—. Volviste a la tienda antes de cerrar, ¿para qué?

—Se me había olvidado comprar chicles.

Estábamos casi al lado de un aparcamiento. Se abrió el portón hacia arriba y salió un coche. Cuando volvía a bajar, Garzón estuvo rápido y metió al chico de un empujón en el garaje. Yo me colé detrás. La luz eléctrica se apagó automáticamente. Nos veíamos en la penumbra. Ahí el chico se asustó de verdad.

—¿Por qué volviste a la tienda? Suéltalo de una puta vez.

—Yo no tengo nada que ver con las drogas.

—¿Drogas, quién ha hablado de drogas? —pregunté en un susurro.

—Por ahí dicen que el dueño de la tienda anda en la droga.

—Y tú eres su jodido camellete, ¿verdad? —gritó el subinspector.

—¡No, no, os juro que no! —Dolcet empezaba a estar fuera de sí, casi lloraba.

—¡En vaya lío estás metido, chaval! Tu vida a tomar por saco, ya ves qué fácil.

—¡Yo no he hecho nada, no tengo nada que ver con la tienda ni con el dueño! —Ya tenía la voz rota por el llanto, por el miedo. Intervine de nuevo.

—¿Qué fuiste a hacer a las dos de la tarde del martes a la tienda de ultramarinos? Apuesto a que Dámaso te pidió que llevaras un paquetito de heroína a alguna parte.

—¡No, no, no era droga, era una carta, sólo un sobre con una carta dentro, para dársela a una mujer!

—¿Cómo?, explícate.

—Primero me pidió que le prestara mi móvil para hacer una llamada. Le dije que no, justamente por si era algo de droga. No quería que el número quedara marcado en mi teléfono. Entonces me dijo que volviera al mediodía y me daría una carta para una mujer, que era un asunto de amores y nada más.

—Y tú lo hiciste encantado de la vida, ¿no? ¡Viva el amor!

—Me daba cien euros por el recado —confesó bajando la cabeza y la voz—. Me enseñó una nota escrita moviéndola en el aire sin que yo pudiera leerla, entonces la metió en el sobre y lo cerró. Dijo: ¿ves? Una carta y nada más.

—¿Puso algo en el sobre?

—No, pero me aprendí la dirección: Virrey Amat, 25, 3.º 2.ª.

—¿Llevaste la carta?

—Sí, tomé la línea 5 de metro y la llevé. Llamé al timbre y tardaron mucho en contestar, pero al final, cuando dije que iba de parte de Dámaso, me abrieron. Salió una mujer y sin quitar la cadena de la puerta me preguntó qué quería. Le di el sobre, dijo gracias y cerró.

—¿A qué hora fuiste?

—Llegué sobre las cinco de la tarde porque primero fui a mi casa y comí.

—¿Cómo era la mujer?

—Pues morena, alta.

—¿Qué edad le calculaste?

—Pues no sé, más o menos como tú —dijo.

—¿Tenía acento francés?

—No sé si era francés, pero extranjero sí era, no reconozco los acentos de todos los idiomas, ¿entiendes?

—¡Háblale de usted a la inspectora y a mí también! ¿Nadie te ha enseñado que...?

Le tiré fuertemente de la manga a Garzón. Apreté el botón de la puerta.

—¡Déjese de hostias ahora, Fermín, vámonos!

Aún tuvo tiempo mi compañero de enarbolar su dedo una vez más para soltar:

—Y como te vayas de la lengua sobre esta conversación vendré a hostiarte personalmente, ¿comprendes? Seas menor o la momia de Ramsés. ¿Entiendes?

Lo vimos alejarse blanco como un papel. Garzón contempló su figura larguirucha con cara de perro al acecho hasta que desapareció por una esquina.

—Relaje la mandíbula, Fermín, la presa ya se ha ido.

—No puedo soportar a esta generación de chavales capaces de venderse por unos euros.

—Ya escribirá una epístola moral a las nuevas generaciones; de momento no estamos en eso. Hay que darse prisa.

—¿Llamo al teniente?

—Todavía no. Quiero que hagamos primero una inspección ocular.

Salimos a toda velocidad hacia la calle Virrey Amat, que no nos cogía cerca. Evidentemente, carecíamos de la orden judicial prescriptiva para entrar en el piso, pero el juez que instruía el caso en ningún momento nos había puesto la más mínima pega, de modo que ya nos la daría *a posteriori*.

El inmueble era alto y de aspecto humilde. Llamamos al tercero segunda, pero nadie respondió. Lo intentamos con el timbre contiguo y una voz de mujer se dejó oír. Parecía una anciana.

—Somos de la policía, abra, por favor.

Funcionó el automático sin que quien lo había activado dijera ni una palabra. Subimos a pie, desestimando el ascensor. Tal y como me imaginaba, una señora mayor esperaba en el descansillo. Tras ella, otra mujer de la misma edad atisbaba en silencio.

—¿Ustedes son de la policía? ¿Qué ha pasado?, ¿a quién buscan?

—De momento, señoras, cierren la puerta y quédense en su casa. Dentro de un rato hablaremos con ustedes.

—¿Estamos en peligro?

—No, por supuesto que no. Vuelvan adentro, luego las avisamos.

Obedecieron sin rechistar. Garzón y yo nos quedamos mirando la cerradura de la puerta que nos interesaba. No tenía ningún sistema de seguridad y parecía muy endeble.

—¿Patadón? —preguntó el subinspector—. Si lo oyen las viejas pensarán que es mentira que seamos polis y llamarán a los colegas, seguro. Puede armarse un buen follón.

—Probemos antes en el buzón de correo de la entrada.

Garzón se lanzó escaleras abajo como una exhalación. Mientras lo esperaba me pareció oír un ligero frufrú detrás de la puerta de las ancianas. Saqué un chicle del bolso, lo mastiqué varias veces para ablandarlo y lo pegué en la mirilla de su puerta. Al poco, el ascensor paró y de él salió un Garzón jadeante. Sonreía.

—Es usted la mujer más lista con la que me he topado jamás.

Me enseñó un manojo de llaves con aire triunfal.

—¿Ha forzado el buzón?

—¿Y usted qué cree? Una buena leche y a otra cosa, mariposa. Siempre será mejor que cargarse la puerta —dijo mientras abría sin ninguna dificultad.

El piso estaba en silencio absoluto. Entramos en el salón, pequeño, con pocos muebles de mal gusto. Estaba ligeramente desordenado, un par de prendas de punto, sin duda de mujer por el colorido, se encontraban tiradas encima del sofá. En la mesita central, una taza de café a medio consumir. Caminamos hacia la cocina y allí sí reinaba un pandemónium descomunal: sartenes, cazos y platos diseminados por el suelo, la mayor parte sin lavar. Abrí la nevera con la ayuda de un pañuelo para no alterar huellas. El interior se encontraba pletórico de todo tipo de viandas: verduras, yogures, carne, zumos... Parecía evidente que el huésped que allí moraba pensaba seguir haciéndolo durante bastante tiempo.

Pasamos al dormitorio principal. Se hallaba lleno de ropa esparcida, la cama deshecha, el armario ropero abierto, y unos zapatos de tacón yacían sobre la alfombrilla. En el cuarto de baño anejo habían sido abandonados productos de higiene, también varios tipos de maquillaje y cremas para el cuerpo y la cara.

Otro dormitorio pequeño era el último lugar para inspeccionar. Sobre una cama pequeña, había una maleta abierta, sin nada en su interior. Martine Marchand había huido precipitadamente, dejando atrás sus pertenencias. Aun sin atrevernos a registrar a fondo, nada daba indicios de que hubiera dejado algún papel, alguna fotografía, cualquier objeto que fuera de interés. Sólo una cosa era diáfana: la mujer que había estado allí era sin duda nuestra francesa y había estado sola, los gorilas que la habían acompañado no habían pernoctado en el mismo lugar. Quizá había prescindido de ellos viendo que el dinero o las drogas que buscaban no habían aparecido, quizá habían regresado a Francia ya.

—Llame a una dotación, Fermín, que hagan un registro en condiciones, huellas, etcétera, y que precinten después.

—Enseguida, inspectora. ¿Llamo también al teniente?

—Sí, cuéntele un poco y dígale que ya puede detener a Dámaso. Nosotros iremos después. Voy a hablar con las viejas.

Quité el chicle de la mirilla y llamé al timbre de las vecinas. No estaban excesivamente alarmadas, incluso me invitaron a pasar. El saloncito de su casa era como un muestrario de manualidades: cuadros hechos con punto de cruz, cojines de bolillos, tapetitos de ganchillo, macetas colgadas de soportes tejidos con macramé. Un auténtico horror. ¡Cuánto se equivocan los que piensan que la modernidad ha llegado a todas partes por igual! Allí vivían aquellas dos mujeres como si el siglo XIX hubiera acabado de transcurrir un mes atrás.

—En el piso de enfrente vivía una señora de unos cincuenta años, ¿cierto?

—Sí, muy guapetona.

—¿Cuánto tiempo estuvo aquí?

—Poco, como un mes o así. Este piso siempre estaba cerrado y nos sorprendió cuando la vimos.

Les mostré la foto del pasaporte falso.

—¿Era esta mujer?

—Sí, está un poco cambiada, pero yo diría que sí.

—¿Hablaron con ella?

—Muy poco, hola y adiós. Era extranjera. Un día yo le pregunté algo, no recuerdo qué, y por señas me dijo que no me entendía, así que si nos veíamos, nos saludábamos y ya está.

—¿Recibía visitas?, ¿vieron a alguien en alguna ocasión?

—Nosotras somos muy discretas y no nos metemos en la vida de los demás.

—Por supuesto que no, pero pudieron ver a alguien por casualidad.

—Nunca vimos a nadie. No es que estuviéramos pendientes de si había movimiento en su casa, pero como usted dice, la casualidad hubiera podido hacer que nos cruzáramos con alguien, oír voces en el descansillo o algo por el estilo, pero no. Yo creo que estaba sola siempre.

—Pero salía a la calle.

—No mucho, pero sí. Iba al supermercado y a veces no estaba en toda la tarde.

—¿Cuándo la vieron por última vez?

—Ayer mismo. Yo vi que salía de casa con una mochila a la espalda. No he vuelto a verla más. Oiga, ¿la han asesinado?

Contestó por mí la otra anciana.

—¡Ay, Manolita, por Dios, no seas tan brutal! Perdone a mi hermana, pero es que se pasa la vida viendo series de crímenes.

Sonreí y les di las gracias. A mi espalda pude oír muy bajito:

—¿Por qué me has cortado? Ahora no sabemos si la han asesinado o no.

20

Por si nos faltaba alguna certeza con la que operar, el piso de la calle Virrey Amat pertenecía legalmente a Dámaso Ibáñez Juárez, nuestro hombre. La complicación, o quizá la ventaja, era que se trataba de un sospechoso compartido con el teniente Montilla. Al llegar a su cuartel, ya nos esperaba con amplia cara de satisfacción. Había cazado a su presa, que ya estaba en prisión preventiva, ahora sólo le faltaba poder cocinarla y comerla después. Aceptó de buen grado que estuviéramos presentes y activos en el interrogatorio, pero yo insistí en que antes de entrar en materia, tuviéramos una reunión nosotros tres.

—Primero vamos a por lo nuestro, Montilla. Se trata de atrapar a una asesina, que es algo muy grave. Luego tú le preguntas lo que necesites en tu investigación. ¿De acuerdo?

—Me parece adecuado a la situación.

—¿Tiene Dámaso abogado?

—Por supuesto que lo tiene. Se llama Rodrigo Galván y es un pájaro de cuenta. Defiende a todos los malhechores que os podáis imaginar. Sólo con que un detenido solicite su presencia ya debería ser una prueba de culpabilidad. Pero Dámaso ha renunciado a que esté presente hoy.

—¿Y eso?

—Supongo que quiere convencernos de su inocencia. Además, lo ha hecho porque es un chulo, aunque si se las ve magras pedirá llamar a su ilustre letrado, ya lo veréis. Aparte de ser un cabrón, Galván es un tío muy bueno en lo suyo. A Dámaso siempre lo ha sacado del atolladero.

Al entrar en la sala no me pareció que el detenido estuviera nervioso o preocupado. Tenía una actitud relajada y en los ojos una mirada chulesca. No abrió la boca hasta que todos estuvimos sentados, sólo entonces hizo la pregunta tradicional.

—¿De qué se me acusa?

—Complicidad en un asesinato —tomé la palabra sin pensarlo dos veces. Su talante sosegado desapareció de un plumazo.

—¡¿Qué?! —preguntó dando un grito y poniéndose en pie—. ¿Se puede saber de qué van ustedes? Si piensan tenderme una trampa están listos, llamaré inmediatamente a mi abogado.

—¿No es complicidad el dar cobijo a una sospechosa de asesinato?

—No sé de qué me habla.

—No nos haga perder tiempo, por favor. Usted le dio una nota a un chaval del instituto para evadir el cerco de vigilancia que le habíamos puesto. Él la llevó a un piso en la calle Virrey Amat que, mira por dónde, es de su propiedad.

—Sigo sin saber de qué habla.

—Hemos registrado el piso y estaba lleno de ropa y enseres de los que usamos las mujeres.

—Sería una okupa, nunca voy por ese piso.

—Las vecinas de rellano la reconocieron en una fotografía. Se trata de Martine Marchand, alias Nathalie Verbeux. Estamos más que convencidos de que la nota que le entregó al estudiante la ponía en aviso para que abandonara ese domicilio. ¿Va sonándole de algo la historia?

Bajó la vista, se estrujó las manos. Alguna lucha interna estaba produciéndose en su interior. Nadie vulneró el silencio. Por fin dijo:

—Bueno, vale, sí, le dejé unos días mi piso. Vino a verme y me dijo que estaba en apuros y que no podía ir a un hotel. Como nos conocíamos le hice el favor. Luego le dije en la nota que se largara porque pensaba poner la vivienda en alquiler. No quería que la poli se enterara para que no me buscaran complicaciones. ¿Y qué?, ¿hacer un favor es delito?

—Esa mujer era una delincuente y usted lo sabía.

—¿Y tengo que cargar con lo que ella haya podido hacer? ¿Eso es complicidad? ¡Venga, no me joda, inspectora! O sea, que si esa tía se hubiera cargado las Torres Gemelas ¿yo sería su cómplice? Me dijo que tenía un problema, pero ¡yo qué sé a qué problema se refería!

—Huía de la justicia y usted le dio cobijo. Obstrucción a la justicia para empezar a hablar.

—De cómplice de asesinato, nanay.

—¿Qué hacía Martine Marchand en Barcelona?

—No me lo dijo ni yo le pregunté.

Inopinadamente, intervino el teniente Montilla.

—La próxima chorrada absurda que contestes te meto en el calabozo de régimen especial.

Aproveché para ahondar en su línea.

—A lo mejor su dependienta dice cosas con mucho más sentido. Creo que es preferible que la interroguemos a ella.

Se levantó de un salto por segunda vez.

—A mi dependienta ni mentarla, no sabe nada de nada.

—Es su amante, ¿verdad? Pues sepa que está tan envuelta en este asunto como usted.

—¡Ni siquiera conocía a la francesa!

—Eso ya nos lo contará ella personalmente. Teniente, por favor, dé orden a uno de sus hombres para que traigan...

—¡No! —me interrumpió con un grito—. A ver, ¿qué coño quieren saber de la francesa? ¿Que le presté mi piso unos días porque tenía un problema? Pues sí, se lo presté, ¿y eso qué prueba?

—¿Qué tipo de problema tenía Martine?

—No me lo contó. La gente no va contando sus problemas por ahí. Yo le debía un favor desde hace un montón de años y dejándole el piso se lo pagué. Eso es todo.

—¿Era un problema de drogas? —intervino Montilla por segunda vez. Dámaso lo miró con odio infinito.

—No, yo con la droga ya no tengo nada que ver.

—Eso ya lo trataremos luego —le devolvió el odio el teniente.

—¿Qué buscaba Martine en Barcelona? —pregunté.

—No lo sé.

Me acerqué mucho a él, lo miré a los ojos.

—Dámaso, estoy investigando un asesinato. Si me dice algo, aunque sea poco, sobre por qué motivo la francesa estaba en la ciudad, me veo con ánimo para que no conste en ninguna parte que usted la escondió y después la alertó para que no la atrapáramos.

—No habla en serio, ¿se cree que soy tonto?

—Será tonto si no aprovecha la ocasión que le brindo. No me interesa en lo que usted ande metido, el asesinato es prioritario para mí. Le juro por mi vida que si me cuenta lo que sabe, cuando el subinspector y yo traspasemos la puerta, todo este lío acabará para usted, también para su amante.

Desvió la mirada hacia el teniente.

—Delante de ese no pienso decir nada.

Montilla apretó la mandíbula y se largó con ira evidente. Entonces Dámaso bajó la voz para decir:

—Martine vino con dos tiparracos de su organización. Buscaban algo que le había escatimado un tío que hacía negocios con ella, un tipo que tenía una furgo de comidas.

—¿Drogas?

—No lo sé.

—¿Dinero?

—Quizá. El caso es que no encontraron lo que buscaban y los dos gorilas volvieron a Francia.

—Pero ella se quedó.

—Sí, se quedó.

—¿Por qué, Dámaso, por qué?

—Quería averiguar quién se había cargado al tío de la furgo.

Garzón y yo nos quedamos tan pasmados que ni siquiera intercambiamos una mirada.

—¿No lo había hecho ella?

—Yo le digo lo que ella largó, no sé nada más. Se lo aseguro, de verdad. Si hubiera cometido ella el asesinato no hubiera venido a contármelo a mí, no éramos amigos. Lo que dijo exactamente es que quería saber quién se había cargado al tío de la furgo, nada más. ¿Va a cumplir su palabra?

—Siempre lo hago.

Abrí la puerta. Montilla estaba esperando fuera.

—Todo suyo, teniente —dijo Garzón.

—¡Eso no es lo que habíamos acordado! —aulló el detenido.

—Conmigo sí. Pero el teniente creo que se guardaba preguntas sobre el tráfico de drogas en general. Eso no me concierne.

Los dejamos a solas. Al salir a la calle, el subinspector comentó:

—Me juego el sueldo de cinco meses a que dentro de un rato llegará el abogado de Dámaso.

—Espero que antes no se hayan agredido mutuamente el teniente y él.

—Inspectora, ¿usted cree que lo que nos ha contado ese tipo es verdad?

Miré al cielo, que estaba claro y luminoso. Tuve la impresión de que no lo había visto durante meses.

—Pues... no sé qué contestarle, Garzón. En cualquier caso, si fuera verdad, eso nos liberaría de un absurdo que nos ha perseguido durante toda la investigación. ¿Por qué matar y después buscar? ¿No sería más lógico al revés? El cadáver de Laurent no tenía señales de violencia o tortura. Nadie estuvo maltratándolo para que dijera dónde estaba la droga o el dinero.

—Entonces se trataba de una venganza.

—Conociendo la ferocidad de la Leoparda, puede que sí. Vino para matarlo y se lo encontró muerto. Fue entonces cuando llamó a sus hombres para que la ayudaran a buscar lo que Laurent le había escatimado. Aunque hay algo un poco absurdo en esa posibilidad, ¿por qué vino ella personalmente y no encargó el asesinato a sus secuaces?

—Mire, inspectora, si se trata de encontrar absurdos, en este caso tenemos dónde escoger.

Un absurdo sobre otro, llevaba razón.

Hice el informe sobre el hallazgo del piso que Marchand había ocupado, sobre el interrogatorio a Dámaso. Obvié los detalles heterodoxos, al fin y al cabo cargarse un buzón de correspondencia era una nimiedad.

Aquella noche llegué a casa más temprano de lo que solía hacerlo en los últimos tiempos. Estaban los tres hijos de Marcos viendo la televisión.

—¡Ya hemos acabado todas las tareas! —se justificó Hugo con anticipación.

—¡Vaya, Petra, qué alegría verte! Creí que habías fallecido en el peligroso ejercicio de tu profesión —soltó Teo con su sorna característica.

Sólo faltaba la reacción de Marina, que fue de índole práctica.

—Petra, la asistenta ha cocinado acelgas para cenar. Y yo ya he comido acelgas en el colegio. ¿No podríamos variar, preparar cualquier otra cosa?

—¿Y qué hacemos con las acelgas? —dije distraídamente, abrumada por la variedad de temas que proponían mis hijastros.

—Las llevas a comisaría y amenazas con ellas a un sospechoso que estés interrogando y no quiera cantar.

—Muy gracioso, Teo.

—Anda, Petra, enróllate bien y cocinamos otra cosa —imploró Marina zalameramente.

—Veré lo que puedo hacer, pero supongo que no se os habrá pasado por las mientes que yo vaya a currar a la cocina mientras os quedáis aquí repantingados.

—Bien pensado, las acelgas no estaban tan mal —bromeó Hugo.

—¿Queréis que os confiese una cosa? —dije apagando la televisión—. La próxima vez que me case, me aseguraré de que mi prometido no tiene hijos.

Por el pasillo reían, se empujaban, gritaban «¡Abajo las acelgas!». Pensé (sólo un momento) que al volver a casa después del trabajo quizá era más energético aquel follón que tomarse a solas un whisky con hielo.

Hervimos unas patatas después de que los chicos las pelaran con idénticos lamentos que los que deben oírse en un cuartel militar y luego las mezclamos con las acelgas y las corté en una concienzuda juliana. Finalmente, las refreí con unos ajos. En el microondas había filetes empanados.

—Esta cena es digna de un zar de todas las Rusias —argumenté al servir.

—No está mal —comentó Teo.

—¿Y tú por qué no cenas, Petra?

—Espero a vuestro padre. Nosotros cenaremos caviar.

Se miraron entre ellos sin comprender.

—Pero papá ha llamado diciendo que no vendría a cenar, tiene un compromiso. ¿No te ha avisado?

Fui en busca del teléfono móvil. Revisé mensajes, llamadas perdidas y wasaps. No había nada. Era la primera vez que Marcos no me prevenía de una ausencia. Lógico, quizá, mi vida en los últimos tiempos no había respetado horarios ni citas.

—Se habrá olvidado —comentó Marina al ver mi perplejidad.

—Se habrá olvidado, sí —repetí distraídamente.

Cené cualquier cosa charlando con los chicos. Más tarde me fui a la cama acompañada de un libro. Tenía la firme intención de esperar leyendo a que Marcos llegara. Sin embargo, el cansancio que mi cuerpo acumulaba no me lo permitió. Ni siquiera le oí cuando se acostó, y cuando me desperté por la mañana se había marchado ya. «Este es un modo perfecto para que los matrimonios funcionen —pensé—. Un poco drástico, quizá.» Ni pretendiendo ser divertida ante mí misma, me hizo la menor gracia mi reflexión.

21

Por fin llegó a nuestras manos algo que, debo confesarlo sinceramente, habíamos olvidado por completo. Sentí cierto remordimiento al ver el informe sobre mi mesa. Garzón, que reaccionaba de modo muy diferente al mío, convirtió el remordimiento en furia reivindicativa.

—¡A buenas horas, mangas verdes! ¿Por qué tiene que ir todo tan lento en este país? Pides una cosa y se la proporcionan a tus herederos. ¿Cómo vamos a funcionar bien? Parece que en España el año tenga trece meses, el mes cuarenta días y el día veintisiete horas. ¡La vida es larga, no os preocupéis!

—¿En algún momento de los últimos días usted se había acordado de reclamar el informe?

Me miró con gesto de falsa sorpresa y una sonrisa irónica estrangulada bajo el bigote.

—¿Yo?, ¿olvidarme yo del informe del móvil de Bob? ¡Cada día y cada noche he estado pensando en él!

Me eché a reír y él me siguió abiertamente.

—Hay que ver, inspectora, en las pelis la policía sigue unos planes meticulosos paso a paso y sin saltarse ninguno. ¿Y sabe qué pasa entonces? Pues que la gente lo ve y se lo cree. Luego nos critican diciendo que los españoles trabajamos a salto de mata. Como si el salto de mata no fuera consustancial al trabajo de la poli, aquí y en Sebastopol.

—Sí, la mata es básica en nuestra labor.

Una mirada mutua bastó para que riéramos de nuevo. Luego nos dispusimos a estudiar el informe de las navegaciones y las llamadas del pobre Bob.

Sus navegaciones por internet desde el móvil eran tan poco interesantes como las que habíamos comprobado en su ordenador portátil. El conjunto se componía básicamente de agenda para visitar sitios de cocina, de recetas y noticias de prensa sobre restaurantes. La única diferencia era que en el teléfono, lógicamente, no figuraba ninguna contabilidad. Pasamos a inspeccionar las llamadas, centrándonos en las de los días previos a su suicidio. No había demasiadas. Podía observarse, por comparación con fechas anteriores, cómo las llamadas a sus distribuidores habituales de productos alimentarios, y las realizadas o recibidas por ayuntamientos de diversos lugares, iban disminuyendo hasta su desaparición total. Adiós al tiempo feliz en el que de la caravana salían apetitosos olores.

—Un hombre realmente sin amigos —comentó Garzón.

—Su modo de vida comportaba ciertas renuncias. Pero tenía a su socio, algunos compañeros de caravana, sus clientes... Había creado un cierto equilibrio en su vida social.

—Que se jodió cuando perdió la caravana. Pero

era un hombre muy poco luchador. Yo hubiera intentado volver a empezar.

—La vida es cansada, Fermín.

—¡Nos ha jodido! No me lo diga a mí, que no he llegado a tener tranquilidad hasta casi en la vejez. ¿Sabe lo que se le ha metido ahora a Beatriz en la cabeza? Que en cuanto me jubile nos iremos a hacer un crucero por el Caribe.

—¡Caray, Garzón, eso sí es lujo y esplendor!

—A mí al principio no me hacía ninguna gracia. Eso de estar encerrado en un barco tantos días..., pero resulta que hay cine, sala de fiestas y, lo más importante, varios restaurantes distintos. Claro que esos lujos, como usted dice, puedo permitírmelos gracias a las riquezas de mi esposa, porque con mi pensión de poli jubilado...

Mientras me hablaba y yo le escuchaba con relativa atención, fui repasando los números telefónicos del informe hasta encontrar algo en lo que, a bote pronto, no habíamos reparado.

—Mire, Fermín, aquí hay una llamada que hizo Bob dos días antes de suicidarse. Corresponde a una tal Elisenda Monclús.

—Me suena un montón.

Nos quedamos ambos pensando con pareja intensidad y empezamos a hablar casi a la vez.

—¡La caravana de los vegetales! Lo de Monclús me había despistado —me ganó por segundos Garzón—. ¡Joder!, ¿y eso qué significa?

—Localice a los vegetarianos a ver dónde coño están.

Gracias a los cielos se encontraban en la ciudad.

Habían plantado su caravana en la explanada de la Feria de Montjuïc. Iríamos a hablar con Elisenda a media mañana. Descartamos en un principio hacerla venir hasta comisaría, no había motivo aún para oficializar nada. Además, así la cogeríamos desprevenida.

La explanada estaba relativamente llena de gente. Se celebraba una feria de complementos de moda: bolsos, adornos para el pelo, guantes... Garzón estaba alucinado de que semejantes productos, completamente marcianos en su vida, congregaran el suficiente potencial económico como para dedicarle una gran feria.

—Hay especialistas en moda que juzgan los complementos como más importantes que la propia ropa —contribuí a su sapiencia.

—Pues vaya —fue su enigmático comentario.

Expositores y clientes tomaban café o almorzaban en las caravanas. En la que era nuestro destino vimos que estaban sirviendo zumos de frutas. Sólo Javier estaba a la vista, y cuando nos acercamos nos miró con una cara que expresaba cualquier cosa menos cordialidad. Esperamos con paciencia que acabara de cobrar un zumo de piña.

—Hola, inspectores, ¿otra vez por aquí? —fue su saludo forzado, y enseguida añadió—: ¿Se sabe algo del asesino?

—Algo se va sabiendo —respondió el subinspector, que estaba misterioso aquel día.

—Queremos hablar con Elisenda —concreté.

—Ha entrado en el recinto de la feria para llevar un pedido, no creo que tarde mucho. A lo mejor yo puedo ayudarles también.

—La esperaremos, no se preocupe —contesté gélidamente.

—En ese caso, permítanme ofrecerles algo: un zumo, un poco de pastel de zanahoria y deliciosas empanadillas... —se explayó, cambiando de actitud.

—Lo único que me apetece a estas horas es un buen café, y no sé si de eso tienen ustedes —afirmó mi compañero.

—¿Cómo que no tenemos buen café? Nuestro café es natural y de comercio justo. Lo que pasa es que no utilizamos marcas comerciales, está hecho de modo tradicional.

—Espero que no sea de calcetín, como antes se decía —soltó Garzón con una risita. Javier replicó la risita con otra más falsa todavía. Por fortuna, en ese momento apareció Elisenda y la conversación dejó de declinar. Su gesto al descubrir nuestra presencia fue más de sorpresa que de fastidio.

—¡Hola!, ¿qué hacen por aquí?

—Queremos hablar un momento con usted, Elisenda.

—Sí, no hay ningún problema, adelante —dijo, algo desconcertada.

—Mejor con un poco de privacidad.

Saltó el marido para sugerir:

—Entren en la caravana, en la mesa estarán bien.

—Estaremos mejor al aire libre, detrás de la caravana —atajé enseguida.

La ubicación propuesta no le hizo maldita gracia a Javier porque no se enteraría de la conversación, que era justo lo que yo pretendía.

Elisenda seguía teniendo su habitual apariencia de fragilidad a la que en aquellos momentos se añadía un rictus de turbación.

—Elisenda —comencé en tono muy calmado—, Bob le llamó por teléfono hace poco, ¿verdad?

Pensó un instante, como rebuscando en su mente. Luego dijo tranquilamente:

—Sí, no recuerdo el día concreto, pero es verdad que no hace mucho me llamó.

—¿Qué le dijo en esa llamada?

—¿Qué me dijo? Pues no sé..., quería saber cómo estábamos y contarme que él se encontraba bien dentro de lo que cabía.

—¿Puede recordar exactamente sus palabras?

Su confusión inicial pareció aumentar, titubeó varias veces para formar las frases.

—No sé qué decirle, inspectora, fue una llamada normal. Dijo que hacía tiempo que no nos veíamos, que nos echaba de menos, que de momento no podía volver a su trabajo, me preguntó por algunos compañeros de otras caravanas... En fin, las cosas que se cuentan entre amigos.

—¿Le habló de él, de su situación actual?

—Algún comentario sí que hizo: que estaba un poco triste, pero que ya se le pasaría, que remontaría de aquel bajón, que probablemente se compraría otra caravana... Poco más.

—¿No se despidió de usted?

—¿Despedirse?, bueno, al fin de la charla, como es lógico.

—No me refiero a eso. —Hice una pausa durante la cual ella me miraba con candidez—. Elisenda, a

Bob lo han encontrado muerto en un pequeño bosque cerca de Barcelona. Se suicidó colgándose de un árbol.

Su cara se crispó, dejó los ojos en blanco durante un segundo, se puso muy pálida. Temí que fuera a caerse al suelo de golpe, pero lo hizo despacio, como si su cuerpo fuera perdiendo la firmeza de los huesos poco a poco. Quedó de rodillas, encorvada sobre sí misma y entonces empezó a convulsionar. Lloraba a lágrima viva. Sin duda desconocía la noticia, ni la actriz más eximia de la historia hubiera podido improvisar semejante escena de dolor. Entonces, como si las mentes de marido y mujer se hubieran comunicado telepáticamente, apareció Javier detrás de la furgoneta sumamente alarmado.

—¿Qué pasa?, ¿qué le han hecho? —preguntó uniendo alarma a un inicio de ira.

Se agachó, la levantó ayudado por nosotros. Le decía al oído palabras dulces de consuelo. Me lanzó una mirada de odio que era una pregunta directa a la que yo contesté:

—Hemos informado a Elisenda de que Bob se ha suicidado.

La sorpresa se pintó en el rostro de aquel hombre con un trazo firme y directo.

—¿Cómo ha dicho?

—Se ahorcó, se colgó de la rama de un árbol. Su esposa ha reaccionado así cuando la hemos informado. Nadie le ha hecho nada.

—¡Todo esto es una locura!

—Para que no siga siendo una simple locura queríamos hacerle unas preguntas a Elisenda, él la llamó poco antes de morir, pero no creo que ahora sea el momento adecuado. Volveremos mañana.

—¿Y qué quieren preguntarle?, ¿ella qué puede saber?

—Es pura rutina de la investigación. Será sólo un momento.

Nos largamos sin decir adiós. Frente a la caravana vegetariana había un par de personas esperando. Garzón retrocedió.

—Voy a advertirles que tienen clientes, no quiero que ese tipo nos acuse también de joderle el negocio.

Cuando volvió pregunté:

—¿Qué hacían ahora?

—Nada, lo mismo de antes, él la consolaba con besitos en la mejilla. Me ha dado las gracias por avisar y ha dicho que enseguida atendería a los clientes.

En el coche comenzó nuestro cambio de impresiones. Garzón hizo la primera jugada.

—Yo juraría que ni ella ni él sabían nada del asunto de Bob. ¿Está de acuerdo conmigo?

—Por completo. Sus reacciones eran auténticas. Sólo hay un punto que me intriga: ¿no ha sido la reacción de ella algo desmedida? Estaba un poco sobreactuada, como dicen ahora.

Oí el runrún de los pensamientos de mi subalterno.

—¿Cree que tiene algo que ver con el asesinato de Laurent o quizá con el suicidio de Bob? —preguntó por fin. Le respondí con otra pregunta.

—¿Cree que el asesinato y el suicidio tienen que ver entre sí?

—Podrían tener que ver incluso con la guerra civil. Cualquier cosa me parece posible y absurda al mismo tiempo. ¿De verdad vamos a interrogarla de nuevo?

—Sí, mi duda es si debemos contarle algo sobre la nota que dejó Bob.

—En caso de estar implicada, decirle algo es un riesgo porque descubrimos nuestras cartas, aunque también puede inducirla a actuar con precipitación y meter la pata.

—¿Usted sabe cómo se siente un pulpo en un garaje, Fermín?

—Me hago una idea.

—Yo, también.

Fuimos a reponer fuerzas a un bar. La cerveza helada me pareció una bebida propia de los dioses, lo más sofisticado que había probado jamás. Me gusta mucho la cerveza, pero soy lo suficientemente racional como para no anteponerla a un buen cava o champán. Cuando eso me sucede, cuando una birra me parece lo más de lo más, es indicio seguro de que estoy llegando al colmo de mi preocupación profesional. Aquel caso había explotado y se había atomizado de tal manera que aún flotaban en el aire las esquirlas de su deflagración. Ninguna revelación importante, ni un faro guía que seguir. Para colmo, también estaba fragmentado el personal de investigación. Nuestros compañeros de la Policía Nacional, con la colaboración de la policía autonómica, buscaban a Martine Marchand. La Guardia Civil interrogaba a un sospechoso que había surgido por la derivación hacia las drogas en el caso. Los gendarmes franceses estaban avisados para abortar la entrada de Marchand en su país. Por último, estábamos el inspector Garzón y yo tras la estela de un suicida que había dejado una pista vaga, falsa quizá. Nosotros éramos, en el fondo, los que teníamos un cometido menos concreto, más impreciso. ¿Cómo no iba a lanzarme sobre una cerveza fría intentando que el placer de beberla solapara la sensación de desastre, de fracaso, de ridículo también? De repente, el sabor que me había parecido sobrenatural un minuto antes empezó a amargarme el paladar.

Al subinspector debía sucederle un proceso parecido cuando se enfrentaba a un bocadillo de chorizo porque, mirándolo de reojo, comprobé que elevaba los ojos al cielo como dando gracias por aquel pequeño placer. Sin embargo, ningún síntoma daba a entender que súbitamente dejara de apetecerle en absoluto.

El inconveniente de aquellas compensaciones gastronómico-alcohólicas era lo efímero de su duración. Cuando hubimos acabado con el refrigerio nos miramos a los ojos y casi al unísono dijimos:

—Hay que decírselo. Tiene que saber lo de la nota, aunque levantemos alguna liebre.

Yo añadí:

—Hoy mismo la llamamos a comisaría para que venga a declarar.

—Sí, inspectora, el factor sorpresa siempre puede ayudar y lo de ir a comisaría no se lo espera. Además, así evitamos que venga el borde de su marido a incordiar, tendrá que quedarse a cargo del negocio.

—El borde sólo quiere proteger a su mujer.

—No es sólo eso, parece que nos odie, desde el principio parece que nos odie a los dos.

—Sí, puede que no le caigamos bien.

Unas horas después, habiendo elaborado una lista de preguntas entre los dos, fui yo quien telefoneó a Elisenda.

—¿Declarar?, ¿declarar otra vez?

—Lo de antes ha sido una conversación entre usted y yo. Ya le dije que necesitaríamos nuevas charlas.

—¿Y por qué en comisaría...?

—Elisenda, declarará usted como testigo por si puede ayudarnos, no está detenida, ni tampoco investigada... ¿Dentro de una hora le va bien?

Llevaba el mismo vestido de la primera conversación, vaporoso y estampado con florecitas multicolores. Supuse que era un refuerzo para el negocio esa forma de vestirse haciendo referencia a las delicias del campo. Se la veía tan debilucha y cohibida como de costumbre, quizá era una artimaña adquirida con los años para que, de entrada, la gente se dirigiera a ella de modo delicado.

Garzón fue quien tomó la palabra. Anunció someramente que se disponía a leer una nota que Bob nos había dirigido antes de catapultarse al otro mundo. La chica puso tal cara de asombro que una vez más pensé en la imposibilidad de que su reacción fuera impostada. No se fabrican actrices así. Mientras el subinspector procedía, yo no perdía detalle de los más mínimos gestos o movimientos musculares que se produjeran en el rostro de nuestra invitada. No, una actriz tan buena no se puede fabricar de la noche a la mañana, porque la impresión que saqué de mis atisbos faciales correspondió exactamente con lo que dijo.

—No entiendo absolutamente nada, inspectores, se lo digo de verdad. No sé por qué Bob les pide disculpas ni... Nada, no entiendo nada.

—¿Sabe si Bob estaba metido en drogas junto con Laurent?

—Creo que ya se lo dije una vez, Bob nunca me contó nada de eso.

—Sin embargo, eran lo suficientemente amigos como para que la escogiera a usted como la última persona a quien llamó antes de suicidarse.

—Verá, inspectora, Bob era un hombre muy divertido, muy tierno también, pero interiormente sufría mucho. Siempre me contaba que no había tenido suerte en la vida: desengaños amorosos, fracasos profesionales, la autoestima por los suelos...

—Sí, eso nos lo contó a nosotros también, y en cuanto a su autoestima, resulta fácil deducir que alguien que se cree Superman no decide colgarse de un árbol. Lo que nos interesa saber es qué confidencias le hizo a raíz de su estado de ánimo.

—¿Confidencias?

—¡Cosas concretas! —casi bramó el subinspector a punto de perder la paciencia.

—Parece un contrasentido... —continuó la muchacha un tanto atemorizada—, pero por más que habláramos de ese tipo de cosas privadas, nunca pasábamos de ahí: comentarios generales, consuelos con lugares comunes: hay que animarse, uno debe aprender a cuidar de sí mismo..., ya saben, ese tipo de frases.

—¿Y usted, qué le contaba usted? —se me ocurrió preguntar de repente.

—¿Yo? —preguntó sorprendida—. Yo era normalmente quien lo consolaba, quien le decía que todos los seres humanos valemos igual, que él era muy talentoso y con el negocio de la furgoneta lo hacía muy bien...

—O sea, que usted tampoco le contaba ninguno de sus problemas en concreto.

—¿Problemas míos?

—¡Sí, suyos! ¿O es que usted no tiene problemas, Elisenda? —gruñó Garzón ya sin ningún recato.

—¡Todo el mundo tiene problemas, desde luego! El trabajo es duro, siempre hay que estar al día e inventando recetas, la vida moderna... —Miró al subinspector temiendo sin duda un bufido que intentó atajar añadiendo con rapidez—: A mí me hubiera gustado tener una ocupación más acorde con mis estudios y, desde luego, en la que hubiera podido pensar en tener niños. Con nuestro modo de vida actual resulta imposible aspirar a crear una familia.

—¿Y qué le decía Bob?

—Que la familia era una institución del pasado y que más valía tener libertad —dijo sonriendo, e inmediatamente se echó a llorar—. ¡Pobre Bob! Todo este asunto lo trastornó por completo: el asesinato de su socio, la pérdida de su querida caravana. La vida es muy injusta, él era muy buena persona y merecía un poco de felicidad.

—¿Quién le destrozó la caravana, Elisenda?, ¿qué buscaban allí?

Se secó las lágrimas y me miró con estupefacción.

—¿Cómo voy a saberlo, inspectora? Si hubiera tenido esa información, ¿cree que me la habría guardado?

—¿No le hizo Bob ningún comentario, no tenía alguna sospecha, alguna teoría sobre los culpables? ¿No le comentó nada en esa llamada telefónica?

Negó tristemente con la cabeza, bajó la voz hasta que se convirtió en un susurro.

—Él cargaba con todas las culpas de lo malo que le traía el destino, y al final, ya ven, le echó un pulso fatal al destino y, por desgracia, no lo ganó él.

—Puede marcharse —dije de improviso.

Ella, despacio, serenamente, se levantó, nos saludó con una inclinación de cabeza y salió limpiándose la cara con un pañuelo.

Los ojos de Garzón se me clavaron con la firmeza de dos dardos en una diana.

—La deja marchar, pero sabe que está mintiendo, ¿verdad?

—No, no estoy segura de si miente o no.

—¡Pues yo sí estoy seguro! Siempre he tenido la sensación de que en este puto caso miente hasta el apuntador. Dos socios que no se contaban nada, dos amiguetes y vecinos de trabajo que tampoco se decían nada importante. En fin, ¿qué era aquello, un monasterio trapense donde sólo hablaba Dios?

Dicho esto dio un salto hacia la ventana.

—Me lo imaginaba, mire, inspectora.

Vimos cómo Elisenda cruzaba la calle y Javier la recibía con un beso, se tomaban del brazo y empezaban a caminar.

—¿Lo ve, inspectora? El cabrón del maridito ha

sido capaz de cerrar el negocio en hora punta con tal de venir a ver si le hemos hecho daño a su mujercita.

—¿No haría usted algo así por Beatriz?

—¡Yo tengo que trabajar para recibir un sueldo! A este parece que le sobre el dinero, ¿no? Además, no se pueden establecer comparaciones sobre lo que hacen los demás y lo que haríamos nosotros.

—¡Pues deberíamos comparar todo el tiempo! A usted le parece sospechoso que personas cercanas no se cuenten cosas importantes, pero si se pone a reflexionar, ¿qué es lo que hacemos usted y yo?

—Nosotros sí hablamos de nuestros problemas.

—¡Bah, cosas superficiales!

—¡Yo le conté la bronca de las cortinas con mi mujer!

—¡Ya ve, tampoco es una confidencia muy profunda!

—¿Qué quiere, que le cuente qué tal hemos follado el día anterior?

—¡Fermín, y pensar que a veces creo que se ha pulido usted un poco! Pero no, sigue siendo el ser más basto, ordinario y soez que anda por el mundo.

—No crea, a veces me encuentro a otros iguales que yo.

22

Mi vida privada seguía desaparecida por completo, o sería más correcto decir que yo había desaparecido del escenario, dejando a los otros actores representar a su aire la función, una función, por cierto, en las que las partes de guion que me correspondían estaban muy limitadas: «Buenos días, buenas noches, hoy no vendré a comer, hoy no vendré a cenar, un beso, un abrazo, luego hablamos, estoy muerta de sueño, adiós». Con semejantes líneas, las réplicas tampoco alcanzaban un nivel shakespeariano. Pero mucho antes de hacerme a mí misma ningún tipo de reproche, me aplicaba la conocida frase, tan original: «Así es la vida del policía». A pesar de su trivialidad, e incluso insensatez, la sentencia me funcionaba como mano de santo. Pues bien, aquel maldito día en que el teniente Montilla me llamó urgentemente desde comisaría, determinó el comienzo de un periodo en el que el devenir de los acontecimientos personales en los últimos tiempos pareció una balsa de calma y placer familiar comparado con lo que se nos venía encima en el devenir profesional.

—¿Inspectora Petra Delicado?

—¡Presente! —no pude por menos que contestar en vista de la marcialidad que llegó a mis oídos.

—Persónese lo antes posible en el número 12 de la calle Marie Curie. Es un almacén.

—¿Qué ocurre, teniente?

—Dámaso ha cantado ahora mismo. En el almacén está la Marchand. Mis hombres ya van para allí, y yo también, naturalmente.

Esa última precisión me rompió el alma al tiempo que acababa de despertarme del todo. Que el teniente hubiera enviado a sus hombres sin duda significaba que se aproximaba al citado almacén la propia División Mecanizada Brunete, haciendo que hasta las cucarachas de las calles huyeran, espantadas por el estrépito.

Obvié la ducha y, por supuesto, el desayuno y salí del dormitorio como una ventolera. Marcos abrió los ojos.

—¿Adónde coño vas? ¡Son las cinco de la mañana!

—Te llamaré cuando pueda.

—¡Ah, magnífico, lo celebraré!

No estaba para ironías a aquellas horas intempestivas. Las cinco de la mañana, cierto, ni siquiera me había fijado, tan pronta estaba siempre a la llamada del deber. ¿Y a aquellas horas había cantado Dámaso?, ¿qué era, una especie de gallo al amanecer?

Puse la dirección en el GPS y volé hacia allí. Como el tráfico era muy escaso, no tardé mucho en llegar. No estaba la Brunete, pero bloqueando la calle ya podían verse varios vehículos de la Guardia

Civil. Afiné la mirada desde lejos, buscando al subinspector, pero a bote pronto no conseguí verlo. Quien brillaba en todo su esplendor era el teniente Montilla. Daba órdenes, hablaba por el móvil, se movía a derecha e izquierda como una fiera sin libertad. Al alcanzarlo, cortó con brusquedad su conversación telefónica y me sonrió abriendo los brazos.

—¡Por fin, Petra, por fin lo hemos cazado! ¡Y con toda la pesca, además!

—¿Lo?, ¿a quién han cazado, teniente?

—Dámaso ha cantado como le dije antes y ha soltado la dirección del alijo. Entre, entre y verá lo que hay ahí.

Estaba pletórico, sonriente, feliz como un niño en Navidad.

—¿Y la francesa? —pregunté gélidamente.

—Mis hombres aún están inspeccionando el lugar. El almacén tiene un sótano interior al que se accede por una trampilla.

—Pero no la han encontrado todavía.

—No, cierto, todavía no ha aparecido.

—¿Y dónde piensa que puede estar, en el interior del excusado, emparedada detrás del papel pintado?

—No entiendo su tono ni dónde quiere ir a parar.

—Pues está muy claro, teniente, usted ha ido a resolver su caso, ha trincado al culpable y encontrado una guarida donde había droga. El tema de la francesa como posible asesina de nuestro caso le ha dado exactamente igual.

—¡Pero si la he llamado! La deducción era que esa mujer estaría aquí, al ladito de la droga.

Uno de los guardias llamó al teniente.

—¡Señor!, ¿puede venir un momento?

No dudé en ir con él. En el interior del amplio almacén se veían montones de cajas de cartón apiladas por todas partes. Los hombres de Montilla iban abriéndolas y tirándolas a un lado, estaban todas vacías. El teniente me indicó el camino hacia la trampilla que daba acceso al sótano. Bajamos por unas escaleras de madera muy empinadas. El guardia que había llamado a su jefe enseguida señaló hacia una esquina.

—Mire, teniente, allí hay un jergón, una mochila y enseres de baño. Parece que alguien se ha alojado aquí.

—Sí, es obvio que han pernoctado —sentenció el teniente.

El sótano estaba repleto de bolsas llenas de polvo blanco.

—Un alijo importante, ¿eh? —me soltó el guardia civil.

—Sí, y una ausencia importante también: la francesa.

—Bueno, ya ve que, probablemente, se escondía aquí, ahora ya pueden sacar sus conclusiones.

—¡Cojonudo, teniente!, usted trinca el alijo, empapela a su hombre más buscado y a nosotros nos queda la migaja de que, a lo mejor, la francesa se escondía aquí, incluso puede que haya huido alertada por el follón que han armado sus hombres.

—¡Esa acusación no es justa, Delicado! Le doy

mi palabra de honor de que en los interrogatorios preguntamos mil veces a Dámaso dónde demonio estaba la sospechosa. El tipo no lo sabía, de verdad que no lo sabía. Dudo mucho de que tuviera ni idea. Ya había cantado, inspectora, nada le costaba soltar el paradero de esa tipa. La francesa era una de sus principales clientas. Él traía la droga desde Marruecos hasta aquí y ella se las componía para llevársela hasta Francia. Ya no tenía motivo para protegerla, de haber sabido dónde estaba, lo hubiera soltado.

—¿Y por qué dormía en el almacén?

—Tendría una llave. El almacén debían utilizarlo los dos.

—Está bien, no nos pongamos nerviosos. Supongo que, por lo menos, habrán avisado al subinspector Garzón.

Montilla miró a su hombre, trasladándole la pregunta con una mirada.

—¡Claro que se le avisó! Lo hice yo personalmente, señor. Lo que ocurre es que no ha comparecido.

Me extrañó, pero el teniente estaba tan entusiasmado con su alijo y su culpable confeso que continuó dándome la tabarra.

—Por la pinta, yo diría que es material de alta calidad. Sabía que Dámaso estaba en activo todavía y la cosa no ha hecho más que empezar, ahora irá cantando nombres de clientes, vamos a dar con una red potente, ya verá. —Se fijó en mi cara de pocos amigos y añadió—: Por un poco no cogemos a la francesa durmiendo.

—Me sorprendería, le repito que con el cristo

que deben haber armado habrá tenido tiempo de escapar.

—Sólo hubiera podido colarse por la minúscula ventanita del lavabo que hay abajo, pero mandé a un par de hombres a la calle de atrás y por allí no salió nadie.

—¿La ventana estaba cerrada?

—Sí —dijo con tan poca convicción que estuve segura de que había aventurado la respuesta.

—Tiene reja —participó el guardia civil.

En ese momento se oyeron gritos en la parte superior y una voz bajó por la escalera berreando.

—¡Teniente, venga enseguida, se han oído tiros en la parte de atrás del edificio!

Emprendimos una carrera enloquecida que acabó en la calle trasera adonde daba el almacén. Allí vi a tres guardias civiles agachados sobre algo que sus cuerpos impedían ver. Me acerqué más. Era Garzón. Estaba de rodillas. Su brazo derecho empuñaba la pistola reglamentaria, en la manga izquierda de su americana había un roto del que manaba un poco de sangre. Me arrodillé junto a él.

—¡Fermín! —susurré.

—No es nada, todos tranquilos, tranquilos, es sólo una rozadura. Y no hace falta que intenten seguirla, hace ya un poco que salió corriendo.

—¿A quién, a quién no debemos seguir? —le pregunté en voz baja.

—Era ella, inspectora, la francesa, seguro que era ella: alta, morena, fuerte... Me disparó.

Montilla se puso a dar órdenes a todo el mundo como un demente:

—¡Inspeccionen la zona!, ¡busquen el casquillo de la bala!, ¡llamen a una ambulancia!

—¡Por Dios, qué manera de mandar! —dijo el subinspector por lo bajo. Luego añadió en voz más baja aún—: Ya le contaré lo que ha pasado. A ver si este tarado deja de pegar esos alaridos.

—Pero ¿se encuentra bien?

—¡Y cómo coño quiere que me encuentre bien! ¡Se me ha escapado, la he tenido a tiro y se me ha escapado! Sólo la duda de si era ella o no me impidió pegarle un tiro en la pierna.

—Tranquilícese, Fermín. Hizo bien. Imagínese que le pega un tiro en la pierna a la presidenta de la Asociación de Amas de Casa, hubiéramos tenido un problema, ¿no cree?

—No me haga reír ahora, que me duele el brazo. Suba usted conmigo en la ambulancia. Si me acompaña el teniente, es capaz de ordenar que me operen a corazón abierto. ¡Y que no avisen a Beatriz, por favor! No vayamos a cagarla del todo.

—Seguiré a la ambulancia en mi coche.

La herida del subinspector no revestía mucha importancia. La bala sólo lo había rozado y arrancado un poco de tejido muscular. «Un pedacito de carne», como decía él. No fue nada complicada de curar, mucho más compleja resultó la explicación que Garzón me dio sobre los hechos que acababan de suceder.

Salimos del hospital y, aunque el médico le había advertido que no bebiera alcohol porque le había inyectado un antibiótico, mi testarudo compañero insistió: «Necesito un whisky, pare en el primer bar que vea». Fue inútil que le repitiera los consejos de rigor, que a mí misma me tocaba las narices darle: «No sea imprudente, espere un rato para beber...». El último fue: «Pida una cerveza en vez de un whisky», pero tampoco sirvió. Paré y aparqué el coche. Nos sentamos en la terraza de un garito bastante inmundo que descubrí al pasar. Para no dejarlo solo en su irresponsabilidad, yo pedí un whisky también; por eso y porque, francamente, lo necesitaba después de tantos momentos de tensión. El whisky era horrible, pero al menos consiguió que el subinspector arrancase a hablar con cierta serenidad.

—Todo ha partido de un error. El tonto del haba que me llamó por teléfono para que fuera al almacén pronunció fatal el nombre de la calle Marie Curie y yo entendí Marià Cubí. ¡Claro, con esa puta manía de escribir los nombres de las calles en catalán!

—Le recuerdo que estamos en Cataluña, Fermín.

—¡Zarandajas, y qué más dará! Lo pones en una lengua que entienda todo el mundo y adiós muy buenas.

—¿Puede continuar con el relato antes de echar las culpas de su error al mismísimo papa de Roma?

—Bueno, pues el caso es que la cagué, hablando en lengua internacional. Llegué a la calle Marià Cubí de los cojones y allí no había ningún dispositivo de la Guardia Civil. Llamo al pelanas que me había avisado y logro entender cuál es la verdadera dirección. Cojo el coche a toda leche y allá que me voy. Pero cuando ya estoy en las inmediaciones, ¡toma castaña!, me topo con un millón de coches oficiales cortando el paso, aparte de un jaleo de cojones en el tráfico general provocado por el séptimo de caballería que ha organizado el teniente.

En ese momento no pude por menos que echarme a reír, pero la mirada de mi subalterno me reconvino, de modo que opté por moderarme y escuchar.

—Bien, reculo como puedo y voy hacia las calles de atrás, pensando que allí podría aparcar el coche. En efecto, dejo el coche en un hueco y me encamino a pie hacia la dirección. En ese momento, veo cómo una mujer sale de un portal contiguo al edificio donde estaba el follón. Me mira y se para un momento. Entonces la reconozco, le doy el alto y ella echa a correr. Empiezo a seguirla, pero ella saca una pistola y me dispara. Me puse de rodillas para repeler la agresión y aún pude pegar un tiro al aire, pero de nada sirvió, como ya sabe bien.

—Parece evidente que saltó por la ventana trasera y, en vez de empezar a huir a la desesperada, esperó para asegurarse de que todo estuviera despejado escondida en un portal. No contó con su retraso, Fermín, ni con que usted apareciera por la parte de atrás.

—Muy lista, la cabrona.

—Hay algo que no cuadra, los hombres de la Guardia Civil dijeron que la ventana trasera tenía reja.

—Sería de quita y pon.

El subinspector acertó por completo. Según se comprobó después, la reja no estaba fijada a las paredes, sino únicamente encajada. La francesa no había tenido más que apartarla y volver a ponerla después. Todo previsto para huir en aquel almacén de droga.

Ni que decir tiene que Montilla estaba exultante. No quise preguntarle con qué métodos había obtenido la confesión de Dámaso, si bien él mismo dijo que había ejercido presiones que incluían serias amenazas a su amante. En esta ocasión estaba seguro de que ningún abogado, por más marrullero que fuera, sería capaz de librarlo de su merecido legal. Además, los interrogatorios continuarían con la aquiescencia del juez hasta que todo el entramado saliera a la luz y los cómplices afloraran también, con nombres y apellidos. Aquello podía ser el comienzo de una redada internacional de dimensiones colosales. Eso debía pensar el teniente, esa esperanza sin duda tenía porque, de ser así, aquello supondría una gloria indecible para él: felicitaciones, un ascenso, una condecoración..., quién sabe qué cosas más.

Le recordé con toda la sutileza de la que fui capaz que Garzón y yo esperábamos nuestro turno para interrogar a su bien guardada presa. Para mi asombro, no reaccionó bien.

—Sí, Petra, por supuesto, por supuesto que tendrá su ocasión de hablar con el pajarito. Lo que pasa es que, si mezclamos elementos en medio de una investigación, puede resultar muy nocivo para esclarecer los hechos. Vete a saber qué escapatorias puede encontrar ese tiparraco en las preguntas que le formulen ustedes.

—¡No me jodas, Montilla! Sabes que llevamos entre manos un asesinato, y esa mujer es la clave.

—¿Y crees que Dámaso sabe dónde está ahora?

Ella estaba en el almacén que había abierto con llave propia, y eso debía tratarse de su último recurso. ¿Cómo podía reubicarla o protegerla si lo hemos metido preso? No, imposible, a esa mujer la tenéis a tiro. Ya carece de lugares donde esconderse, la frontera la tenéis controlada... Caerá, estará a punto de caer. Sólo es preciso decirles a tus hombres que mantengan los ojos más abiertos. De hecho, Garzón estuvo a puntito de trincarla, pero falló.

Me miró malévolamente, su tono llevaba implícito un claro retintín. Se me erizaron los pelos como los de un gato agresivo.

—Te estás comportando de manera miserable, Montilla, que lo sepas, y que sepas igualmente que a tu pajarraco lo vamos a interrogar.

—Tendrás que aportar la orden de un juez y, tal y como están las cosas, tu juez se verá obligado a ponerse de acuerdo con el que lleva mi caso.

—La traeré, no te inquietes. ¿Y todo esto lo haces para colocarte más medallas delante de los superiores? ¡Qué bajo que caen algunos, no me lo puedo creer!

Garzón se enfadó bastante con el teniente cuando le conté la precedente conversación, pero se enfadó mucho más conmigo porque no le había llamado gusano, hijoputa y maldito cabrón. Cuestión de matices.

Y bien, si todo se complicaba hasta el exceso en aquel abominable caso, ¿por qué diantres iba a variar de un día para otro? Montilla llevaba razón, algo tan simple como obtener una orden para interrogar a un individuo que ya estaba enchironado no fue coser y cantar. El juez que instruía nuestro caso nunca nos había puesto ninguna dificultad de cara a nuestras acciones. Era más bien el clásico tipo que aplicaba el *laissez faire*, pero en esta ocasión debía ponerse de acuerdo con el colega que llevaba el *affaire* de Dámaso y ahí entraban las diplomacias jurídicas que siempre provocaban la misma consecuencia: un enlentecimiento asegurado.

Tanto yo como el subinspector éramos conscientes de que el teniente debía haber estado susurrando lindezas al oído de su juez con el propósito de entorpecernos; de modo que tomamos la resolución de hacer lo propio con el nuestro. El pobre hombre, que no era joven ni bragado, se ponía nervioso cada vez que le llamábamos por teléfono o nos presentábamos en su despacho. Nunca nos envió al infierno ni nos dijo una mala palabra, aunque quizá hubiera sido mejor, porque la letanía que nos soltaba era desalentadora a más no poder: «Ustedes saben cómo son estas cosas», «veremos de qué modo se puede arreglar».

El acoso al que sometimos a aquel bendito magistrado alcanzó su cénit con una frase que le dirigió Garzón.

—Señoría, dese cuenta de que, a medida que pasa el tiempo, ya no es que demos ocasión a que la sospechosa huya, sino que puede cometer otro crimen, y si no lo comete, es seguro que alguna tragedia tendremos que lamentar.

El juez dio un respingo parecido al que di yo. Se quedó un momento en suspenso y sentenció:

—¡Caramba, subinspector, eso es muy alarmante! Me emplearé a fondo en buscar una solución.

A la salida, mi subalterno se subía por las paredes.

—¡Buscar una solución! ¡Mierda y mil veces mierda! ¿Es que la justicia no se puede ejercer con lógica y rapidez?

—Quizá esta vez ha tocado usted alguna fibra sensible con lo del nuevo asesinato y las tragedias, por falta de tremendismo no quedará, ha puesto toda la carne en el asador.

Lo que yo injustamente denominé como tremendismo resultó ser un simple espejo de la realidad.

23

Estábamos Garzón y yo cumpliendo con la sagrada obligación de todo trabajador español que conozca sus derechos: el café de las once en el bar. En La Jarra de Oro no cabía nadie más: mesas ocupadas, barra atestada y el barullo que tantos españoles juntos suelen producir. Por poco no oí mi teléfono cuando sonó.

—Dígame.

Era el jefe de una de las brigadas móviles que tenían nuestro aviso de detención.

—Inspectora Delicado, hemos encontrado a la sospechosa.

Le di un codazo al subinspector, metí la mano libre en el bolso para ir sacando dinero y pagar rápidamente. Al mismo tiempo le dije al policía que estaba en línea:

—No me dé la dirección verbalmente, mejor escríbala en un wasap. ¿O está detenida en dependencias?

—Inspectora, la sospechosa no está detenida en ninguna parte, está muerta. Acaban de encontrarla hace un rato, ya hay gente nuestra allí.

—¿Cómo ha dicho?

—Sí, lo que acaba de oír, la han asesinado, al parecer. El cuerpo lo encontró un trabajador que iba hacia Mercabarna. Es en la Zona Franca, le mando la dirección.

Esperé un instante a que en la pantalla del móvil apareciera el wasap requerido. Durante ese espacio de tiempo Garzón estuvo con la boca abierta, incapaz de reaccionar. Deduje que había oído la conversación.

—Calle Longitudinal número nueve. Zona Franca —leí en voz alta.

—Pero, inspectora... —balbució mi compañero. Enseguida lo interrumpí.

—No me pregunte nada, no me hable. Mejor callados los dos.

Cumplir mi orden no le costó demasiado. Observé durante la conducción hasta qué punto estaba absorto, de qué manera su mirada se perdía a través de la luna del coche. Sólo lanzó una exclamación cuando hubimos llegado y topamos con el amplio operativo que ya estaba desplegado en plena calle.

—¡Cojones, aquí ya está todo cristo!

Con zancadas decididas que evidenciaban mi mal humor me acerqué al grupo y pregunté quién estaba al mando, enseñando mi placa. Un inspector de paisano se me acercó enseguida. Nunca lo había visto antes.

—¿Eres Petra Delicado?

—¿Por qué no se me ha avisado antes? —fue mi contestación.

—Petra, se tardó un poco en hacer la identificación y atar cabos. No llevaba ningún documento encima.

Vi cómo los de la Científica fotografiaban el cadáver.

—Pues un poco más y me la encuentro con la autopsia hecha.

—Ya sabes cómo van estas cosas, Delicado.

—Sí que lo sé, mal.

Llegamos hasta donde trabajaban los hombres de blanco. El forense también estaba presente y, según me informaron, el juez acababa de marcharse, habiendo firmado todo lo firmable. En el suelo yacía la víctima. Sentía una gran curiosidad por descubrir los rasgos de su cara, que la muerte había desdibujado ligeramente. Aun así, pude vislumbrar que sus facciones eran regulares, proporcionadas, sin duda hermosas. Tenía cejas elevadas y curvas, que le daban un aspecto angelical a su frente, contrastando severamente con una boca grande, rectilínea, que mostraba una determinación poderosa, aun siendo ya cadáver. El cuerpo era grande, musculoso y el cabello negro azabache, tal y como nos la habían descrito más de una vez. Allí estaba la mujer fugitiva, la desalmada malhechora capaz de marcar a un tipo con un cuchillo, la presunta asesina de Pierre Laurent. Ni siquiera me di cuenta de que tenía al forense justo al lado.

—Lleva más de siete u ocho horas muerta —dijo—. Un navajazo muy certero en el corazón, sin señales de autodefensa que se puedan apreciar. Para mí, que la han trasladado quizá ya moribunda hasta aquí. ¿Ve?, tiene un golpe importante en la parte derecha de la cabeza que le afecta un poco la cara, como si la hubieran tirado desde un vehículo, también hay rozaduras en la misma parte del cuerpo. No hay rastros de sangre, es evidente que la cuchillada no se la asestaron aquí. Pero, en fin, la autopsia dirá.

Garzón estaba casi más afectado que yo. No hablaba, probablemente porque no tenía nada que decir, punto en el que coincidíamos por completo, pero al menos yo renegaba y maldecía, si bien en un tono de voz lo suficientemente bajo como para no armar un escándalo. Los destinatarios de las invectivas se extendían desde los tópicos abstractos: «¡Este caso está endemoniado!, ¡por qué me metería yo a detective!», hasta la concreción individual más absoluta: «¡Joder con el puto juez!», «¡cuando vea al teniente me lo cargo!», «con tanto retraso hemos dado pie a que suceda esto».

Cuando todo el cortejo fúnebre policial se hubo disipado, el subinspector y yo nos miramos.

—¿Un cafelito, inspectora?

—¿El café aclara las ideas?

—Eso dicen.

—Pues entonces que sean dos.

Garzón buscó en su móvil.

—En la calle 5 hay un bar que se llama Punt de Trobada.

Allí que nos plantamos poco después en busca de inspiración y consuelo, pero sobre todo siguiendo una tradición que se había ido forjando con el tiempo: entrar en un bar cuando realmente te encuentras perdido en una investigación.

—¿Qué le parece esta novedad, Petra?

—La cafeína tarda un poco en hacer efecto, no me agobie.

—¿Dámaso la ha mandado matar por medio de alguno de sus hombres?

—¿Primero la protege y luego se la carga? No tiene sentido.

—Dámaso se dio cuenta de que la francesa ya no tenía adonde ir, de manera que de un momento a otro la íbamos a cazar. Ella contaba con información, y ya sabe: mujer muerta no habla.

—¿Y cómo dio la orden desde la cárcel?

—Quizá fue algún otro preso a quien le pidió el favor.

—Otro preso, imposible, el cabrón de Montilla lo tiene incomunicado mientras el juez le permita continuar con los interrogatorios.

—¿Algún policía corrupto?

—Fermín, deje de pegar tiros a voleo.

—¡Es que no tenemos presa a la que apuntar!

—La fase de hipótesis dejémosla atrás, es obvio que no se puede elaborar una historia con lógica.

—Pero, inspectora, ¿quién?, ¿quién se ha podido cargar a Martine Marchand y por qué?

—La fase de preguntas sin respuesta también es inútil. Ahora no podemos andarnos con prisas, no pretenda llegar en avión, es el momento de caminar pegados a la tierra, paso a paso. ¿Cuál cree que debe ser el primero?

—Ir a hablar con el comisario Coronas. Este tema tan grave no se le puede presentar en un simple informe escrito.

—De acuerdo, hágalo usted. Y de paso pídale que meta presión para una autopsia rápida.

—Como de costumbre.

—No, esta vez necesitamos mucha más presión, como una olla a punto de reventar.

—Utilizaré el símil, aunque está un poco visto. ¿Y qué hará usted?

—Ir a hablar con el maldito juez que instruye el maldito caso.

—Inspectora, por favor, le ruego que no se me ponga demasiado brava con él. Los jueces últimamente están muy poseídos de su función y...

—Esté tranquilo, si recurro a las manos procuraré no dejarle señales.

El juez, por más que yo lo hubiera denostado en un momento iracundo, no era mala persona. De mediana edad y mediana complexión, debía andar también mediado de carácter porque enseguida comprendí que era él quien temía enfrentarse a su colega y prefería dejar pasar un poco de tiempo hasta que la situación se resolviera por sí sola.

Se quedó de una pieza cuando le conté que nuestra sospechosa había aparecido asesinada. Aproveché su desconcierto inicial para entrar en materia sin dilaciones.

—Usted, señor juez, que ha sido informado puntualmente de todas las incidencias de este caso, debe comprender la importancia capital que tiene para nosotros interrogar inmediatamente a Dámaso López.

—¿Es sospechoso del crimen?

—Quizá sí.

—Estando en prisión incomunicada no parece posible que...

No iba a liarme en una discusión bizantina con él. Primero, porque hubiera sido inútil. Segundo, porque aquel tipo ya me tenía hasta las pelotas y empezaba a sentir unos deseos irreprimibles de machacarlo sin piedad.

—Oiga, señoría. No me atrevo a decir que el asesinato de la ciudadana francesa Martine Marchand se haya producido como consecuencia de la dilación en interrogar a Dámaso López. No me atrevo a decirlo porque no sé seguro si ha sido así. Sin embargo, tengo la certeza de que nuestro caso, que acumula ya dos víctimas mortales en estos momentos, necesita de su firma inmediata para que podamos resolverlo de una maldita vez.

Su reacción hubiera podido ser airada, no se le habla de ese modo a un juez, pero se trataba de un hombre débil y alguna duda debía albergar su conciencia, porque serio y sin proferir ni una palabra se puso a escribir la orden requerida. Cuando acabó, sin ninguna expresión reconocible en el rostro, me dio el papel diciendo:

—Aquí tiene la orden, espero que sirva para algo. Hablaré con mi colega para que no haya malentendidos. —Hizo una pausa mirándome a los ojos—. A veces yo también pienso que el guante blanco que utilizamos entre nosotros los jueces indica una cierta soberbia corporativa.

Alguna vez había pensado que los hombres débiles suelen ser inteligentes. Las preguntas siempre se me acumulaban frente a aquella constatación: ¿la debilidad te lleva hacia la inteligencia para compensar la falta de carácter? ¿La inteligencia te señala que la llamada debilidad no es sino prudencia? ¿La debilidad llega a convertirse en un arma poderosa para quien sabe usarla? En cualquier caso, le di las gracias al juez y le prometí que seguiría puntualmente informado de nuestros movimientos en la investigación.

—¿Cómo logró convencerlo? —me preguntó el subinspector.

—Justo como usted me previno para que no lo hiciera.

—¿Se puso brava?

—Le di una hostia.

Me miró con escepticismo y media sonrisa.

—¡Ay, inspectora, podría incluso creerla!

—Si no me cree, le voy a dar un ejemplo de que soy muy capaz.

—¿Cómo?

—Dando otra hostia.

—¿A quién?

—Al teniente Montilla.

—Eso me lo creo más.

No había ninguna necesidad de que nos entrevistáramos con Montilla, pero yo sentía el deseo placentero de hacerlo, de restregarle la jodida orden judicial por las narices. Además, sería un modo de advertirlo seriamente de que cualquier intromisión por su parte a partir de aquel momento daría lugar a una queja oficial por la mía. A ver quién se llevaba el gato al agua.

Fui yo sola para hablar con él, no quería que Garzón me recriminara mi actuación, cualquiera que esta fuera. Se quedó sorprendido al verme, me hizo pasar a una sala vacía del cuartel. Naturalmente, ya estaba informado de que se había emitido la orden del juez. Aparentaba naturalidad, pero no me dejé arrastrar a una conversación de tipo cortés y rutinario, entré al trapo con rapidez.

—Ya has podido comprobar adónde ha llevado tu cabezonería, teniente.

—No sé a qué te refieres.

—Lo sabes muy bien, has dado lugar a que se produzca un asesinato.

—Oye, Petra, deja de soñar. ¿Qué crees que va a contarte Dámaso sobre ese asesinato?

—Hablas como si nunca hubiera tenido ninguna relación con la francesa.

—Y tú hablas como si el tipo no estuviera detenido y aislado.

—¡Detenido, aislado y contestando únicamente a tus preguntas, que dudo incluyeran a Marchand!

—A las tuyas no va a saber contestar, te lo garantizo. Dámaso ni ha matado ni ha mandado matar a tu sospechosa. Esa es la realidad con la que vas a encontrarte.

—¡Es posible que lleves razón, él no ha podido ordenar ningún crimen, pero quizá me proporcione pistas!

—Pues adelante, ahora ya tienes el permiso para interrogarlo. Pero te voy a advertir una cosa, querida colega: espero, de verdad lo espero, que no interfieras para nada en mi investigación. Dámaso aún tiene mucha información que necesito para destapar por completo su red.

—Lo más lamentable de todo este sainete, teniente, es lo que se intuye tras él: la rivalidad entre cuerpos policiales. Eso que todos negamos de boca para afuera, resulta que existe de verdad. Una pena, en serio, una pena.

Tal y como había previsto, acusó mi golpe como un auténtico derechazo en la mandíbula. A un defensor de la ley y el orden tan públicamente formalista como él, aquello le sentó peor que mal. Me miró con furia no disimulada y dijo en voz baja:

—Mejor dejémoslo así.

—Gracias por recibirme.

Cuando mi subalterno quiso saber qué tal había ido la entrevista, hubiera podido recurrir a la fantasía para hacerlo reír, pero lo cierto es que enseguida me salió una frase que era mi verdadero resumen final.

—Según él, Dámaso no ha tenido nada que ver con el asesinato de Martine.

—¿Han hablado todo el rato de eso?

—No, y ahora me doy cuenta de que es justo lo que hubiéramos tenido que hacer: intercambiar información, pedirle que me explicara por qué está tan seguro de que Dámaso no tiene ninguna responsabilidad en el crimen, de que no ha podido utilizar ningún intermediario, incluso hacer juntos alguna hipótesis. ¿Y en vez de colaborar qué hemos preferido? Enseñarnos las plumas erizadas amenazadoramente como gallos de pelea.

—Bueno, al menos él se ha librado de la hostia que usted le tenía asignada.

Me entristecí de pronto. Una persona no pierde su

condición de ser humano en el trabajo. Donde deberían reinar la calma, la frialdad, la razón y la experiencia, sigue ardiendo la hoguera de las vanidades, la desconfianza, el amor propio herido y la banalidad. Me privé de comentarle a Garzón aquellos pensamientos porque sabía lo que hubiera respondido: «No somos santos», y hubiera estado en lo cierto.

Antes de que pudiéramos elaborar ninguna estrategia de cara al interrogatorio de Dámaso, tuvimos una grata sorpresa: las influencias de nuestro comisario habían surtido efecto, el propio doctor Jordi Rosselló llamó diciendo que ya había realizado la autopsia del cadáver de Marchand, estaba escribiendo el informe y se brindaba a encontrarse con nosotros si queríamos comentarlo con él.

—¿Usted piensa que a partir de ahora irán encadenándose los golpes de suerte, Petra? —se le ocurrió al subinspector preguntarme.

—Estoy convencida de ello —dije sin estarlo.

—Yo también —respondió sin pizca de convicción.

El doctor Rosselló tenía un lío considerable sobre la mesa de su despacho: papeles, fotografías, discos de ordenador...

—Disculpen esta desorganización, pero las prisas son malas consejeras, y desde que hay presunción de crimen machista ponemos ese caso a la cabecera de la lista y a veces las cosas se hacen deprisa y corriendo.

Su comentario nos desconcertó, luego me di cuenta de que era evidente que se negaba a admitir que había sucumbido a las presiones de los superiores. El subinspector había empezado a decir: «Pero...» cuando le toqué ligeramente un brazo al tiempo que le lanzaba una mirada asesina. Algo notó el forense porque lanzó rápido su pregunta.

—Porque se trata de un crimen machista, ¿no?

—Presunción, presunción —atajé como pude—. Su dictamen nos ayudará a determinarlo.

Y bien, Martine Marchand había perdido la vida a causa de una puñalada asestada con la suficiente fuerza sobre la zona cordial como para afirmar que no sufrió en absoluto. Su corazón no pudo resistir un golpe tan certero y brutal. No había signos de lucha en defensa propia. Quien la atacó lo hizo cara a cara y a corta distancia. El cuerpo presentaba algunos golpes y rozaduras que nada tenían que ver con la causa de la muerte. Sin duda se habían producido por una manipulación posterior, probablemente el asesino trasladó el cadáver en algún vehículo y lo dejó caer sobre la calzada. Sin embargo, debió tomar precauciones porque no se había hallado ninguna prueba incriminatoria analizable: ni pelos, ni hilos, ni fibras de ningún tipo. La víctima no había ingerido ninguna sustancia tóxica ni alcohol, apenas había comido.

—¿Cuánto tiempo transcurrió desde que la mataron hasta que la encontraron?

—No estoy seguro, inspectora, pero calcularía no menos de tres horas.

—La asesinaron sobre las tres de la mañana.

—Algo así.

—¿Usted cree, doctor Rosselló, que la «técnica», vamos a llamarla así, de la puñalada es la misma que la de la última autopsia que usted realizó para un caso nuestro? La de Pierre Laurent, otro ciudadano francés. No sé si la recuerda.

—Por supuesto que la recuerdo, no hace tanto de eso, pero creí que estábamos tratando un caso de violencia de género.

—En fin, puede existir alguna relación —improvisé. El médico me miró con desconfianza y en un tono que traslucía cierto escepticismo sentenció:

—Lo de las técnicas asesinas no deja de ser un argumento de ficción, inspectora Delicado. Todo depende de la postura de atacante y atacado, de la situación emocional: más fuerte, más flojo el ataque... Sin embargo, si lo que me pregunta es si hay posibilidad de que ambas puñaladas las haya ejecutado una misma persona, le contestaré que sí, es posible, aunque quizá con la misma seguridad podría asegurarle lo contrario.

Asentí varias veces con la cabeza. Roselló nos acompañó hasta la salida amablemente e hizo algo que detesto: nos deseó suerte. Cuando alguien a quien has pedido ayuda profesional te desea suerte como despedida es como si dudara de la eficacia de tu trabajo, lo cual resulta descorazonador.

En la calle escuché el esperable comentario de Garzón.

—¡Joder con el comisario Coronas, mintiendo también tengo influencia yo!

—No creo que mintiera, lo de la violencia de género se lo ha inventado Rosselló para justificar la celeridad y salvar la cara frente a nosotros. Aquí todos tenemos la piel muy fina.

Por la noche, todo el mundo en mi casa dormía cuando llegué, una costumbre ya. Noté que los niños estaban presentes porque olí la colonia de Marina. Entré en su habitación. Ya tenía once años, pero seguía durmiendo como un bebé, profundamente, con el cuerpo desmadejado y la cabeza fuera de la almohada. Crecía rápido y cada vez iba consolidándose la belleza que prometía en su primera niñez. Pensé que hacía un montón de tiempo que no hablaba con ella, que no escuchaba con atención sus aventuras en el colegio, los desencuentros con su madre sobre banalidades diarias ante las que, aunque me hicieran gracia, siempre evitaba reír. Obviamente, me estaba perdiendo algo por culpa de aquel caso intenso y obsesivo, pero no podía evitarlo. No se trataba de que el deber, con sus llamadas, fuera devolviéndome a la senda de la investigación. Al contrario, era yo quien no abandonaba los pasos en la misma dirección decidiéndolo por mí misma y las llamadas de mi conciencia hacían ahora referencia a mi vida personal. Los zarpazos de la culpa, de los que siempre había logrado escapar, estaban alcanzándome de lleno. Debía zafarme de ellos como pudiera. Una de las razones por las que me juré desde la infancia no tener hijos era la culpabilidad que veía proliferar entre las jóvenes madres con quienes me topé: todas sufrían por las ausencias familiares que suponía cumplir con su trabajo: «Pobres criaturas, un día ni me reconocerán», pero si se dedicaban con más brío a la crianza de los niños, los remordimientos venían del lado profesional: «Si no le das duro al trabajo, acabarás en la mediocridad». Un horror que yo había solventado no pariendo. Pero el destino, que es arrogante y puñetero, me había conducido al mismo lugar, aun sin reproducirme. No, se acabó, pensé, una niña es una niña nada más, y si mi corazón no me había impuesto estar más a su lado era porque tenía un corazón que me conocía bien. Yo estaba en mi salsa buscando a los culpables de dos asesinatos, preguntándome por qué se había suicidado Bob, qué demonio sabía Dámaso. Cerré la puerta y me fui a la cama. Sería cuidadosa para no hacer ningún ruido que despertara a Marcos, del mismo modo que él lo haría por la mañana en atención a mí.

24

La preparación estratégica de un interrogatorio, en especial si está conducido por dos personas, siempre resulta complicado de plantear. Tienes la impresión, mientras lo haces, de que los derroteros por los que se desarrolle la sesión quizá no coincidan en absoluto con tu esquema inicial. Aun sabiendo eso por experiencia demostrada, el subinspector y yo tuvimos nuestra pequeña reunión antes de meterle mano a Dámaso.

—¿Alguien le ha informado de la muerte de Marchand? —le pregunté.

—Teóricamente no. Se supone que al tipo lo tienen aislado.

—No creo que el juez le deje a Montilla tenerlo aislado mucho más tiempo. De cualquier modo, déjeme la baza a mí. Yo se lo soltaré en el momento en que juzgue que puede causarle más conmoción.

—¿Piensa de verdad que se conmocionará al enterarse?

—No sé en qué medida, francamente, pero eran amigos. Él le dio cobijo y la protegió hasta el último momento.

—Suponiendo que lo hiciera por amistad.

—Hasta las bestias salvajes tienen su corazoncito.

—Que suelen utilizar para atacar con más virulencia.

—¡Ay, Fermín, si va a llevarme la contraria todo el rato, mejor lo interrogo sola!

—Perdone, inspectora, estaba haciendo de abogado del diablo, pero la cosa está clara: usted lleva las riendas y yo salgo al remate si veo que se le despista alguna jugada.

—Y si se pone impertinente, usted le pega el capón, siempre verbal, entiéndame bien.

—¿Ponemos en marcha la técnica clásica «policía bueno, policía malo»?

—Mejor la técnica «policía hijoputa en ambos casos».

—Suele ser siempre la mejor.

La sala de la prisión destinada a los interrogatorios no era demasiado deprimente. Cuando Dámaso López compareció, debidamente custodiado, el funcionario me preguntó si requeríamos su presencia y yo le contesté que no. El reo no tardó en hablar, antes de sentarse o ser preguntado exclamó:

—Mi abogado ya ha conseguido que deje de estar en régimen de aislamiento, desde ayer estoy con los demás. Lo próximo que conseguirá es que salga de aquí.

—Enterados, Dámaso, ¿algo más que comunicarnos?

—Sólo una pregunta. ¿Qué coño quieren de mí? Les aseguro que ya he tenido bastante con el jodido teniente. Se le va a caer el pelo en cuanto mi abogado le eche encima los perros de la ley.

—¡Eso es casi poético!... «Los perros de la ley», muy bonito, sí.

—Repito: ¿qué coño quieren de mí?

—No tenemos nada que ver con el teniente. Nuestro asunto es otro: Martine Marchand.

—¿Aún andan con eso? Parece que a la policía española le pagan por no hacer bien su trabajo, ¿no? Pues de mí poco van a sacar. No tengo ni puñetera idea de dónde está la francesa. ¿Cómo quieren que me entere de algo estando aquí aislado como un criminal?

—Por eso no se preocupe, nosotros sí sabemos dónde está.

Se quedó mirándome sin comprender.

—¿Y entonces qué hacen aquí?

—¿No le interesa saber dónde está su amiga?

—No, bastante tengo con lo mío. Cada palo que aguante su vela, ya hice bastante por ella, no puedo hacer más.

—Martine está en la morgue, Dámaso. Alguien se la ha cargado de una puñalada y no sabemos quién es.

El impacto de la noticia en su cara fue evidente. Contrajo todas sus facciones en una mueca de sorpresa y dolor. Tardó un poco en volver a hablar.

—¿Esto qué es?, ¿una trampita de mal gusto para que hable? Pues podían ahorrársela porque no sé nada de ella.

Saqué el fajo de fotografías que llevaba preparadas, se las tendí y empezó a mirarlas con desconfianza. A medida que pasaba las imágenes del cadáver de Marchand sobre la camilla de autopsias, su rostro iba perdiendo el color. No llegó al final. Tiró las fotografías sobre la mesa y se tapó los ojos. Pensé que quizá lloraba, pero no, cuando volví a ver su cara esta sólo traslucía horror.

—¡Hijos de la gran puta! Pero ¿quién es capaz de algo así?

—Eso es lo que queremos saber, Dámaso, y usted puede ayudarnos.

—¡No, yo no sé nada! Se lo dije al principio y se lo repito ahora.

Su voz sonaba al borde de la desesperación. Supuse que no sólo gravitaba sobre él la turbación de la noticia que le habíamos dado, sino también el desgaste emocional causado por varios días de prisión incomunicada.

—No sabe nada, pero le proporcionó cobijo a Martine hasta que le fue posible. ¿Por qué?

—No sé si se puede decir que éramos amigos. Yo le tenía bastante admiración. Había conseguido buenos negocios y, aunque la perseguía la poli francesa, la tía entraba y salía del país sin despeinarse. A pesar de ser una mujer, tenía unos cojones como un toro. Se las gastaba fuertes, sin piedad para quien no se la merecía.

—Sí, algo hemos oído de eso. Terribles venganzas, ¿no?

—Este mundo de la droga es muy chungo. Yo lo sé de cuando me dedicaba, que ahora ya estoy limpio, por más que se empeñe el jodido Montilla.

—Eso a nosotros no nos interesa. Siga, ¿y qué más?

—¿Cómo que qué más? ¡Ya les he dicho que no sé nada más! Ella vio que ustedes la estaban buscando y que lo tenía crudo para irse, así que yo le di protección porque me caía bien, también porque ella se había portado bien conmigo en otros tiempos.

—¿Y qué más?

—Oiga, ¿usted no tiene oídos o no entiende el español?

Garzón vio llegado su momento de darle un toque. Levantó un dedo en el aire.

—¡Eh, tranquilo, colega! Habla con respeto o se te va a caer el pelo. Aunque vas bien jodido, aún tienes cosas que perder, ¿de acuerdo?

—¡Pero es que no sé nada más!

—Creemos, Dámaso, que el asesinato de Martine puede estar conectado con el de Pierre Laurent.

—Pues yo no sé nada de ninguno de los dos.

—De acuerdo, muy bien, de acuerdo, usted no sabe nada de los asesinatos, pero sabe cosas de la francesa que no ha querido decir. ¿Por qué fue a la caravana de Laurent la noche en que lo asesinaron? Porque no lo mató ella, ¿verdad?

Empezó a restregarse los ojos, murmuró que le dolía la cabeza.

—¿Tampoco saben eso? ¡Pues se le habría ocurrido hasta a un niño de diez años!

Garzón se tensó, pero le hice un gesto para que le permitiera seguir hablando sin interrupciones. Como si sintiera un cansancio infinito continuó:

—Estaban liados, inspectora, estaban liados, ¿qué otra cosa podría ser? Cuando ella venía por aquí follaban bien a gusto. Él era por lo visto un pichabrava, así que se lo montaban los dos de maravilla.

—Pero, al margen de eso, hacían negocios con la droga, ¿no?

—De poca importancia, pero sí, de esa manera fue como se conocieron.

—¿Qué buscaban ella y los matones que trajo de Francia?

—Parece que el pichaloca se la jugó con una partida entera de material, coca, creo recordar. No encontraron la droga ni de coña. Ahí le tocó pagar al otro imbécil.

—¿Qué otro imbécil?

—¡El socio de Laurent! Buscaron en la caravana y se la jodieron por si sabía algo y no quería soltarlo. Ya le digo que la francesa era la hostia.

—¿El imbécil estaba también en el asunto?

—No, creo que no.

—Pero sí sabía que su socio estaba liado con Martine.

—¡Pues claro, joder! Se conocían y todo. Es difícil vivir con un tío y no saber con quién está follando, aunque era tan tonto que yo lo vi una vez con Martine, le pedimos que le llevara un paquete con dinero a Laurent diciéndole que eran ingredientes de comida. Martine le soltó que yo era su hermano. ¡Hay que joderse! ¡Se lo tragó! ¿Era imbécil o no?

Miré a Garzón, estaba tan avergonzado como yo. Aquella información nos había calado hondo, debíamos haber insistido con Bob, era obvio que sabía más de lo que declaró. Proseguí, sin embargo, con un esfuerzo para no dejarme amilanar.

—O sea, que cuando Martine fue a la caravana la noche del asesinato, ¿iba a pedirle cuentas de la partida de droga desaparecida?

—No había desaparecido todavía. Iba a pedirle cuentas porque había recibido protestas de sus clientes. La droga que pasaba por el francés estaba cortada con algo, adulterada, quiero decir. Para sacar más provecho la mezclaba con tiza o con algún producto químico, exactamente ella no me lo contó. Se presentó por la noche y se lo encontró fiambre. Por eso buscaba la droga y, de paso, a quien se había cargado a su novio. Ahí sí que tuvo una debilidad de mujer. Decía que ella estaba segura de que Laurent no la había traicionado. El tío que se lo había cargado se había llevado la droga. Martine me juró que se arriesgaría al máximo para saber quién era el asesino y dónde tenía el material.

—Pero si la droga estaba cortada, él sí había estado pegándosela.

—¡Eso mismo le solté yo! Pero nada, no quería atender a razones: él era un santo con una polla divina y en paz. Debilidad de mujer, que le ha costado la vida, por cierto.

—Dámaso, lo que acaba de contarnos nos ha ayudado, ahora dígamelo con toda sinceridad, ¿tenía ella alguna sospecha de quién había matado a Laurent?

—Ninguna, ni puñetera idea tenía.

—¿Y usted?, ¿la tiene usted?

—Le juro que no. Todo lo que les he contado es lo único que sé.

—Espero que sea verdad, realmente no está usted en situación de mentir por algo que ni le viene ni le va.

—Ya que les he ayudado, supongo que se lo comunicarán al juez: que he colaborado con la policía. Eso me beneficiará. No quiero volver a verle la jeta a Montilla.

—Lo haremos, no se preocupe, en cuestión de jetas el juez es muy sensible.

Y bien, nuestro escenario había cambiado, o al

menos se habían introducido nuevas aportaciones en su decoración. En medio de un tema tan sumamente prosaico como las drogas, aparecía como por arte de magia el amor, o el sexo, o ambas cosas a la vez. Sin embargo, aquel descubrimiento no aclaraba nada. Sí, de acuerdo, habíamos encontrado una rosa en un erial, pero ¿tenía ese hallazgo algún significado? La reacción a bote pronto era preguntarse qué pintaba tan bella flor en aquel lugar, pero no se sabía qué contestar a una pregunta que sólo indicaba desconcierto.

La conversación que mantuvimos con el subinspector tras el interrogatorio de Dámaso versó sobre la misma inquietud: ¿adónde nos conduce el nuevo dato? Empezaron nuestras preguntas al aire: «¿Quién podía querer matar a Laurent por motivos relacionados con el amor o el sexo? ¿Un rival? ¿Tenía Martine algún novio, alguien que pretendía sus favores y se enteró de su *affaire* con el francés?».

—No daba la impresión de que la francesa fuera el tipo de mujer que se dejaba controlar por un amante celoso. Más bien parecía que hacía siempre su voluntad —respondí a la pregunta aérea de Garzón.

—Que ella no se dejara controlar no significa que alguno de los canallas de su entorno se encaprichara de su persona y...

—Eso está bien visto, Fermín, realmente el medio en el que se desenvuelve toda esta gentuza no permite muchas conjeturas románticas.

—Sí, pero no nos centremos tanto en la parte emocional de la cuestión. Según el tío este, quien se cepilló a Pierre Laurent se llevó con él bastante material. Eso no tiene nada que ver con los sentimientos.

—Quizá aprovechó la ocasión, o quizá si se trataba de una venganza personal por haberse follado a su amada, quiso llevarla a cabo con todo tipo de agravantes.

—No sé, inspectora, yo al principio pensé en un asunto pasional, pero ahora la veo a usted demasiado colgada de la nueva interpretación sentimental. ¿Y si no tuviera nada que ver? Martine pudo encontrarse a su amante fiambre por alguna razón que nada tuviera que ver con ella. De hecho, buscaba al asesino, al asesino y la droga, por supuesto.

—Realmente, si hubiera sido un amante despechado quien se cargó al francés, ella hubiera sospechado su identidad, no lo hubiera buscado tan a la desesperada como lo hizo: acudiendo a las ferias, aun a riesgo de que la reconocieran, trayendo consigo a sus forajidos, jodiéndole la caravana a Bob...

—Por cierto, me gustaría saber qué pito toca en todo esto Bob, también llamado el Imbécil.

—No creo que tuviera muchos pitos que tocar. Y de lo de «el imbécil» habría mucho de que hablar, el tío bien nos engañó: no sabía nada de los negocios de su socio, desconocía que su documentación fuera falsa... ¡Y nos lo tragamos todo, joder!

—Según el jodido Dámaso, no estaba implicado en el negocio de las drogas, pero bien le destruyeron la caravana por si acaso guardaba el alijo allí.

—Eso no lo convierte en sospechoso, siendo socios en el restaurante ambulante, sería bastante normal pensar que pudo hacerle el favor de guardarle temporalmente la farlopa. Por eso fueron a revisarle el vehículo.

—Una revisión a conciencia. El auténtico motivo por el que decidió poner fin a su vida. ¡Es verdad que era imbécil!, ¿no? Suicidarse por una cosa material.

—Todo es materia, Fermín, todo es materia.

—Menos el amor, inspectora.

—Dejémoslo; se suponía que en este caso, la inclinada a romanticismos era yo.

—Entonces, inspectora, ¿nos quedamos con esa hipótesis? ¿Un admirador o quizá un examante misterioso se cargó a Laurent por celos?

—¿También se la ha cargado a ella? Le recuerdo que en nuestra mochila hay dos muertos.

—Sí, ahí culmina su venganza.

—¿Un asunto de violencia de género mezclado con tráfico de drogas?

—¿Por qué no?

—¿Y por qué sí? Es una hipótesis construida en el aire.

—La primera que nos hemos atrevido a hacer en toda la investigación.

—Muy bien, se la acepto. Un auténtico monstruo de violencia y malos instintos ronda a su examante y su nuevo amor. A los dos se los cepilla muy limpiamente y, encima, se lleva droga para los gastos. ¿Ese monstruo nunca ha sido visto por nadie? A Martine la reconocieron algunos feriantes, otros la vieron rondar por las ferias cuando ya se la buscaba policialmente. Hay quien vio a sus secuaces cuando estaban en Barcelona y, sin embargo, ¿al monstruo quién lo vio?, ¿nunca nadie, en ninguna parte? ¿Y cómo sabía el puto monstruo que Laurent dormía con la puerta abierta o que la cerradura estaba estropeada?

Habrá que volver atrás, Fermín. Alguien tiene que haberse percatado de la presencia de un hombre extraño que rondaba por allí.

—¿Volver atrás significa...?

—Sí, tendremos que localizar de nuevo a todos los feriantes que estaban juntos la noche del asesinato y los días posteriores, es necesario volver a interrogarlos enfocando las preguntas desde otro punto de vista más amplio.

—¡Me lo temía! —exclamó Garzón llevándose las manos a la cabeza—. Voy a hacerle una confidencia, inspectora. En las últimas semanas he tenido una pesadilla recurrente. Cuando me despertaba, tenía el cuerpo sudado y el corazón me latía con fuerza. ¿Sabe cuál era?

—Sí, por supuesto que lo sé. Debido a la evolución de los acontecimientos en la investigación se veía obligado a localizar a cada uno de los feriantes, dondequiera que se encontrara, y volver a interrogarlos uno a uno.

—¡Exactamente! Pero eso es terrible, inspectora, un trabajazo increíble.

—Póngase en marcha, Fermín, queda mucha tela por cortar.

—¿Y no podríamos comprarnos un traje hecho?

Sonreí, y con el dedo índice apuntando a la puerta lo conminé a ponerse en acción. Intenté que ese gesto demostrara seguridad y convicción, aunque yo también pensaba que aquello sería un coñazo insufrible y no tenía la más mínima certeza de que fuera a servirnos de algo.

25

Recuperamos la lista de feriantes gastronómicos con sus correspondientes teléfonos de contacto. ¡A saber dónde pararía cada uno de ellos! «¿Habíamos abandonado demasiado pronto aquel entorno?», me pregunté ejerciendo mi tradicional autocrítica destructiva. «¡No y mil veces no!», me respondí. La investigación había sido exhaustiva y no fuimos capaces de sacar más información. Volver atrás representaba un riesgo: perder el tiempo miserablemente, pero aquel caso, que ya se me antojaba eterno, bien podía dilatarse un poco más. El dilema ahora era por dónde empezar a preguntar, y la pregunta también se las traía: ¿vio usted a un fantasma alguna vez?

—Yo empezaría por los que estén más cerca —afirmó Garzón.

—No me parece una decisión muy ortodoxa. En el mismo plan podríamos empezar por el que sirva la comida que más le guste a usted.

—Tampoco estaría mal. ¿Qué le parece si buscamos al gallego? Parecía el jefe moral del grupo.

—Pero el grupo como tal ya no existe y quizá no tenga ganas de hablar.

—Da igual, inspectora. El que tiene cualidades de líder siempre hace su papel.

—Eso es una verdad como una casa, Fermín, y le felicito por la reflexión. Espero de verdad que no le haya surgido porque le esté apeteciendo el pulpo *á feira*.

—No lo descarte, sinceramente.

El gallego tenía plantado su bastión en una feria gastronómica de Mollet. El subinspector estuvo protestando un poco por aquel protocolo que habíamos cumplido muchas veces ya: tomar el coche, buscar el lugar, calcular una hora buena para el encuentro y presentarse sin avisar, cosa que había decidido yo.

El momento escogido no resultaba perfecto, el patrón tenía la caravana abierta al público, pero la clientela era abundante y no le sentaría nada bien tener que abandonar su puesto un rato para atendernos dejando sola a su mujer. Seguimos la estrategia de confundirnos como unos clientes más y pedimos cerveza y una tapa del pulpo ansiado por Garzón. Nos reconoció enseguida, saludándonos sin el menor entusiasmo o cordialidad. Él mismo sirvió la comanda y, mientras la degustábamos tranquilamente, se acercó en el primer instante que tuvo libre.

—Supongo que no vienen sólo a comer pulpo, ¿no?

—¿Puede dedicarnos un momento?

—Ya ven cómo tengo de lleno el garito. Es mi trabajo, ya saben, y el trabajo es sagrado.

—El nuestro es investigar y tiene una cosa especial: cuando lo ejercemos, los demás tienen que parar de trabajar y atendernos, ¿comprende? Es lo que marca la ley.

Se lavó las manos y se las secó con un paño. Habló con su esposa y nos hizo un gesto hosco para que lo acompañáramos a la parte trasera de la caravana.

—¿Qué quieren saber ahora?

—La sospechosa que andábamos buscando ha aparecido asesinada.

No se inmutó, pensó un par de segundos y se encogió de hombros.

—No me sorprende. ¿Y?

—¿Vio alguna vez a algún hombre extraño rondando la caravana de Pierre Laurent? ¿O quizá vio a la sospechosa acompañada de un hombre en alguna ocasión? Parece ser que el francés mantenía una relación sentimental con ella.

Se echó a reír teatralmente.

—¡Relación sentimental!, tiene gracia. En esa caravana siempre pasaban cosas raras, había ambientillo, según cuentan.

—¿Qué tipo de ambientillo?

—¡Bah, rumores! Estos campamentos acaban siendo como un patio de vecinos, todo el mundo dice la suya, y nunca te puedes fiar. Yo voy a mis cosas y no presto atención.

—¿Qué rumores?

—Ustedes ya los saben, *carallo*, a ese francés le gustaban más las tías que un pastel, y se le daban bien al condenado, según dicen por ahí. Parece que tenía una novia en cada puerto, ¡que le gustaba follar, vaya!

—Lo habíamos entendido, sí. ¿Qué decían en concreto esos rumores?, ¿tenía Pierre Laurent alguna amante que sus otros compañeros pudieran identificar?

—¡Y yo qué sé, inspectora! Soy un padre de familia que se gana las castañas trabajando como un animal. No tengo tiempo de prestar oídos a chorradas.

—Entonces, ¿cómo sabe los rumores que corrían?

—A veces, por la noche, después de cerrar las ferias, estamos tan hechos polvo que nos juntamos unos cuantos y tomamos una cerveza. Ahí es donde oí de las aficiones del francés, pero nadie dijo nada concreto, ¡qué va! La mayor parte de los cotilleos son milongas que la gente se inventa. Nos reímos un rato y a dormir. Además, como este tío era extranjero y bastante antipático, pues muchas bromas y chismorreos le caían a él.

—¿A quién podemos preguntar que estuviera fuerte en habladurías?

—Pepa Darder es la que siempre cuenta más cosas, es muy cachonda. Vende quesos con denominación de origen. A base de quesos hace canapés, tortillas, *soufflés*... Le va bastante bien.

—¿Sabe por dónde puede parar ahora?

—¡Ah, ni idea! Hace tiempo que no coincidimos.

—La encontraremos. Tenemos su teléfono.

—Pues yo no lo tengo, ya ven. Oiga, no le digan que lo de los cotilleos se lo he contado yo, igual me toma manía. A nadie le gusta tener a la policía rondándole.

—Muy amable por su parte. Gracias por la información.

—Son quince euros.

—¿Por la información? —preguntó sorprendido el subinspector.

—No, por la tapa y las cañas que se han tomado.

Me disculpé por el olvido, saqué mi billetera y pagué nuestra deuda. De camino al coche llegó el inevitable comentario de Garzón, que ya esperaba.

—¡Qué cabrón este tío! No sabe nada, no ha visto a nadie, no se acuerda de nada, pero cobrarnos la cuenta no se le despista.

—Es lo normal. ¿Ha cogido la lista de los contactos?, ¿la lleva apuntada en el móvil?

Se dio el clásico golpe en la frente de quien ha olvidado algo crucial. No le di tiempo a buscar una excusa o a emitir una lamentación.

—Llame a comisaría, que nos localicen a Pepa Darder.

Dimos una vuelta por la feria gastronómica de Mollet sin reconocer a ninguno de los feriantes que estaban presentes el día de la muerte de Laurent, quizá simplemente no los recordábamos. A Garzón el fallo de memoria le vino de perlas. Fuimos picando aquí y allá y nos vimos obligados a poner coto a las cervezas de acompañamiento si queríamos llegar enteros adonde quisiera que fuéramos a parar.

Al cabo de un rato sonó el teléfono de mi compañero. Habló brevemente, afirmó, dio las gracias y volvió a hacer un gesto tradicional con las manos: se las llevó a la cabeza con cara de espanto.

—¡La madre que la parió! —dijo—. En Lleida ni más ni menos. La cotilla está en Lleida, en una muestra alimentaria.

—¿Se encuentra en condiciones de conducir? A mí no me apetece.

—Si lo dice por la cerveza..., podría competir en Monza, pero irnos ahora me da una pereza...

—La pereza cada vez ocupa más espacio en su personalidad, deberá tomar medidas.

—De momento mediré los kilómetros del viaje. Claro que un poco de queso como postre puede ser un acicate importante.

Mientras íbamos por la autopista me adormecí. Oía a lo lejos los ruidos de la conducción, algún carraspeo de mi compañero, pero era incapaz de volver en mí. Acabé por perder la consciencia por completo y me sobresalté cuando Garzón zarandeó mi brazo sin piedad.

—¿Qué pasa?

—Que ya hemos llegado, inspectora. Estaba usted como un tronco. ¡Y mira que el viaje no es corto!

—¿Por qué no me ha despertado antes?

—Me gustaba tenerla ahí, tan indefensa, es algo que no suele pasar. He aprovechado para hacer comentarios machistas.

—¿Más de los que hace cuando estoy despierta?

—Ni se los imagina.

—¿Dónde estamos?

—En un parking, a cinco minutos a pie de la Muestra Alimentaria.

—¿La qué?

—Inspectora, ¿se encuentra bien? Esto es Lleida,

investigamos dos asesinatos y yo soy el subinspector Garzón, siempre a su servicio.

—Sí, déjese de coñas, estoy bien. Pero no sé qué vamos a preguntarle a esa mujer de los quesos. Debería haber estado pensando en vez de dormir.

—Vamos a entrevistarla en su calidad de cotilla, y si lo es de verdad, hablará ella sola sin necesidad de que le preguntemos.

—Últimamente está usted muy perspicaz.

—Sólo es mi perspicacia natural, que usted no ha apreciado hasta ahora.

No comprendía la capacidad de mi compañero para mostrarse siempre dispuesto a bromear, siempre despierto, siempre en forma, ajeno a las debilidades que nos aquejaban al resto de los humanos.

El recuerdo de Pepa Darder no lo tenía nada claro en la mente. El grupo a quienes interrogamos en los días posteriores al asesinato de Laurent era numeroso y el aspecto de Pepa no tenía nada de particular: cerca de los cuarenta años, pelo lacio teñido de rubio, ojillos vivos y maliciosos..., un aspecto de lo más convencional.

Pepa no pareció contrariada por tener que hablar con nosotros, sí sorprendida, por supuesto, había pasado tiempo suficiente como para que el recuerdo de nuestra investigación se hubiera disipado, o al menos hubiera dejado de despertar interés morboso en los feriantes.

—¿Y qué quieren saber? —preguntó con todo descaro.

—Primero queremos que sepa usted. Martine Marchand, la mujer francesa que habíamos estado buscando y que rondó varias veces por las instalaciones donde ustedes paraban, ha sido asesinada.

—¡Joder! —musitó.

—Se lo contamos para que vea la trascendencia de la cuestión.

—No, si la trascendencia ya la veo, pero no entiendo qué tengo que ver yo en eso. Además, ¿ella no era la asesina del francés? ¿Y ahora van y la asesinan a ella?

—Nosotros somos quienes hacemos las preguntas. Nos han dicho que usted solía estar bastante al tanto de las circunstancias personales de sus compañeros.

—¿Y quién les ha dicho eso? —saltó como una autómata. Garzón le paró los pies.

—Oiga, Pepa, la inspectora ya se lo ha dicho bien claro. Aquí quien hace las preguntas somos nosotros, así que usted contesta lo más claro y rápido posible. ¿Me capta?

—Sí, sí, ¡qué barbaridad! No hace falta que la tome conmigo. Lo que pasa es que estoy muy harta de la fama de chafardera que me han puesto. Yo sé las cuatro cosas que sabe todo el mundo, lo que ocurre es que a veces las comento y los demás se callan como putas.

—Vale, la entendemos. Pues de las cuatro cosas, empecemos por la número uno. ¿Cree usted que la francesa y Laurent estaban liados?

—No me sorprendería nada, la verdad. Pierre ligaba mucho. Yo lo veía a veces vacilando con las clientas. Alguna noche había visto algún que otro coche que se paraba cerca de su caravana, bajaba alguien e iba para allá.

—¿Sabe qué hacía?, ¿entraba en la caravana, volvía a salir poco o mucho rato después?

—Ya les digo que yo no soy una chismosa. Para saber eso hubiera tenido que quedarme despierta, salir de mi caravana y ponerme a esperar para ver si pillaba algo. Yo no hago esas cosas ni de coña. Para enterarme de algo tenía que ser que me lo encontrara por casualidad, así que sólo sé eso, lo que a veces pasaba por ahí.

—Pero las cosas incompletas que veía por casualidad tienen una o varias interpretaciones.

—De acuerdo, pues yo me privaba de hacer interpretaciones. Sólo me imagino que Pierre ligaba porque las tías le ponían ojitos y él se dejaba querer, pero no los he visto meterse en la cama para hacer sus cosas. Me expreso, ¿no?

—Sí, se expresa. ¿Qué interpretación se le podría dar al hecho de que coches llegaran en la noche y depositaran un pasajero cerca de la caravana de Pierre?

—Ni idea, oigan, ni idea, y se lo digo muy en serio, no lo sé. Hay una cosa que siempre pensé y es que en la caravana del francés y Bob había un ambiente raro. Y si me preguntan qué quiere decir eso les contestaré que no lo sé. Es una sensación que yo tenía. No debía ser la única, además, porque corrían cotilleos a veces tontos, como que Pierre y Bob estaban liados. Para que vean que la gente habla por hablar. Oiga, ¿por qué no les preguntan a sus amigos los vegetarianos?

—¿Qué pasa con ellos, también le producen alguna sensación extraña?

—No, pero ponían muchas veces al lado su furgoneta, y Bob charlaba con Elisenda muchas veces también. Digo yo que vería más el que estaba más cerca, ¿no?

—Pero nada de sensaciones, ¿no es eso?

—Elisenda y el marido son buena gente. No vayan a cotorrearles ahora que yo los he señalado por algo en particular, a ver si vamos a liarla por una gilipollez.

Garzón sonrió de través. Como lo conocía bien, enseguida supe que estaba al borde de su aguante. No me equivoqué, le soltó desabridamente:

—La policía no tiene por costumbre cotorrear ni tampoco liarla. Justamente es lo contrario de nuestro deber: desliar lo que está liado. Espero que le haya quedado claro por si hemos de volver a interrogarla.

—Muy clarito, sí, señor. No se mosquee conmigo, es sólo mi manera de hablar. ¿Quieren probar un poco de queso? Me entró ayer un gorgonzola que está de muerte.

Muy mal debía haberle caído la testigo al subinspector, porque se privó del gorgonzola y contestó con sequedad:

—No, muchas gracias, para muertes ya tenemos suficientes.

El cónclave posterior que mantuvimos mi subalterno y yo fue breve pero intenso. No estábamos seguros de que lo que había relatado la cotilla oficial tuviera un valor intrínseco para la investigación, pero ninguno de los dos se había quedado con la impresión de que mentía.

—De acuerdo, Garzón, pero ¿y las ocultaciones? Puede haberse callado detalles que supongan algún riesgo para ella, como por ejemplo los asuntos de drogas.

—Yo creo que ella sabe perfectamente que Laurent trapicheaba, quizá lo sabían todos los que tuvieron alguna relación con él, pero si lo confiesa, de alguna manera podemos hacerla pringar por no habernos avisado.

—Sin duda lleva razón, pero si no son drogas, ¿de qué otro modo deben interpretarse las visitas de coches en mitad de la noche? ¿Quizá estamos hablando del monstruo que lo asesinó?

—Concluyendo, que lo único que nos ha aclarado esta tía es que Laurent ligaba bastante y que recibía visitas intempestivas de madrugada, que nosotros atribuimos al tráfico de droga o a un enemigo en la sombra. Suposición sobre suposición.

—Bueno, son suposiciones que vienen a corroborar ideas anteriores. Eso no está mal.

—¡Bah, caca de la vaca! Sólo dijo una cosa interesante la chismosa, y encima nos puso en ridículo. Vayan a la caravana vegetariana porque es la que estaba más cerca. Si llegaban coches por la noche, los vecinos cercanos debían verlos, ¿no?

—No se lo tome tan a la tremenda. Si no hemos ido todavía a interrogarlos es porque ya sabemos qué van a decirnos esos dos: Pierre era muy reservado, sólo hablábamos de cosas banales, nosotros no entramos en la vida de los demás...

—¿Y las visitas nocturnas de los coches tampoco las oían? Localice a esos dos, subinspector.

—A sus órdenes, inspectora, aunque con la racha que llevamos seguro que estarán en casa Dios, en el último confín de Cataluña.

Desconozco si era por la racha que atravesábamos o porque Dios se había mudado de casa buscando la paz, pero el caso es que el subinspector estaba en lo cierto, la caravana de Javier y Elisenda estaba en unas jornadas festivas en Tortosa, en plenas Terres de l'Ebre, confín sur de la comunidad. Decidimos visitarlos al día siguiente por la mañana, nuestro espíritu viajero no daba para más en aquella ocasión.

26

Salimos pronto por la mañana. Conducía Garzón, canturreando. Me sorprendió que no renegara como de costumbre por aquel desplazamiento temprano. Como estaba medio dormida, intenté despejarme enhebrando una conversación.

—Le veo muy feliz, subinspector. Creí que eso de coger el coche y hacer millas le sentaba fatal.

—Y en efecto así es, pero hoy casi me apetece alejarme de Barcelona y del hogar.

—¿Puede saberse el motivo?

—Bronca con Beatriz.

—Las broncas conyugales siempre son una buena razón para huir, cuanto más lejos, mejor.

—Otra vez está con lo de que últimamente no me ve el pelo, y que si soy un brazo de la justicia al cien por cien, pues mejor me caso con la justicia, que como lleva los ojos vendados le dará lo mismo verme el pelo o no.

—Hay que reconocer que su esposa tiene un excelente sentido del humor —dije riendo.

—Sí, el problema es cuando lo usa en contra mía. ¿A usted Marcos no le hace recriminaciones laborales?

—Pues no lo sé, como casi no nos vemos...: yo no voy a casa en todo el día y él parece que estuviera evitándome.

—Será para ahorrarle broncas.

—Es posible. En su día llegamos a una especie de acuerdo verbal. Yo le aseguré que para mí era muy importante el trabajo, y le advertí de que se trataba de un trabajo muy especial que en muchas ocasiones no respeta horarios ni vida familiar. Le rogué que eso nunca se convirtiera en un nido de problemas. Lo aceptó, aunque estoy segura de que ahora anda cabreado, pero como es tan racional, prefiere no caer en la tentación de hacerme reproches o montarme números.

Garzón me miraba de reojo, estupefacto. Sin duda aquella historia de acuerdos y estipulaciones conyugales era algo demasiado artificial para sus estándares diarios. De la estupefacción pasó a un gesto de aprecio afirmando con la cabeza.

—Sí, puede que Marcos sea muy racional, pero usted no le anda a la zaga.

—Oiga, Fermín, ambos hemos dejado atrás dos divorcios. No es cuestión de fiarlo todo a la fuerza del amor.

—Pero si justamente le estoy diciendo hasta qué punto me parece bien que las cosas se pacten anticipadamente. Pero claro, luego surgen detalles, la letra pequeña del contrato y...

—Los detalles no se pueden pactar, Garzón, lógicamente. Hay que ponerse de acuerdo en cosas globales e importantes.

Siguió conduciendo en silencio, absorto en la carretera, pero yo sabía que estaba pensando en lo que acabábamos de hablar. Se corroboró mi intuición cuando dijo:

—¿Y usted cree que es demasiado tarde para que yo llegue a un acuerdo de esos con Beatriz?

—Beatriz ya se ha dado cuenta de lo importantes que son para usted sus deberes policiales.

—Sí, pero yo pactaría otras cosas.

—¿Como por ejemplo?

—Pactaría que no quiero saber nada de la decoración del hogar, ni comer comida saludable, ni recibir en casa a algunos amigos de mi mujer, más pijos que la hostia.

—¡Detalles! —solté echándome a reír.

—Para mí no lo son. Primero habría que pactar lo que son cosas importantes y lo que usted llama detalles.

—Nos metemos en una discusión sin fin, subinspector, mejor dejémoslo. Supongo que deberíamos estar contentos con la flecha que nos lanzó Cupido y eso es todo.

—¡La flecha que nos lanzó Cupido!, nunca en la vida la había oído decir algo así. Es poético.

—Es cursi, pero hoy no doy para más. ¿Cuánto falta hasta Tortosa?

—Unos ochenta kilómetros.

—Llegaremos casi a la hora de comer.

—Pues cojonudo, he leído en internet que en Tortosa hacen unas morcillas artesanales de arroz y piñones que son una gozada espiritual.

—¡Una gozada espiritual! ¿Ve? Usted también tiene ramalazos poéticos, y además no son cursis.

—En eso lleva razón, las morcillas superan de lejos a Cupido.

Llegamos, en efecto, cerca de la una y media, una hora perfecta para nuestros propósitos. Según la experiencia adquirida durante el caso, llegar a una zona de caravanas gastronómicas cuando se hallan a pleno rendimiento, conduce a que los propietarios te miren con mala cara y no estén por la labor de contestar preguntas. Por consiguiente, me dejé llevar por las búsquedas que mi compañero había realizado en la red y acabamos en una loma donde había una zona residencial y algunos restaurantes. El que Fermín había encontrado servía comida típica de la región y sí, entre los platos destacados en la carta, figuraban las famosas morcillas llamadas «baldanas», que ordenamos sin dudar. Garzón pidió una botellita de vino tinto y, por un momento, logró que se nos olvidara por qué habíamos llegado hasta allí. Fue una comida deliciosa, con buen ambiente y buen yantar. Ni un momento hablamos de la investigación, no parecía haber lugar para muertos, suicidios o sangre, más allá de la que contenían las baldanas. Al final, tomamos café y yo, aguijoneada por mi conciencia, empecé a inquietarme un poco y se lo hice saber a mi compañero de mesa. Él miró el reloj.

—Es pronto todavía, tenemos tiempo para un chupito final.

—¿Chupito también? ¿Y no llegaremos al trabajo medio cocidos?

—Utilizaremos la mitad que nos queda cruda para trabajar.

—No sé si me parece adecuado.

—No le parece adecuado porque le gusta machacarse, inspectora. Relájese, no por sufrir más se trabaja mejor.

Emitido semejante dictamen moral, pidió a la camarera dos chupitos de orujo blanco muy seco. Nos los bebimos de un tirón, sin el menor síntoma de autoflagelación o sufrimiento.

El joven matrimonio se repartía las labores cuando llegamos. Ella servía a los clientes rezagados mientras él iba recogiendo y limpiando el menaje utilizado. La reacción facial de ambos al vernos fue como la que siempre habían tenido frente a nuestra presencia. Elisenda sonrió levemente y pareció azorarse, mientras que Javier nos recibió con cara de pocos amigos. Nos dirigimos a él y su bienvenida pareció digna de un funeral.

—¿Siguen a la gente por todas partes?

—Sólo cuando tenemos que interrogarlos —respondí con tan poca cordialidad como la que él había empleado.

—Pues aún estamos en plena faena, tendrán que esperar un rato.

—Nuestro tiempo tiene tanto valor como el suyo, así que aparque lo que está haciendo y atiéndanos inmediatamente —le espetó Garzón.

Probablemente, no esperaba una réplica tan dura, porque cambió de actitud al segundo, dirigiéndonos una sonrisa que no tenía aspecto de sincera.

—Bromeaba, señores. ¿Ya han comido? Si les apetecen tengo hechos unos canelones de calabacín y huevo duro que han salido muy ricos.

—Muchas gracias, acabamos de comer —dije bastante perpleja por su cambio radical.

—¿Y postre?, ¿han tomado postre? Como homenaje a la zona en la que estamos, Elisenda ha preparado *pastissets*. Son una especie de empanadillas rellenas de cabello de ángel. La receta tiene origen medieval, son muy típicos de aquí. Pueden interrogarme mientras los prueban.

Ante mi sorpresa, el subinspector aceptó la invitación. Mientras Javier iba en busca de los dulces, se lo recriminé con una mirada, pero él sacó su móvil y se puso a disimular buscando algo en Google. Comentó:

—¡Vaya, eso de los *pastissets* no lo tenía controlado! Voy a mirar si de verdad son de origen medieval o se lo ha inventado este tío.

No me hacía ninguna gracia que Garzón ampliara su cultura gastronómica frente a un testigo que ejercía de anfitrión. Crear climas de confianza puede venir bien en algunos interrogatorios, pero en otros suele desvirtuar los roles de cada cual.

Llegaron los *pastissets*, Garzón hincó el diente en uno y todo fueron alabanzas y buen rollo. Corté de raíz aquella confraternización preguntándole a Javier:

—¿Se han enterado del asesinato de Martine Marchand?

—¿Quién es? —contestó distraídamente.

—La sospechosa del asesinato de Pierre Laurent, ¿recuerda?

—¿Y la han matado a ella también? Eso es terrible, inspectora. ¿Saben ya quién ha sido?

—No, todavía no, pero sí hemos sabido que entre Pierre y Martine existía una relación sentimental. Y ¿sabe qué le digo, Javier? Que me extraña mucho que ni usted ni su esposa estuvieran al tanto de ello con el contacto, y podría incluso decirse la amistad, que existía entre ustedes.

—Pero a eso ya le contestamos en su día. Pierre era un hombre muy cerrado, nunca contaba cosas propias, ¿cómo podíamos estar informados de sus relaciones sentimentales?

—Esa mujer debía de aparecer de vez en cuando por la caravana de Pierre y Bob. Es sabido por todo el mundo que ustedes solían colocar su caravana junto a la de ellos. ¿Nunca, ni una sola vez la vieron, aunque fuera de refilón?

—No, no la vimos. De haber sido así se lo hubiéramos dicho cuando ustedes la buscaban.

—Otro tema: hay testigos entre algunos propietarios de caravanas, cercanas a la del francés, que aseguran haber visto cómo de madrugada se acercaban coches y él recibía visitas a esas horas intempestivas.

Por primera vez se exasperó un poco y volvió a su hosco tono inicial.

—Inspectora, mi mujer y yo trabajamos como bestias toda la jornada, usted misma puede verlo. Este trabajo es exigente: hay que comprar alimentos diariamente, elaborarlos, servirlos, limpiar... ¿De verdad piensa que cuando llega la noche estamos en condiciones de ponernos a fisgonear qué pasa fuera? Mataron al pobre Pierre y no nos enteramos, eso le da una idea de que por la noche hacemos lo mismo que la mayor parte de la gente: dormir, sólo que con mayor intensidad que la mayoría.

—Muy bien, felicidades por su facilidad para el sueño reparador. Dígale a su esposa que venga.

—Está atendiendo a los últimos clientes, tendré que suplirla yo.

—Adelante, a usted ya no le necesitamos.

Se largó de mal talante, la tregua de los dulces, medievales o no, había sido breve. El hecho de que le ordenáramos que se presentara su mujer había empeorado todavía más su mala disposición hacia nosotros. Seguía protegiendo a su tierna rubia.

Elisenda estaba como siempre, lánguida y vulnerable. Cuando le comunicamos el asesinato de Martine se echó a llorar. Entre lágrimas dijo:

—¿Nunca se acabará esta pesadilla? ¿Por qué la gente se odia, se ataca, se matan unos a otros? ¿No será nunca posible que haya un poco de amor?

Nos quedamos bastante descolocados ante aquel arranque buenista. Cuando hubo acabado su pequeño duelo por la naturaleza humana, pasamos a hacerle las mismas preguntas que le habíamos formulado a su marido. No se apartó ni un ápice de lo que había dicho él, aunque el estilo resultaba muy distinto. Suspiraba de vez en cuando, casi volvió a llorar cuando le contamos sobre los amoríos de las dos víctimas y exclamó: «¡Y ahora muertos los dos!», pero en definitiva: no sabía nada de la vida de Martine, mucho menos de su ligamen sentimental con Pierre, y jamás oyó coches o individuos que visitaran en la noche a Laurent. Punto final. Nos despedimos. Ella nos dio la mano, flácida y helada.

Yendo hacia el coche, el subinspector comentó:

—Esta chica está fatal, cualquier día entra en una depresión. No me extraña que nunca se entere de nada.

—Elisenda es un poco mística, Fermín, y los místicos nunca se enteran de nada concreto, piensan en abstracto, supongo que es su manera involuntaria de librarse de meter los pies en el barro.

—¡Coño, ahora la mística es usted! ¿Qué quiere decir con eso?

—Si en vez de decirle «meter los pies en el barro» le dijera «embadurnarse de mierda», ¿lo entendería mejor?

—Pues debo pertenecer por completo al populacho, porque sí, ahora sí la he entendido a la perfección.

Iba conduciendo yo, y justo habíamos salido de la ciudad camino de la autopista, cuando el subinspector exclamó pegando un salto en el asiento:

—¡Coño, Petra, tenemos que regresar! ¡Me he olvidado el móvil en la caravana de esos dos!

Pegué un frenazo, busqué alguna salida lateral y la enfilé para dar la vuelta. No despegué los labios en toda la maniobra, lo cual hizo que la culpabilidad que sin duda sentía mi compañero alcanzara su cota máxima. Dijo entre dientes:

—Lo siento, créame que lo siento de verdad, pero al irse el marido y venir la mujer me despisté por completo.

—¿Sabe dónde lo ha dejado?

—Sí, en la mesita portátil donde comimos los *pastissets*. Debió de quedarse debajo de una servilleta de papel.

—¡Dejarse el móvil! Demasiada confianza en los testigos —tuve la maldad de decir. Garzón no respondió.

De nuevo en el parque municipal comprobamos que el paisaje de la caravana había cambiado. El servicio al público ya no funcionaba, habían echado la persiana metálica. Era ahora Elisenda y no Javier quien se ocupaba de la limpieza de los enseres. Lo primero que hizo el subinspector fue suspirar de alivio al comprobar que la mesita donde habíamos estado no había sido recogida. Se dirigió hasta ella, levantó una servilleta y, tal y como su memoria le había indicado, allí estaba su teléfono móvil. Elisenda nos miraba embobada. Garzón le enseñó el aparato. «Lo había olvidado», aclaró. Yo me acerqué a Elisenda y le pregunté:

—¿Ya no está su marido?

—Ha tenido que salir.

—Con urgencia, por lo que veo.

—Bueno, se tiene que ingresar la recaudación en el banco y esas cosas, siempre hay recados que hacer.

Asentí y nos largamos, esta vez de modo definitivo o, al menos, eso cabía esperar.

27

El comisario Coronas nos convocó a una reunión. Según él, nuestros informes hacía tiempo que eran una mierda. Se refería al contenido o, mejor dicho, a la falta de él. El caso no avanzaba hacia una resolución y el tiempo se hacía eterno. Le replicamos que no existía presión mediática, por lo que las circunstancias obraban a nuestro favor en cuestión de presiones. Eso lo dijo Garzón, yo me lo hubiera callado ladinamente, ya que me imaginaba la reacción que, en efecto, se produjo.

—¡No, claro!... —bramó el comisario—. Si los periodistas no aprietan, tenemos todo el tiempo del mundo, ¿verdad, subinspector? Llevan un siglo mareando la perdiz y les recuerdo que hay mucho trabajo en esta comisaría y que dedicar tanta atención a un solo asesinato es un lujo que no podemos permitirnos.

Incomprensiblemente, Garzón volvió a cagarla otra vez.

—¡Pero, comisario, los asesinatos ya son dos!

—¡Cojonudo! Para que el plazo de resolución no se haga excesivo, lo más práctico es ir añadiéndole muertos al expediente.

—Lo que quiere decir el compañero... —intenté una interpretación que aliviara tensiones, pero Coronas me interrumpió.

—Sé perfectamente lo que ha querido decir, a ver si ahora entienden lo que voy a decir yo. He puesto a su disposición todos los medios, he pedido ayuda a policías extranjeras, he esperado tranquilamente sin darles ningún ultimátum, les he visto ir y venir como una lanzadera por todo el territorio catalán. Sé, además, que han entrado en colisión con algún miembro de la Guardia Civil y que han creado conflictos a los jueces. ¿Y todo para qué?

—Hemos hecho avances, señor —dije después de aquel chorreo.

—Seguidos de sus correspondientes retrocesos. No, no puede ser, ya está bien. Si en un plazo razonable no encuentran a los culpables, tendré que tomar decisiones drásticas.

—¿Le pedirá al juez que cierre el caso, señor? —se apuntó por fin un tanto el subinspector. Coronas quedó descolocado un momento. Yo ataqué por mi parte.

—Si lo que está pensando es relevarnos, me permito humildemente apuntar que los nuevos responsables también seguirán trabajando en lo mismo, con la circunstancia agravante de que habrá que hacerles informes exhaustivos de cualquier cosa.

Me miró con una energía más ficticia que real.

—En primer lugar, inspectora, usted no ha hecho nada humildemente desde el mismo día en que la parieron. Y en cuanto a cuáles sean mis decisiones, no tengo por qué avanzarles nada, cuando las tome ya se enterarán. Pueden retirarse.

Nos retiramos cada uno con una sensación diferente. Garzón parecía Napoleón abandonando Waterloo. Yo no estaba tan abatida.

—¿Qué hacemos ahora, inspectora?

—Vamos a cruzar a La Jarra de Oro y tomaremos una cerveza.

—¿Le parece adecuado?, ¿y si el jefe nos ve cruzar la calle por la ventana de su despacho?

—No creo que se asome, estará pensando en sus decisiones secretas.

Sentados uno junto al otro en la barra, dimos el primer sorbo a la cerveza helada. Garzón peleó un poco dando soplidos a la espuma pegada a su bigote y por fin me miró de reojo.

—Muy tranquila la veo.

—No puedo morderme las uñas y beber al mismo tiempo.

—Puede tomárselo a broma, pero Coronas estaba cabreado de verdad.

—Tocaba una bronca para que veamos que sigue el asunto con interés, pero va de farol.

—Eso mismo debían decirle a Judas y mire usted lo que pasó.

Solté una carcajada comedida sólo para que viera cómo apreciaba su humor sacrílego, pero mi mente navegaba por otros mares. Busqué un número en el contacto de mi móvil y lo tecleé. Garzón no se atrevió a preguntarme qué hacía. Mi llamada no obtuvo respuesta.

—¿Volvemos al trabajo, Fermín?

—¿Y por dónde empezamos?

—Por el final. Como usted sabe bien, el método inductivo funciona así.

—¿Ese no era el deductivo?

—Olvidemos las teorías y vamos a preparar los informes, que cuanto más abstrusos sean, mucho mejor.

Volamos cada uno a nuestro espacio laboral y, antes de empezar a hacer especialmente farragosa la información que debía redactar con el objetivo de que fuera más extensa, llamé a mi compañero.

—Oiga, Fermín, remóntese al pasado de este caso y haga un resumen por apartados: detenciones, interrogatorios, colaboraciones con otros cuerpos..., póngale un número a cada breve descripción, lo incluiré todo en el informe. Esas cosas siempre impresionan, a ver si el comisario se da cuenta de que no hemos estado tocándonos... En fin, cada cual sus atributos más íntimos.

—Entendido, inspectora. Me pongo a ello. ¿Y usted?

—Yo muy bien, gracias. Cuando acabe, márchese. Ya nos veremos mañana.

Empecé con mi labor dudosamente literaria. Cada hora la interrumpía para llamar al teléfono de Javier, alias el Vegetariano. La respuesta era siempre la misma, una voz femenina tipo estándar que repetía: «El teléfono al que llama está apagado o fuera de cobertura».

Con tanta autointerrupción unida a lo difícil que me resultaba dar datos por escrito de por qué considerábamos importante la revelación de que Laurent mantenía un vínculo sentimental con Marchand, se me hizo muy tarde. Acabé sobre las diez de la noche. Ya no había nadie en comisaría, exceptuando el retén mínimo habitual. Garzón había desaparecido silenciosamente, tal y como le pedí. Era inútil volver a llamar a Javier, pero decidí contactar con su mujer antes de regresar a casa. Tardó un poco en contestar.

—¿Elisenda? Soy Petra Delicado.

Su voz sonó despistada y etérea.

—¡Ah, sí, inspectora, dígame!

—Llevo toda la tarde intentando hablar con su marido, pero su teléfono está inactivo. ¿Está ahí con usted, puede pasármelo?

—No, en este momento no está.

—Supongo que a esta hora tienen ustedes un montón de trabajo. ¿Está sola para hacerlo?

—Sí, estoy yo sola. Ya tenía los platos preparados desde esta tarde. Ahora los serviré y ya está. Puedo apañarme perfectamente.

—¿A qué hora llegará Javier?

—Ha tenido que salir de viaje.

—¿De viaje?

—Bueno, sí. Ha ido a comprar unas conservas vegetales que reponemos de vez en cuando. Son unos productos artesanos que elabora un campesino en la provincia de Teruel. La finca está muy aislada, por eso no tiene cobertura en el teléfono.

—¿Y a estas horas aún está allí?

—Suele quedarse a dormir en el camino.

—De acuerdo. Dígale que me llame mañana, por favor.

—Buenas noches, inspectora.

Recogí mis cosas en estado de mosqueo. ¿Era raro que Javier acudiera a proveerse de conservas artesanas? No. ¿Parecía fuera de lugar que se quedara a dormir en algún hotel del camino existiendo una distancia considerable entre el punto de arranque y el de destino? No, parecía bastante normal. Y, sin embargo, la ausencia de Javier justo después de haber visitado al matrimonio me llenaba de una sospecha que no podía determinar con claridad.

En mi casa había silencio total. No nos tocaba, al parecer, visita de los hijos de Marcos. En la cocina encontré una nota escrita por él: «Llegaré tarde. No me esperes para cenar». Era la frase que habíamos intercambiado más veces en los últimos tiempos, tanto él como yo. En fin, nada nuevo bajo el sol, tampoco iba a ponerme a llorar. Tenía un hambre canina y ni siquiera me había dado cuenta. Miré en el horno y descubrí un arroz cantonés listo para calentar. Nuestra asistenta era una mina. Cené procurando no pensar en nada, y para ayudarte a tener la mente en blanco, nada como la televisión, de modo que la encendí. De basura en basura, estuve cambiando de canal. Por fin, en uno estatal, hallé algo que no me provocaría un corte de digestión: un programa sobre diseño de jardines. El jardín tipo inglés, frondoso y desordenado. El francés, milimetrado y tendente a la geometría. La hierba verde intenso que crece durante el verano en los techos de las casas noruegas..., imágenes relajantes, paz y aburrimiento a partes iguales. Con los últimos bocados de arroz me adormecí. Desistí de tomar postre y, dejando la mesa como una pocilga, llegué hasta el dormitorio. Tuve el tiempo justo de ponerme el pijama y enfilar la cama; un instante después, había perdido por completo la consciencia.

Garzón se presentó al día siguiente en comisaría como un niño que acude a una excursión escolar. El pobre no sabía la excursión que le tenía preparada.

—Deberíamos regresar a Tortosa.

—¿Cómo? —exclamó perdiendo la sonrisa. Le relaté mis llamadas del día anterior. Pensó un momento y, lleno de buen criterio, apuntó—: ¿Está segura de que la feria sigue activa? A ver si nos presentamos allí y no queda ni cristo. Será mejor que llame antes a Elisenda.

—No, quiero ver la situación tal y como esté, contando con el factor sorpresa de nuestra llegada.

—En ese caso llamaré al ayuntamiento para preguntar si ha terminado el evento.

Estaba decidido a agotar todas las posibilidades antes de ponerse en camino. Llamó delante de mí, y sólo por la cara que se le puso adiviné que la feria seguía en su sitio.

—No levantan el campo hasta dentro de dos días.

Intenté mejorarle el ánimo en vez de pegarle cuatro voces, que era lo que una buena jefa hubiera tenido que hacer.

—El otro día nuestra comida fue muy rápida. Como hoy saldremos más pronto, si quiere podemos reservar en un buen restaurante donde hagan algo de su gusto —dije.

Una lucecilla tenue iluminó su mirada. Sacó el

teléfono del bolsillo, buscó un restaurante y no tardó casi nada en encontrarlo.

—Cuando vayamos en camino, llamaré. Siempre será un premio de consolación.

No se olvidó. Yo iba conduciendo mientras él hizo la reserva. Se mostró de nuevo lo suficientemente conforme como para pensar en el trabajo.

—¿Usted cree de verdad que estos dos andan metidos en el meollo, inspectora? Sinceramente, no dan el perfil de asesinos ni de coña.

—No adelante acontecimientos, Fermín. Yo no he dicho que hayan cometido ningún asesinato. Es posible que Javier se largara por las razones que ella me dio ayer, pero todo me parece extraño, y en un caso donde las pruebas hay que buscarlas debajo de las piedras, no podemos descuidar ni el más pequeño guijarro.

—A mí lo que continúa sin parecerme claro es que nunca se enteraran de nada ni vieran nada. Vale que estuvieran muy cansados después del currelo, pero no ver nunca nada...

—En su descargo podría decirse que, considerando a Laurent su amigo, no quisieran dar detalles banales para no dañar su reputación.

—Diga cosas en contra de esos dos, no en su descargo. Ya me parece lo bastante inútil este viaje como para que vaya dándoles salidas.

Hubiera debido enfadarme con él por ese comentario malicioso, pero preferí callar. Los enfados te obligan siempre a hablar demasiado.

Los caracoles no son, ni con mucho, mi plato favorito, tampoco eran la especialidad de la región.

Sin embargo, figuraban en la carta del restaurante y Garzón los pidió. Sólo viendo cómo el subinspector los olía, los sacaba de su concha, los saboreaba, los sorbía y ponía los ojos en blanco, pensé que había valido la pena ordenarlos. Era tal su devoción por aquellos animalillos cocidos sobre una superficie metálica que estuve convencida de que el viaje había dejado de parecerle una inutilidad.

Como aún quedaba tiempo libre, tomamos crema catalana y un excelente café.

—Son las dos treinta. A esta hora encontramos la caravana abierta seguro. ¿Vamos allá, subinspector?

—De buen grado me echaría una siesta, pero comprendo que es mucho pedir.

Tal y como nos habían indicado en el ayuntamiento, la feria gastronómica estaba en pleno ejercicio. Sólo había desaparecido una cosa de ella: la caravana vegetariana de Javier y Elisenda. Simplemente, ya no estaba. El espacio que había ocupado se encontraba completamente vacío. Nos acercamos sin decirnos ni una palabra, con los ojos muy abiertos, como si de pronto la camioneta fuera a materializarse ante nuestros ojos. Llegamos a la parcela desocupada y, en una mutua reacción estúpida, miramos a derecha e izquierda como niños jugando al escondite.

—¿Y esto? —pregunté, abundando en la estupidez.

—Se han largado. Usted llevaba razón, esos dos no son trigo limpio.

Inmediatamente, nos repartimos las furgonetas presentes y empezamos a preguntar. Todo el mundo reconoció haberse sentido sorprendido al ver que faltaban sus vecinos de negocio. Según me contaron, abandonar su puesto antes de que acabe el evento era algo que nadie solía hacer. El alquiler de la parcela que ocupaba cada cual costaba bastante dinero. Por añadidura estaba la cuestión contractual. El ayuntamiento o quienquiera que fuera la entidad organizadora no veía con buenos ojos una deserción y se corría el riesgo de que, en ocasiones posteriores, se negaran a dejar trabajar de nuevo al desertor. Garzón regresó de su encuesta con una información parecida a la que había recopilado yo. Ambas indagaciones coincidían en otro punto importante: nadie había visto a «los vegetarianos» recoger los bártulos y marcharse.

De común acuerdo con mi compañero, habíamos dejado aparte a una testigo para poder acudir juntos a visitarla: Pepa la cotilla, que también había desplegado sus manjares en aquella demostración gastronómica. Nos esperaba, creo que incluso se encontraba un poco alarmada al ver que no formaba parte de los breves interrogatorios individuales que veía desplegarse a su alrededor. De hecho, lo dijo en cuanto vio que llegábamos a su quesería ambulante.

—¡Vaya, pensaba que se olvidaban de mí!

—Al contrario, la hemos dejado para el final.

Me miró con desconfianza.

—¿Ah, sí? ¿Y por qué?

—Porque sabemos que tiene usted un sueño ligero y suele despertarse cuando los demás están como troncos.

Mi excusa pareció contentarla.

—Pues en eso lleva usted mucha razón. Esta madrugada me desperté al oír un motor que se ponía en marcha y me asomé a la ventana de mi vehículo para tener la seguridad de que no era algún intruso. Ya ven que estoy un poco lejos, pero vi claramente cómo la caravana de Javier y Elisenda se largaba muy despacio, casi sin cambiar de marcha para no alborotar. ¡Y llevaban las luces apagadas! No las encendieron hasta no salir del recinto de la feria.

—¿Qué hora era?

—Las cuatro y diez. Lo miré expresamente. Estaba oscuro como boca de lobo.

—¿Iban los dos en la furgoneta?

Mi pregunta la sorprendió. Se quedó callada, se encogió de hombros.

—A ellos no los vi, sólo la furgoneta que salía.

—Gracias, Pepa. Levantan el campamento muy pronto, ¿no?

—Sí. Yo cogeré un par de días libres, para descansar.

—¿Y adónde irá después?

—A Barcelona otra vez. Hay una feria que...

La interrumpí suavemente.

—Si queremos contactar con usted, le haremos una llamada, ¿de acuerdo?

—De acuerdo. Ya saben que lo mío es cooperar con quien me necesita.

De regreso al coche, Garzón renegaba como un gañán.

—Cooperar, ¿no te jode? ¡Maldita chismosa!

—Para una pista que nos dan y una tipa que cumple con su deber ciudadano...

—¿Una pista? ¡Está claro que se han largado! ¿No ha visto su espacio vacío?

—Pero se han largado de noche, subrepticiamente, sin usar ni los faros de la furgoneta. Eso es una pista importante. Hay que pasar aviso de búsqueda inmediatamente.

—Será fácil, una camioneta es más fácil de encontrar que un coche.

—Fantástica deducción, Fermín. A no ser que la metan en un garaje o la hundan en el fondo del mar.

—¿Es que tiene alguna teoría?

—Ninguna. Ni Einstein se las vio tan crudo con la suya.

—Tiene todo el camino de vuelta para pensar.

—Muy bien, para poder pensar más claramente, conducirá usted.

28

Durante toda mi vida profesional me había tocado investigar más de un caso difícil. Sin embargo, no recordaba ninguno en el que el pálpito de estar cerca de una resolución estuviera tan alejado de una comprensión lógica. ¿Javier y Elisenda eran los asesinos de las dos víctimas? ¿Por qué? No se me ocurría ninguna razón. La elaboración de hipótesis estaba atascada. Había algo que unía a todos los implicados, pero no se me ocurría qué podía ser. Algo, o quizá varias cosas, se nos habían escapado en aquel proceso demencial en el que habíamos andado de un lado a otro, entresacando mínimos indicios que sólo servían para indicar un camino sinuoso y oscuro que no llegaba a una meta final. Ninguno de los teléfonos del «matrimonio vegetariano» daba señales de vida. Con aquel capítulo de la historia no habíamos contado.

El operativo de búsqueda de la furgoneta se puso en marcha a todo gas. Por fin, Coronas se convenció de que íbamos tras algo importante. Al menos teníamos dos prófugos a quienes perseguir y eso siempre confiere mucha moral. Se alertó a todas las patrullas de la Guardia Urbana de la ciudad. Se contactó con las dotaciones de carretera de la policía autonómica. Nuestros hombres visitaron todos los parkings públicos, alertando a los propietarios por si aparecía la furgoneta en algún momento. A pesar de la intensidad de la búsqueda y de la colaboración de tantos cuerpos policiales, pasaron veinticuatro horas y la camioneta no había sido localizada. Cabían dos posibilidades: o el vehículo había sido ocultado en algún almacén o aparcamiento privado, o había salido de Cataluña y corría por España en dirección desconocida. Había sido el comisario quien ordenó que no se pasara orden de captura a Tráfico en todo el país hasta que no hubiera transcurrido un día completo. «Finalmente, no sabemos si estamos tras la pista de un asesino. Se trata sólo de una conjetura», dijo. Lo hubiera agredido con sumo placer, pero en puridad llevaba razón. Dio la orden de búsqueda, pero lo hizo de mala gana. Temía quedar en ridículo frente a sus superiores. Quizá seguía alentando la idea de que los prófugos no eran más que dos *neohippies* a los que habíamos acosado en exceso y reaccionaban con miedo. Pero yo no dudaba de que en aquellos jóvenes estaba el quid de la cuestión, de todas las cuestiones en realidad.

Garzón se mantenía al margen de cualquier polémica, no acababa de definir su postura. Mientras yo era incapaz de controlar mi nerviosismo, él se paseaba de un lado a otro por comisaría pidiendo noticias, haciendo comentarios, pero siempre empleando el estilo parsimonioso de absoluta tranquilidad del que suele gozar.

Al tercer día de funcionamiento infructuoso del operativo general, decidí quedarme por las noches en comisaría, durmiendo de cualquier manera sobre un viejo sofá. No ganaba gran cosa con ello, pero al menos tenía la impresión subjetiva de estar haciendo algo. Cuando se lo comuniqué a Marcos por teléfono, poniendo énfasis en los momentos especialmente tensos que vivíamos, no se inmutó demasiado.

—De acuerdo, está bien.

—Pero lo comprendes, ¿verdad?

—Sí, sí, no hay problema. Entiendo la situación.

Hubiera deseado una reacción más efusiva por su parte, y hablo de efusiones negativas, de protestas por no poder vernos. Tampoco hubiera estado mal un poco de curiosidad, por más vetadas que le tuviera las preguntas sobre cualquier investigación. No, lo que dijo fueron frases neutras pronunciadas sin la más leve vehemencia. Lo suyo fue, simplemente, enunciativo y racional. ¿Tanto mejor? Quizá no.

Al final de ese tercer día, cuando yacía en aquel mueble obsoleto que nadie sabía de dónde había salido, pero que plantificaron un buen día en mi despacho, no fue el teléfono lo que me sacó de mi sueño reparador, sino un policía de guardia que entró por la puerta. Como no esperaba semejante intromisión, pegué un salto que casi me tiró al suelo. El policía no había hecho mucho por llevarme a un tránsito suave hacia la vigilia. Pegó un berrido infrahumano:

—¡Inspectora Delicado! Los de la patrulla del barrio de Sants quieren hablar con usted. ¿Le paso la llamada?

—Pásela.

—Les he dicho que estaba durmiendo, pero contestan que es importante.

—¿Y por qué no han llamado a mi móvil?

—¡Ah, eso sí que no lo sé!

No me dio tiempo ni de acercarme al lavabo para echarme un poco de agua por la cara, aunque si lo que pretendía era despejarme un poco, la noticia que el responsable de la patrulla me comunicó lo consiguió por sí sola.

—Inspectora. Estamos en Sants, en la confluencia de la calle Cáceres con la calle Sant Medir. Los servicios municipales de limpieza han encontrado un cadáver cosido a puñaladas. Su identidad coincide con la de uno de los sospechosos que estamos buscando, los de la furgoneta de comida. Se llama Javier Martínez.

—¿Están seguros de ese dato?

—Llevaba encima el carnet de identidad.

—Supongo que ya han avisado al forense y al juez. Llamen inmediatamente al subinspector Garzón.

—No tenemos su móvil, tampoco el de usted. Por eso contactamos con su centralita. Un fallo enorme viniendo la orden de su comisaría, ya lo sé.

Esta vez sí pasé por los lavabos, aunque ya me encontraba alerta, necesitaba que el agua se llevara consigo el montón de ideas absurdas y preguntas extrañas que me impedían pensar con normalidad. Conduciendo hacia el lugar de los hechos, había logrado que sólo permanecieran las preguntas en mi mente. ¿El cadáver llevaba el carnet de identidad? ¿Cómo era posible que lo hubieran asaltado en un lugar tan poco discreto aunque fueran las tres de la mañana? ¿Y la furgoneta y Elisenda dónde estaban?

Como sorprendentemente había sucedido en los últimos días, llegué yo antes que Garzón al escenario del crimen. Tampoco estaban aún presentes el forense ni el juez. El jefe de la patrulla se llamaba Valdés y era listo como un águila. Deseé que nadie se presentara antes de que él concluyera con sus aclaraciones, precisas y bien explicadas.

—Verá, inspectora, este hombre estaba en un almacén pequeño que hay en ese entresuelo, justo ahí delante. La puerta está abierta. Hemos dado una ojeada sólo para comprobar que no había nadie en el interior, pero les he dicho a los hombres que no entren para no alterar pruebas. Alguien ha arrastrado el cuerpo hasta aquí, en medio de la calle. Mire, el rastro de sangre desde el almacén es enorme.

El cadáver correspondía efectivamente a Javier. Estaba destrozado. Las puñaladas le habían desfigurado la cara y la sangre seca manchaba su cuerpo por todos lados. Llevaba una camisa blanca hecha jirones. Pasé un buen rato mirándolo con la fascinación que provoca la muerte violenta, muy violenta en este caso.

—¿Interrogamos ya a los vecinos, inspectora, o es demasiado pronto?

—¿Han buscado por los alrededores?

—Sí, calles desiertas. Son las tres de la madrugada.

—Como ninguno de los vecinos ha salido a husmear, supongo que no habrán visto u oído nada.

—O si lo han oído, preferirán estar callados.

—Exactamente, Valdés. Esperaremos un poco

para los interrogatorios domiciliarios. Total, enseguida llegará todo el mundo: la Científica, el forense, el juez...

—Habrá que cortar la calle al tráfico. Como son dos arterias importantes se liará un buen follón.

—Le pediré al juez que ordene el levantamiento lo antes posible.

En ese momento se presentó el subinspector. Le habían informado someramente del crimen, pero fue verme y precipitarse sobre mí para freírme a preguntas. Lo transferí a Valdés.

—Él le cuenta, Fermín. Yo estoy cansada.

Para subrayar mi estado, me senté en el bordillo de la acera. Se me agolpaban los pensamientos, pero ni uno de ellos tenía la menor validez. Me faltaba información. Como empezaban a circular algunos coches, Valdés avisó a la Guardia Urbana, que tardó poco en llegar. Después ya se produjo el aluvión: la Científica, el forense, el juez y, por último, y sorpresivamente, el comisario Coronas. Yo permanecía sentada en el suelo, esperando que cada cual hiciera su papel. Coronas se me acercó.

—¿Pidiendo limosna, Petra?

—Exacto, comisario, a ver si me cae un poco de información.

Dio media vuelta y me dejó sola de nuevo. Observé cómo se movía entre la barahúnda que se había formado. Hablaba con unos y con otros, preguntaba, señalaba con el dedo. Tenía la actitud que suele adoptar un jefe en las ocasiones especiales: parecía saberlo todo cuando en realidad iba en busca de noticias. Tras una somera inspección del forense, el comisario instó al juez a iniciar un levantamiento rápido. Este estuvo de acuerdo enseguida. No era deseable organizar un desorden público en plena calle cuando las pistas principales debían encontrarse en el interior del pequeño almacén. Metieron el cadáver en su funda y lo cargaron en una ambulancia para trasladarlo hasta su penúltima morada: el Anatómico Forense.

—Infórmeme de todo en tiempo real —me dijo el comisario como despedida.

El juez y él tomaron el mismo coche para marcharse. Una vez desaparecidos los personajes más prescindibles para la investigación pura y dura, abandoné mi postura sedente y entré en el almacén donde trabajaba la Científica. Antes, abordé al forense, que no era otro que el doctor Rosselló, que ya recogía sus cosas.

—Apuñalamiento múltiple. No sé si puede llamarse ensañamiento patológico o simple ataque de furia. No sé si eso será discernible cuando haga la autopsia. He pedido encargarme yo mismo y les aseguro que esta vez no tardará en estar lista. La he reclamado personalmente para darle prioridad absoluta.

—¿Es que hay algo especial en esta muerte?

—Mi curiosidad, Petra. He seguido un poco los entresijos de este caso y le aseguro que no veo nada lógico en él.

—En eso estamos igual.

—No es una buena noticia oírla decir eso.

—No, no lo es. Veamos si su ciencia esclarece algo.

—Confiar excesivamente en la ciencia es un error. Si el hombre estuviera compuesto sólo de materia, no le diría que no. Sin embargo, las emociones, la maldita psicología y todo lo que contiene el cerebro, aparte de las neuronas, no hace más que incordiar.

Me sonrió con desánimo y le devolví la sonrisa intentando que fuera menos vacilante que la suya, aunque no lo conseguí.

—La llamaré en cuanto tenga resultados —dijo alejándose.

El operativo de la calle había desaparecido por completo. Se habían tomado todo tipo de muestras del lugar exacto donde el cuerpo había yacido y un servicio de limpieza echaba agua a presión sobre la acera, llevándose por delante la sangre diluida. Sólo permanecíamos *in situ* los compañeros de la Científica, todos dentro del almacén, Valdés con su patrulla, a la que se habían añadido unos cuantos hombres más, y por supuesto Garzón, que buscaba inútilmente explicaciones en mi mirada. En vez de comentarios o certezas, sólo recibió órdenes de mí.

—Ocúpese de todo lo externo con Valdés y sus hombres: interrogatorios de los vecinos del inmueble, los operarios que lo encontraron, algún posible vecino de edificios cercanos..., ya sabe. Yo voy a hablar con los colegas de blanco, si es que me dejan entrar en el almacén. Si hay algún testimonio interesante por ahí fuera, lo selecciona y me lo trae. Le esperaré en la calle.

Desde la puerta del almacén, que era poco más

que una habitación grande, llamé al jefe de la Científica.

—¿Puedo pasar? Tendría que hablar un momento contigo, también echar una pequeña ojeada.

—Entra, inspectora, y colócate aquí. A ser posible no te muevas y por supuesto...

—No tocaré nada, eso ya lo sé.

La actividad que ejercía el equipo era la que ya había contemplado otras veces: fotografías, toma de muestras... Dejé vagar la mirada por la estancia, un lugar destartalado con las paredes apenas encaladas. Había un amplio tablero de madera colocado sobre dos caballetes, en la superficie adiviné la presencia de varios objetos, pero a la distancia que me encontraba no podía distinguir qué eran. En un rincón se acumulaban unas diez o doce cajas de cartón, todas ellas abiertas. En el suelo, la sangre abundaba, cubriendo casi todas las losetas. El jefe se me acercó con su atuendo espectral.

—¿Ya has hecho una mínima inspección ocular? Te explico un poco. A la víctima la apuñalaron ahí, en ese círculo que hemos marcado. Parece que intentó huir y volvieron a apuñalarla casi en la puerta, esta vez por la espalda; el forense ha estado de acuerdo con nuestro dictamen. Los análisis dirán si toda la sangre es de la víctima o hay también del agresor. Hemos recogido algún pelo. El asesino lo acribilló a puñaladas.

—¿Qué son los objetos de encima de la mesa?

—Instrumentos de química. Y en aquellas cajas hay bolsas de cocaína, a falta de análisis, claro está. Yo juraría que es todo el equipo que se necesita para adulterar droga, pero sería mejor que lo comprobara un especialista.

Una luz fuerte y clara me estalló en el cerebro, un auténtico fogonazo que iluminó recovecos oscuros. Ahora los veía con nitidez. Javier era químico de formación. El cometido de Laurent era pasar la droga que le llegaba desde Marruecos y debía reexpedirla hasta la organización de Marchand en Francia. Pero un buen día tuvo una idea genial: con la ayuda de Javier, que sabía mucho de mezclas, podía reenviar alguna partida convenientemente adulterada. Hasta que la francesa se enteró. El jefe de la Científica interrumpió mis deducciones.

—Se diría, inspectora, que la víctima, o quienquiera que fuera, ha dormido aquí. Debajo de la ventana hay unas mantas. ¿Cuántas noches? Imposible saberlo.

—¿Qué ocurrió después del crimen?

—Bueno, lo que todos hemos visto. El asesino arrastró el cadáver hasta la calle y allí lo dejó tirado, sin quitarle el carnet de identidad, era lo único que llevaba encima.

—Tenía la intención de que fuera encontrado sin dificultad.

—Me pregunto por qué, inspectora.

—Es una pregunta tan oportuna que hasta me la hago yo también. ¿Me mandarás los resultados de todo lo que encontréis?

Mi última pregunta era de contestación obvia y previsible, pero no se me ocurrió otra manera de acabar la conversación. Salí a la calle y busqué un bar con la mirada. Naturalmente, había uno muy cercano y justo acababa de abrir. El café y las tostadas me parecieron lo mejor que había tomado jamás. Y bien, ¿estábamos cerca de un final definitivo o más alejados que nunca? Javier era cómplice de Laurent. Ambos habían montado un negocio paralelo, y además de adulterar la droga, muy probablemente despistaban algunas cantidades para redondear ganancias. En su arriesgado viaje a España, Martine buscaba esa droga o dinero o quizá el laboratorio clandestino que se ocupaba del trabajo sucio después de la muerte de Laurent. En cualquier caso, ¿quién seguía estando vivo en todo aquel asunto?, ¿quién seguía teniendo motivos para matar después de que ella hubiera sido asesinada? Hice una llamada de móvil para preguntar si habían encontrado la furgoneta vegetariana. Contestación negativa. Llamé de nuevo a comisaría, esta vez para averiguar si el teléfono de Elisenda emitía alguna señal. No, silencio absoluto. ¿Sabía ella que habían asesinado a su marido? ¿Dónde estaba?, ¿quizá había conseguido huir del asesino de Javier que iba también a por ella? Pedí un segundo café y me sumí no en mis pensamientos, sino en un estado de total estupefacción. Tras más de una hora, me llamó el subinspector.

—Petra, las diligencias que ordenó están completadas.

—¿Hay testimonios?

—Le he seleccionado dos. El presidente de la comunidad de vecinos y el hombre de la limpieza municipal que encontró el cuerpo. ¿Dónde va a interrogarlos?

—Llévelos a comisaría, será lo más práctico. Yo también voy para allá.

El presidente era un hombre muy mayor, pero perfectamente lúcido. Lo que contó nos resultó de bastante interés. Dijo que Javier tenía alquilado el pequeño almacén, que iba de vez en cuando por allí, pero que nunca se supo para qué lo utilizaba.

—¿Nadie le preguntó? —inquirí.

—No había ninguna razón para meternos en su vida. El chico nunca molestó a nadie, pagaba los gastos de escalera puntualmente y era muy educado, por lo que me pareció las pocas veces que coincidí con él.

—¿Vio en alguna ocasión una u otra actividad en el almacén?

—No entiendo lo que quiere decir.

—¿Le llegaban paquetes, tenía visitas?

—Nunca vi nada, pero es que mi piso está en el ático, vivo solo desde que murió mi mujer. Pueden preguntar a los vecinos que están más cerca de la entrada al edificio, a lo mejor ellos sí pueden contestarle.

Miré a Garzón, que estaba de pie junto al testigo. Negó con la cabeza.

—Ya lo hemos hecho, pero nadie se fijó.

—No me extraña, como ahora la gente recibe tantos paquetes por Amazon, internet y todas esas cosas, no sé quién se iba a fijar —dijo el testigo.

—Le agradecemos mucho su ayuda. Tendrá que volver otro día a firmar su declaración.

—Vendré, no se preocupe, tengo mucho tiempo libre. ¿Puedo hacerle una pregunta, inspectora?

—Adelante, dígame.

—¿Quién pudo matar a un chico tan joven y tan majo?

—No lo sabemos aún, pero cuesta creerlo, ¿verdad?

—El mundo va cada vez peor.

—Nunca ha ido demasiado bien, si leemos los libros de historia.

Se encogió de hombros con resignación. Lo vi alejarse, sentí pena por él. Cuando falleciera podría decirse con certeza que el mundo había empeorado un poco más.

El siguiente testigo estaba más nervioso que un flan y su declaración resultó inútil. Sólo se dedicó a quejarse y exclamar letanías sobre su mala suerte.

—¡Tenía que tocarme a mí, joder! Me acerco a los contenedores y veo a un hombre tirado en el suelo todo lo largo que era. Al principio pensé que sería un borracho y fui para donde estaba, pero enseguida ya me di cuenta de que tenía sangre por todas partes y me entró un yuyu de cojones. Casi tuve un ataque de nervios. ¡Hay que joderse, no había visto nunca un muerto así tan deshecho! No es plato de gusto, ¿eh?

—¿Hubo algún detalle que le llamara la atención, aparte del muerto en sí mismo?

—¿Le parece poco detalle?

—¿Vio a alguna persona por los alrededores o quizá alejándose del lugar?

—Yo no miraba para ninguna parte, los ojos se me iban para la sangre. Bajó el compañero del camión y él sí miró a un lado y a otro. «Aquí no hay ni Dios», dijo, eso fue lo que dijo, me acuerdo perfectamente.

Miré de nuevo a Garzón y él volvió a asentir con la cabeza.

—Eso es todo por el momento, puede marcharse. Ya le avisarán para que venga a firmar su declaración.

—¿A firmar?, ¿y qué coño voy a firmar si no vi nada?

—Encontró el cadáver, ¿no? Pues eso tiene que contar y firmar, es facilito y obligatorio, le recuerdo.

—No, si yo hago lo que me toque hacer.

—Pues lo que tiene que hacer ahora es marcharse. Muchas gracias.

Mi paciencia había llegado al límite. Cuando salió el testigo me encaré con Garzón.

—¿Se puede saber por qué carajo me ha traído a este tío?

—Encontró el cuerpo, inspectora.

—Sí, llenito de sangre y le dio un yuyu que no veas, pero ¿qué hay de interesante en el testimonio de ese maldito patán?

—Con todos los respetos, Petra, de vez en cuando le sale a usted una vena clasista que no me la puedo creer.

—¿Clasista?, ¿qué tiene que ver el clasismo en esto?

—Como es un funcionario de la limpieza sin cultura, cualquier cosa que diga la pone a usted de los nervios.

—¿Ah, sí? El señor que ha declarado antes es un obrero jubilado. No puede decirse que pertenezca a la élite intelectual, pero no dice chorradas, ¿comprende? A mí lo que me pone de los nervios es la gente tonta, sin más, y la que no tiene cultura, también. ¿Por el hecho de que trabajes como funcionario de limpieza no puedes leer algún puto libro de vez en cuando, ver un programa cultural en la tele, comprar algún maldito periódico? No, fútbol, bar y noticias de cotilleo, eso es lo que hay. ¡Vaya país de mierda el nuestro, Garzón!

—Está diciendo cosas que no le corresponden, Petra. Creo que se encuentra muy alterada.

Me apreté los ojos con los dedos.

—Lleva razón, Fermín, alterada de verdad. Acumulamos muertos en un caso infernal del que todavía no soy capaz de entender gran cosa. Todo pasa delante de nuestras narices sin sacar nada en limpio. ¿Usted no está alterado? Créame que le admiro de corazón.

—Pero siempre hemos estado en el buen camino, inspectora.

—¿En qué camino?, ¿en el que va directo al abismo?

—El camino que nos ha traído hasta aquí nos llevará hasta el final.

—Sí, cuando sólo quede uno vivo, ese será el asesino.

—Algo así. ¿Sabe lo que le pasa?, que no ha desayunado ni tomado un café. Ahora nos arreamos un bocatilla y lo verá todo más claro.

—¿Meterme otra vez en un tugurio? Casi prefiero caer en el abismo sin mirar.

Me tomó del brazo con toda confianza, impulsándome hacia el bar del que acababa de salir. Ese era mi destino: entrar y salir de los bares a por cerveza o café. He conocido destinos peores, nada que objetar.

29

Aquella noche me fui a la cama tarde. Marcos dormía ya. Estaba tan cansada que tuve el tiempo justo de derrumbarme sin abrir siquiera mi parte del embozo. A las tres de la madrugada vibró mi móvil sobre la mesilla de noche. Me levanté de un salto y salí al pasillo para no despertar a mi marido. Bajé al salón. No reconocí el número que aparecía en la pantalla.

—Dígame.

Nadie respondía.

—Dígame.

Ni una palabra del otro lado. Tras mi tercer imperativo oí una voz de mujer, floja, titubeante.

—Inspectora, soy Elisenda. Necesito hablar con usted.

—¿Dónde está?

—Tengo aparcada mi furgoneta en el parking del aeropuerto de El Prat. Ahora le escribiré el sector y el número y se los mando por wasap. ¿Puede venir ahora mismo? Venga sola, por favor.

—¿Está sola usted también?

—Le aseguro que sí.

Mi primer pensamiento fue ponerme la gabardina sobre el pijama y salir corriendo. Luego recapacité y me vestí. Mientras conducía, hacía cábalas sobre lo que me esperaba. ¿Qué iba a contarme Elisenda? ¿Sabía algo del asesinato de Javier? ¿Conocía al asesino y pensaba denunciarlo o, más probablemente, temía por su vida?

El aparcamiento de El Prat presentaba un aspecto fantasmal a aquellas horas. Inconcebible que a ningún policía se le hubiera ocurrido buscar la furgoneta allí. Encontré el lugar indicado en el wasap y, en efecto, allí estaba el *food truck* vegetariano. Aparqué detrás del vehículo. Había luz en el interior. Preparé la pistola porque no podía estar segura de a qué iba a enfrentarme. Antes de llamar a la puerta, esta se abrió. En el quicio estaba Elisenda, pálida, desmelenada, con los ojos un poco idos. Le temblaban las manos.

—Siéntese, inspectora, por favor. Voy a preparar café. Lo que tengo que contarle es muy largo.

La observé mientras manipulaba la cafetera. Sus movimientos eran lentos e inseguros. Era evidente que había tomado tranquilizantes o alguna otra sustancia que le daba un aire zombi. La pistola seguía en mi bolsillo, muy a mano. El pequeño lugar se llenó de un agradable olor a café. Llenó dos tazas y se sentó frente a mí en la minúscula mesa. Empezó a hablar. No me miraba, tenía los ojos semicerrados y la cabeza hundida entre los hombros.

—Inspectora, estoy segura de que ya han encontrado el cuerpo de mi marido, ¿verdad?

—Sí, así es —dije asombrada.

—Lo maté yo.

El corazón empezó a palpitarme con fuerza y pesadez.

—¿Lo mató usted misma con sus propias manos o tuvo a alguien que la ayudó?

—No me haga preguntas, por favor. Yo se lo cuento todo de un tirón, y si al final no ha entendido algo, entonces sí le contestaré a lo que quiera saber.

Se le trababa un poco la lengua, pero se expresaba con bastante claridad. Me encontraba muy despistada sobre qué demonio pensaba contarme. Arrancó sin preámbulos.

—Javier en realidad no estaba nada contento con nuestra vida, con la suya en particular. Yo era feliz con mi caravana y el negocio nos iba bien, pero mi marido tenía más aspiraciones que no podía cumplir. Decía que lo que ganábamos era una mierda y que así no se podía ahorrar ni un euro para poder cambiar de manera de vivir alguna vez. En el fondo se consideraba un pringado, un feriante de tercera, peor que un representante comercial sin éxito. Él había estudiado en la universidad y hacer lo que hacíamos, que a mí me parecía bonito, a él le parecía una humillación. Los hombres son así, me entiende, inspectora, ¿verdad?

—Sí, la entiendo.

—Javier se hizo muy amigo de Pierre Laurent. Coincidíamos al principio por casualidad en las ferias, pero luego los dos se coordinaban para tener las caravanas en el mismo evento y siempre una al lado de la otra. Ustedes ya saben toda la historia de Laurent, ¿verdad? Le mandaban la droga desde Marruecos y él se la pasaba a Martine Marchand, que estaba muy vigilada en Francia. Un día se le ocurrió mejorar el negocio y cortar la droga aquí. Se lo propuso a Javier para que lo ayudara con las adulteraciones porque era químico, y mi marido aceptó, encantado de la vida. En los últimos tiempos se atrevieron a ir a mayores y le robaban a la francesa algunos envíos de droga. Yo siempre pensé que, más que por el dinero que ganaba, aquello era para Javier como una especie de venganza contra la sociedad. «No me dais un buen trabajo como químico, pues vale, me convierto en delincuente y encima ya no soy un desgraciado feriante sin más.» Lo entiende, ¿verdad, inspectora?

—Lo entiendo muy bien.

—Pierre era un donjuán. Le gustaban mucho las mujeres y a ellas les gustaba él. Javier me contó que estaba liado con Martine y a veces ella, arriesgándose a que la detuvieran, venía a verlo para follar con él. Perdone la manera de decirlo, pero no hay otra más clara. Lo malo del atractivo de Pierre fue que...

Se interrumpió, tragó saliva, bebió un sorbo de café. Continuó en voz más baja.

—Lo malo, inspectora, lo verdaderamente malo fue que yo también me lie con él. No voy a intentar justificarme, pero mi marido tenía mal concepto de mí: «Eres una depresiva insoportable», me recriminaba, y es verdad que lo soy. También pensaba de mí que era débil, conformista, poquita cosa como mujer. Me trataba con desprecio, a veces era incluso violento, aunque no siempre, claro está. Pierre era amable, pícaro, me decía que era la chica más dulce del mundo. Nos veíamos de vez en cuando en algún hotel, en el tiempo que yo tenía destinado a hacer las compras. ¡Vaya imbécil que soy!, ¿no? Sabía perfectamente que estaba liado con la francesa, que disparaba sobre cualquier mujer que tuviera a tiro y, sin embargo, ahí estaba yo, oyéndolo decir que era la chica más dulce del mundo y follando con él como si me lo creyera todo. Eso sí que no se entiende, ¿verdad, inspectora?

—No lo sé, quizá sí. Las mujeres somos muy especiales en cuestiones de amor. Prosiga, Elisenda, por favor.

—Como no podía ser de otra manera, la francesa se enteró o sospechó del enjuague que se traía Laurent con la droga. Lo llamó por teléfono diciendo que, aunque la cazaran en la frontera, estaba dispuesta a venir a verlo para «charlar tranquilamente sobre sus negocios». Pierre se acojonó muchísimo y se lo contó a Javier. Nunca le había dicho antes que Martine era una tipa cruel, sanguinaria, dispuesta a cualquier cosa, una profesional temida en el mundo del narcotráfico. ¿Sabe cómo la llamaban?

—La Leoparda.

—Exacto, eso es. Mi marido se acojonó mucho más cuando supo con quién se la había estado jugando y se cabreó con Laurent por no haberle advertido desde el principio. Pierre le juró y perjuró que ella no sabía nada de su participación en las adulteraciones, que Javier no existía para la Leoparda. Le pidió que no se deshiciera de nada, que conservara todo el material en el almacén que habían alquilado en Barcelona y pagaban entre los dos, ya sabe, el sitio donde yo lo maté.

Oírla hablar con tanta calma sobre el asesinato de su propio marido me paralizó un instante, pero Elisenda siguió con su relato, y ahora sí me miraba a la cara mientras hablaba.

—Le aseguró a mi marido que controlaba la situación. Recibiría a su amante francesa, le daría un buen revolcón, lo negaría todo y, como la cantidad no era excesiva, ella olvidaría la presunta traición. Por supuesto, Javier no se creyó nada de eso y, simplemente, pensó que Pierre lo señalaría con el dedo frente a la narco y echaría todas las culpas sobre él. Es terrible decirlo, pero yo estuve de acuerdo en eso, parecía un montaje, una trampa muy clara para mi marido. El día que ella apareció por la feria y compró tantas cosas, Javier estaba pendiente de lo que sucedía entre los dos. No le pareció que hubieran tenido tiempo de hablar de nada, pero estuvo seguro de que habían concertado una cita. Esa misma noche...

Las lágrimas hicieron su aparición por primera vez. Lloraba y permanecía callada. La ayudé a terminar la frase casi de manera instintiva.

—Me imagino lo que pasó, Elisenda. Esa misma noche, Javier entró con un cuchillo en la caravana de Pierre y lo asesinó. Martine acudió horas más tarde y lo encontró muerto.

Lloraba y lloraba sin parar.

—¿Usted estaba al tanto de lo que su marido iba a hacer?

—Sí.

—¿Nunca pensó en disuadirlo, incluso en avisar a la policía?

—No tenía fuerza moral para hacerlo, inspectora.

—No la entiendo.

—Es que hubo otra complicación.

Nuevas lágrimas. Yo estaba en ascuas y aquellas pausas que hacía para llorar empezaban a impacientarme, pero me encontraba frente a una confesión en toda regla y lo suyo era callar, ser firme pero tierna a la vez.

—¿Se acuerda de Eduardo Castillo, inspectora?

—¿Bob, el socio de Laurent?

—Sí. Bob y yo hablábamos muchas veces, nos teníamos cariño. Él me había comentado que estaba un poco harto de los ligues de su socio. No le gustaban los donjuanes, quizá porque nunca tuvo pareja y sentía un poco de celos viendo el éxito y la actitud despreocupada de Pierre. La tarde en que llegó Martine como clienta, Bob enseguida la identificó como una de las queridas de su socio. Supongo que, vaya a saber por qué razón, le afeó su conducta al compañero y discutieron. Bob era un buen hombre, incapaz de causarle daño a nadie, pero ese día hizo algo impensable. Movido por una cólera que nunca solía sentir, me delató.

—Ahora tampoco la entiendo.

—Fue a encontrarse con Javier y le dijo que Pierre y yo éramos amantes.

—¿Y cómo pudo enterarse de eso?

—Se lo había contado yo tiempo atrás. Necesitaba hablarlo con alguien, me sentía culpable. Él era muy buen tipo, me escuchaba, aunque siempre me recomendaba que dejara la relación. No sé qué pudo pasarle por la cabeza para convertirse en un…, no sé cómo expresarlo.

—¿Delator?

—Sí, eso es.

—¿Bob conocía las actividades con la droga de su socio?

—No sabía ningún detalle concreto, tampoco quería saber. Se enteró de más cosas al empezar ustedes la investigación, claro está. Cuando Pierre apareció muerto, él enseguida pensó que Javier lo había matado por celos, por venganza de marido engañado y cargó con la culpa de haber provocado aquel desastre. Si se hubiera mantenido callado… Pierre hubiera seguido vivo. En el fondo, algo de razón llevaba al sentirse culpable. Aquella… ¿cuál es la palabra?

—Delación.

—Sí, delación, fue la gota que colmó el vaso. Si Javier había tenido alguna duda de cargarse a Laurent, ahí se le disipó. Fue a por él con todas las ganas, cargado de razones, ciego de ira.

—¿Y usted?, ¿qué pasó con su marido, cómo reaccionó?

—Me dijo que me daría tal cantidad de hostias que no lo olvidaría jamás, pero no en aquel momento porque vendría la policía y sería difícil de justificar el verme marcada. Pero cumplió su amenaza poco a poco, me abofeteaba con fuerza por cualquier tontería, por cualquier error en el negocio por pequeño que fuera. Me odiaba. Lo demás ya lo sabe usted: llegó Martine, lo encontró muerto, debió volverse loca de resentimiento, se trajo a tipos de su banda, rondó varios días por las ferias donde estábamos..., quería saber quién había matado a su amante y dónde estaban su dinero y su droga. Se cargaron la caravana de Bob... Un desastre, inspectora, un desastre.

—¿Quién mató a Martine, Elisenda?

Volvió a mirar al suelo, suspiró amargamente.

—Javier, inspectora, Javier.

—¿Ella pudo localizarlo?

—No. Antes de hacer desaparecer el móvil de Pierre, mi marido había copiado todos sus contactos. Él la llamó.

—¿Por qué la mató?

—Cada vez estaba más nervioso. Ustedes aparecían por las ferias, preguntaban, indagaban... Se obsesionó. Por las noches imaginaba que Martine vendría en su busca y lo liquidaría sin mediar palabra. Creía que asesinarla era el modo de borrar por completo aquella historia de su vida. No había pruebas contra él, Bob se había suicidado, sólo quedaba un peligro ambulante: la francesa. Si la policía la pescaba, declararía cosas, aflorarían detalles, vendrían deducciones... Si la mataba, ya nadie podría relacionarlo con el caso.

—Una muerte inútil. ¿En esta ocasión usted también conocía sus intenciones?

—Sí, lo sabía, y no me sorprendió, Javier había entrado en la rueda de la muerte. Una vez que has matado a una persona dicen que te vuelves como una especie de monstruo y que ya no te importa volver a matar. Creo que es lo que le pasó a él.

—No sé si es una explicación muy científica,

pero sí es verdad que quien mata al cabo de un tiempo se da cuenta de que le ha resultado más fácil de lo que nunca había pensado.

—Luego llegaron ustedes, estrechando el círculo cada vez más. Después de su última visita ya no pudo resistir los nervios y el miedo. Se refugió en el almacén que nadie tenía localizado. Yo debía encargarme de ocultar la furgoneta durante unos días, quitarme de en medio. Luego sacaríamos billetes de avión para algún país hispanoamericano y huiríamos los dos de aquí.

—No les hubiera resultado nada fácil llevar a cabo ese plan, se lo aseguro.

—A mí ya me daba igual ese plan o cualquier otro. Me he pasado la vida huyendo de algo, inspectora. Me casé con Javier para huir de mi familia, que era terrible conmigo, con todos mis hermanos en realidad. Hui años y años de la idea de abandonar a mi marido. Siempre creía que se produciría algún cambio en él, que finalmente me querría y me respetaría... Después vino todo lo que acabo de contarle. Huir, huir y huir. No, eso se ha acabado para mí. Sólo necesito un poco de paz.

—¿Por qué no nos llamó, por qué no lo denunció, por qué convertirse en una cómplice? Ahora usted también es una asesina. ¿Era necesario apuñalarlo, quitarlo de en medio con tanta saña?

—Javier merecía morir. No lo apuñalé en un ataque de furia, fui al almacén armada y decidida a matarlo. Cuando lo tuve delante no me costó seguir con el plan, ni me asusté cuando empecé a clavarle el cuchillo tantas veces, cuando vi la sangre. Al contrario, sentía una gran serenidad. Ahí sí acababan las huidas y los odios. Él había matado y yo puse punto final a su locura. Se acabó, se cerraba el círculo. Arrastré el cadáver hasta la calle para que ustedes pudieran encontrarlo pronto.

—Tomó la justicia por su mano.

—La justicia nunca ha existido en mi vida. Nadie fue justo conmigo.

—Sabe lo que le espera ahora, ¿verdad? Tiene una idea de los cargos que pesarán sobre usted.

—Me los imagino. Me juzgarán y me llevarán a una cárcel de mujeres, seguramente para un montón de años. Eso es justo lo que quiero, inspectora. Estaré muy tranquila allí. Ya he pensado que me ofreceré como voluntaria para la cocina, que es en el fondo lo mío. Viviré feliz.

—¿Por qué no acudió a la policía inmediatamente después de cometer el crimen? ¿Pensaba callarse y luego recapacitó? ¿Por qué dejar el cadáver de su esposo en medio de una calle?

—Quería que lo encontrara la policía, tirado como una basura, y me escondí porque no quería declarar en una comisaría delante de un tipo que no conocía de nada, quería hablar con usted. Usted es una mujer y seguro que me comprende.

No respondí. Ella insistió.

—Porque usted me comprende, ¿no, inspectora?

—Que llegue a comprenderla no significa que la disculpe o justifique su acción.

—Pero el que comprende ya está disculpando un poco, ¿no le parece?

—Me temo que las cosas no funcionan así. Voy a

detenerla, Elisenda. ¿Quiere que le diga sus derechos?

—No hace falta.

—Hará una declaración formal en comisaría y más tarde ante el juez.

—Sí, inspectora, haré lo que tenga que hacer.

La trasladé a comisaría sin hacer uso de las esposas, no eran necesarias.

Hacerle la síntesis de todo aquello a Garzón me costó bastante tiempo. Entre sus preguntas aclaratorias, sus exclamaciones de incredulidad, las de asombro y las de escándalo, me vi interrumpida en varias ocasiones. Sin embargo, rehacer el relato en mi mente me fue útil para escribir el informe. Luego vinieron los comentarios.

—¿Se da cuenta, Petra? Al «imbécil» de Bob la culpabilidad lo devoraba, pero se sentía atado de pies y manos para hacer cualquier movimiento más concreto. La única pista fiable fue la que nos encaminó a Dámaso. No era tan bobo en realidad, a Dámaso sólo lo había visto en una ocasión y, como nos seguía, lo reconoció en su tienda el día que se cargó el cristal.

—Sin duda Bob era un tipo raro, una mentalidad fuera de lo común.

—Era lo que ahora llaman un perdedor.

—En el fondo, todos lo somos, Fermín, vamos perdiendo cosas hasta que con la muerte lo perdemos todo.

—¡Joder, inspectora, a eso le llamo yo optimismo! Se pierden unas cosas, pero se ganan otras, y al final te mueres, claro. Aún no conozco a nadie que se haya quedado como simiente. Además, le advierto de que debería estar un poco más alegre, ¡el caso está resuelto!

—Pero hemos dejado un reguero de muertos peor que en la batalla de Verdún.

—¿Acaso nos los hemos cargado nosotros? La gente se quita de en medio los unos a los otros, inspectora. Seguimos matándonos lo mismito que en las cavernas, pero nuestro trabajo es averiguar quién mata a quién y por qué razones, nada más. Así que no se ponga tan triste y filosófica porque no corresponde. ¿Qué le parece si nos arreamos un copazo?

—Su solución a los problemas siempre es la misma, pero debo reconocer que un copazo nunca es mala idea.

Tomaría el copazo con mi compañero, lo saborearía y disfrutaría, pero dudaba de que en esta ocasión mi tristeza se disipara totalmente. Continuaba pensando en Elisenda, aquella frágil asesina victimizada, en aquel caso diabólico donde nos habíamos movido como rapaces, en círculos aéreos que iban acercándonos un poco más hasta la presa, la cual se nos brindó, indefensa, en un descampado. ¡Pobre Elisenda, toda la vida huyendo sin conseguir mover los pies del mismo sitio, exactamente como sucede tantas veces en las pesadillas!

Desestimé hacer cualquier declaración directa a los periodistas. De eso se encargaría la portavoz oficial, una bella muchacha que, con su presencia moderna y un tanto angélica, solía contrarrestar la sordidez de los detalles que hacía públicos.

El comisario Coronas no nos felicitó de modo

formal como suele hacerse cuando algún equipo de investigación resuelve un caso difícil, pero me llamó a mí sola para decirme que la confesión final de Elisenda había sido una baza muy bien jugada por mi parte. Yo, que me sentía bastante asqueada de todo aquello, le aseguré que mi juego había sido inexistente, Elisenda me había confesado todos los entresijos de la historia de modo voluntario, sólo porque yo también soy una mujer. Sin embargo, para Coronas aquella explicación no era suficiente.

—Déjese de historias, Petra, no se haga la humilde. A cada cual hay que reconocerle sus méritos, y es evidente que usted supo ganarse la confianza de la chica. Al final, remató con una confesión, y lograr una confesión, saber dirigirla hacia los puntos cruciales, requiere sabiduría y buena práctica. Enhorabuena.

Asentí sin el menor entusiasmo. ¡Enhorabuena!, más buena hubiera sido la hora para mí de no haberme hecho cargo de aquel caso que mezclaba gente malvada con pobres desgraciados. Pero en fin, así es la vida, expresión que sólo se emplea cuando la vida es una auténtica mierda.

Le pedí al comisario unos días de permiso y me los concedió. Quizá recuperando mi vida familiar olvidara antes aquel tiempo de trabajo arduo e intenso. Garzón dijo que a él no le hacía falta ningún puñetero descanso y siguió en comisaría, feliz y contento. Envidié una vez más su condición de duro pedrusco, siendo consciente de que el más duro de los pedruscos es un diamante. Ser resistente es la mejor virtud de un policía.

Coda final

La primera noche que tuve libre invité a cenar a todo el clan: Marcos y sus tres hijos menores. Hacer venir al mayor desde Londres me parecía impropio de una celebración con motivos tan poco importantes: mi descanso y la resolución de un caso. Además, los chicos siempre escogían una pizzería para cualquier evento gastronómico, pero el londinense tenía ya gustos más sofisticados por razón de su edad, de modo que hubiera renegado a base de bien. No, ya lo sumaríamos en Navidad a un ágape con más sustancia.

Reunir a los tres muchachos en un día que no figuraba como «nuestro» en el calendario de visitas estipuladas siempre resultaba conflictivo. Sin embargo, yo me empeñé en que fuera así. Por las especiales circunstancias del último caso hacía bastante tiempo que no los veía y me apetecía que aquello fuera como un reencuentro y, en cierto modo, como una disculpa por mis reiteradas ausencias del que era, en fines de semana alternos, su propio hogar.

Los chicos comprendieron mis razones y se mostraron muy contentos por la variación de la rutina. Cada uno de ellos peleó por sus derechos no estipulados con sus respectivas madres para que les dejaran venir. Yo les había prometido que, en cuanto concluyera la cena, los llevaría en coche hasta sus casas.

—Espero que sea de madrugada —dijo Teo en su registro irónico habitual.

—Las pizzerías cierran pronto —respondió Marina, llena de sensatez.

—Pero, después de las celebraciones, los adultos se toman un gin-tonic. Tú no sabes eso porque aún eres una enana que no tiene edad de salir.

Marina, que pasaba de la racionalidad al insulto con gran rapidez, aunque sin abandonar nunca su tendencia a la síntesis, respondió:

—Gilipollas.

Hugo hizo por una vez de mediador, si bien utilizó una salida inesperada.

—No os peleéis. A lo mejor no hace falta gin-tonic y nos dejan pedir cerveza con la pizza.

Marcos, que estaba bastante distraído aquella noche, sintonizó un momento con el resto para sentenciar:

—Mientras yo sea vuestro padre, cosa que parece bastante inamovible hoy por hoy, ninguno de vosotros beberá alcohol hasta que haya cumplido los dieciocho años.

—Pero la cerveza tiene una graduación muy baja y dicen que es estupenda para la salud —argumentó Hugo.

—También es bueno para la salud hacer cien flexiones cuando te levantas por la mañana y dudo mucho de que estéis por esa labor.

—Es que aún no tenemos dieciocho años —dio Teo una vuelta de tuerca.

—Y si te enteraras de que beben cerveza cuando no los ves, ¿tú qué harías, papá? —preguntó la niña no muy inocentemente.

—Se lo contaría a Petra y ella los detendría.

Marina puso cara de felicidad y, volviéndose hacia los gemelos, les soltó:

—¡Hala! Esa sí que no os la esperabais, ¿eh?

Los chicos la miraron con desprecio. Teo apostilló:

—Si Petra intenta detenerme, me pondré a berrear diciendo que sufro maltrato y como soy menor...

Marcos se llevó las manos a la cabeza.

—¿Será posible que nunca nunca jamás podamos llevar en la mesa una conversación interesante y madura? ¿Es que no se os ocurre ningún tema que no sea una chorrada?

—El fútbol —señaló Hugo. Su padre puso cara de sufrimiento.

—La prostitución infantil —apuntó Teo. Su padre se puso serio y lo amenazó moviendo el índice.

—¡El medioambiente! —exclamó Marina. Su padre respiró con placer.

—¡Ese sí es un buen tema!

—Esta niña cada vez está más cursi y más pelota —rezongó Teo.

La cosa hubiera podido enzarzarse de nuevo, pero, afortunadamente, aparecieron las pizzas con su variedad de coloridos y su intenso olor a callejón romano, de modo que los chicos se olvidaron de cualquier cosa que no fuera comer.

Es curioso, pensé, a veces me hartaba de aquellas accidentadas comidas y perdía internamente la paciencia. Sin embargo, ese día, probablemente debido al periodo sin frecuentar a los chicos, me divirtieron sus piques y sus inofensivas bromas.

Tras la cena no hubo gin-tonics, tampoco ningún otro tipo de despedida alcohólica o sobria. Como los chicos tenían sueño y al día siguiente madrugaban, dejé a Marina en casa de su madre y a los gemelos en la de la suya. Marcos arguyó que le dolía la cabeza y se fue en taxi al Poblenou, donde nos encontraríamos poco después.

Me esperaba en el salón, donde había preparado una cubitera, una botella de bourbon y dos vasos.

—¡Vaya! —exclamé—. Veo que no predicas con el ejemplo. ¿Eso es alcohol o son hierbas medicinales?

—Siéntate, Petra. Me gustaría charlar un rato contigo y en los últimos tiempos no he tenido muchas oportunidades.

—Viendo cómo has preparado el escenario, el tema debe ser importante.

—Lo es, o debería decir lo es y no lo es.

—Está bien, dame tiempo para colgar la gabardina y entrar en el lavabo. Vuelvo enseguida.

Mientras realizaba esas acciones empecé a especular sobre qué demonio pensaba decirme mi marido. Enseguida, me di cuenta de que se trataría de algo que había olvidado en aquellos días de jaleo: la puñetera casa en el campo. ¿Tan pronto volvía a la carga? Si aquello era tan crucial para él, ¿qué podía contestarle?, ¿que necesitaba pensarlo un poco más?, ¿que no me agobiara con la toma de decisiones recién acabado un lapso de trabajo tan angustioso?

A mi regreso, Marcos ya había servido las copas. No se le veía nervioso, él raramente lo estaba. Yo me encontraba más bien incómoda, porque me parecía inoportuna la elección del momento para cualquier confidencia. Me senté, cogí mi whisky, le di un sorbo y abrí las manos en señal de aquiescencia.

—Heme aquí dispuesta a conversar.

—¿Puedo pedirte que no me interrumpas mientras te cuento?

—Eso es darte mucha ventaja, pero en fin...

—No estoy bromeando, Petra.

—Sí, ya lo veo, pones cara de empleado de pompas fúnebres. ¡Adelante, te escucho! ¿Y si tengo preguntas?

—Al final.

—Como en una rueda de prensa.

Torció el gesto porque yo continuaba usando la ironía festiva y por fin se arrancó a hablar.

—Petra, han ocurrido cosas en estos meses. He conocido a una chica muy joven y estamos saliendo.

Empecé a notar un intenso hormigueo de alarma en la nariz y las puntas de los dedos de las manos. Él prosiguió, como si le urgiera soltarlo todo.

—No es lo que inmediatamente se puede concluir: no me he enamorado de ella ni ella de mí. Es la típica aventura que ni siquiera tiene como principal componente la sexualidad. Tú ya sabes cómo funcionan esas cosas, es más bien tu propia inmadurez la que te lleva a la ilusión de estar viviendo algo juvenil, algo que ya no te corresponde por edad. Parece una bobada, pero se disfruta intensamente, incluso sabiendo que es un autoengaño, un síntoma de vanidad y de decadencia.

Me miró como esperando una respuesta, aunque

sus reglas eran que yo no debía interrumpir. Procuré que la expresión de mi cara no se alterara en absoluto, lo tenía bien ensayado de los interrogatorios policiales. Marcos volvió a hablar.

—Puedes dar por seguro que yo continúo queriéndote y que no pienso en dejar nuestra relación. Lo único que te pido es un poco de tiempo, quizá apenas dos meses, para plantear nuestra convivencia de otra manera. La chica de la que te hablo está instalada en la casa que compré. No se ha hecho ninguna reforma, apenas el mínimo acondicionamiento de una sola habitación y un baño. Ella sabe que lo nuestro es muy pasajero y que romperemos en cualquier momento. Está de acuerdo. El plan sería que yo pasara algún día con ella y el resto contigo, en esta casa, como siempre. Pasada la aventura, quizá sería un buen momento para reacondicionar la casa en serio y que los dos viviéramos siempre allí. Ya ves, Petra, me resulta completamente imposible engañarte llevando una relación paralela, no es mi estilo. Dime qué te parece todo esto con total sinceridad.

El primer whisky se había acabado y serví más en ambos vasos. Lo miré con frialdad.

—Por lo que acabas de explicar ya me has engañado, ¿o es que la chica se ha instalado esta misma mañana? ¿No me engañabas cuando reacondicionabas esa habitación?

—Petra, llevas un tiempo casi completamente ausente de esta casa. Tu trabajo era lo único importante para ti. No encontré la ocasión de hablar contigo seriamente sin que tu mente estuviera en otros asuntos.

—Muy bien. Voy a recapitular tus palabras para estar bien segura de que entiendo lo que me planteas.

Lo que quieres es hacer simultáneo nuestro matrimonio con un ligue sin que eso altere nada. ¿Es así?

—Durante un periodo muy corto, que en ningún caso se prolongará. La chica no tenía dónde vivir y está buscando piso. Quizá ese sea el plazo.

—Y el motivo por el que necesitas esa especie de tregua marital es porque no puedes privarte del placer ocasional de convertirte en un ser tan ilusionado como un adolescente. ¿Cierto? No hay amor, no hay sexo, sólo ilusión ficticia.

—Decirlo así es una manera de desvirtuar las cosas.

—Llevas razón, hay otro modo de decirlo. Lo que deseas es vivir tu aventura sin la sensación de culpa que puede provocarte un engaño y sin perder tu estatus oficial de marido legítimo. ¿Así está mejor?

—Petra, ni tú ni yo somos niños, tanto tú como yo venimos de dos matrimonios, fallidos uno tras otro. Sabemos cómo es la vida, el amor, los instintos y las relaciones emocionales. Conocemos nuestra propia personalidad y ya no tenemos edad para envolvernos en ilusiones futuras.

—¿Y cuáles son las ilusiones futuras, las que conciernen a nuestro matrimonio o las de tu nueva pareja?

—¡No es mi nueva pareja, sólo una historia temporal con fecha de caducidad predeterminada!

—¿Y para una corta historia sin importancia montas una organización tan compleja: rehabilitación de una habitación y de un lavabo? Encima, te presentas aquí proponiéndome un apaño. No lo entiendo, Marcos, de verdad.

—¿Hubieras preferido que no te dijera nada?

—Sí, por lo menos me hubiera evitado enterarme de tu plan tortuoso.

—¡Plan tortuoso! ¿Te has olvidado de quién eres, Petra? La Petra a quien yo conocí, aquella con la que me casé, era una mujer progresista, que despreciaba los convencionalismos sociales, que pensaba en amar y vivir con libertad sin colgarse al cuello los yugos absurdos con los que carga la gente. ¿Qué ha pasado?, ¿de repente has cambiado de arriba abajo?, ¿te has vuelto una esposa del sistema o es que me engañaste desde el principio sobre cómo eras en realidad?

Se sirvió whisky él solo, e inmediatamente lo hice yo en mi vaso. Elevé un poco la voz.

—¡Un momento, un momento! ¿De qué coño me estás hablando, qué tiene que ver la progresía y la libertad con la componenda que pretendes? ¡Pero si lo tuyo es un clásico de los inicios del siglo pasado! El maridito aparca a su amante en una casa de su propiedad y sigue viviendo respetablemente con la esposa legítima en el domicilio conyugal. Doble familia y doble moral. Un clásico. ¡Tu plan es cojonudo, todo un ejemplo de amor libre y modernidad! ¡Es puro *Fortunata y Jacinta*! Pero yo no soy la esposa fiel y dócil que aguanta cualquier cosa por conservar a su marido. Y ella, esa chica..., estoy segura de que si acepta tus condiciones es por dos motivos: o anda corta de dinero o espera que ese plazo temporal que te has sacado de la manga vaya prolongándose más y más en el tiempo hasta la conquista definitiva del carcamal. Por supuesto, el carcamal eres tú.

—¡Estás perdiendo los papeles, Petra! ¡Ni en una ocasión me has preguntado quién es esa chica, cuándo y cómo ha entrado en mi vida, a qué se dedica! ¿Te parece eso racional, piensas que es un modo de hacerse una idea de la situación?

—No, no te lo he preguntado, ¿y sabes por qué?, ¡porque me importa un carajo quién sea tu enamorada temporal, me la sopla, me la refanfinfla, me da exactamente igual! Sé algo de ella que seguro que es verdad: es una chica que no tiene tu altura económica, tu estatus social ni tu cultura, una chica ante la que puedes mostrar tu superioridad, exhibirte como un pavo presuntuoso, demostrarle que su juventud no es nada comparado con tu figura de poder. La vanidad de los tíos, Marcos, la jodida vanidad de los tíos que no tiene fronteras, que es grande como la extensión del desierto, e igual de estéril además. Tú no te libras de ella. No me hables de ilusiones que ayudan a vivir, a rejuvenecer un tiempecito para resurgir con más fuerza después. Nada de eso cuela. Tú necesitas que una nena acabe pensando que le ha tocado la lotería por estar contigo.

—Todo eso no deja de ser un montón de lugares comunes de una vulgaridad espantosa que yo hubiera juzgado impropia de ti.

—Pero ahora caes en la cuenta de que soy una tipa vulgar y corriente. Es verdad, siempre lo he sido, aunque por lo menos no soy tan sibilina y ridícula como tú: «Verás, querida, voy a proponerte un pequeño plan...».

—¡Basta, Petra, estás poniéndote histérica!

—Es verdad, calma. Recapitulemos: me cuentas tu problema de aburrimiento y falta de ilusión y me das tu receta para solucionarlo. Naturalmente, como mínimo, quieres saber lo que pienso yo. Pues bien, mi opinión ya te la he dado, ahora te digo cuál es la respuesta a tu planteamiento: no. Vete con esa chica, acaba las obras de tu casa campestre e instálate con ella allí. Y si es verdad que al cabo de un corto tiempo te has cansado de esa relación banal, puedes hacer lo que te plazca menos volver por aquí. Lárgate, la esposa moderna y progresista se ha convertido en una maruja insoportable. Supongo que pensar eso te reconfortará.

Marcos me miró con una animadversión que no recordaba haber descubierto nunca en sus ojos. Cogió la botella de bourbon, que ya casi habíamos vaciado, y la estampó contra el suelo. Luego salió de la casa dando zancadas y pegó un portazo tan violento que los cuadros colgados de las paredes dieron un pequeño salto y las copas dentro del aparador tintinearon como campanillas. Oí mi coche ponerse en marcha —recordé que él había venido en taxi— y partir a toda velocidad. El hombre tranquilo por antonomasia, el que no perdía nunca la ecuanimidad y evitaba toda exaltación, se había puesto como un basilisco. Aun así, había tenido el cuajo de murmurar antes del magno portazo:

—Ya hablaremos otro día como personas, hoy veo que no puede ser.

Que saliera llevado por las furias no me pareció mal. Que hiciera añicos la botella fue casi una curiosidad antropológica. Sólo aquella frase final, entredicha en voz baja, que pretendía aún demostrar su racionalidad, me sacó de mis casillas. Me maldije por no haber reaccionado como él, no haberlo seguido hasta el coche con celeridad y lanzarle algo duro sobre el capó: un cenicero decorativo, un jarroncito con flores que había en el recibidor. Todo hubiera sido entonces todavía más grotesco, más propio de una asquerosa serie televisiva o de un folletín, perfecto en su cutrez.

Saltando sobre los trozos de vidrio de la botella, mi cabeza giraba como un ciclón. Ni siquiera sabía si debía dejar de beber o seguir haciéndolo. Sin darnos cuenta y con compulsión habíamos acabado con el whisky. Renuncié a la ginebra o el vodka. No, me inclinaría por una cerveza fresca que me devolviera cierta claridad mental, aun conservando algunas brumas que me impidieran cualquier atisbo de desesperación.

Toda recapitulación, tal y como yo la entiendo, empieza por el autoanálisis, después ya vienen los juicios y consideraciones sobre las actitudes ajenas. Y bien, ¿era yo en realidad una falsa progre, convencida de que no pertenecía a la mayoría convencional cuando en realidad me regía por las mismas reglas ortodoxas de los demás? ¿Había llegado acaso a una edad en la que se olvidan las convicciones propias y sólo se actúa temiendo perder lo que se tiene? ¿Pasadas unas semanas o meses me reafirmaría en la reacción que había tenido aquella misma noche o me echaría a llorar cada dos por tres loca de añoranza? Primera batería de preguntas sin respuesta inminente, sería necesario desmenuzarlas y responderlas tras haber efectuado una profunda meditación. Segunda batería de preguntas: si Marcos volvía para plantear de nuevo aquel pacto infamante e imposible, ¿lo mandaría otra vez al infierno y con las mismas cajas destempladas o intentaría hacerlo razonar amorosamente? ¿Y si volvía diciéndome que «pelillos a la mar», que se había equivocado por completo y todo seguiría como siempre? En caso de no dar señales de vida, ¿lo llamaría yo?

Bien, ya tenía material de meditación suficiente para cuando me encontrara más serena. En cualquier caso, tomé una decisión inmediata y firme: ni hablar de ponerme a llorar como una Magdalena en aquel momento, eso hubiera sido impropio de mí. Tenía sueño, pero ningunas ganas de levantarme, ir a la habitación, asearme, ponerme el pijama y ocupar mi lugar en la cama semivacía. Así que me retrepé en el sofá, encogí las piernas y me dispuse a pasar a la inconsciencia allí mismo. Por causa del licor derramado, el salón olía a rayos, como un maldito figón de mala muerte, como una destilería clandestina. Quizá mejor, así podía imaginar entre sueños que había pasado una noche de juerga y desenfreno, sin más.

A una hora indeterminada de la noche, todo estaba oscuro aún, me pareció que habían llamado a la puerta. No confié en mis percepciones, entontecidas por el alcohol, y me quedé donde y como estaba. Llamaron otra vez. Sólo entonces mi mente empezó a funcionar: al otro lado de la puerta estaba sin duda Marcos, y vendría en son de paz y reconciliación, puesto que no había utilizado su propia llave y esperaba mi permiso para dejarlo entrar.

Sin mucho brío, más bien arrastrándome un poco, llegué a la puerta y la abrí de par en par. ¡Oh, sorpresa!, allí se encontraba el subinspector Garzón. Me tapé los ojos con las manos.

—¡No, por favor, Fermín, tenga piedad! Me imagino lo que viene a contarme. Elisenda se ha suicidado en la prisión, ¿acierto?

Mi subalterno no contestó ni dio un paso al frente para poder entrar en la casa. Estaba inmóvil y pétreo como un moái de la isla de Pascua.

—¡Pero entre, no se quede ahí pasmado!

No entró, se limitó a empezar a hablar con voz temblorosa.

—Petra, los de Tráfico han dado parte de que su coche ha sufrido un accidente. Al ver que lo conducía Marcos, me han llamado a mí.

En la larga pausa que hizo yo intentaba comprender el sentido de sus palabras.

—¿Está en el hospital? —pregunté.

Garzón negó lentamente con la cabeza. Yo asentí lentamente con la mía. Entonces el subinspector me puso una mano en el hombro, sentí su calor. «¡Ay, Petra! —pensé—, siempre huirás del recuerdo de esta noche. En el fondo, todas las mujeres huimos de algo, y tú te convertirás en una más.» En ese momento comprendí que el calor de la mano de mi compañero era el mayor consuelo que tendría durante años, quizá el único en realidad.

Vinaròs, 12 de septiembre de 2023